WITHDRAWN FROM ✓ T5-ASA-088
TSC LIBRARY

Power Play

THE MIDDLE AGES SERIES

Ruth Mazo Karras, Series Editor
Edward Peters, Founding Editor

A complete list of books in the series is available from the publisher.

Power Play

The Literature and Politics of Chess in the Late Middle Ages

Jenny Adams

PENN

University of Pennsylvania Press
Philadelphia

Copyright © 2006 University of Pennsylvania Press
All rights reserved
Printed in the United States of America on acid-free paper

10 9 8 7 6 5 4 3 2 1

Published by University of Pennsylvania Press
Philadelphia, Pennsylvania 19104-4112

Library of Congress Cataloging-in Publication Data

Adams, Jenny, 1969–
    Power play : the literature and politics of chess in the Late Middle Ages / Jenny Adams
        p.   cm. (Middle Ages series)
    ISBN-13: 978-08122-3944-7 (alk. paper)
    ISBN-10: 0-8122-3944-X (alk. paper)
    Includes bibliographical references and index.
        1. Literature, Medieval—History and criticism. 2. Chess in literature. 3. Chess—
History. I. Title. II. Series: Middle Ages series
    PN687.C53 A33   2006
    809'933579—dc22   2006042135

For Jeff

Contents

We see we cannot play at chess but that we must give names to our chess-men; and yet, me thinks, he were a very partial champion of truth that would say we lied for giving a piece of wood the reverend title of a bishop.

—Philip Sidney, *Defence of Poesy*

Introduction:
Chess in the Medieval World

In the opening pages of *Roman van Walewein*, a Middle Dutch romance from the thirteenth century, King Arthur calls his court together for one of his legendary banquets. As the assembled company finishes the meal, a magic chess set floats in through an open window and settles on the floor, bedazzling the onlookers. Yet the knights hesitate to touch it, and the board and its pieces soon fly back out the window.[1] Bewitched by the set, the king offers to bequeath his land and his title to the knight who retrieves it. When no one moves, an exasperated Arthur declares that he will fetch the set himself, prompting Walewein, Arthur's nephew and favorite knight, to intervene and accept the mission. His pursuit of the chess set occupies the rest of the poem.[2]

In the world of romance, where tests of a hero's prowess most often revolve around jousts or battles, the magic chess set comes as somewhat of a surprise. What exactly is it *doing* in the castle? Why do the poem's authors, Penninc and Pieter Vostaert, make it the story's central focus?[3]

We can start to answer these questions by looking at the ways the game represents a type of political order conspicuously missing from Arthur's court.[4] Indeed, the game's first notable characteristic is its opulence. The ivory chessboard, inlaid with gems and precious stones, is "more valuable than all of Arthur's kingdom."[5] The pieces themselves, which today still reflect a medieval social hierarchy, stand in rows, ready to be moved to action. By contrast, the silence of Arthur's knights, who not only fear the board but also make no move to retrieve it, exposes the problems of a community where even the promise of a rich reward fails to provide motivation for the quest at hand. That only one knight, Walewein, accepts the challenge indicates a general apathy, or worse, a weakness, on the part of Arthur's men.[6] Arthur's offer of his kingdom also hints at the court's troubles, reminding us of the king's failure to produce an heir. Because he has no son, he must find a successor to ensure the stability of his realm.

As the narrative progresses, the chess game and the order it embodies slowly become attainable. Walewein soon finds the board at the castle of

King Wonder, who rules over a completely harmonious community impervious to attack. No longer floating, the set rests between Wonder and his son, and the two men play as Wonder's knights joust nearby, an action loosely parallel to the action on the board. Eager to retrieve the chess set, Walewein soon leaves Wonder's kingdom to find a magic sword, comes back later to trade the sword for the chess set, and finally returns to Arthur's court, where he and Arthur begin to play. The discord previously plaguing Arthur's court vanishes, and in a mirror of the match between Wonder and his son, the game confirms Walewein's role as king-elect.[7] By retrieving the game Walewein has become the heir apparent, and the chess set provides a physical reminder of the ties between the two men as well as a reaffirmation of the knight's role in the newly stabilized kingdom.

As I argue in the pages that follow, chess games in literary texts such as *Walewein,* as well as in more straightforwardly political treatises from the late Middle Ages, encoded anxieties about political organization, civic community, economic exchange, and individual autonomy. Just as the chess set in this poem becomes symbolic of the newfound stability of Arthur's court, so too the actual game in real life was seen to model an ideal civic order based on contractual obligation and exchange. Later in this introduction I will return to the nature of this civic imagining and its implications. But I first need to offer a bit of background on chess, since its arrival in Europe and subsequent transformation underlies the symbolic weight the game acquired over the course of late Middle Ages.

Most likely originating in the Indian game *chaturanga,* chess spread through Persia and later though Arab cultures in the sixth and seventh centuries, eventually reaching the Latin west by 1000 A.D.[8] Within several generations chess had spread throughout Western Europe, and surviving manuscripts that reference the game exist in nearly every European language.[9] When chess first entered Europe, most of its rules were carried over directly from the contemporary Arabic game.[10] The game was played on an uncheckered board with the "noble" pieces placed on the back row and the pawns on the row in front of them. The king, knight, rook, and pawns moved as they do in modern chess, and the movement of these pieces remained, with the exception of some regional variation, essentially static.[11] The queen and bishop, however, originally advanced in a very limited way: the bishop could leap diagonally over any adjacent diagonal square to the square beyond it, while the queen, also confined to a diagonal progression, moved only one square at a time.

That medieval culture *wanted* to see itself in the game is most indicative in the changes Western players and writers made to the pieces and the rules.

In a departure from its Eastern predecessors, medieval chess in Europe featured a queen rather than a counselor, a judge or bishop rather than an elephant, and a knight or horseman rather than a horse, names that made the game correspond to social classes of the cultures that played it. Particularly striking was the change of the Arabic *firz*, or *firzān*, a word that describes a male counselor, to the European queen, or *regina*.[12] And while the name was retained in a modified form in some languages (most notably Spanish, French, and English), almost all European cultures changed the gender of the piece in what can only be a conscious attempt to map its own social structure onto the game.[13]

Allegorists went even farther than players, pushing the similarities between the game and society beyond the simple resemblance of social roles. For writers such as Jacobus de Cessolis and the anonymous author of *Les Echecs amoureux*, or the *Chess of Love*, chess in the late Middle Ages became a way to model political order as well as a way for individuals to imagine their own civic identities. Even for writers like Penninc and Pieter Vostaert, who used the game in the context of romance rather than allegory, chess provided a way to (re)configure human interaction and institutions as well as a means to show the ways such institutional power could be ordered.

If chess had remained a marginalized game, such interest on the part of a few authors would be less remarkable. But in fact, testaments to the game's popularity appear in a variety of places. Although only a few medieval chess pieces have survived from the medieval era—the most notable are the Lewis Chessmen and the inaptly named "Charlemagne Chessmen"—many wills and inventories make reference to the game.[14] The numerous extant chess problem sets (diagrams of boards with pieces set up to achieve a checkmate in a given number of moves), the frequent references to it in romances, and popular philosophical allegories of the game also confirm that chess was a central part of the culture.[15] Such references indicate that both men and women played chess. And while the game was idealized as a noble activity, the occasional portrayal of lower-class chess players in medieval romances suggests that the game extended beyond the aristocracy.[16] Nor was the game confined to the dominant Christian culture; a small number of Hebrew works make reference to the game.[17]

In addition to depicting chess as widely played, writers were quick to assert the game's privileged status.[18] The set in *Walewein*, encrusted with jewels and radiating a luminous glow, represents an otherworldly object that floats above the members of the court. King Alfonso X's thirteenth-century *Libros des ajedrez, dados y tablas* (*The Book of Chess, Dice, and Backgammon*), a sumptuously illustrated volume of game problems, offers even more straightforward praise. The treatise begins with a story of a king in India, who has a number of conversations with three philosophers. When asked to provide the king with the most essential virtue (implicitly, the virtue most important for ruling a kingdom), each philosopher has a different opinion: one argues for the primacy of reason, one promotes daring as the most advantageous quality, and one insists on a mix of intelligence and daring. To support their arguments, they each create a game: the first, chess; the second, dice; and the third, backgammon. As the narrator confirms, the first philosopher wins the argument: "And because chess is a more intelligent and honorable game than dice or backgammon, we speak in this book first of it."[19] As with the floating set in *Walewein*, Alfonso's treatise prioritizes the game as superior, exemplary, and desirable, and his collection of problems emphasizes the importance of skillful play on the part of a king.

As evinced by Alfonso's chess book and by *Walewein*, writers capitalized on the game's mimetic qualities. Although these generically different works are separated by language and geography, both emphasize the ties between the game and the political order.[20] Modern readers might dismiss as an entertaining flourish the legend that opens Alfonso's treatise. However, this myth of origins serves to validate Alfonso's own choice to commission the manuscript; the moral value of chess merits the volume's lavish expense. Or rather, wise kings will recognize the game's superiority and make the game a central part of their court. Such is also the case with *Walewein*, where King Arthur, recognizing the game's value, not only initiates the quest for the magic set but also articulates the game's connection to political order when he promises that the knight who fetches it will be heir to Arthur's throne.

The connection between learning to play chess and improving one's ability to govern one's kingdom (and, implicitly in *Walewein*, one's self) reached its fullest expression in Jacobus de Cessolis's late thirteenth-century *Liber de moribus hominum et officiis nobilium ac popularium super ludo scachorum* (*The Book of the Morals of Men and the Duties of Nobles and Commoners, on the Game of Chess*).[21] The *Liber* is a treatise, intended as advice to princes, that narrates the story of a ruler who through his knowledge of chess ceases his tyrannical ways, becoming a benevolent leader and, according to Jacobus, a better one. The game functions in this text as an instrument of reform rather than as a simple reminder of social hierarchy or a site of repentance. At the same time, the *Liber* does not use the game to address itself to the king alone but seeks to absorb all people in its symbolic domain. Thus while the king may function as either the primary audience or the center point for the game in the *Liber*, the *Roman van Walewein*, and Alfonso's chess book, the symbolism of chess works to disperse political and social power among the members of the civic body. Or to rephrase this according to the logic of the game, the king may be the most important piece on the board, but the other pieces have freedom of movement independent of the monarch and thus can affect the outcome of the game. Nor was the king the only person who could improve himself through chess. Jacobus suggests that anyone who learns the game should be able to master his or her role in the civic body and the rules that govern his or her actions. In more than one manuscript copy of the *Liber*, the text itself is followed by a set of chess problems like Alfonso's, a pairing that emphasizes the correlation between the *Liber*'s moral tales and the act of play.[22]

In looking at chess in this fashion, I am engaging with scholars of late medieval literature who have looked at medieval political order and its impact on individual identity and autonomy.[23] Along the way I aim to answer a variety of questions about the intersections between the medieval cultural understandings of the game and of political responsibility. How does chess break with earlier models of secular government, in particular the state-as-body model that dominated political discourse? What are the political and cultural implications of a game with pieces designed to match European social roles? Why did allegorists repeatedly promote the similarities between the game and real life, in some cases differentiating the pawns so that each could represent a specific trade? Ultimately, I argue that the Middle Ages were not uniformly hierocratic and autocratic, but were also capable of producing a civic order dominated by "associational forms."[24]

At the same time I will suggest that discourses of association were often constrained by the metaphor of an organic polity, which sought to temper the radical reimagining of the political body. I also consider the ways that categories imposed by the chessboard, which mirrored the rise of trades and professions, undermined notions of individual autonomy.[25] Or, to put this another way, it is difficult to answer the questions posed above without considering the relationship of the game to the individual who played it or to the person reading the allegory. If the board offered a panoptic view of civic order, where was an individual's place on it? What was a person's relationship to his professional identity, or for that matter, to the other professions represented as pieces on the board? If "the confrontation of the subject with the determinations of the exterior, present world" formed one of the central tropes of late medieval writing, then a close look at chess, a game that in many instances asks the player to assume a specific professional and/or psychological identity, is long overdue.[26]

While *Power Play* responds to previous work on political order and its relationship to individual identity, it also tries to account for the act of play as a cultural pastime. In the opening chapter of *Homo Ludens*, the first extended study of the cultural significance of play and games, Johan Huizinga defines play as a voluntary activity that takes place in a physically defined space separate from "real" life. It proceeds according to fixed rules and has a beginning and end, even though the activity itself can be repeated. When following a game's strictures, players may become absorbed in the game itself; yet they never forget that they are playing and thus that their actions are not "real." Engaging in play, Huizinga argues, is not necessarily a means to a specific end; the act of play itself leads to the general evolution and betterment of mankind. Or, as he claims in his foreword, "civilization arises and unfolds in and as play."[27]

Several decades after the appearance of *Homo Ludens*, the French sociologist Roger Caillois offered an extended critique of Huizinga in his own book *Man, Play, and Games*. Although still willing to see play "as a free and voluntary activity" that is "carefully isolated from the rest of life," Caillois is more suspicious of games and refers to them as pastimes of "pure waste," in which "nothing has been harvested or manufactured, no masterpiece has been created, no capital has accrued."[28] Nonetheless, he argues, play itself has merit, and he devotes his text to a classification of games according to their characteristics. According to Caillois, all games fall into four basic categories: *agon*, a game of competition; *alea*, a game of chance; *mimicry*, a game of simulation; and *ilinx*, a game one plays internally, characterized by a feeling of dizziness or disorientation.[29] In making such classifications Caillois intends to establish "the foundations for a sociology *derived from* games."[30]

Despite their different attitudes toward play and games, both Caillois and Huizinga understand play as a sphere of activity that can be analyzed in situ and isolated from the "real" world. Whether on a tennis court, on a chessboard, or in a theater, the game creates a space of fantasy that, while in dialogue with the world outside it, remains tightly sealed off from that world.

In more recent years postmodern scholars have increasingly called into question this separation between games and "real" life. For Judith Butler and other gender theorists who have convincingly shown gender roles to be products of an extended performance (another form of play), the division between the two spheres is a convenient fiction. In the field of anthropology, Clifford Geertz has examined the ways that a game can both explain and reinforce social organization and status markers. In "Deep Play," his well-known essay on cockfighting in Bali, Geertz writes: "What sets the cockfight apart from the ordinary course of life, lifts it from the realm of everyday practical affairs, and surrounds it with an aura of enlarged importance is not, as functionalist sociology would have it, that it reinforces status discriminations . . . but that it provides a metasocial commentary upon the whole matter of assorting human beings into fixed hierarchical ranks and then organizing the major part of collective existence around that assortment."[31] For Geertz, the cockfight in Balinese culture works as "a simulation of the social matrix, the involved system of cross-cutting, overlapping, highly corporate groups," where a citizen is taught "what his culture's ethos and his private sensibility (or, anyway, certain aspects of them) look like when spelled out externally in a collective text."[32]

Academics have not been alone in recognizing the slippage between the "real" world and the world of play. Although perhaps not yet willing to acknowledge the extent to which individual identity is upheld (or one might even say policed) by performative play, popular culture has itself become obsessed with the permeability of the "real" and the "fictional," and reality TV shows like *Survivor, American Idol,* and *The Apprentice* challenge our ability to distinguish between the two. In each case, the game bleeds freely and uncontrollably into the "real" world of the contestants, having material ramifications on their lives and changing their identities.

But, as I will argue, this self-aware blurring between the "real" and the game is not an exclusively modern (academic or otherwise) phenomenon. Medieval society, which mapped its social hierarchy (or at least one fantasy thereof) onto the game of chess, changing its nomenclature with the rise of professions and shifting demographics, used play to similar ends. Chess is especially interesting because it gave instruction on citizenship and on moral autonomy, functioning as a medium for the articulation and exercise of power. What set this game apart from "the ordinary course of life" was the space it opened for an individual to imagine his (or her) relationship both to the political body and to the singular bodies therein.[33]

Before describing my project further, I should add that the questions I pose carry with them risks of generalization and also of specialization. In an effort to combat the former, I have tried to confine the first half of my analysis to two allegorical works (one produced in Italy and the other in France), and the second half to the ways in which fourteenth-century English writers reacted to the allegorical traditions initiated by these two earlier texts. Nevertheless, this has left me little room to consider the ways chess, as it spread throughout Europe, took on features specific to individual locales. The twelfth-century Lombards, for example, played chess under rules that differed slightly from most regions in France, Italy, and Germany, and the German word for the pawn, *bauer* (farmer), has a cultural resonance that differs from the French word *pion*, or pawn.[34] Such variations surely reflect different understandings of the game.

By the same token, my specific focus on the game's political and economic discourses has not permitted me to expand on the game's various symbolic registers, even those that might seem pertinent to my project. In his early thirteenth-century *Les Miracles de Nostre Dame*, for example, Gautier de Coinci uses chess to depict a contest between God and Satan. Here the devil, a master player, tries to trick mankind with his false moves, such as his plucking of Adam and Eve from paradise. Just as the game appears to be lost, God makes "such a Virgin queen / That he was mated and undone."[35] The game in this instance seems less about political order than about a way to rewrite the story of Mary as a representation of divine intellect. In the *Avowing of King Arthur*, a fifteenth-century English text, chess becomes a way to code various vectors of sexual desire. Near the end of the narrative Arthur decides to test to his knight Baldwin, who has vowed never to feel jealous. Arthur goes to visit Baldwin's castle and, in an echo of the romantic trials of Gawain in *Sir Gawain and the Green Knight*, sends Baldwin hunting for a day. After Baldwin leaves, Arthur goes with one of his knights to visit Baldwin's wife in her bedroom. He commands her to open the door; then, after she admits him to the room, he orders his knight to strip and get into the bed with her. Assuring Baldwin's wife that no harm will come to her, the King commands his knight, on the pain of immediate death, to stay on his own side of the bed. Arthur then plays chess with another woman in the chamber until the hunting party comes home the next morning, at which point he tries to trick Baldwin into jealousy.[36]

In these moments I see lessons on political order that echo those found in more explicit allegories. Gautier's emphasis on Mary as a queen involved in earthly affairs—"She knows the secret of all good plays / And is so adroit when she plays / Her friends she pulls from all bad spots"—offers a reminder of God's interest in earthly affairs rather than divine ones.[37] This is no passive virgin queen, but one who takes care of man in his daily existence. Similarly, the *Avowing* carries with it a lesson on political control. The king has ordered the lady to play with him and has commanded his knight to enter the bed, and these commands remind us of Arthur's power to manipulate whatever bodies are at hand. Ultimately, then, the match between Arthur and the lady is intended as an explicit lesson on the nature of political control, a control that Arthur himself sees as synonymous with the power to control the bodies of others.

The allegories found in the *Miracles* and *Avowing*, two seemingly disparate metaphors, are thus not wholly exempt from the political discourses I have attended to. Yet crucially, they embed the game in still other symbolic systems. If I have minimized or omitted works like these, it is only because their references are too brief to lend themselves to substantial analysis or because the game's political valences are not nearly as strong as others circulating through it.

In short, generalization and specificity do not have to be pitfalls. Just as I see tight thematic focus as a way to help clarify my overall argument, I see broad chronological overview as a way to register historical continuum and change. And while my project does not account for specific changes in the game's rules, it does look closely at specific texts, and in studying these texts I respect local differences. A work like Jacobus's *Liber* was read and understood in various ways at different times by different cultures, and I have aimed to show and account for these varied receptions. Like Mary Carruthers, who describes her own work on medieval memory as a project "concerned with elementary assumptions and the commonplaces which underlie the practices" she studies, I offer a general examination of a larger cultural phenomenon rather than an isolated study of one instance of its expression.[38] Like Carruthers, I hope to focus on the "commonplaces." Chess enjoyed an immense popularity throughout Europe, and the game articulated emerging notions of citizenship, power, and political order that spread throughout the West over several centuries.

While chess itself provides the primary strand uniting the varied cultures that I discuss, literary connections between the cultures themselves provide another. To quote David Wallace, "no magic curtain separated 'medieval' London and Westminster from 'Renaissance' Florence and Milan."[39] Authors in late fourteenth- and early fifteenth-century England eagerly read and took inspiration from Italian and French writers, some of whose careers overlapped their own. Chaucer's literary debts to Jean de Meun, Boccaccio, and Petrarch have been well documented by readers in this century and in Chaucer's contemporary England. Lydgate, the darling of the Lancastrians and prized by his peers as one of the greatest English poets, made his career by translating, imitating, expanding, or continuing earlier Continental works. Underlying this shared literary tradition was the Church, whose customs still patterned the daily lives of most Western Europeans.

Nevertheless, it is important to note that generalizations about literary similarities should not overwhelm an acknowledgment of cultural difference, in particular the variations in political organization. Italy, which had already begun to organize itself into independent city-states or communes a century before Chaucer started to write, had a political organization that differed from its northern neighbors. Some communes had a local government that neatly replicated the top-down despotism exercised on a larger scale by the Germanic-Italian emperor. In cities like Florence and Genoa, however, political power was becoming reconfigured. One could not legitimately label twelfth-century Genoa as a democracy; nevertheless, the city "did not have a king, strong archbishop, or lord to create by fiat markets, laws, rules, or anything to regulate the local economy."[40] Although most experiments with shared power would eventually fail, by the fourteenth century turning into despotic or oligarchic regimes, the early thirteenth century saw "a stronger and more impartial executive, the *podestá*" in charge, and basic rights were extended to an ever increasing group of citizens.[41]

This increased dissemination of power had social, economic, and cultural repercussions, and facilitated the production of texts that would probably not have appeared had the Italian lands grown into a unified nation. Dante's *De monarchia*, which argues for a strong, centralized secular power, offers a negative view of these changes and criticizes the papacy, which often used the power of the *popolo minuto* (lower classes) to advance its own causes. By contrast (and as I demonstrate in this book), Jacobus de Cessolis uses his *Liber de moribus hominum et officiis nobilium* to embrace and promote a society in which a wide variety of tradesmen and professions enjoyed a certain amount of political autonomy. Although adapted by French poets and translated twice into French, his *Liber*, which reformulated the structure of political power and addressed itself to a diverse body of readers, did not find full expression in England again until Caxton published it in 1483.[42]

Chapter 1 of *Power Play* offers a study of Jacobus's late thirteenth-century *Liber*, one of the most popular works of the late Middle Ages. I argue that this treatise, in popularizing chess as model of a civic organization, demonstrates a fundamental break with previous representations of political order, the most popular of which was the allegory of the human body. Whereas the state-as-body model saw the members of civic group bound by organic ties, the chess allegory conceives of its members as a contractually bound group.[43] In the *Liber* each piece corresponds to a specific trade or group, with all pieces being interdependent; just as the knight needs the blacksmith (represented by the second pawn) on the adjacent square, so too does the king depend on the money changers (represented by the fourth pawn) placed in front of him. This shift in representation does not yield complete independence for the members of a civic community. Instead, the chess allegory encodes a different technology of social control organized primarily around associational and professional ties; rather than having their actions dictated by the "head" of the state, who directed the actions of the body politic, members of a civic community are seen as beholden to a set of rules particularized to their own social station.

At the same time that Jacobus was using the game to model social structure, the popular practice of playing chess for a stake threatened to undermine his allegory. The *Liber* takes great care to detach the game from the more suspect pastime of dice, an activity associated exclusively with gambling. By identifying the eighth pawn, the one farthest to the king's left, as a dice player and condemning his gambling pursuits, Jacobus tries to preserve the noble tenor of chess. Nevertheless, the text at points has trouble containing the association of chess and gambling. The late thirteenth century saw a proliferation of chess problem sets such as Alfonso's, which were used by gamblers and non-gamblers alike. As noted above, in several manuscript copies of the *Liber*, a series of chess problems is attached to the text. This coupling complicates the treatise's positioning of the game as an ideal model and disrupts Jacobus's attempts to seal off the game from the impurities that come with real-life play.

Chapter 2 continues this discussion of the chess allegory's internal tensions, tracking them into the anonymous fourteenth-century *Les Echecs amoureux*, a poem that uses and reworks Jacobus's chess allegory. Rather than seeing the pieces as representations of professional trades, the *Les Echecs* poet imagines a chessboard where the pieces correspond to the emotions of two lovers, who play the game in a garden. Yet shortly after the male suitor loses his match—he is mated in the left corner by the lady's queen, a piece that carries the image of a balance on its shield—Pallas Athena appears and launches into a lecture drawn from Aristotle's *Politics*. Pointing to the connections between romantic love and social stability, she expatiates on the importance of a well-governed household, which in turn provides the bedrock of a well-governed city. In short, mastery of the chess game is tantamount to mastery of one's own sexual desires, and the lover's mate on the sinister side indicates his failure to understand his responsibility to the social body. In a Commentary on the poem, written shortly after the poem itself, Evrart de Conty emphasizes the game's double valence. For Evrart the game functions simultaneously as a metaphor for human desire and as a model of social hierarchy, and he repeatedly notes that the chess pieces, in addition to symbolizing the lovers' emotions, represent the social classes, trades, and members of the civic body.[44]

Thus while poet and commentator accept Jacobus's allegory of chess, both also worry about what makes a good citizen in a political body decreasingly conceived as a natural one and increasingly conceived as either organized around economic factors or simply pragmatic ones. In a response to the *Liber*, the *Les Echecs* poet and commentator embed the chess allegory within a discourse of nature. Now representative of human emotions, the pieces are no longer bound by contractual ties but by organic (or at least psychologically determined) bonds. And while the lover, like Jacobus's player, has the power to move his own pieces independently, this freedom is soon shown to be illusory; the player is always bound by rules, in this case those of the natural world. At the same time, the poet's use of the lover's body, which he imagines as an embodiment of civic order, also challenges the state-as-body allegory, a model that had resurfaced in fourteenth-century political writings. No longer is the king the head of the political body; instead the bodies of all lovers resemble a complete and independent political order.

Just as the practice of gambling on chess complicates the *Liber*'s model of stable community, so too does it pose a challenge to the *Les Echecs* poet and commentator, who imagine romantic love as a process of mutual exchange and equality. The poet, who narrates the players' opening forays before setting up the closing moves, never acknowledges the custom of wagering on the game even though he models his endgame on a contemporary chess problem. At the same time, his choice of a draw as the ideal outcome (an ideal established in a game that precedes the lovers' match) deliberately sidesteps the issue and suppresses the discourses of exchange and desire surrounding the game. Not only did players use chess to gamble, but several stories from this and the previous century feature a match between two lovers in which the woman's virtue is quite literally at stake. Thus only when the game has no winner does sexual desire remain contained and safe. On his part, the commentator discusses the ramifications of gambling directly, demonstrating its dangers and emphasizing the importance of a tied game. In this way the commentator addresses the problems posed by gambling more explicitly than Jacobus, who never describes a game in progress. By acknowledging the potential for unequal exchange, however, the *Les Echecs* poem and Commentary undercut their own positioning of the allegory as a stable model for virtuous love and harmonious civil order.

It is this anxiety about economic exchange (and in particular the potential for loss) that I follow into fourteenth- and fifteenth-century English literature, the focus of Chapter 3 and, more generally, of the second half of this book. Instead of using the game as a metaphor for social order, works such as the pseudo-Chaucerian *Tale of Beryn* feature matches that facilitate the trade of material goods. Whereas Jacobus and the *Les Echecs* author emphasize the game's power to create an orderly society and moral behavior, the *Tale of Beryn* uses chess games as negative examples that show the ways individuals try to negotiate the world of commerce (a world that contains elements of risk and chance), the ways that they often fail, and the impact of that failure on the stability of the civic community. Unlike the static game found in Jacobus's allegory, and unlike the idealized tied game in *Les Echecs*, the *Beryn* poet describes games in action and exposes the material, economic ramifications of the mate. Actual games or discourses of gaming become ways to represent commerce gone bad and to emphasize the threat of inequality lurking behind any type of trade.[45]

Indeed, chess in the *Tale of Beryn* becomes so detached from proper political order that the story ends with the banishment of the "fals lawe" that has produced it. Abolishing this law eliminates the game-like aspects of commerce and thus ensures that economic exchanges benefit the community as a whole. Indeed, the centralization of power, expressed in *Les Echecs* by the return to the state-as-body ideal, marks the *Tale of Beryn* as similar to *Les Echecs*, even if chess itself no longer contributes to the state's consolidation. It is thus no coincidence that, like *Les Echecs*, the community's stability comes from (and is mirrored in) a controlled sexual union, and the *Beryn* poem ends with a marriage that cements a new political order, uniting it around two bodies, Beryn's and his new bride's, who serve as microcosms of the larger order.

Chess in England, however, did more than allegorize the danger of individual exchanges. In Chapter 4, I consider the ways that chess by the mid- to late fifteenth century again became a model for political order, as well as a way to define and question the power of the monarch within that order. I first look at Hoccleve's *Regement of Princes*, a *speculum regis* written for Prince Henry of Wales (later to become King Henry V) that borrowed heavily from the *Liber*. Although he uses the *Liber* as his primary source and at points acknowledges the overarching allegory, Hoccleve primarily mines it for exempla. Rather than mapping social order by class or profession, Hoccleve devotes his text to the king alone, listing fifteen qualities important for a ruler and using a host of stories and aphorisms to demonstrate the value of each.

Appearing as part of a flurry of such advice texts, Hoccleve's poem demonstrates an unease about the license and limits of a king's authority at the same time that it imagines monarchy as a complex of power hedged about by contractual constraints.[46] Importantly, Hoccleve does not drop all references to Jacobus's text, and in his first mention of the *Liber* he capitalizes on the political implications of this allegory for the monarchy. When introducing Jacobus's work, Hoccleve jokingly insists that despite his knowledge of a king's "draght" (move or education), he himself has never learned all the "draghtes" (moves or tricks) needed to succeed in the "eschequeer."[47] By punning on the double meanings of the words "draght" and "eschequeer," Hoccleve effectively foregrounds the slippage between the game and real life; the Exchequer is not only a checkered board that dominates Hoccleve's primary source, it is also the office that owes him his paycheck. Hoccleve follows this joke by encouraging the king to learn the game, and in particular the king's move, a skill which will "profyte" poet and king alike.[48] Thus while Hoccleve has dropped the larger organizational structure of Jacobus's treatise, he does not abandon the allegory wholesale. In punning on the game's economic implications, he brings the symbolic power of chess in line with the *Tale of Beryn*, where a game leads to disastrous consequences. Yet rather than shun chess, the *Regement* suggests that the king must embrace the game's "draghtes" and master them as part of a noble education.

In addition to its cameo appearance in Hoccleve's *Regement*, the entire *Liber* itself appeared sixty years later in English. Published as *The Game and Playe of the Chesse* by William Caxton in 1474, it was the second English text that Caxton printed while still in Bruges. Caxton then printed the text a second time in Westminster in 1483. As I argue, Caxton's choice to translate and print the *Liber* meant that English readers now had full access to Jacobus's ideas of a rule-based (and contractually bound) community, and thus could find an alternative to the state-as-body model of political order. Unlike Christine de Pizan's *Book of the Body Politic*, an early fifteenth-century *speculum regis* that recycled John of Salisbury's organic model of the state, the *Liber* reflects a model of government built on a "latticework" of position taking; the king, no longer the head of the kingdom, is merely another piece on the board, upon which he like his "subjects" can be moved as needed. Caxton highlights this shift in the prefaces to his two editions. After dedicating the first printed version to a nobleman, Caxton uses his second preface to direct the text to the people of England, and stresses the text's applicability to all readers.[49] This new preface and the addition of the woodcuts that had not appeared in the first edition make the *Liber* much less of an affirmation of hierarchical authority, and Caxton reaffirms the increasing role of all classes and professions as arbiters of power. In short, with Caxton's second edition of the *Liber*, the text had once again come to symbolize an alternative model of political organization.

Chapter 1
(Re)moving the King: Ideals of Civic Order in Jacobus de Cessolis's Liber de ludo scachorum

I shall then suggest that ideology "acts" or "functions" in such a way that it "recruits" subjects among the individuals (it recruits them all), or "transforms" the individuals into subjects (it transforms them all) by that very precise operation which I have called interpellation *or "hailing," and which can be imagined along the lines of the most commonplace everyday police (or other) hailing: "Hey, you there!"*
—Louis Althusser

Jacobus de Cessolis's *Liber de moribus hominum et officiis nobilium ac popularium super ludo scachorum* (*The Book of the Morals of Men and the Duties of Nobles and Commoners, on the Game of Chess*; henceforth the *Liber*), one of the most widely circulated texts of the late Middle Ages, opens with a story of a king named Evilmerodach who rules over Babylon.[1] True to his name, Evilmerodach is a tyrant. He has come to power by killing his father, Nebuchadnezzar, chopping the body into three hundred pieces, and giving the pieces to three hundred birds to eat. This violent assassination troubles Philometer, a philosopher in the city, who, at the request of the city's residents, agrees to instruct the king in the art of humane governance.[2] To this end Philometer creates the game of chess, which he first teaches to Evilmerodach's nobles. When Evilmerodach sees his men playing, he wants to join them, and Philometer teaches him the rules. Evilmerodach then asks Philometer why he has created the game, to which the philosopher responds that he wants to teach the king how to live a virtuous life.[3] Playing chess, Philometer claims, will teach the king the art of proper governance.

This introduction to the game in the *Liber*'s first book lays the groundwork for the rest of the treatise. Books 2 and 3 contain chapter-by-chapter descriptions of the pieces, or as constituted by the allegory, the different types of people who inhabit a well-ordered kingdom. Beginning with the chess king, Jacobus describes the physical attributes of each piece in detail and narrates stories to illustrate the virtuous behavior each piece/citizen should exhibit. The "noble" pieces in book 2 are treated separately from the "common" pieces in book 3 (Table 1). Yet Jacobus devotes a great deal of energy to each, spelling out the importance of his (or in the case of the queen, the only female piece on the board, her) contribution to the common good. The eight pawns in book three symbolize trades as varied as innkeeper, farmer, smith, and notary, and as the *Liber*'s exempla repeatedly demonstrate, the virtue of each group is crucial for the well-being of the community as a whole.

In the fourth and final book, Jacobus explains the game's rules, after which he informs his readers that Evilmerodach shed his evil ways once he mastered chess: "so that the king who had formerly been wicked and disorderly, became just" ["ut rex qui prius erat inordinatus et impius, iustus fieret"] (163–64). But Jacobus does not stop with the king's conversion, which he uses as an example for all men. "Therefore," he adds, "let us all have recourse to the One who is virtue from whom virtue and grace flows" ["Igitur ad illum recurramus qui est virtus a quo virtus manat et gratia"] (164).

The pairing of the narrative of Evilmerodach's rise to power with the *Liber*'s extended chess allegory allows Jacobus to introduce themes and tensions fundamental both to his work and to the idea of civic order. Nebuchadnezzar's mutilated corpse indicates the importance of the king's physical being as both a somatic entity and a representation of the larger realm. That Evilmerodach not only kills his father but, as graphically depicted in Caxton's 1483 edition of the *Liber*, destroys the dead body systematically and publicly, highlights the importance of the ruler's body just as it exposes the new ruler's depravity (see Figure 1). In an outdoor landscape framed by a thin line that can barely contain the scene's chaos, birds swirl around the dismembered body as the executioner gazes to a point outside of the frame. It is not enough for Evilmerodach to seize the kingdom; he fragments the previous ruler and destroys all order as a means to secure his own power.

In response to this barbarity Philometer creates chess as a model of civic order based on reason and law. Again the woodcut in Caxton's edition captures the thrust of the text it accompanies, in this case showing the balance and stability found in Philometer's ideal civic community (see Figure 2). Whereas the first illustration appears with almost no border, the second is enclosed by two pillars, with two windows furnishing a second inner frame. Philometer sits alone in the room at the table adjusting the pieces as he contemplates the moves most suitable for each. The patterned floor beneath him emphasizes the connection of the game itself to the real matter of ruling; life is so much like a chessboard that Philometer becomes quite literally a piece on one. At the same time, the picture positions the reader as a player, and the philosopher stares out of the frame as if inviting him to play.

This opening story promotes a narrative of progress from disorder, represented by Evilmerodach's tyranny, to order, represented by the chess set. Upon closer examination, however, this idea of progress relies on an antinomy that collapses under the weight of the dead body at its center. Just as the new

TABLE 1. Jacobus de Cessolis (thirteenth century), *Liber de moribus hominum et officiis nobilium ac popularium super ludo scachorum*

Book 1
Under which king the game was invented
Who discovered chess
Reasons the game was invented

Book 2 (back row)
The king
The queen
The bishops (judges)
The knights
The rooks (vicars/legates)

Book 3 (front row from R → L)
First pawn (farmers)
Second pawn (smiths and carpenters)
Third pawn (notaries and wool workers)
Fourth pawn (merchants and money changers)
Fifth pawn (doctors and apothecaries)
Sixth pawn (tavern keepers)
Seventh pawn (toll keepers and custodians of the city)
Eighth pawn (wastrels, players, and messengers)

Book 4
On chess
On the moves of the king
On the moves of the queen
On the moves of the judge
On the moves of the knight
On the moves of the rook
On the moves of the pawns
The epilogue

king divides the old king's *literal* body, so too does Philometer divide the *figurative* body politic into multiple and somewhat autonomous pieces. Or rather, Philometer's chess set imagines an ideal community as a place where the body of the king no longer stands as the lone representative of the realm. Like Evilmerodach's destruction of his father, this act is violent. Yet by pairing these acts—the murder of Nebuchadnezzer followed by the creation of the chess set—the narrative displaces the implicit violence of the latter onto the explicit violence of the former. Evilmerodach's homicide absorbs the reader's attention, and his depravity gives license to any solution.

In looking at the *Liber* I will examine the ways the chess allegory captures a different technology of power emerging in the late medieval world, a power organized less around overt force and more around coercion, exposure, and shame. This form of power, articulated in Jacobus's *Liber*, does not offer a system that makes its subjects any more free. Nor does it protect them from the violence or chaos of a tyranny like Evilmerodach's. Rather, it

Figure 1. First woodcut from Caxton's 1483 edition of *The Game and Playe of the Chesse* (book 1, chap. 1). Newberry Library folio inc. 9643.

relies on the coercive abilities of the secular state, which in turn exists as a matrix of social forces and lacks any one person at the center. Inherent in this power is a violence, however sublimated, that is not so far removed from that of the framing story itself. If Nebuchadnezzar's butchered corpse serves as a reminder of tyrannical rule, so does that body warn us of what can happen to any orderly community whose members do not constantly police each other and themselves.

As I will also argue, the *Liber*, in using chess as a metaphor for the body politic, demonstrates a fundamental shift in the ways medieval peoples had begun to conceive of themselves and their relationships to their civic community. Before the *Liber* the predominant metaphor for the state was the human body, which represented types of people as parts subordinate to the body as a whole.[4] Whether a king or a court functionary, members of the kingdom were imagined as parts of a biological organism with physical and physiological relationships to the other members of the body politic. If the head of

Figure 2. Second woodcut from Caxton's 1483 edition of *The Game and Playe of the Chesse* (book 1, chap. 2). Newberry Library folio inc. 9643.

a body decided that the body should walk, the feet would have to follow. By contrast, the chess allegory imagines its subjects to possess independent bodies in the form of pieces bound to the state by rules rather than biology. If the chess king advances, the pawns are not beholden to do the same. Nonetheless, this representation of subjects as independent of a central authority should not be mistaken for complete freedom. Philometer does not merely invent a game. He uses the chess set to build a taxonomic chart of civil society, and in doing so creates a social matrix that asserts its control over the subjects it contains. Unlike the more explicit physical bonds that subjugate the members of a physical body, the relationships modeled by the chess game carry with them a power that aims at psychological as opposed to physical control.

This shift from physical to nonphysical coercion appears most clearly in Jacobus's encouragement of all men to learn the game. By claiming its readers as potential players, the *Liber* offers everyone a fantasy of objective self-perception. Having a view of the entire board, one can make decisions for the good of the whole community while also looking out for one's own interest. Yet at the same time a player is now responsible for his own moral choices and ethical conduct. A knight playing the game cannot move himself to all positions but must act according to the virtues listed at the beginning of his chapter. Failure to do so will place both his body and his community in jeopardy. Nor will this failure be hidden, but it will be exposed publicly on the board. Under the state-as-body metaphor, a foot cannot see itself and thus cannot correct its own behavior. By contrast chess thematizes the exposure of individual bodies for the scrutiny of all. If one can see one's own "self" on the board, other players can see one's own "self" too. Thus rather than offering an opportunity for free movement, the act of playing demands that a subject police his or her own actions.[5]

At the same time that the *Liber* asserts this type of control, it tends to mask its own mechanisms of power and to suppress the game's own internal potential for chaos and violence. Although explaining the rules, Jacobus never describes a game in action; the board and its pieces remain static, a frozen grid of figures with lists of virtues attached to each. When played, however, chess was (and is) a game of war that necessarily results in a king's figurative death. By explaining the pieces' various moves in his final chapter, Jacobus opens the door to the symbolic violence implied by this conflict. If a virtuous reader decides to play, what should we make of the death of his king? Jacobus never offers an answer. Nor does he explicitly address the common use of the game for gambling, a practice that still enjoyed popularity in the fourteenth century even though it had been outlawed on several occasions at various universities throughout Europe.[6] Thus at the same time that Jacobus repeatedly admonishes individuals to work toward the general good of the *res publica*, his fellow residents in Lombardy were busy using the game to different ends. Such discord gestures toward the violence in the *Liber*'s narrative of the game's creation. The game ostensibly teaches Evilmerodach the art of rule. However, Nebuchadnezzar's dead body demonstrates that the young king has already learned how to grasp power. Thus instead of "correcting" him, the game teaches him how to manipulate more precisely the apparatus of state power even as it teaches him that he, too, is a subject.

In arguing for this larger cultural shift, I should note that I am not positioning the *Liber* as the sole force behind more general cultural changes, in particular a rising concern about moral autonomy.[7] The establishment of mandatory confession by the Fourth Lateran Council of 1215, and the subsequent rise of penance manuals, handbooks elaborately detailing the facets of mankind's moral and psychological life, testify to the Church's newfound interest in and attempts to control individual interiority.[8] Confession, which forced individuals to articulate an interiority, necessarily gave shape to the very interiority it demanded, just as penance manuals, written to help the faithful access their own proclivities to sin, scripted the sins themselves as well as an internal reaction to them. The proliferation of these handbooks and the increasing importance attributed to the act of confession invested the Church with a tremendous amount of spiritual authority over believers.

Yet while many scholars have examined the role of penance and penance manuals when considering the history of subjectivity, few scholars have, in narrating this history, considered the role of works like the *Liber*. Like the penance manuals of the same era, the *Liber* takes an interest in the relationship between an individual and a collective body just as it manufactures the imagined interiority of the different types of people in the collective body itself. To borrow some terminology from Althusser, the chess game, as used by Jacobus, "'recruits' subjects among the individuals," marshaling them into professional categories and defining their relationships to the state.[9] The reader is "hailed" as member of the system in which he becomes a subject of and subjected to the exigencies of the game. Thus, while this chapter is a starting point for a more extended discussion of medieval chess and the way the game both produced (and was produced by) identities in the late Middle Ages, it also offers an overdue examination of the *Liber*, a text that historians and literary analysts have more or less ignored.

Cities, States, and the Italian Communes

Jacobus's *Liber* enjoyed a tremendous popularity in medieval Europe. Translators quickly reproduced it in both prose and poetry in almost every Western European vernacular, including German, French, Italian, Spanish, Catalan, Dutch, Swedish, and Czech, and an English version was the second English work printed on William Caxton's press in Bruges.[10] H. J. R. Murray's claim that the *Liber*'s circulation in the fourteenth century "must have almost rivalled that of the Bible itself" may exaggerate the point. Nevertheless, the fact that over three hundred manuscripts and incunabula are still extant suggests that his sentiment was not ill-founded.[11]

Given the popularity of the *Liber* one might expect a commensurate amount of information about the author himself. Yet the details of Jacobus's life remain scanty, and even the most recent scholarship has done little to pin down the where, when, and why of the text's production.[12] More concrete evidence would be needed to corroborate any particular narrative of origins. Still, a few minimal, although important, observations can be made about the historical forces that might have affected its composition.

Such historical contextualization serves two ends. First, it allows us to see some of the material and historical forces in which the *Liber* was embedded and to which it was responding. Jacobus's was a culture dominated by interfamilial warfare and organized by contractual bonds, which helps to explain the author's decision to jettison an organic metaphor for a nonorganic one. The composition of the *Liber* most likely took place in the last quarter of the thirteenth century, a time when the Italian communes experienced a tremendous amount of political turmoil and violence. With this violence came fundamental changes in the organization of civic communities, which increasingly sought a form of governance based on disinterested contracts rather than on kinship. In other words, Italy began to embrace the type of governance that lies at the heart of Jacobus's political model.[13]

Second, reading the *Liber* against other texts of its period allows us to chart more precisely the ways the work rewrites secular power. Jacobus's choice of subject and the text's composition date indicate that he was influenced by the many *specula* in circulation. The *Liber* aims to correct a king, a correction that comes through its many examples of virtuous behavior. Nevertheless, although Jacobus addresses the nature of kingship and the importance of virtue to the good of the realm, his treatise differs radically both in its audience and in its use of the chess game as an organizing metaphor for the state. By replacing the allegory of the state-as-body, the standard metaphor for political organization, and by addressing his text to all men, Jacobus reflects a larger cultural shift in the ways people imagined their relationship to the civic order. Or rather, by configuring the state as a chess game, Jacobus offered a vision of a secular order organized around contractual agreements rather than one organized around a centralized authority and sustained exclusively by kinship ties.

Although earlier scholarship positioned him as a writer in France, Jacobus de Cessolis most likely lived in Italy; the name Cessolis presumably derived from the northern Italian district of Cessole, an area very close to Genoa in the region of Lombardy.[14] The only concrete detail about his life appears in the *Liber*'s introduction, where he refers to himself as a Dominican friar.[15] Jacobus's familiarity with Lombard chess rules suggests that this is where he learned to play the game. It may also indicate that he composed his treatise here, although such an assumption seems more conjecture than anything else.[16] Better evidence for the author's Lombard connections appears in a Genoese cartulary written between 1317 and 1322, which names one Jacobus de Cessolis, Dominican, as a curate of Jacobus de Levanto, the Inquisitor of Lombardy and March of Genoa.[17]

In Jacobus's Italy, most cities were run by a *podestà*, the rough equivalent of a modern-day city manager, who tended to the daily workings of the city he served.[18] Hired from outside the city, the *podestà* usually held office for one year, after which his contract expired. In addition to his quotidian duties, the *podestà* was charged with keeping the peace between the city's large noble families. Such monitoring became increasingly difficult in the middle of the thirteenth century when the rise of the Guelf and Ghibelline factions exacerbated the already heightened inter- and intracity tensions between families. The Guelfs, the party of the tradesmen or *popolo*, supported the Church over lay authority, while the Ghibellines, usually made up of nobles, felt contrarily. Yet the philosophical significance of each was quickly forgotten as the composition of each group fluctuated. Not only did individuals shuffle their allegiances, whole cities would change from Guelf to Ghibelline (or vice versa) if it became materially and/or politically expedient to do so.[19] Like the earlier feuds between noble families, clashes between the two groups often had bloody consequences. One 1268 Ghibelline outbreak in Mantua resulted in a general slaughter of Guelfs that included children and the elderly.[20]

In Genoa, a coastal city isolated from its land-locked neighbors by a mountain range, political change may have taken place at a different pace, although it was no less contentious. Genoa had gained its status as an independent commune sooner than its neighbors had, and a 1056 charter granted its citizens the right to exercise their own justice without the supervision of neighboring nobility.[21] By the mid-eleventh century, the Genoese were governing themselves, having successfully escaped the notice of the imperial power, under whose auspices the Genoese ostensibly functioned, and of other powerful communal factions in northern Italy.[22] For the next century the city faced political strife from without and within. A protracted battle with Pisa in the early part of the thirteenth century was followed by an attempted revolt by a faction within the city in 1227, which was made while the *podestà* was away in the city of Lucca.[23] Several decades later, Genoa would see a more clearly defined assault by the Ghibellines on its predominantly Guelf rulers, but at this point the division between the two groups was not clear. As Steven A. Epstein has observed, the rise of the *popolo*, "a general phenomenon in most thirteenth-century Italian cities, was as yet feeble and tardy in Genoa."[24] And up until the mid-thirteenth century, the *popolo* had quietly supported the city's leaders. But a contraction in the shipping industry, the backbone of the Genoese economy, contributed in 1255 to a large-scale economic crisis and paved the way for a revolt. In 1257 the common people of Genoa, led by Guglielmo Boccanegra, a wealthy but nonnoble tradesman, rose up against the government.[25] During the next fifty-four years the city prospered financially yet floundered politically as various groups vied for power.

Although this government was not produced by democratic idealism, a much larger and diverse group of people enjoyed political power under Boccanegra's regime than they had under the previous *podestà*s, and the continued civil unrest testifies to a dispersion rather than a concentration of authority. An illustration of this can be seen in Genoa's reconfirmation of its pact with Manfred of Sicily, which was signed in 1257 by Boccanegra, the *podestà*, the *parlamento*, the *anziani* (a council of elders), and the consuls of the craft guilds. Again, Epstein notes that "no previous official act of the commune had included the guilds or their leaders as institutions or people having any say in the affairs of government."[26] Similarly, at the end of the treaty of Nyphaeum, a trade agreement made with the Byzantines in 1261, a variety of Genoese groups swore to uphold the accord, each signing his name and listing his trade. This diverse list included an innkeeper, a spicer, a draper, a dyer, a butcher, a barber, a cutler, and a smith, a list remarkably similar to the trades that Jacobus assigns to his eight pawns (see Table 1).[27]

Just as Jacobus's treatment of tradesmen as an integral part of a civic order reflects the political situation of late thirteenth-century Genoa, his decision to minimize the clergy's role on the board—the pieces commonly known as bishops are portrayed in the *Liber* as a community's judges—reflects the Church's decreased power over secular affairs. Tension between secular and papal powers had already started to build when the Church, worried about the increasing independence of monarchs and unwilling to submit to local taxation laws, began to assert its position at the head of a hierocracy, arrogating to itself ultimate authority over worldly affairs.[28] Aligning itself with the *popolo*, it tried to reclaim or secure its territory and used the power of excommunication to intimidate secular rulers. By this point, however, most rulers had abandoned the idea that the king was subject to God's vicar on earth in anything but spiritual affairs. Seeing taxation as a prime way to fund wars of expansion, secular authorities had no qualms about fighting against the Church-backed *popolo* in a quest to extend their domains.

This conflict came to a head in 1296 when Pope Boniface VIII published his famous *Clericis laicos* bull in an effort to prevent Philip IV of France ("Philip the Fair") from taxing local clergy.[29] Although this quarrel was quickly patched up, tensions boiled over again in 1301 when Philip arrested a bishop, a challenge to the tradition of clerical immunity from secular courts. Unlike the earlier squabble, this problem was not resolved so easily, ultimately leading to Boniface's excommunication of Philip in 1303 and, shortly after Boniface's death, to the removal of the papacy from Rome to Avignon in 1305, where it would remain for the next seventy-three years.

The altercations between Philip and Boniface triggered a flood of writing about the nature of secular power and its relationship to the papal state. James of Viterbo, the archbishop of Bourges, and his teacher Aegidius Romanus (Giles of Rome), the archbishop of Naples, were probably the most notable supporters of the hierocratic position. Of these two, Aegidius held the more dogmatic position on papal power. His *De ecclesiastica potestate*, written in 1301 or 1302, positioned the pope not only as the supreme authority on earth but also as the arbiter of secular power; any ruler not sanctioned by the Church would automatically be illegitimate.[30] By contrast Dante Alighieri and Marsiglio of Padua, who did not enjoy any benefits of papal preferment and who had first-hand experience with the disorder of Italian communes, offer a radically different view of secular governance, which both saw as having supremacy over papal power in worldly affairs.[31] In his 1313 *De monarchia* Dante puts forth the idea of a "temporal monarchy," a governance of one ruler over the entire world: "'Temporal monarchy' . . . is the political supremacy of one . . . over all things temporal, or . . . all things that are measured by time."[32] He goes on to argue that this ruler can either be invested with power from a higher authority (i.e., God and not the pope) or from general election. And finally, he systematically refutes all claims by papal supporters of the pope's supremacy on earth.[33]

That Jacobus blithely omits all mention of the Church's role in secular rule all but confirms at least two things. First, the altercations between the late thirteenth-century pope, Boniface VIII, and the recalcitrant King Philip help us further determine the *Liber*'s composition date. Had he been writing after 1296, Jacobus would have likely known about the struggles between Boniface VIII and Phillip and would have realized that a treatise addressing a monarch's power (without any acknowledgment of the papacy) might be seen as endorsing a secular rule unfettered by papal restrictions. Given that late thirteenth-century Genoa was a predominantly (even if not uniformly) Guelf commune and dependent on papal support, such an endorsement of the king's power would have likely proved career-threatening. Secondly, because Jacobus does not feel the need to engage in these debates, he feels free to reimagine the state in a way that broke with past representations of the political order, which had imagined the state as a human body.

This second point is striking, as political writers engaged in the conflict between Boniface and Philip consistently drew upon the state-as-body allegory to buttress their positions.[34] Marsiglio, after comparing the parts of the state to the habits of human bodies, claims "the state and its parts established according to reason are analogous to the animal and its parts perfectly formed according to nature."[35] Dante, who spends the bulk of the *Monarchia* dismissing the papal powers, makes several asides on the "nature" of the civic community and, like Marsiglio, uses the allegory of the body to describe the state. James of Viterbo, who subsumes the secular state within the body of the Church, similarly resorts to metaphors of the human body, where "certain members are divisible, and are divided into other lesser members: as the hand into fingers, and the fingers into joints."[36] In short, for these writers, the state-as-body metaphor offered an image of organic order and cohesion, and this discourse of the "natural" could be used to support the arguments of each side. For Marsiglio and Dante, the secular state naturally had the monarch at the head; for Aegidius and James, the body of the state was naturally bound by the body of the Church.

Bodies of Power

While the use of the body as an allegory for political order may be, as Leonard Barkan has argued, "heuristic, idealized, and propagandistic rather than empirical, literal, or concrete," its popularity betrays a faith in the power of this particular image and in the ideology it embodied.[37] It is, in short, difficult to use a "propagandistic" metaphor unless the metaphor itself has currency with the writers using it and the audience reading it.

Part of the appeal of the state-as-body comparison no doubt came from its grounding in scripture.[38] Although Plato and other classical writers often compared the state to a somatic being, Paul's description of the Christian community as analogous to the body that "is one and has many members" helped to give the metaphor weight in subsequent centuries.[39] Indeed, this passage, found in Corinthians, provided a template for later writers, who worked to refashion the metaphor to their own ends. Paul writes:

For the body does not consist of one member but of many. If the foot should say, "Because I am not a hand, I do not belong to the body," that would not make it any less a part of the body. And if the ear should say, "Because I am not an eye, I do not belong to the body," that would not make it any less a part of the body. . . . As it is, there are many parts, yet one body. The eye cannot say to the hand, "I have no need of you," nor again the head to the feet, "I have no need of you." On the contrary, the parts of the body which seem to be weaker are indispensable, and those parts of the body which we think less honorable we invest with the greater honor, and our unpresentable parts are treated with greater modesty, which our more presentable parts do not require. But God has so composed the body, giving the greater honor to the inferior part, that there may be no discord in the body, but that the members may have the same care for one another.[40]

Here Paul makes a compelling case of the interdependence of the members of a community. Christians, like the eyes and hands, need each other, not just for mutual comfort but for basic survival. And while Paul admits to a hierarchy among parts, he insists that each must "have the same care for one another."

That this image was easily adaptable to secular ends is readily seen in the writings of Aegidius Romanus, who first used the metaphor to validate secular political power and then used it again to support the papacy. Roughly twenty years before his *De ecclesiastica potestate* (*On Ecclesiastical Power*), Aegidius Romanus, later to be one of the most enthusiastic supporters of papal authority, composed *De regimine principum* (*On the Government of Princes*) (ca. 1280), at the request of King Philip III. An advice manual for Philip's son, the future ruler, Philip IV, *De regimine* repeatedly draws on the trope of the state as a human body. But unlike his later *De ecclesiastica*, which sees civic order as subject to papal authority, *De regimine principum* imagines a body of state with the king as its head. The text consists of three lengthy books, each of which examines a certain aspect of the community's organic order. The first book explains the king's virtues and passions, crucial to the role of the "head" in dispensing justice. The second discusses the organization of the king's household, which, like the realm, is a body of its own. The third surveys the king's rule of his kingdom, the largest part of the body with many members necessary to the health of the whole.

Aegidius's *De regimine principum* came as part of a flurry of *specula regis*, or mirrors-for-magistrates, written at this time.[41] Various *specula* appeared in such great numbers during the second half of the thirteenth century that some scholars suggest this age produced "the true *miroir au prince*."[42] In addition to *De regimine principum*, Vincent of Beauvais's *De morali principis institutione* (*On the Education of Princes*) and *De eruditione filiorum nobilium* (*On the Education of Noble Women*) (both ca. 1260), Aquinas's *De regno ad regem Cypri* (*On Government to the King of Cyprus*) (ca. 1265), and Ptolemy of Lucca's *De regimine principum* (*On the Government of Rulers*) (a continuation of Aquinas's *De regno* that appeared between 1300 and 1305) were composed in a time span of roughly thirty years. Along with these Latin texts, a number of vernacular advice books also appeared, including *L'Enseignement des princes* (*The Education of Princes*) (1240) by Robert of Blois, the anonymous *Libro de la nobleza y lealtad* (*Book of Nobility and Royalty*) (1250–60), and the anonymous Old Norse *Konungs skuggsjá* (*King's Mirror*) (1240–63). Fueled by the thirteenth-century interest in political theory, William of Moerbeke produced the first Latin translation of Aristotle's *Politics* in 1278, which later writers used as a source for their own works.[43]

Like Aegidius in *De regimine principum*, each of these authors uses the human body as the predominant metaphor for civic organization; in doing so each emphasizes the naturalness of a community's hierarchical ordering and the elevation of some of its parts over others. Under this schema different members of a civic community had little independent mobility or identity. In a human body a foot could not wake up one day and be a stomach. Similarly, in a civic body an illiterate farmer was expected to spend his life working the land; he could not abruptly decide to become a tax collector. While these works varied in the powers and virtues they assigned to the ideal monarch, none questioned the monarch's place in the center as the "mind" or "soul" of the kingdom.[44] In short, although writers may have disagreed about the relative strength of a body's different parts, the image of the state as a naturally occurring and physiologically functioning unit held sway.

In drawing on this trope, thirteenth-century writers were, like Aegidius Romanus, echoing the ideas of Paul. Yet in a more immediate context, many were enlisting (and responding to) John of Salisbury, whose *Policraticus* mapped a detailed relationship between the various parts of the stately body. John, who launched his bureaucratic career as a secretary for Archbishop Theobald of Canterbury, was appointed in 1155 as King Henry II's chancellor.[45] Although he had supported Henry in his battle against King Stephen for the English throne, he soon became a vocal opponent of the king's policies toward the Church. He was temporarily exiled from the court in 1156, at which point he began to write the *Policraticus*. (The *Policraticus*'s subtitle, *Of the Frivolities of Courtiers and the Footprints of Philosophers*, suggests the ambitiousness of John's project.) In its first incarnation the *Policraticus* offered both a philosophical study of happiness and a diatribe against the type of indulgence John had witnessed among the members of Henry's household. After John returned to court, he expanded the text to include advice for courtiers on how best to counsel the king, a subject that ultimately led him to meditate on the nature of the entire political body.

John's discussion of the body politic lies at the heart of the *Policraticus*—this section comprises the bulk of books 4, 5, and 6—and it is here that John's state-as-body metaphor receives its fullest explication.[46] In a lengthy section of book 5, John describes the state as "a sort of body which is animated by the grant of divine reward and which is driven by the command of the highest equity and ruled by a sort of rational management."[47] The position of the head is occupied by the king; the heart by the senate; the ears, eyes, and mouth by the governors; the hands by the officials and soldiers; the flanks by king's assistants; the stomach by the treasurers and record keepers (i.e., the members of the Exchequer); and the feet by the peasants, who are bound to the land.[48]

Although John hierarchizes the parts of the body, he (again like Paul) also repeatedly stresses the interdependence of the various components of his physiological model. If one organ fails, the entire body is jeopardized. To demonstrate this, John uses the example of the tyrant. When the magistrate oppresses his subjects, he explains, it is as though the head of the body grows so large that its members cannot sustain it at all, or not without grave consequences.[49] Similarly, the feet are crucial to the body's well-being, because they support the parts above them. Like organic human bodies, the state by nature functions in certain ways preordained by divine forces. If any part of the political body does not follow its proper natural function, the body becomes infected and eventually dies.[50]

John's idea of government is not exactly one of subordination and rule. Although the allegory of the body imposes a rigid set of restrictions on individual autonomy, he tries to allow for a certain measure of liberty among the members of a body politic. John's endorsement of tyrannicide in the case of unjust governance offers a case in point. That a subject is "permitted to slay" a ruler "whom it is permitted to flatter" indicates that said subject has some power of reasonable discrimination and freedom of action.[51] Yet at the same time the model put forth by the *Policraticus* remains antithetical to most notions of equality, and John's gestures toward shared power are undercut not only by the allegory itself but also by his focus on the head and the heart to the near exclusion of all other parts. That John addresses *Policraticus* to the officers of court, and that much of his focus remains on the king, underlines the power discrepancy between noble and commoner.[52] Even the soul, which represents the priesthood's task of tending to the body's spiritual side, remains subordinate to the king's power.

Thus while the *Policraticus* may gesture toward granting autonomy to the body politic's various parts, it does not stop to consider the matter of individual choice. In accordance with its genre, this *speculum regis* offers a mirror for the king alone to police his own actions, the other body parts having only the power of physical motion. Except in the case of tyrannicide, the members of the civic body are not, for John, capable of decision making, a power that resided exclusively in the head. And even in this case, the parts would need to form a collective group as a virtual body working in concert to achieve the ruler's ouster. In John's discussion of individual freedom, he highlights this limited capacity for freedom even more strikingly; at the same time that he praises liberty as important to a kingdom, he argues that liberty should be used moderately, especially among the vulgar.[53]

John's vision of the state-as-body endured, even as economic changes began to sweep aside traditional notions of social hierarchy, and even as the rise of the merchant class and the growing power of guilds produced "a form of social organization not dependent on blood ties."[54] A surprisingly flexible metaphor, the image at times promoted the state as a collective of parts ruled by a head and at times as a body with somewhat autonomous members. Thus, while the whole body still had a sphere of action higher than its individual parts, those parts began to take on a capacity for action that did not necessarily impact the larger order.

This increased emphasis on an individual's self-regulation within the state-as-body metaphor appears most clearly in Aquinas's thirteenth-century *De regno*.[55] At first, this text seems only to reproduce John's model. Presenting the Aristotelian argument that man is, by nature, a social and political animal, Aquinas claims that individuals cannot survive in isolation.[56] In addition to his natural need for community, man has been blessed with reason, a facility that dictates a division of labor as the most efficient way to organize a polity. This is, he points out, much like the organization of the human body: "Among the members of the body there is one which moves all the rest, namely the heart: in the soul there is one faculty which is pre-eminent, namely reason" ["In membrorum enim multitudine unum est quod omnia movet, scilicet cor; et in partibus animae una vis principaliter prae-sidet, scilicet ratio"].[57]

As John does in the *Policraticus*, Aquinas in *De regno* draws on the image of the body to justify the state's "natural" hierarchies and the interdependence of its various parts. At the same time he expands the king's power, vesting the community's "heart" with both the faculty of reason and the responsibility for spiritual guidance; as mind and soul, the ruler holds together the diverse elements of the body. This subtle yet important switch moves the king away from a role of participatory decision maker to one of spiritual shepherd. Just as the king is to the body politic, so too is the soul to the body and God to the world.[58] Thus while the king should look on the persons in his kingdom "as the members of his own body" ["sicut propria membra"], he aims more at preserving its overall welfare rather than controlling its individual parts, who must *by their own volition* act virtuously.[59] Ultimately, one's own virtue enables one to live a good life ("virtus enim est qua bene vivitur").[60]

Aquinas placed a similar emphasis on individual responsibility in his *Summa theologica*. When discussing the nature of the body politic, Aquinas observes that the whole of a community cannot be truly good unless each of its members is virtuous: "So it is impossible for the welfare of the community to be in a healthy state unless the citizens are virtuous."[61] Indeed, laws cannot monitor all things, "but only the graver vices from which the majority can abstain" ["sed solum graviora, a quibus possibile est maiorem partem multitudinis abstinere"].[62] The community, in other words, depends on its individual citizens to monitor their own behavior.[63]

The increasing emphasis on individual sovereignty grew out of and reinforced fundamental changes in the image of kingship itself. In *The King's Two Bodies* Ernst Kantorowicz demonstrates the ways the king's person, in both the Middle Ages and the Renaissance, was simultaneously viewed as an individual body and also as a corporate body politic, and he traces this metaphorical doubling to an earlier era that saw the king's body as a "twinned" person, "one descending from nature, the other from grace."[64] The king was, in essence, both a man and a representative of Christ. In the thirteenth century, however, this "Christ-centered" image of the king began to change, becoming by the end of the thirteenth century a "Law-centered" and still later a "Polity-centered" kingship. No longer did the prince enact divine will. Instead, he derived his power both from God and from his people: *populo faciente et Deo inspirante*.[65] Moreover, the prince himself was now subject to Justice, which ruled through or in his body.[66] The king's second body had become, in essence, the body politic. Texts like the anonymous *De regno* and Aquinas's *Summa* support Kantorowicz's arguments, and both works emphasize the king's role as an embodiment of God's will and also as subject to God's law.

Yet unnoted by Kantorowicz are the ways that this transition to law as the primary regulatory force in society helped to increase a subject's responsibility for his or her own behavior.[67] Or rather, subjects (and the king was now included in this category) became increasingly called upon to exercise sovereignty over their own actions, and the secular state acquired a power increasingly based on psychological coercion. At the same time, most of the *specula regis* written at the end of the thirteenth century, while emphasizing the importance of individual self-regulation, stop short of addressing the subjects themselves. *De regno*, subtitled "to the king of Cyprus," is ostensibly aimed at an audience of one, and Aquinas's thoughts in the *Summa* form only a part of an extended academic meditation on the nature and purpose of theology. Thus, while both texts may vest the parts of a given body politic with more responsibility than the *Policraticus*, they do little to make this responsibility available to the full spectrum of society, focusing instead on those at the top, be they the lawmakers or the king.

This reluctance to endow a community's subjects with autonomy and responsibility does not appear in Aegidius Romanus's *De regimine principum*, a work composed roughly fifteen years after *De regno*.[68] In *De regimine* Aegidius specifically addresses his text to all men, encouraging his readers to strive for the same virtues as the king: "Therefore in moral teaching we must use evidence and examples. . . . For though this book is titled 'of the teaching of princes,' all people will be taught by it. And although not every man may be king or prince, every man should desire to make himself worthy to be a king or a prince."[69] In case the reader misses his appeal to "all people," Aegidius repeats this injunction soon after, stating that he seeks to show how a king, "and so how every man," should rule himself.[70] Later in the text Aegidius compares the state to a human body. But although he acknowledges some parts as higher than others, he stresses the corporate nature of the whole. The state like "a body is made up of divers limbs joined together," and every part must be willing to sacrifice itself for the good of the whole.[71] For Aegidius, the body symbolizes the importance of diversity to a community rather than that of hierarchy or place. Just as the body has many limbs, so too does a city have many artisans. Just as the body's parts are all unique, so too is a city made up of different types of professions. Nor does Aegidius confine his analogy to the state as a whole. He also uses it to show the cooperative nature of a body politic's smaller parts, such as the army. As he observes: "the army is like a body, just as the limbs help each other so too do the men help each other." Although Aegidius's use of the human body foregrounds a physiological justification for a unified state, *De regimine principum* does not dwell on the biological forces behind the allegory. Instead the power of nature is replaced with the power of justice, a force that governs the relationships between the two parts, and between all the parts and the whole. This is, Aegidius observes, like a foot and an eye; each needs the other to walk in the right direction. Inequality or lack of cooperation will make the body sick.[72]

Nevertheless, although Aegidius addresses all men, his treatise was composed for, and officially addressed to, one person: Prince Philip, soon to be Philip IV, one of the most powerful and ruthless rulers of the late Middle Ages.[73] *De regimine principum* may dissect, analyze, and explicate the body of the state, yet it ultimately rebuilds it as a whole and reestablishes Philip as the central power in the realm. Early in book 2, Aegidius insists that "each citizen should know how to rule his own house and demesne, not only because such ruling is to his own profit, but also because such ruling contributes to the common profit, as in the profit of realm and city."[74] This encouragement to support the "common profit" works to mask the book's larger project, which advises Philip on ways to maintain the kingdom for his own benefit. In sum, Aegidius urges the citizens in his imagined community to embrace their autonomy while denying them the means or incentive to do so; the king is still the only essential member of the body politic and the actions of his subjects have only a limited effect on the working of the larger order.

Objective Subjectivity

As the squabbles between papal and secular powers continued to intensify, as the rulers of the Italian city-states battled for power, and as writers struggled to maintain the fiction that these republics, like the human bodies they contained, were naturally formed and divinely inspired, Jacobus composed his *Liber*. While the authors of late medieval *specula regis* typically cast the state as a biological entity—not only did they compare the state to a body, but John of Salisbury, Dante, Marsiglio, Aquinas, and Aegidius all see man as political by nature—Jacobus embraces an ideal of civic order produced by human invention. Philometer, upon seeing Evilmerodach's tyranny, manufactures a solution; he does not lecture about a ruler's natural duties or about the intrinsic order that should hold sway over Babylon. Moreover, he never addresses the *Liber* to a single ruler or privileges a king as the text's most important audience. In his *Prologus* Jacobus stresses this point, noting that "many people both secular and clerical" had tried to persuade him to compose the treatise on chess and that he had finally given in to their requests (3).[75] In the bulk of the *Liber* Jacobus continues to focus on the state as a whole, taking care to account for all groups of people, from nobles to commoners ("nobilium ac popularium"), that comprise a community, and his chess game proposes to teach all people to master virtuous behavior.

Such a mastery of one's own actions is fundamental to this alternative model of civic order. As discussed above, the traditional state-as-body model cast civic community as a physiologically rather than contractually based entity. Bound to the base of society, feet (the farmers) could not simply walk away from the kingdom. Their position at the bottom of the body came from God and symbolized their subordination to the rest of the body. Farmers, like feet, were also seen as incapable of deep thought and thus were encouraged to rely on the head, the king, to take care of them. By contrast, Jacobus uses his chess allegory to break down the monarch's body, which he replaces with individual bodies, each having a certain amount of autonomy within the larger civic order. Rather than serving as feet, the farmer appears as a pawn that sits in front of the rook (or, as depicted in the *Liber*, the king's legate) at the far right of the board. Because he provides food for the entire community, he is tied to the legate and to the rest of the kingdom. But at the same time, he is a body in his own right—the piece is "made in the human form" ["in humana specie factus"] (74). As such, his contributions to the kingdom come from practical necessity rather than biological obligation. Thus, as Jacobus reminds us several times, farmers must have *utilitas* for the community and must behave in certain ways that benefit the common good.

This depiction of citizens as independent bodies, tied by contract to the political whole, raises unsettling questions. To continue with the example of the farmer, how can one be sure that he will live virtuously, honor his contracts, and contribute his share to the collective whole? If the farmer does not live a moral life, if he cheats his customers or refuses to plow his fields, his immoral behavior could in turn affect the health and welfare of the entire community.

Jacobus tries to solve this problem through the structure of the game itself, which allows him to use the power of shame and the threat of exposure to encourage a reader/player to monitor his own actions. The stories in each chapter illustrate proper behavior via numerous exempla and *senten-tiae*; a knight reading the *Liber*, for example, would see a model of his ideal behavior.[76] Yet at the same time, the public nature of this representation raises the possibility for shame and exposure. Or rather, the knight is not the only one able to look at his piece. We, too, can see the ways he should act. We, too, can judge if he has acted correctly. The exempla themselves further highlight this potential for exposure, and many show how improper behavior is ultimately revealed and punished.[77] In such stories, moral transgressions become externally marked, scarring the transgressor's body and becoming the sole marker of his identity. In short, the individuals in Jacobus's stories make what seem to be personal decisions. But when their vices spill over from their personal relationships to the other members of the community, the fabric of society is threatened.

The process of identification described above, the ways in which a reader/player is positioned as a citizen in a contractually bound body, resembles that found in Althusser's description of a modern state. As Althusser would have it, the state continually presents its citizens with a fantasy of their relations to each other and to their production. We internalize this fantasy because the state, through various mechanisms, presents it to each of us as individuals. We are, in short, each "hailed" as a member of a larger system (see the quote that opened this chapter), and we accept such hailing as it confirms and validates our position in the larger whole.

Althusser's model, which grows out of (and is aimed at) the mechanics of a capitalist system, depends on a worker's alienation from his own means of production and thus differs in scale and nature from an allegory of medieval political order. Moreover, whereas Althusser does not endorse the type of state control he describes, Jacobus sees individuals as necessarily embedded in (and as answering to) the concerns of a community as a whole. Nevertheless, Jacobus, like Althusser, is interested in the ways professional identity constructs a political order and in the ways that this political order in turn constructs and confirms individual identity. A reader of the *Liber* is called on to identify himself as a specific "type" of member of the civic body and, after he has done so, to police his own behavior.

The text does this hailing primarily through its vivid descriptions of the pieces, which encourage a reader/player to recognize himself as a figure on the board.[78] The description of the first pawn is emblematic of this concern:

Fuit autem sic formatus: nam fuit in humana specie factus, habens in manu dextra ligonem, quo terra foditur. In sinistra habet virgam, qua armenta et cetera talia animalia diriguntur. In corrigia seu in cingulo, habuit falcem seu sarculum, quo vineae seu arbores putantur, et eis superflua decidunter. Ad haec tria omnis agricultura reducitur. (74)

[Thus he was formed: He was made in the shape of a human, having in the right hand a shovel with which the earth is dug. In the left he has a rod, with which the herd and the other such animals are directed. In the shoe string or belt, he has a scythe or a cutting tool with which the vines or trees are trimmed and extra growth is cut down from them. All agriculture can be reduced to these three things.]

Although most chess sets of the time, even the more expensive ones, used simple, nonanthropomorphic markers for the pawns, Jacobus here and elsewhere insists that these eight pieces be *in humana specie factus.*[79] Each chapter in book 3, the book that treats the *populares,* contains some version of this phrase—*in forma humana* (the chapter on the smiths), *in humana specie fuit* (the merchants/money changers), and so on—to remind the reader of the piece's human shape. Nor is Jacobus content to note that the pieces are human, for he continues each portrait by listing instruments that identify an individual's trade. Just as the farmer holds a rod to herd his animals, the smith holds a hammer to pound his iron and the innkeeper holds a loaf of bread to offer to his guests. Although Jacobus does not feel the need to specify the human forms of the *nobiles,* which were apparently already implicit, these pieces like the *populares* are marked by their professional responsibilities. The knight, for example, sits "on a horse," and "he must have a helmet on his head, and a lance in his right hand" ["super equum . . . debet enim habere galleam in capite, hastam in manu dextra"] (39). In his left hand he holds a sword, and his combined equipment signifies his readiness to fight. In this way he and the other chess figures are not only doubly defined as human, each possessing a human form and tools, but are also marked by their ability to contribute to the common good. Thus portrayed, each piece is first and foremost a member of the community.

If these detailed descriptions foreground the importance of each individual's membership in the civic body, the explanation of each piece's placement highlights the interconnectedness of the community's members. The farmer sits in front of the rook "because it is necessary for the king's vicar to provide food for the whole kingdom" ["quia regis vicarium per hunc oportet toti regno necessaria providere ad victum"] (73). Just as the other citizens depend on the farmer for their sustenance, the farmer needs the legate (behind him) to distribute his wares and the knight (behind him and to his right) to protect his crops. The second pawn, the smith, sits in front of the knight "because the knights need to have bridles and footwear, saddles and armor" ["quia milites indigent habere frena et calcaria, sellas et arma"] (80). But he also notes that the smith is responsible for precious metals, and in this way he is linked to the merchant two spaces away.[80] Third in line is a single piece that represents both the notaries and the wool workers. Both of these groups contribute to the creation of texts, an art essential for the judges who sit on the back row (behind the notaries and next to the king) and "compose laws at the mandate of the ruler" ["leges de mandato principis condere"] (31). The money changers, placed strategically in front of the king, sit next to the notaries. And next to the money changers are the physicians and apothecaries, who tend to the queen and her ladies. And so on. Depicted by Jacobus, each piece produces a good or service for the *res publica*, and his professional responsibilities link him to the community's other members. In short, contractual ties, which in turn depend on individual behavior, hold the pieces together.

At the same time that the pieces' descriptions may highlight their individualistic natures, Jacobus does not make them detailed to the point of exclusion. The knight's arms mark his social group rather than a particular order or family crest, while the judges are called upon only to enforce laws justly without any articulation of what those laws might be. In the row of *populares*, the pieces all have instruments specific to their trades rather than ones specific to a particular guild or to a particular region. Almost any reader can find his or her piece easily and insert himself or herself in the most appropriate category. If the readers/players do not see themselves as a member of the board, they are merely moving pieces in an abstract game and the didactic thrust of Jacobus's lesson is lost.

Given the *Liber*'s totalizing view of civil society along with its invitation to readers (or auditors) to identify themselves as members of it, Jacobus must have conceived of a broad audience for his book. After all, the text addresses itself to a farmer and the king with equal urgency; each merits his own lengthy chapter, and each chapter contains exempla that stress the importance of virtuous behavior. Obviously, Jacobus's ideal of total inclusion does not mean that the text itself had to be known universally in order to assert its ideal civic structure. Yet while not everyone played chess or possessed the ability to read a text of this sort, all men were by default participants in the imaginary civil order. And although farmers were probably neither the intended nor primary audience, the work's tremendous popularity reveals a wide readership, which, given a large number of extant vernacular editions, most likely included members of the trade classes. That the *Liber* was translated into almost every Western European vernacular (as listed earlier in this chapter) testifies to its availability to the laity. In short, because the *Liber* envisions a *universal* ability for individuals to recognize the difference between virtuous and nonvirtuous behavior and to govern their own actions accordingly, it must necessarily address the civic community as a whole rather than simply parts of it. To do the latter would be to contradict the very operation of moral autonomy the text articulates.

A reader's ability to identify himself (or herself) in the text and game of the *Liber* holds the promise of objective detachment and of autonomous action. If one can see oneself as one *really is*, one can *know* oneself and one's place in the social matrix. A knight looking at himself on the board, for example, would not simply see his identity mirrored, but would also be able to touch and move "himself" across the board. Proper self-regulation in turn leads to additional rewards, and many of the *Liber*'s exempla highlight the material profits of consistently good behavior.

These incentives appear clearly in the chapter on the fourth pawn, which represents a community's money changers and merchants. Here Jacobus recounts the story of Obertus Guterinus, a money changer from Genoa.[81] Obertus is an honest money changer. But one day a duplicitous merchant comes to Obertus insisting that, although he has no receipt of deposit, he has left 500 florins in Obertus's care. Because Obertus runs an honest business and believes in the integrity of others, he gives the money to the merchant, who proceeds to parley 500 florins into 15,000 florins, which he then bequeaths to Obertus after his death. The merchant's deception is by no means praiseworthy, and Jacobus does not condone his swindle. Yet the merchant ultimately atones for his sin by repaying the "loan" with a more-than-commensurate amount of interest. More significantly, Obertus's commitment to honesty results in a sizable reward rather than a punishment. If the merchant's duplicity had instead led Obertus to sin himself, the effects would have rippled throughout the larger community, infecting all of his subsequent deals.

In the chapter on the notaries and wool workers, Jacobus offers an even more powerful incentive to practice the virtue of friendliness.[82] He tells the story of two merchants, one from Baldach (another name for Babylon) and one from Egypt, who develop a strong friendship through their trades. When the Baldacharian falls desperately in love with the Egyptian's fiancée, the Egyptian gives his bride away to save his friend from heartbreak. Later, when the Egyptian is accused of murder, the Baldacharian comes to Egypt and offers to die for him. This action impresses the Egyptian judge so greatly that he grants the Egyptian merchant a full pardon.

Jacobus offers a similar lesson on friendship in his chapter on the knights. After advising knights to be faithful to one another, Jacobus tells the story of Damon and Pythias, two knights who were best friends.[83] When the King of Sicily condemns one of them to die, the other stands in as a surety while the accused goes home to arrange his affairs. The condemned man returns on the day of his execution, an act that impresses the king, who excuses both men and asks to be their friend. In each instance friendship proves literally life-saving. Yet the friendship exhibited by these men is also publicly recorded for all to see. In this way the merchants and knights reading the *Liber* are prompted to act virtuously both for personal gain and for public glory.

Public exposure, however, does not always lead to glory, and while the ability to see oneself "from above" allows one to reap the rewards of behaving virtuously, it also shows the potential for shame for those who act immorally. The ever-lurking threat of punishment suggests that the autonomy promoted in the *Liber* is at best conditional. If readers/players can see themselves in the game, then so too can everyone else, and in seeing them, measure them by the same exacting standards articulated by Jacobus. Although ostensibly free to accept or reject the game's lessons, a reader/player inevitably risks being publicly humiliated if he does not adhere to the virtue embodied by his piece. Because the objects of shame are communally determined, shame distributes power over the social hierarchy, giving a community license to determine individual values, decisions, and self-understanding. Jacobus uses its power both to regulate the actions of reader/player and, more tacitly, to validate the game itself.

Such an example of public shame appears shortly before the story of Obertus, when Jacobus tells a tale about a woman who hoards her gold. After her death the gold she has squirreled away is discovered, and the bishop orders the townsfolk to throw it into the pit with her corpse. Yet this act fails when the body begins to cry despondently, attracting the attention of the people in the town and causing the local bishop to take action:

Cum autem multis diebus vicinos multipliciter molestasset, de episcopi mandata ad eam extumulandam venitur, apertoque tumulo aurum collatum et liquatum in ipsius os igne sulfureo reperitur, ut verum sit illud: Aurum sitisti, aurum bibe. Corpus autem avarissimae mulieris fetidissimum acceptum ex tumulo in cloacam proiecit. (101)

[However, because it (the voice) troubled the neighborhood for many days, the bishop gave them leave to open the sepulcher. And when they had opened it, they found all the gold melted with fire full of sulfur in her mouth, so that it is true: "You thirsted after gold, now drink gold!" And they took the most rotten body of the most covetous woman out of the tomb, and it was cast out in the sewer.]

Here gold functions as both an object of avarice and its embodiment. Its discovery leads directly to the exposure of the old woman's sin, which is then inscribed on her corpse, her mouth symbolically announcing its own vice. The entire thrust of the story underscores the inevitability of exposure; the woman's attempts to hide her gold and her greed fail. Immediately after death her own body betrays her, foreclosing all possibility of secrets or privacy.

The chapter on the tavern keepers, represented by the sixth pawn, contains a similar lesson on public exposure. In this chapter's final exemplum Jacobus tells the story of a father and son who go on a pilgrimage to the shrine of St. James in Galicia, Spain. When they stop one night at an inn, the innkeeper plants a silver cup in the son's bag and in the morning accuses him of stealing. The son is hanged for the crime, after which the father pays a fine and continues on the pilgrimage alone. On the way home the father travels back by the same inn and sees his son's corpse still hanging outside. The body talks to the father, revealing the crime and explaining that St. James has tended to his dead body. The father fetches the judge, who summons the innkeeper. The innkeeper soon confesses that he acted "on account of avarice and greed" ["propter avaritiam et cupiditatem rerum"], and he is subsequently put to death (121). In both of these stories sinful acts and the shame they bring have the power to reach beyond death and back into a living community.

Such threats of shame and exposure are not confined to the members of *populares*, but are universal. In the chapter on the queen, Jacobus, admonishing noblewomen to guard their chastity, recounts the story of Rosimond, a former duchess of Lombardy whose husband has died in war. When Catinus, the King of Hungary, comes to attack her lands, she becomes sexually aroused and offers to relinquish her kingdom if he will marry her. Catinus agrees, and they wed. On the first night Catinus fulfills his marriage debt. Then, on the second, he hands her over to twelve other Hungarians, ostensibly to be raped by all.[84] On the third night he impales her on a spear from her genitals to her mouth and displays her outside, stating, "Such a lecherous wife, who betrayed her city on account of her concupiscence, should have such a marriage" ["Talis libidinosa uxor, quae propter concupiscentiam civitatem suam prodidit, talem debet habere maritum"] (30). The last story in the chapter on the queen, the story's narrative power rests as much on the threat of public display as it does on Catinus's brutality. While Rosimond's death is decidedly horrific, the exposure of her body underscores the civic nature of her offense, which lies in her willingness to sacrifice the common good in the interest of personal desire. In contrast to their mother, Rosimond's two daughters manage to avoid the Hungarians by stuffing rotten chickens under their armpits. The smell causes the invaders to recoil in disgust and allows them to escape. Having successfully guarded their virtue, they are rewarded: one becomes the queen of France and the other the queen of Germany. In this case civic responsibility is rewarded with the power to rule.

The respective actions of Rosimond and her daughters highlight the power of choice given to each member of the community.[85] The three women face a common danger. One chooses to sacrifice the realm to fill her lust; she is subsequently humiliated before all. Two choose to protect themselves, and they are ultimately rewarded with kingdoms of their own. Each woman acts independently of a higher authority, making her decision as an autonomous thinking member of the political community. That the daughters' rewards are earthly, rather than divine, testifies to the significance of proper choice in the human world rather than in one beyond. Similarly, Rosimond's lust, while sinful in itself, is not punished by divine authority but by Catinus, whose speech emphasizes the impact of her actions on the civic community, and her body serves to warn everyone of what can happen to those who betray their *civitatem*.

Although the danger of exposure becomes a means to control all members of the body politic, it exercises a particular power over the king, the first of the chess pieces discussed and the only one that directly corresponds to a character in the framing story. Philometer may teach the nobles to play, yet Jacobus records only the game's effects on Evilmerodach. That Jacobus charts Evilmerodach's progress—he turns from evil tyrant to benevolent ruler—brings the *Liber*, despite its implied universal audience, closer to the model of a proper *speculum* addressed to a single king. Within a treatise that promotes the idea of equal responsibility for moral choice and nearly equal freedom to move around the board (i.e., to affect the common good), Jacobus still emphasizes the importance of the king's actions even as he highlights the ways that this imagined ruler, like his citizens, is subject to the regulating power of public surveillance. Indeed, while the king may exercise more power than the other members of the civic community, he is also more exposed to public scrutiny and thus more threatened by the potential for shame.

We are reminded of the ruler's importance in the opening description of the chess king:

Rex sic formam accepit a principio. Nam in solio positus fuit, purpura indutus, quae est vestis regalis, habens in capite coronam, in manu dextra sceptrum in sinistra habens pilam rotundam. Nam super alios obtinet et accipit dignitatem, quam praetendit corona capitis. (13)

[Thus the king receives the form of a prince. For he is in his own place, dressed in purple, which is royal clothing, having a crown on his head, in his right hand a scepter, and in his left a round ball. For above all he is given and receives dignity, which the crown on his head shows forth.]

Like the *populares* and the other *nobiles*, the king's physical appearance confirms his proper role in the social order. Unlike the other pieces, however, the description places a decided emphasis on the ruler's inner virtue. The orb signifies the realm and people over which he rules; the scepter denotes his authority as a judge; and the purple robes reflect his noblesse. In short, the king is literally clothed in virtue, a condition suggesting that any deviation from a virtuous life would leave him both literally and figuratively naked.

In addition to his clothing, the king's actions are exposed for all to see. In one of the first exempla set out for the king, the emperor Alexander arrives at a city and declares that he will attack it. When his former teacher Anaximenes comes out from the city to beg the emperor's clemency, Alexander cuts him off midsentence, vowing to do the exact opposite of whatever the philosopher requests. Hearing this pronouncement, Anaximenes immediately asks Alexander to destroy the city, and the emperor realizes that he has been tricked. Still, he must stop his attack: "although he was angry, he would rather let got of his anger at the city than go against his oath, and thus the safety of the city was obtained by virtue of one oath" ["maluit enim iram voluntatem, quam habebat contra cicitatem [*sic*] dimittere, quam contra iuramentum venire, et ita salus urbis unius iuramenti beneficio obtenta est"] (17). Here individual desire is subordinated to a public vow, and the reader is reminded that verbalized (i.e., externalized) promises form part of one's public identity. In order for Alexander to be a man of his word, he cannot act out his internal desires; to go back on his promise would be to open up the potential for shame.

So important is the king's virtue that the potential for shame and the power of public surveillance reach into the framing story. By making Evilmerodach's psychology visible to the tyrant, Philometer also makes it visible to the king's court. Evilmerodach's conversion is theatrical and public, and the philosopher teaches the king the nature of the moves in front of the court's nobles. Yet Evilmerodach's eventual mastery of the game has *two* audiences— one in the narrative (his nobles) and one outside of it (the readers)—and Jacobus reminds his readers that to play the game is to expose oneself to scrutiny. Or rather, the only way one can see one's own weaknesses is to display them publicly. Thus while one may be free to move, this freedom will always be checked by fear of exposure and the possibility of shame. An incorrect "move" is never an innocent one.

The extension of shame into the framing narrative in turn allows Jacobus to validate the game itself, and he uses the power of external perspective to legitimize chess as a medium for moral instruction and an objective test of virtue. Recounting the history of the tyrant's rise to power, Jacobus first outlines Evilmerodach's vicious behavior. Evilmerodach's depravity established, the author then offers a solution through the mouth of the philosopher. Because we as the audience members have already accepted Jacobus's evaluation of Evilmerodach as a tyrant, we have no problem accepting Philometer's remedy. Or rather, Jacobus does not simply offer his readers a seemingly objective view of themselves but calls on them to sanction the story of the game's creation. Our attention diverted to Evilmerodach's excesses, we never question the *Liber*'s authority or the authoritative viewpoint offered by Philometer. Because Philometer's view resembles our own—after all, most readers would agree that one should not feed one's father to the birds—the story validates our own moral stance. Evilmerodach's refusal to question the game or his teacher, and his acceptance of it as an objective, authoritative means of self-improvement only reaffirm this.

Above I have tried to emphasize the ways Jacobus's allegory broke with previous representations of the body politic. It is, however, important to note that the *Liber* also diverged from earlier texts that use chess as a metaphor for civic life, and a quick look at these texts reveals that Jacobus's originality lay less in the creation of the game-as-state metaphor—this had already been done—than it did in the ways he used the game to conceive of individual autonomy.

One such work, the thirteenth-century *Quaedam moralitas de scaccario* (which Murray retitled the "Innocent Morality"), uses the chess game to represent the intrinsic problems of earthly life, and to some extent the author's ideas about social order resemble those espoused by Jacobus.[86] According to the *Quaedam*'s allegory the world resembles a chessboard. Both the world and the game are ruled by a king, and both consist of interdependent units—people in the world and pieces that represent people in the game—working together to survive. Although occupying different social stations, the pieces, like the people they represent, form a single community and face a common fate. The king's law binds his subjects, and the author implies that the social order will fail if the pieces/people do not fulfill their respective roles.

Yet unlike the *Liber*, which emphasizes the need for virtues among members of a civic body, the *Quaedam* uses the game to show human depravity. Of the pieces described, only two exhibit virtue: the king and the rook. An embodiment of absolute law, the chess king can capture in all directions. As his representative, the rook roams throughout the kingdom in a straight line, enforcing the king's just rule. The remaining three noble pieces are inherently corrupt or inclined toward profligate behavior: the queen moves diagonally because women take things through unjust seizure; the knight's ability to move along two axes signifies his legal power to collect rents and his illegal practice of extorting supplementary money for personal gain; and the *aufins*, or bishops, always move obliquely, because every cleric profits by cheating. The author's depiction of the pawns, which represent an undifferentiated mass of common men and laborers, is ambivalent. These pieces move in a straight line symbolic of their innate tendency toward honesty. But upon reaching the eighth line, the pawn/commoner becomes a *fers*, or queen, and starts to move aslant, "which shows how hard it is for a poor man to deal rightly when he is raised above his proper station" ["set (*sic*) cum capere vult, obliquat, quia cum cupit aliquid temporale vel honores consequi"].[87]

This last element illustrates just how differently the chess allegory works in the *Quaedam* than it does the *Liber*. Because the author of the *Quaedam* views the game as demonstrably sinful, he never encourages anyone to learn it. Instead, because the world is by default a type of chessboard with all individuals trapped on the board as pieces, the game as a whole demonstrates mankind's tendency toward social *dis*order. Thus rather than teaching virtue, the act of play exposes our inherently corrupt practices. If the pawn reaches the eighth square, usually the sign of skill, the piece gains powers that are, metaphorically, injurious rather than beneficial to the common good.

Near the end of the allegory the author ultimately rejects the board altogether, shifting his focus from the chess pieces to the player who moves them. He concludes:

In isto autem ludo diabolus dicit *eschek...* insultando vel percuciendo aliquem peccati iaculo qui [*sic*] percussus nisi cicius dicat *liqueret*, . . . ad penitenciam et cordis compunctioni transeundo, diabolus dicit ei *Mat*, . . . animam secum ad tartara deducendo, ubi non liberabitur.

[In this game the Devil says, "Check!" while cursing or striking anyone with the barb of sin, [and] unless he more quickly says, "Clear," by passing to the penance of a sorrowful heart, the Devil says, "Mate!" leading his soul off to the lower levels of hell where it will not be freed.][88]

Although used initially as a representation of social order, chess by this point has become a test of an individual's virtue. If any person—the text has now conflated the player and the reader—falls into sin, he will lose both the game and his soul. And while the *Liber* emphasizes individual virtue, the *Quaedam* author isolates the question of virtue to the player himself, who must repent for his inherently sinful behavior and prevent his fall by repudiating the game. In the end, then, the *Quaedam*'s chessboard represents a fallen world that is neither wholly positive nor entirely negative. Even though the game ostensibly offers a player more than a simple reflection of his condition, it leaves little room for choice. Instead, the author can only encourage the reader/player to reject the game and the worldly temptations it represents, or rather, to realize that divine forgiveness alone can save him. Only faith allows an individual to escape the game altogether, and his repentance brings about a guaranteed victory.

For us the *Quaedam*'s use of the game to represent a sinful life is as far removed from the state-as-body allegory as it is from Jacobus's ideal of social order. This was not, however, the case for some medieval readers. In its various surviving versions the *Quaedam* is attached most often to John of Wales's thirteenth-century *Communiloquium,* a vast handbook for preachers that discusses the relationship between a community and its various members.[89] Much like Jacobus, John gears his texts toward a large audience, likely comprised of preachers but also nominally including all members of society. Also like Jacobus, John tries to instruct a body of citizens about the prince and about their own relationship to the prince's kingdom rather than instructing a prince himself. Finally, the *Communiloquium,* like the *Liber,* relies heavily on examples to demonstrate virtuous behavior. A staple authority for both texts is Valerius Maximus—the *Liber* attributes forty-eight stories to Valerius's *Factorum et dictorum memorabilium* (Memorable Deeds and Sayings); the *Communiloquium* contains sixty-five such references—with Seneca predominating in each.[90]

Jenny Swanson, a leading scholar on John of Wales, has argued that the *Communiloquium* does not meet the strict definition of a *Fürstenspiegel* ("mirror of princes").[91] Nevertheless, as Swanson herself points out, the first and longest section of the *Communiloquium* follows many tropes of the *speculum regis* genre. Comparing political order to a physical body, John describes the state from the head (the prince) to the feet (the workers), and discusses the duties of the various members of a kingdom. In an almost exact copy of the *Policraticus,* the *Communiloquium* casts the officials and judges as the eyes and ears; the republic's council functions as its heart; the soldiers as its hands; and the workers as its feet. The *Communiloquium* also follows the state-as-body tradition in that it gives the prince a special place in the "respublica."[92] And even if John of Wales feels that "*everyone* has a duty to be involved in the state," his use of a physiological metaphor and his belief in the state as a naturally occurring entity mean that everyone had little choice.[93] Thus while John takes a keen interest in a kingdom's social order, the attention he gives to the king and his use of the body metaphor bring the *Communiloquium* in line with the other mirrors composed at the end of the thirteenth century.

That the *Quaedam* was bound with the *Communiloquium* suggests a perceived relationship between the two texts, a relationship most likely created by their similar interest in political order. While one used the metaphor of chessboard and the other the human body, each could account for a community's distinct parts while simultaneously showing the need for unity; just as all pieces are part of a game, so too are all organs and parts essential to a properly functioning body. John of Wales's *Communiloquium*, though using a traditional metaphor for a republic that offered little autonomy to its subjects, still encourages all people to live a virtuous life. Similarly, in the anonymously authored *Quaedam*, the chessboard, like a somatic body, reflects a human condition. Yet as discussed above, in the *Quaedam*'s chess allegory the "game" is not a real game but a means to represent corruption and salvation. The contest has only one right move, which happens the moment the player stops exercising his or her own will and turns the chessboard over to God. Not only are all other moves difficult to make, but they seem futile as a common fate will come to all both on the board and off it.[94] Submission, one quick move that takes the player away from the game at hand, becomes the only moral act possible on the board.

While *Quaedam* uses the game to represent social deterioration, Galvano de Levanto's *Liber sancti passagii Christicolarum contra Saracenos pro recuperatione Terrae Sanctae* uses the game in a way that more closely resembles Jacobus's *Liber*. An obscure writer, Galvano authored several medical tracts currently housed in the Bibliothèque Nationale.[95] (According to Casimir Oidin, who found a reference to Galvano in the *Commentarii de scriptoribus ecclesiae antiquis*, Galvano worked as the doctor for Pope Boniface VIII but later quit the medical profession to enter an order.) In addition to his medical writing, he produced the *Liber sancti passagii*, a text dedicated to Philip the Fair that listed reasons and ways to recapture the Holy Land. Written shortly after the Western crusaders had been forced from Acre in 1291, the *Liber sancti passagii* contains two parts preceded by a lengthy introduction in which

Galvano explains how the rules of chess can be used to help teach kings the way to reconquer the Holy Land. The first part of the treatise, which follows this opening section, is essentially a *speculum regis*. In the second part of the work Galvano turns his attention to his primary topic, articulating the need for Christians to recapture the lands they have recently lost in the battles at Acre in 1291.

Perhaps foreshadowing Jacobus, Galvano discusses the citizens of a state as a series of chess pieces, proceeding through them in hierarchical order (i.e., starting with the king and ending at the rook). Yet in a departure from the *Liber*'s political redistribution of power, Galvano devotes the majority of his treatise to the king, taking care to elaborate the qualities that make a strong monarch. Also unlike Jacobus, Galvano does not individuate the pawns, and he spends only two chapters on their moves and their qualities. Thus while Galvano offers a model of state similar to that in Jacobus's *Liber*, any autonomy offered by his chess allegory is subsumed by his focus on the king, the most important piece, who alone possesses the power to recapture lost territory and thus unite the kingdom.

In Engreban d'Arras's "Ch'est li jus des Esques," a 298-line verse fragment from the late thirteenth century, the author also compares human society to the pieces of a chess set.[96] As in the *Liber*, the chess pieces/subjects in Engreban's poem struggle together as a community. Yet unlike the community members described by Jacobus, these noble pieces/subjects watch without compunction as their non-noble counterparts get taken. Only at the game's end is the situation reversed. At this point, the pieces are all put in a sack, with the heaviest falling to the bottom and the lightest resting comfortably on them.[97] Instead of embodying the ideal community, chess here ultimately shows the irreparably fallen state of man and echoes the *Quaedam* with its reminder that "all pieces have a common fate which levels all the ranks."

Natural Bodies and Common Profits

To this point I have shown how the *Liber*, with its focus on individual virtue and its appeal to everyman as a reader, deviated from other models of social order in circulation at this time. Instead of casting the state as a human body, Jacobus compares it to a chess set. Instead of representing a fallen world, this particular chess set becomes a model for civic order. And instead of portraying the king as the sole arbiter of law in a civic community, the *Liber* imagines this power as dispersed in a public sphere: everyone is an independent subject and as such must monitor his or her own behavior, even as that behavior is being monitored by the community as a whole. Although it would be a mistake to hail Jacobus's chess allegory as a complete revolution in the history of political thought, the *Liber*'s modes of representation suggest significant changes in the way people had started to conceive of themselves and their relationship to the civic body.

Yet even as Jacobus rejects traditional models of civic order, at various points he invokes discourses of nature and of the state as an organic body that hearken back to earlier ideas about civic organization. Why, after crafting an allegory of community that opposes earlier models of statehood, does Jacobus borrow earlier discourses of the state-as-body?

As I will argue in the remainder of this chapter, such moments reveal Jacobus's own anxiety about using this particular metaphor to represent civic organization. Chess, while considered by many writers to be noble, was often played at this time as a gambling game. And gambling, an act by which one party benefits at the expense of the other, poses problems for Jacobus's allegory. In a game with a stake, one person will lose, and this loss disrupts the mutualism, social harmony, and productivity the allegory seeks to capture. Only by relegating gambling to dice playing, a "profession" that Jacobus builds into the allegory itself, can one sustain the image of chess as a noble pastime that will teach Evilmerodach to live virtuously. Situated liminally on the left (sinister) side of the board, the dice-playing pawn acts as a repository for vice itself. It is no accident that this piece lies farthest from the first pawn, a farmer, whose contribution to the *communitas* forms the foundation of society's well-being.

Links between chess and gambling appear as early as the eleventh century. In a letter addressed to the pope-elect Alexander II in 1062, Peter Damian, the cardinal-bishop of Ostia, requested permission to withdraw to a monastery because he was so disgusted by a fellow cleric who played the game for a stake. In the letter Damian narrates the story of a recent trip he has taken with a bishop from Florence. Arriving at their lodgings one night, Damian withdraws to the quarters reserved for the priests while the Florentine bishop sits down in a spacious house with a crowd of travelers. The next morning a groom comes and announces to Damian "that the . . . Bishop had taken the lead in chess."[98] Damian immediately becomes furious and runs off to upbraid his companion:

Rectene, inquam, tuique erat officii vespere in scacchorum vanitate colludere, et manum, Dominici corporis oblatricem, linguam inter Deum et popolum mediatricem sacrilegi ludibrii contaminatione fedare? Praesertim cum canonica decernat auctoritas, ut aleatores Episcopi deponantur?

[Was it your duty at evening to take part in the vanity of chess, and to defile your hand, the offerer of the Lord's body, and your tongue, the mediator between God and His people, by the contamination of an impious sport, especially when canonic authority decrees that Bishops who are dice-players [*aleatores*] are to be deposed?"][99]

The bishop of Florence quickly retorts that "*scachus* [chess] is one thing, and *alea* [dice] another."[100] When Damian informs him that both dice *and* chess are species of *alea*, and therefore subject to the same restriction, the Florentine bishop concedes and accepts a penance.

For these two men, the argument does not turn so much on the relative merits of chess, but rather on whether or not chess counts as a species of dice. Most likely developed as a means of expediting the game, dice were commonly used to play chess from the eleventh through the fourteenth centuries.[101] According to the bishop from Florence, playing chess without dice exempted it from the canonical laws against dice playing. By contrast, Damian argues that any game that could be played with dice constitutes a type of *alea*.[102]

One could dismiss Damian's reaction as a consequence of his strict self-regime. By nature an ascetic man, Damian throughout his life held suspicions of secular pastimes.[103] His endorsement of flagellation was looked upon as overly zealous and lacked support among many of his peers. The strict penance he imposes on the bishop—three recitations of the Psalter, washing the feet of twelve poor men, and giving these men each a gold coin—offers more evidence of his personal austerity than of a particular hatred of chess.

Yet Damian's reaction did not lack precedent. As both bishops make clear, Church decrees had condemned dice playing among the clergy, and the Florentine bishop eventually admits that chess could be considered a form of *alea*. A similar prohibition for the Templar Knights stated "chess and dice are to be execrated" ["scacos et aleas detestantur"].[104] Dice was almost always associated with gambling, and as such it had particular resonance with the clergy, who often reminded their parishioners that soldiers gambled at the foot of the cross for Christ's seamless robe after dividing his clothes.[105] Like the threat gambling poses to the political body, gambling in this instance metaphorically threatens to divide the unified Church, represented here by Christ's mystical body.

If chess represented a form of pure recreation, clerical bans on the game might seem unusually stringent. But in fact, it was *not* uncommon for chess players to use dice specifically to expedite the game in the case of gambling.[106]

Nor had gambling on chess games stopped by the time Jacobus composed the *Liber*, and the sudden proliferation of problem sets (short descriptions of nearly completed games with a designated number of moves to mate) in the late thirteenth century suggests that the practice of chess gambling had actually increased. Near the end of the thirteenth century, three large collections of problem sets appeared: Alfonso X's 1283 *Libros del ajedrez, dados y tablas* (*Book of Chess, Dice, and Backgammon*), the 1290–1300 *Bonus socius* (*Good Companion*) and its contemporary *Civis bononiae* (*Citizen of Bologna*).[107] James Magee speculates that problems became popular at this time because "there was a demand for a quick, decisive ending adaptable to gambling purposes."[108] Murray, although reluctant to connect problem sets to wagering practices, nevertheless confirms the widespread practice of chess gambling when he observes that "chess was usually played for a stake" and that "probably there was no game played in the Middle Ages in which it was not the ordinary rule to increase the interest by this simple device of attaching a prize to the victory and a penalty to the defeat."[109]

Even if nongamblers consulted problem sets, many of the problems address themselves specifically to the gambler. The introduction to one manuscript of the *Civis bononiae* collection makes the purpose of the diagrams quite explicit. After listing several ways to trick your opponent, the author warns: "Again, you ought to appear cautious in wagering and to note carefully whether he takes the problem with a tremulous voice, or after a moderate amount of consideration, or whether he is ready to wager large sums, or whether he wished to take other problems which have been set up, or whether he refuses to take other positions which are to be set up, for all these things show whether he knows the problem or not."[110] Here the focus is neither on the chess game nor on the intellectual challenge of the problem sets. Instead, the author concerns himself entirely with the stake, specifically with how to read external signs as representative of internal conditions. If your opponent speaks "with a moderate amount of consideration," this may indicate that he has not seen the game before and believes himself to have an assured victory.

However, at the same time that wagers were being made on the board, many writers busied themselves condemning such practices. In the introduction to Alfonso X's *Libros del ajedrez, dados y tablas* the author refers to chess as the "best" of all games.[111] In the pseudo-Ovidian poem *De vetula*, the narrator claims that the game is "noble and honorable" ["noble et honourable"] and that those who gamble on chess "dirty and sully the game" ["tout le gieu laidist et mehaingne"].[112] For this writer, a wager was not a natural part of chess but an element that a player brought to the game. His argument here resembles that of the Florentine bishop who, when debating the matter with Damian, initially insists that a chess game played without dice (i.e., not for a stake) does not qualify as a gambling game at all.

In Piacenza, a town in the heart of Lombardy, this attempt to separate dice playing from the chess game finds expression in a late twelfth-century pavement mosaic in the choir of San Savino (Figure 3a, b). At the center of the mosaic lies Fortune's wheel, supported by Atlas. To the left of the wheel are two panels. The upper panel contains two battling men while the lower panel shows one man with a cup and a cane standing behind a seated figure who appears to be engaged in some activity. While the activity is not completely verifiable, William L. Tronzo, who has compared this image with others like it, offers convincing evidence that the men are playing dice. [113] The location of both panels on the sinister side, one depicting war and the other depicting debauchery, clearly marks these scenes as negative examples. The pictures also contrast sharply with the two panels on the right side of the mosaic. On this side the upper right hand panel contains a king seated on a throne. Above him floats the word REX, and he points to a book inscribed with the word LEX. Above the book is the label IUDEX, an indication of his just rule. The panel below this shows a man seated at a chessboard who appears to be instructing his opponent (now represented only by an arm) in the art of the game. Although the mosaic has suffered considerable damage since its creation, the meaning, if Tronzo is correct, is still clear: drinking and dice, like war, create social discord, while chess provides the foundation for proper rule. [114]

Jacobus follows a similar strategy. Early in his third book, which opens with the pieces on the right side of the board, he emphasizes the need for contractual exchange between members of a community; as noted above, the first pawn, the farmer, is the most important of the *populares* since he must provide food for the kingdom. Yet the moment that he reaches the eighth pawn, who sits on the far left side of the board, the ideal political order devolves into a community gone awry. This pawn, an "embodiment of the wastrels, players, and messengers" ["de prodigiis, ribaldis et lusoribus et cursoribus"] (128) in a community, sits in front of the rook; he has "in his right hand a little money and in his left hand three dice" ["in manu dextra modicam pecuniam, in sinistra vero tres taxillos"] (128). The chapter as a whole narrates the dangers of a lost fortune, and Jacobus notes that it is "a most foolish thing" ["stolidissimum"] to give away money, even to kin, in hopes of recovering it. While moderate spending is acceptable, "a waster of goods is not good for the common profit nor the utility of the realm" ["prodigum autem nec bonum civem nec utilem rei publicae existimamus (*sic*)"] (132).

In order to demonstrate the dangers of lopsided exchange and to validate a world united by contractual (rather than familial) bonds, Jacobus narrates the story of Johannes (or John) Cavazia.[115] John has two daughters each married to a nobleman. Over a series of years he gives his daughters and his sons-in-law large portions of his money. Yet as soon as John's money runs out, his daughters and their husbands spurn him. Realizing his mistake, John borrows a substantial amount of gold from a merchant. He then invites his daughters to dinner, shows them the treasure, and tells them that he will bequeath the gold to them provided that the daughters give away the money he has given them over the previous years. Two days later John secretly returns the money to his merchant friend. Meanwhile, John's daughters, believing they will inherit the gold, give away their fortunes. Eventually John dies, and the daughters discover that their father has left them only a large wooden club with an inscription about the dangers of losing one's wealth.

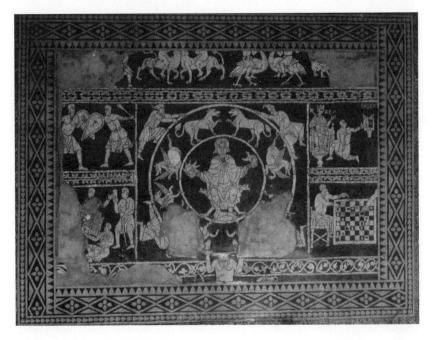

Figure 3a. Late twelfth-century mosaic in San Savino (overview). Photo courtesy of William L. Tronzo.

One of the last of the exempla in the *Liber*, this story illustrates the problems with a society modeled on natural ties. Kinship binds John and his daughters. Yet as evinced by John's experience, such familial bonds are fragile and subject to decay. John's "contract" with his daughters, their care in exchange for his money, lasts as long as John's fortune remains intact.

Figure 3b. Late twelfth-century mosaic in San Savino (close-up).

Once that fortune disappears (i.e., after John has given it to his daughters), the contract ends and his daughters no long tend to him. At the same time, John's deal with the merchant—the merchant loans the money to John for three days as a favor—is based on expediency and exchange. As Jacobus tells us, John has known the merchant for a long time ("ab antiquo"), a relationship presumably established through regular business dealings. Just as John knows that the merchant will loan him the money, the merchant trusts John to return it. As Jacobus argues, both through the story of John and through his rejection of the state-as-body model, natural bonds provide weak glue for social cohesion. Societies built around contractual bonds are, in the end, much more stable than those built on the bonds between family members.[116]

Contractual bonds, however, only work when the two parties making the contract have a shared sense of virtue, a commitment to the common good, and a fortune that is roughly equal. The use of chess for gambling exposes the precariousness of a contractual system, as it suggests that some individuals care more about personal gain than common profit. To elide this problem Jacobus assigns the practice of gambling to dice players. By casting the last pawn as a dice player, he can condemn the practice of gambling while detaching it from the chess game. Jacobus reinforces the connection between dice playing and gambling throughout his chapter by pointing to the many fools who have lost their fortunes in the heat of playing dice.[117] He also takes care never to show a game in progress, or to suggest that anything could be exchanged through the act of playing itself. Yet, perhaps sensing that his treatise may facilitate a practice he condemns, he lapses, at the same moment that he outlines the game's rules, back into the state-as-body comparison.

This invocation of natural order appears as early as the chapter on the smith, where Jacobus notes that "we ought to follow Nature, who shows us that we ought to share profit with each other" ["debemus naturam ducem sequi, et communes utilitates afferre in medium"] (81–82). However, it isn't until the final book, in the chapter on the moves of the king, that Jacobus openly deploys the state-as-body model: "Thus is it important that the king have this nature of all the people, because the virtue of all that is in the members is in the head, and the movement of the whole body in the beginning of life is in the heart, to the end that all are subjected to the king's dignity" ["Merito ergo hanc naturam popularium omnium rex habuit, quia cum omnis virtus, quae est in membris, sit a capite, et motus totius corporis a principio etiam vitae sit a corde, sit et omnes subjecti regiae dignitati"] (143). At this moment Jacobus, summoning up an image that appears nowhere else in his treatise, returns to the idea that political order operates like a human body governed by a king who functions as the body's head. The state, a naturally occurring entity, takes life from such an order, and any violation of it will result in the community's death. It is as if Jacobus, in the middle of describing the moves, suddenly recognizes the potential for play, the commensurate potential for gambling, and finally, by extension, the potential for social discord. By invoking the natural order in this fashion he appeals to an external notion of a top-down social order, one found in the natural world and thus ultimately sanctioned by a divine authority.

That chess furnished a conceptual model for describing the political state demonstrates the significant changes that occurred both in the nature and the representation of secular power in late thirteenth-century Europe. As Roberto Alejandro has observed, citizenship "is 'a sort of club' aiming at the protection of its members from each other. . . . It is not a community of common and organic bonds, but a society of artificial ties created by the legal establishment."[118] If, as Alejandro also claims, citizenship stems from the "universalization of moral autonomy [which] meant that each individual, regardless of social status, became the source of morality," the *Liber*, one of the first political treatises to define the individual as a professional capable of moral sovereignty, was a crucial step in the development of our own identities as subjects of secular states.[119] In his multiplication of bodies—pawns, knights, and legates have replaced feet, arms, and stomachs—and his subsequent treatment of these bodies as producing their own moral codes, Jacobus hints at, if not a redistribution of power, a more complicated apparatus of power governing the relationships between individual subjects and the political body. Although still monitored by a central authority embodied in the king, the political body, as it was represented by the chessboard, suddenly consisted of multiple nodes of authority.

Coupled with this emerging moral autonomy is an increased potential for movement between and among social and professional categories. A reader of John of Salisbury could do little more than identify himself as a part of the political body over which the head reigned supreme. By contrast a reader of the *Liber*, even one identifying himself as a pawn, could enjoy the promise of social mobility in exchange for hard work. If a pawn reached the eighth square, he became a member of the upper class, his new name corresponding to his expanded powers. After explaining this feature of the game, Jacobus himself reminds his reader, "no one must look down on the common people, because we read that they, through virtue and grace, have arrived as the status of emperor or pope" ["Nemo tales populares despiciat, quia tam ad imperium quam ad summum pontificatum, virtutibus et gratiis, legimus eos pervenisse"] (160). Correct moral choices may or may not lead to rewards in heaven. Jacobus, however, is only interested in showing how moral choice can bring communal benefits on earth.

The tremendous popularity of the *Liber* suggests that a new way of thinking about civic communities, about subjects, and about the relationships between these two entities quickly found receptive audiences throughout western Europe. It would be an overstatement to claim that the *Liber* constructed individuals as citizens in most modern senses of the term. However, Jacobus's representation of the members of a political body, each of whom had to be identified by a trade and, more importantly, each of whom was expected to use this trade to a productive end, broke sharply with past notions of political identity. And it is this specific fascination with individual identity, as well as its related interest in individual psychology and autonomy, that will strike a chord with the writer of *Les Echecs amoureux*, Jacobus's most important fourteenth-century imitator.

Chapter 2
Taxonomies of Desire in
Les Echecs amoureux

Marriage, which is necessarily overt, public, ceremonious, surrounded by special words and deeds, is at the center of any system of values, at the junction between the material and the spiritual. It regulates the transmission of wealth from one generation to another, and so underlies and cannot be dissociated from a society's "infrastructures."
—Georges Duby

It is as if the insensible could not yet knock at the doors of the poetic consciousness without transforming itself into the likeness of the sensible: as if men could not easily grasp the reality of moods and emotions without turning them into shadowy persons.
—C. S. Lewis

Sometime in the late fourteenth century, an anonymous poet composed *Les Echecs amoureux* (*The Chess of Love*), a 30,060-line poem that takes as its subject the nature of romantic desire.[1] Much like the poem it emulates, the thirteenth-century *Roman de la Rose*, the story begins with a poet who travels to a garden. Here he meets Venus's two sons, Deduis (Mirth) and Cupido (Love). While in the garden, the poet watches Deduis play chess with a beautiful woman. The game ends in a tie, after which the poet himself plays against the lady, who easily defeats him. Cupido comes to comfort the distraught poet, advising him how best to play the chess game. Cupido's lecture ended, the goddess Pallas Athena appears and chastises the poet for listening to Cupido, insisting that he should follow *une vie contemplative* instead of *une vie voluptueuse*. If this proves too difficult, she adds, he should follow *la vie active*. At this point Pallas starts to outline the components of a civic community, which she sees as the basis for an active life; the poem breaks off when she begins to discuss the importance of economic exchange.[2]

Roughly fifty years after the appearance of *Les Echecs amoureux,* a prose Commentary on the poem began to circulate.[3] Most likely composed by Evrart de Conty, a member of the medical faculty at the University of Paris, the *Les Echecs* Commentary methodically explicates the poem and was used independently as a didactic work in its own right for many years.[4] Like the poem, the Commentary covers a wide range of subjects and includes detailed discussions of the physical universe, music, and philosophy. Chess takes a more prominent place than it does in the poem, and Evrart spends over one third of his Commentary analyzing the various moves in the match between the lady and narrator and the symbolism behind their game.[5] Whereas the poet in *Les Echecs* describes the physical appearance of the pieces, which represent the players' emotions, and gives a description of the game, Evrart spells out in meticulous detail the meaning behind the symbols on each piece (Table 2). On the shields of the lady's two *auphins* (bishops), for example, are pictures of a dove and a pelican respectively, and Evrart interprets these birds as signs of "Generosity of Soul" and "Pity," virtues appropriate to clergymen. The dove found on Generosity's shield "has no gall or bitterness at all in it, and never wounds anything either with its talons or beak" ["n'a point en ly de fiel ne de amertume, n'il ne blesce nulli ne de ongle ne de bec"] (669). For its part, Pity, like the pelican on his shield, who wounds its breast to feed its young, nourishes lovers through difficult times. Working together these two pieces "make lovers live for a long time" ["font vivre longuement les amoureux"] (674) and "protect the lover from misery and despair" ["gardent l'amant de cheir en desesperance"] (674). By tying the pieces' symbols to specific attributes, Evrart draws attention to the connection between outward appearance and inner desires.

Yet the lady's bishops do not represent romantic emotions alone, and Evrart notes that the chess pieces also symbolize the social classes, trades, and members of a civic body. Drawing parallels between the meanings of the pieces in these different categories, he does not prioritize one set of meanings over the other. Instead, the pieces and their insignia function simultaneously within two different semiotic systems. In the description of Generosity and Pity, we see how Evrart describes the bishops as representative of both individual emotions and civic order:

Briefment, ces deux eschecs sont appellés auffins en l'eschiquier d'amours, pour ce que tout aussi que les rocs des eschés representent les lieutenans et les vicaires d'un roy qui a un peuple et une grant communité de gens soubz ly bien ordenee, tout aussi les auffins representent les conseillers et les juges asquelz ces deux auffins sont assez ressamblable.

Nous devons savoir que les juges et les conseillers, du droit de leur office, doivent le roy loyalment conseillier et justement tousdiz le peuple gouverner. Ilz doivent avoir l'oeil tousdiz au bien commun, tenir le peuple en paix tant qu'i leur est possible et faire a chascun droit, sans decliner en aucune maniere . . . franchise et pité samblablement sont conseillers du roy en l'eschiquier d'amours, c'est a dire du cuer de la dame amoureuse, et l'adrescent tousdiz en tous ses mouvemens et en tout ce que elle doit d'amours faire.

[Briefly, these two chess pieces are called bishops in the chess of love because the rooks of chess represents the lieutenants and vicars of the king who has a people and a great community of people well arranged underneath him, so the bishops represent advisors and judges, to which they are quite similar. We should know then that judges and counselors, by the right of their office, should loyally and always justly counsel the king in governing of the people. They should always have their eyes on the common good, keep the people at peace as much as possible, and do [Justice] to each of them without departing from it in any way. . . . [Generosity of Soul] and Pity are in the same way the counselors of the king in the chess of love, i.e., the heart of the amorous lady, and they always direct her in all her movements and in all that she should do in love.] (668–69)

In this passage, as in many others, Evrart compares and conflates the board's symbolic systems, imagining the body of the lady as a mirror of the body politic. Just as a good judge acts mercifully, so too does Pity inspire the lady's soul to pardon a lover's advances and treat him justly. Similarly, Generosity "has no base word or thought in it that could damage anyone, but wishes, as it is said, to help everyone" ["n'a en ly ne vilaine parole ne malvaise pensee qui puisse nuire a autry, ainz veult a tous, come dit est, aidier"] (669). And both advisors have eyes for the common good and justly counsel the king (in this case, the human heart) in governing all the people.

In this chapter I will look more closely at the ways *Les Echecs* and its Commentary amplify the connections between individual desire and social organization, and the ways the two works position romantic love as the foundation for a stable political community. As we saw in the last chapter, Jacobus de Cessolis used the chess game to represent the members of a community, with each piece corresponding to one or more professions. In this fashion his *Liber* encourages the reader/player to see himself both *on* and *at* the board, and this doubled identity gives the reader/player the fantasy of a detached external perspective. The *Liber*'s overt didacticism focuses on professional identity as the lone characteristic that determines a player's place in the political order. Promoting the importance of the common good, the text encourages the reader/player to evaluate his moral condition in terms of political expediency. Ultimately, *playing* the game becomes less important

TABLE 2. The Chess Pieces in *Les Echecs amoureux*. This information is taken primarily from H. J. R. Murray, *A History of Chess*, 556.

Lady's pieces

Pawns:	Youth (moon crescent)
	Beauty (rose)
	Simplicity (lamb)
	Sweet Expression (rainbow)
	Elegance (little ring)
	Good Sense (serpent)
	Goodness (panther)
	Nobility (eagle)
Queen:	Golden Mean (balance)
Knights:	Shame (unicorn)
	Fear (hare)
Rooks:	Sweet Looks (lark)
	Fair Welcome (sea siren)
Bishops:	Generosity of Soul (dove)
	Pity (pelican)
King:	Love (turtle dove)

Poet's pieces

Pawns:	Idleness (dry tree)
	Looking (key)
	Sweet Thought (tiger)
	Delight (blackbird)
	Fear of Failing (leopard)
	Memory (mirror)
	Fine Behavior (swan)
	Good Concealment (owl)
Queen:	Pleasure (moth)
Knights:	Boldness (lion)
	Sweet Speech (harp)
Rooks:	Patience (dove)
	Perseverance (cock)
Bishops:	Desire (ray of fire)
	Hope (ship)
King:	All Lovers (peacock)

than simply *knowing* how to play and *recognizing* oneself as a professional-
ized and productive member of the civic body, one who is contractually and
not organically bound to those around him.

By contrast, the heuristic work of *Les Echecs amoureux* relies on a double
(and sometimes triple) system of representation that joins the individual and
psychological with the professional. Offering an intimate depiction of the
player, the game manufactures and exposes the workings of his inner state
rather than simply typing him by his function in the polity. Instead of encouraging a reader to see himself mirrored as a piece and player, the poem
casts the reader primarily as a player (and metaphorically as a lover). The
chessboard and its figures are "conditions or passions, or motives of the soul"
that exist in *all* people, or at least in all lovers (Jones, 1019). Yet at the same
time, the chess pieces represent the same civic order that Jacobus describes.
If the lady's bishops are her emotions, so too are they the judges in a well-
ordered city.[6]

Thus unlike the *Liber*, where the board exclusively embodies professional
occupations and social classes, *Les Echecs* recasts the civic community as a
collection of subjects who are in turn microcosms of the social body surrounding them. And unlike the *Roman de la Rose*, the closest literary model
for *Les Echecs* and a work that seeks to separate discourses of civic identity
from those of romantic love, the *Les Echecs* poem and Commentary connect
and conflate the two; to be a good lover is to be a member of *la vie active*,
which in this case is the life of civic participation. In sum, by using chess as
an allegory for romantic love and *simultaneously* as an allegory for an idealized community, the poet and commentator turn love into an emotion that
is governed by reason and is also a matter of civic responsibility. Enlisting
the game to taxonomize and expose the psychology of individual desire, the
Les Echecs allegory manufactures a *subject's* (represented here by the lover)
interior "self" and then *subjects* this self to public scrutiny and control.[7] Ultimately, this regulation of heterosexual desire will produce not only equanimity between lovers but equality between citizens.

Or at least this is the allegory's purported ideal, established in the first
chess match between Deduis and the lady, which ends in a tie. But while the
tied game played by Deduis may offer a vision of perfect love and perfect
political order, the realities of the game become all too clear when the *Les
Echecs* lover sits down at the board and promptly loses. His loss reminds the
reader that players do not play to tie but to win, and this goal disrupts the
idea of a harmonious civic community just as it disrupts the ideal of controllable romantic love. Moreover, the tradition of wagering on chess further

complicates the allegorical value of the game as a site of fair exchange. As discussed in the previous chapter, a medieval player not only sought to win the game but often played to profit from it. As I will argue at the end of this chapter, the lover's lost game, which prompts the commentator's warnings against chess gambling, reveals the ways the allegory, despite the best efforts of the poet and commentator, inevitably trades in a discourse of material exchange and individual reward.

Taxonomies of Desire in *Les Echecs* and Its Commentary

From its opening lines, *Les Echecs amoureux* promotes the idea that reason and love are harmonious. Nature, the first person to approach the lover, takes great delight in the physical world, and she claims that men can successfully negotiate terrestrial affairs as long as they follow their reason. Later, when the lover sits at the chessboard, he will forget Nature's stricture, become distracted by his competitor's beauty, and lose the game. However, his failure does not demonstrate the evils of romantic desire but rather shows the dangers of passion. Had he played the "chess of love" properly, he would not have lost the game, which itself functions as a symbol of reasonable love. As Pallas, who later comes to mentor him, points out, reasonable romantic love is in turn essential for the good of the community. On his part Evrart will reinforce these connections even more strongly in his Commentary, and his treatise portrays individual desire as both a foundation for and analogous to political life.

Before mapping the intersections between individual desires and community order, I will look first at the various ways the poet and commentator reinforce the image of the chessboard itself as a place of moral perfection and rational desire. Indeed, the pieces serve as the most obvious marker of the board's idealized status, and their material compositions confirm the ways the game elevates romantic relationships, sanctifying them as divine unions. The poet's pieces, all cast in gold, are pure and noble; the lady's men are made of jewels, the queen carved entirely of ruby, and the king of diamond.[8] The symbolic importance of these materials is made clear in Philippe de Mézières's *Livre de la vertu du sacrement de mariage*, composed between 1384 and 1389. In his treatise Philippe sees marriage between men and women as a mirror of three other marriages: between God and the rational soul, between Christ and humanity, and between Christ and the Church. Philippe portrays none of these marriages directly, preferring instead to represent them by "the marriage of the Fine Ruby to the Fine Diamond, where the ruby is Christ and the diamond is sometimes the Virgin Mary, other times the Church.[9] If the *Les Echecs* author indeed borrowed (and altered) this imagery directly from Philippe's treatise, as seems likely, the pairing of the lady's chess king (the diamond) and chess queen (the ruby) would symbolize their sanctified bond. And even if this imagery does not come from *Livre de la vertu,* the beauty and value of the pieces alone indicate their moral worth and their role as an imitable model for the players.

Whereas the *Les Echecs* poet uses the pieces' iconography to emphasize the ways in which human love can resemble divine love, Evrart's Commentary shows the connections between human love and human reason, and he spends nearly one-third of his analysis on the ways the game captures rational thought. Even before he launches into this analysis, he explains at the onset that "chess can be compared very conveniently to the deed of love, on account of the various and numerous contests one can find there, that most closely resemble battles" ["le gieu des eschez peut estre comparés au fait d'amours tres convenablement, pour les controversies diverses et pluseurs que on y treuve souvent, qui assez proprement ressemblent as batailles"] (9). He then outlines three notable battles of love mirrored in the game: a battle between the lover and his own initial impulse to love; the battle between the lover and his own hope for success in love; and finally, the lover's battle with his lady. The first and second battles, which occur inside the lover, lead directly to the third, in which the lover must reveal his emotions and desires (represented externally by his pieces) in his game with the lady. He will assail her "by amorous glances and by humble prayers" ["par regards amoureux et humbles prieres"] (11); she will defend herself by "hard refusals and fierce rejections" ["de durs refus et de fiers escondiz"] (11).[10]

Later, as Evrart explicates the chess match between the poet and the lady, he further emphasizes the game's potential as a model for reason and insists that the chessboard "can well be taken, and properly enough, *for human thought* which often makes many moves and does different tricks to lovers" (Jones, 973; emphasis mine) ["peut bien estre pris et assez proprement *pour le humaine pensee* ou les amans font souvent moult de traiz et moult de divers tours"] (605). For Evrart, then, the game is a model of perfect reason. The board has formal perfection, and "all its positions themselves are equally square, to fill all the space everywhere in the most orderly way, without leaving anything empty" (Jones, 987) ["tous ses poins mesmes pareillement quarrés, pour le tout remplir de toutes pars plus ordeneement, sanz laissier riens de vuit"] (613). It is perfect musically: "Thus all the five musical harmonies are secretly included in this cubic figure" (Jones, 989) ["Ainsy donc sont les proporcions toutes des .v. consonancies musicaulx secretement comprises et encloses en ceste figure cubique"] (614). It is also mathematically perfect, for the number sixty-four is, as Evrart explains, "a square and a cube and hence serves to measure important figures" (Jones, 981) ["quarrés et cubique, et sy sert a figures notables mesurer"] (608). And finally, because the board itself is perfect, it symbolizes perfect love. Its shape is appropriate because "the four right angles signify the four cardinal virtues by which the loyal lover should be ornamented" (Jones, 976–77) ["les quatre angles droiz pevent segnifier, et raisonablement, les .iiij. vertus cardinaulx dont les amans loyaulx doivent estre adorné"] (606).[11]

Contrasted with the board's perfection is the lover's *imperfection*, which he manifests through his irrational behavior. He publicly demonstrates the inappropriateness of his love when, distracted by his opponent's beauty, he is mated by his opponent in the left corner of the board. As Evrart explains, the board's left side signifies sensuality:

Pour ce donc faint l'acteur qu'il fu ainsy matez ou vergier de Deduit ou senestre angle de l'eschequier d'amours, par la force des traiz de celle damoiselle qui joua contre lui, pour nous signifier que ce ne fu pas fait *du conseil de Raison.* (765; emphasis mine)

[So the author pretends that he was thus mated in the garden of Mirth in the left corner of the chess board of love by the force of the moves of this girl who played against him to signify to us that it was not done *by the counsel of reason.*] (Jones, 1292; emphasis mine)

Here Evrart claims that lack of reason's "conseil" has caused the lover to lose the game. Had he acted reasonably in love, he would not have lost. Indeed, Evrart has already suggested as much in an earlier passage, where he notes that the lover was "more moved and constrained to love her by whom he was mated more for her beautiful manner than for her beauty or for anything else whatsoever he saw in her" (Jones, 1072) ["plus esmeus et plus contrains d'amer celle qui ainsy le mata pour sa bele maniere que pour beauté ne autre chose quelconques qu'il y eust veu"] (655). The message is clear: only when reason controls desire can one play the "chess of love" successfully.

Nevertheless, the fact that the lover's loss indicates "unreasonable" love begs the question: in a game with one winner and one loser, how can one achieve proper love? The answer to this problem lies in the poem's first match. Before the lover sits at the board, the god Deduis plays with the same lady who later plays against the lover. Rather than one defeating the other,

Deduis and the lady end their game in a draw, preserving the equality of the relationship and the balance of power on the board.[12] Their game, which ostensibly features the same pieces used in the subsequent match, is one of romantic love and sensual desire. Nevertheless, the tie helps to prove Evrart's point that "it is nevertheless more natural and much more reasonable for reason to rule sensuality firmly" ["ce neantmoins encore plus naturel chose et trop plus raisonable que raison seignourisse sur sensualité"] (61). Thus, "the main and first end one should seek in love is reciprocation. And so Reason wishes, and it is the law of love and its nature that each of the lovers should devote himself to loving well" (Jones, 975) ["c'est la fin principal et la premiere que on doit querre en amours que reamacion; et pour ce veult raison, et c'est le droit d'amours et la nature, que chascun des amans mecte toute s'entente en bien aussi amer"] (606).

In both *Les Echecs amoureux* and its Commentary, then, the chessboard becomes a medium through which love and reason are harmonized. By learning to play the game properly, the poet will *not* learn to defeat his opponent; instead he will learn to match his love as an equal both in love *and* in virtue. Just as friendship is modeled on fair exchange, so too is romantic love a transaction in which both sides profit, maintaining the stability of the entire system. In this way both the *Les Echecs* poet and commentator refashion romantic love not only as an emotion controllable (and controlled) by reason but also as an act of political importance.

Although both the *Les Echecs* poet and Evrart use the game to symbolize reasonable romantic love, the two authors use different parts of their works to analyze the ways reasonable love leads to civic order. In *Les Echecs* the most concrete links between heterosexual union and civic good appear in Pallas's closing speech, a lecture of roughly one hundred folios (and even at that length, still incomplete) that combines elements of a philosophical treatise and a *speculum regis* in order to specify the attributes of an ideal marital union. Just as love and chess both follow a series of predictable moves, so too must marriage obey a certain set of rules (noted above) established by nature, enforced by mankind, and designed to benefit the civic community. Pallas does not represent political life as the best sort—that is reserved for *la vie contemplative*, which she describes as *la plus suppellative*. Nor is it the worst life, which is *la vie voluptueuse*. But she does equate political life with *la vie active*. In contrast with the other two mode of living, *la vie active* focuses neither on "all the subjects in the world" ["toutez lez sciencez du monde"] nor on the base senses, but "embraces the kings and princes, councilors, the judges, and the people."[13]

At this point Pallas's speech echoes the middle two chapters of Jacobus's *Liber*, and she, like Jacobus, describes the virtues necessary to the various community members she has just introduced. As she lists their attributes, she, again like Jacobus, positions each type of citizen as acting independently of other groups. Good judges, for example, should be merciful and honest. They should also be inclined to leniency if a prisoner shows remorse. On their part, knights must defend the community and look to its common good. And finally the people themselves must live virtuously so that the city remains peaceful. Stressing the economic component of the merchant classes, Pallas notes that the best cities have most of their people "in the middle class" ["de lestat moyen"], which ensures that there is no strife between rich and poor.[14]

Pallas then observes that the state itself depends on the family, and prompted by the lover she begins to address the institution of marriage, describing it as a form of "friendship" and also as the basis for civic order.[15] Insisting that civic communities were built with the family in mind, she claims that no reasonable criticism can be leveled against those who choose to wed.[16] Yet while she views married life as a natural state, Pallas takes great care to detail the numerous regulations governing a marriage bond. A man should be of a certain age when he marries and should not take a wife either too young or too old. He must be the first to get up each morning and the last to go to bed at night. He must govern his wife fairly, giving her "rules and guidelines to live by, and laws that are in accordance with her habits" ["Riegles and manieres de vivre / Et lois a ses meurs accordables"].[17] On her part, the wife must have a variety of assets, not the least of which is monetary. She should also be humble, chaste, and sober. She must manage the household budget and take care not to spend too much money on clothes. Finally, people must take care to marry at an appropriate age and must also avoid marrying a relative.[18] Families that follow these regulations will help to make a stable community.

Whereas the *Les Echecs* poet reserves his discussion of political life for Pallas's speech, the Commentary uses the chess game itself to underscore the interconnections between individual virtue and civic order, an order that Evrart, like the poet, sees as a product of the natural world. On the *Les Echecs* board the pieces represent more than the players' emotions; they also symbolize the citizens of a political community and, at the same time, the cosmological bodies. Just as the lady's chess king represents love, so too does he represent a political ruler and the sun, and his attributes are intraconnected in each system. A lover is not only a state-unto-himself that must be internally harmonized, but any imbalance within his inner state suggests an imbalance in the political state that in turn results in an even larger cosmological disruption. Consequently, the correlations between a subject's constituent parts, the political order around him, and the still-larger cosmological system work to regulate individual passions, and as Evrart draws together three mutually reinforcing allegories, he sketches the parallels between civic order (a structure that is in turn buttressed and naturalized by cosmological organization) and the mechanics of human emotions. Ultimately, a lover must follow the functions of the body politic, and the body politic must follow the motions of the cosmological body, the last of these functioning as the idealized model of natural order that sets the pattern for the first two.

In order to foreground the game's political symbolism, Evrart opens his Commentary by showing the ways that chess mirrors civic community:

Nous devons donc savoir que le jeu des eschez a esté comparé des anciens a pluseurs choses. Aucuns, premierement, ont ce jeucomparé a nostre policie humaine et a la civile communité car tout aussi que en la cité bien ordenee a gens de pluseurs estas et qui ont ars et offices divers, et toutesfois neantmoins, ilz se entraident et se acordent ensemble et tendent tous a une fin ou au moins doivent tendre. (3)

[We begin, then by knowing that the game of chess has been compared by the ancients to several things. First, some have compared this game to our human polity and civic community, because in a well-ordered city there are people of several estates, who have different trades and functions; and they always, nevertheless, aid one another and agree together, and all pursue one end, or at least ought to pursue it.] (Jones, 1)

Stressing the way the game symbolizes a "well-ordered city," Evrart shows how autonomy *and* interdependence are at play on the board. Like the pieces, the members of the civic body come from "several estates" and "have different trades and functions." All, however, "pursue one end." Mutual collaboration and work toward the common good will in turn help the community members "to live in peace among themselves and to strongly resist their enemies" ["a vivre en paix entre eulx et a fort resister contre tous ennemies"] (3).

Similar to Pallas in her lecture on civic order (and also similar to Jacobus in his descriptions of political organization), Evrart fleshes out the details of the chessboard's imagined community. As in the city, "there are in this game several pieces of different sorts with different moves that nevertheless aid one another and maintain one another strongly" (Jones, 3) ["il y a en ce jeu pluseurs eschez de diverses manieres et qui ont divers traiz, qui neantmoins s'entraident et s'entretiennent fort"] (4). The chess king "represents the king who reigns and is the lord of all, and whom all other people in the kingdom must respect and obey" (Jones, 3) ["represente le roy qui regne et seignorist sur tous, et auquel tous les autres de son regne doivent avoir regard et obeir"] (4). A voice for God on earth, only one king can issue laws and commands that must be followed. Similarly, the knights, bishops, and rooks, all of whom are defined in roughly the same terms as in the *Liber*, are "necessary for the good government of the city" ["neccesseres au bon gouvernement de la cité"], as are the pawns, who represent the "common people and craftsmen who know various trades" ["le commun peuple et les gens de mestier qui scevent ars diverses"] (5).[19]

Yet even as Evrart emphasizes the chessboard's connection to the political, the subject of marriage is never far from view. Before discussing the pieces' symbolic values, he cites Aristotle's *Politics* in order to point to one of the most important functions of the state, namely arranging marriages:

car quant les gens demeurent ainsy ensamble en aucune cité ou en aucune ville, ilz s'en alient plus voulentiers par mariage ensamble pour qu'ilz s'entrecongnoissent mielx, par quoy ilz en acquierent plus grant amistié et plus ferme les uns avec les autres, qui est un tres grant bien en la communité. (4)

[for when people live thus together in some city or town, they more willingly tie themselves together by marriage, because they know one another better, by which they have a greater friendship and a strong tie between them, which is a very great good in the community.]

In this manner Evrart exceeds Pallas's emphasis on married life; rather than seeing civic order as supporting the state, he argues that the state itself was created to enable the act of proper marriage. Lest the reader miss this connection between the political and the familial, Evrart adds the sixth cause for a city, which is "to live more virtuously and more according to reason" ["pour vivre plus vertueusement et mielx selon raison"] (4). For Evrart, virtuous people will form solid marriages, and solid marriages will lead to a stable community. Not only does communal living itself create joy (the first reason), but it also allows individuals to aid each other, to protect each other, and to engage comfortably in trade.

In the Commentary a city's interdependence finds its counterpart in the natural world, which itself is naturally balanced and interconnected. The continual change in the sky corresponds to the infinite variation in chess games; the different positions of the planets and stars correspond to the different spaces occupied by the board; and finally, each piece can be compared to a planet.[20] As might be expected, "the king in chess, it is the sun in the sky" ["le roys des eschez, c'est le soleil ou ciel"] (8), as both the king and sun are influential and noble. The queen is Venus among the planets; the bishops, knights, rooks, and pawns are Jupiter, Mars, the moon, and Saturn respectively.[21] Evrart also considers the effects of one system on the other. While the sky "does not give man his virtues or vices, or make him good or bad" ["ne donne pas l'omme les vertus ne les vices, ne elle ne le fait pas estre bon ne malvais"]," the heavenly bodies give everyone "a sort of corporeal disposition" (Jones, 180–81) ["une maniere de corporele disposicion"] that will incline man to make moral choices (117). This parallel between psychological and astrological realms offers yet another reminder that the chessboard's model of desire, which may seem artificial to a casual observer, in fact patterns itself on the natural world.

Although Evrart's prologue lays out connections between romantic love, political order, and the cosmos, he saves his most explicit discussion of these three systems for his analysis of the lovers' chess match. Before narrating the game, he moves through these different symbolic registers, grafting the systems together so that the overlapping meanings reinforce each other. This movement between these registers creates a multilayered structure whereby the different orders become superimposed on each other. Sitting at the chessboard, the players' bodies begin to assume the characteristics of civic and stellar bodies. Or, to borrow from the discussion of the pieces in the prologue, each becomes a mini-state and a mini-universe unto himself or herself.

This conflation of different symbolic systems occurs frequently in Evrart's description of the pieces, and it would take too much space to discuss each instance. Consequently, I will focus only on Evrart's analysis of the lady's chess pieces, where his synoptic descriptions are the most striking. In the opening of this section Evrart describes the lady's collective pieces as symbolic of the virtues essential to love:

Pour quoy nous devons ymaginer que les eschés d'amours dont nous devons parler, ce sont vertus et graces, et condicions ou passions, ou mouvemens de l'ame que les amans portent en eulx mesmez, dont ilz font moult de tours et moult de traiz souvent en leurs pensees, et en sont esmeu en moult de diverses manieres. (628–29)

[Because we should imagine that the chess pieces of Love about which we should talk are virtues and conditions, or passions, or motives of the soul that lovers carry in themselves with which they do many tricks and often make many moves in their thoughts, and are moved by these passions in many different ways.] (Jones, 1019)

Then, in a second passage, Evrart adds to this initial interpretation, claiming that the pawns also represent "the common people of the community," foot soldiers, and "the virtues and conditions" of a lover's soul:

Nous devons oultre aussi ymaginer que tout aussi qu'il y a ou droit gieu et real des eschés .viij. paonnés d'une partie et d'autre, qui representent le gens de pié qui sont voulentiers mis en la bataille ou premier front devant communement, pour l'assault commencier, ou le people commun de la communité, qui usent d'ars divers et de divers mestiers pour l'un l'autre secourre, sy come il est necessité pour vivre mielx et plus souffisaument. (629)

[We should also imagine that as in a right and real game of chess there are eight pawns on each side, which represent foot-soldiers, who are willingly placed in the front line in battle, usually to begin the attack, or the common people of the community, who practice different crafts and trades to succor one another as is necessary to live better and more sufficiently.] (Jones, 1019)

Evrart never prioritizes one system over the other; both exist simultaneously, the function of the pieces and the structure of the game forming a bridge between the romantic and the civic orders. Moreover, this second passage further emphasizes the idea of mutual collaboration. While a pawn might be "moved in a lover's thought" in the game of love, this same piece is also "willingly placed at the front line in battle" in order to defend the good of the whole body. In both cases the individual piece, while able to move autonomously, voluntarily prioritizes the common good over individual gain. A lover should follow this practice of sacrifice as he plays the "chess of love"; only by managing his individual virtues (i.e., by not prioritizing one over the others) can he succeed at the game and preserve the overall virtue of the body politic. In short, Evrart does more than simply compare romantic desire and political order, and he emphasizes the way civic order implies a commitment to the social body as a whole. Moreover, he, like Jacobus, sees this commitment as a matter of personal responsibility, a choice that one must make "voulentiers."

This emphasis on civic responsibility appears throughout Evrart's description of the pieces. Discussing the lady's rooks, Sweet Looks and Fair Welcome, he repeats his previous assertion that chess was "made in the similitude of a community of people of different sorts and several estates, well-ordered together under a king or prince" (Jones, 1085) ["fait a la similitude d'une communité de gens de diverses manieres et de pluseurs estas bien ordenés ensamble soubz un roy ou un prince"] (661). Like the king's legates, Sweet Looks and Fair Welcome serve as the heart's lieutenants and vicars ("lieutenans" and "vicaires"), who are "sent to distant places on [the king's] mission to visit the realm and country and to publish [his] will" (Jones, 1085) ["envoiés en message es parties loingtaines pour visiter le regne et le païz et pour manifester la voulenté du roy et son commandement"] (661). When he turns to the poet's bishops, Desire and Hope, Evrart begins his analysis by reminding his readers that these pieces "in the real game of chess signify the judges and counselors that are in our human polity" (Jones, 1255) ["du droit gieu des eschés segnefient les juges et les conseillers qui sont en nostre policie humaine"] (748). Just as people need to be governed reasonably, "so are desire and hope necessary in love to direct and conduct the lover in what he has to do" (Jones, 1255) ["tout aussi sont desirs et esperance neccesseres en amours pour les amans adrecier et conduire en ce qu'ilz ont a faire"] (748).

As in his opening prologue, Evrart frequently turns from romantic love and civic virtue to a discussion of cosmological bodies, a move that again highlights his reading of the game as representative of both an organic civic order and a natural romantic desire. Describing the lady's pawn Youth, Evrart notes that the new moon on the pawn's shield is an appropriate symbol for this piece because it is dear to the lover's heart, or chess king. The heart, like the king, "is in this little world, that is to say in the human body, prince and king over all the other members, as the sun in the sky is king or prince over all the planets" ["est ou le petit monde, c'est a dire ou corps humain, princeps et roys sur tous les autres members, aussi que le soleil ou ciel est roys et princeps sur toutes le planetes"] (633). Here again Evrart jumps from one symbolic register to another, rewriting the lady's pawn as a literal moon that serves both the lady's heart and the "king or prince over all the planets," the sun, a natural body whose movement has been preset by divine creation. Thus while Evrart's imagined lover may make many moves in a game, only a certain number of those moves may be in accordance with the higher bodies that govern his movements. Or rather, just as God ordered the heavens by means of natural law, so too should reason govern a lover's desire.

Just as it did with the lady's pawns, this conflation of the natural, political, and psychological realms (re)constructs the individual body as a microcosm of the political and cosmological realms, all of them having "a certain ordering among themselves" (Jones, 89) ["certaine ordenance entre elles"] (59). Moreover, in making these connections Evrart, like the poet, positions romantic love as both similar to and essential for the good of the civic body. And while the Commentary never takes account of Pallas's speech—Evrart ends when the lover loses the chess match—his account of the game encapsulates many of points made by the goddess in *Les Echecs* in her lecture to the lover: cities were built around the notion of married couples with children; married couples must live virtuous lives; and the virtues essential for romantic love resemble those essential for civic life. Overseeing these two systems is nature, which ensures that people, both in their romantic desires and their civic responsibilities, follow a virtuous path. If the lady's heart is like a king, so too is it like the sun, which has a natural superiority over the other planets.

Evrart, however, is not content to rewrite romantic love as a natural, self-regulating force. If lovers moved their pieces like the stars moved in the sky, the "chess of love" would hold little danger of excessive desire or passion. And while the rules governing the game may reflect the man-made laws necessary for such regulation, they clearly do not go far enough. This point is evinced clearly by the lover himself, who, while gazing at the lady's Beauty, becomes consumed by lust and neglects to move his pieces properly.[22] This disruption in turn has implications for the political community, which as the *Les Echecs* poet and Evrart have both argued, takes stable desire as its base.

Thus before leaving the lady's pieces, it is worthwhile to take a look at the way Evrart, like Jacobus, uses shame as a regulatory control over the individuals who play the game. "Personified" as one of the lady's pieces, Shame, one of her two knights, sits just behind the pawn Beauty in order to protect it from the lover's attack. His placement on this particular square—he is exposed after the first move when the lady advances Beauty and the lover responds with Looking—points to the ways public exposure can, in the poet's mind, control both external actions and internal state (see Table 2). Lest this be lost on his reader, Evrart uses other parts of his Commentary to remind the reader of the public nature of all action, emphasizing the position of the players in front of an audience that watches the game with interest.

In this emphasis spectatorship and exposure, both *Les Echecs* and its Commentary resemble the *Liber*, which, as we have seen above, features a public chess match and in doing so seeks to regulate behavior by reminding its readers of the constant potential for shame. For Jacobus, a subject is important only insofar as he is a member of an imagined and idealized political community, and the subject's identity derives from what he produces or how he serves. A reader of Jacobus assumes a double vision, a "self" split between piece and player, and a self also exposed to everyone else. In establishing this split, this view from above, Jacobus implicitly invokes shame to monitor a reader/player's actions. A reader of *Les Echecs* and/or the Commentary confronts a similar "self," albeit one divided into sixteen constituent pieces, and the allegory again offers the player an external view from above. Indeed, the reader/player's view from above is even more intimate than that put forth in Jacobus as it allows a magnified view of his inner psychology. Not only can observers watch a player's actions, but they can also see, and thus judge, his very thoughts.

In *Les Echecs* we are reminded of this spectatorship when Deduis, "who is not able to restrain himself," cries out at one point during the match that the lover needs to exercise some self-defense.[23] His exclamation not only highlights the lover's exposure but also indicates that his moves are constantly being monitored and evaluated. Pallas's post-match lecture turns on a similar threat of exposure and judgment, and she reminds the lover that his civic duties concern the members of the entire community. Because the marriage bond provides the bedrock for civic order, an individual's conduct with his wife is necessarily a public affair in which the community as a whole has a stake.

This threat of exposure in turn fortifies the Commentary's attempt to taxonomize, naturalize, and regulate human emotions. The lover's loss makes the impropriety of his love visible to everyone from Pallas, who comes to lecture him, to Evrart, who examines the lover's psychology in great detail. By continually drawing attention to his own position as external critic, Evrart intensifies the already scopophilic nature of the game itself. Revealing the poet's "secret" symbols—and he uses this word repeatedly—he creates a new public, namely his readers, to monitor the lover's progress toward improvement.[24] In a section titled "Why write fiction?" ["Pourquoi écrit-on des fictions?"] (22), he takes care to explain that symbolism and metaphor allow a writer to expose the truth about a subject. Given this, he warns his reader that one should know that

l'aucteur de la rime dessusdite faint et dit moult de choses qui ne sont pas a entendre a la lectre, ja soit ce que elles soient raisonablement faintes, et qu'il y ait aucune verité soubz la lettre et la fiction secretement mucie. (22)

[the author of this poem, as has already been suggested, pretends and says many things that are not to be taken literally, although they may be verisimilitudinous, and that there may be some truth secretly hidden beneath the letter and fiction.] (Jones, 32)

In this way Evrart affirms his power to reveal the truth behind the symbols, exposing things for what they really are.[25] A late fifteenth- or early sixteenth-century edition of the Commentary starkly emphasizes Evrart's position as an observer (Figure 4). Created for Louis de Savoie, the text opens with a frontispiece that shows the chess game in progress. Although the *Les Echecs* game takes place in a garden, this artist relocates the match in an interior room recessed within a building. Inside, the lady, ostensibly flanked by Deduis, plays the game against her opponent, and all three are absorbed in the game. While no crowds surround the board, the game is being observed (secretly, it seems) by yet another observer, the commentator, who sits in a larger room nearby and peers in on the game. His location between the reader and the game suggests that only he can read the game, which "pretends to say many things that are not to be taken literally" ["faint et dit moult de choses qui ne sont pas a entendre a la lectre] for us (32). Nonetheless, the reader too can see the actions taking place in the enclosed space. After all, once the reader has finished Commentary, he, like Evrart, will also know both the symbols of romance and the symbolic nature of language itself. In short, Evrart ensures that everyone can read the telltale markers of love both in the text and in the world.

The poem's investment in the regulatory power of shame was not lost on John Lydgate, whose 1408 translation of *Les Echecs* amplifies the game's potential for public humiliation. When Deduis and the lady begin to play in Lydgate's version,

. . . folke gan drawe to anoon,
Of the gardyn everychoon,
Croude aboute hem environ
To seen a ful conclusyon,
Which of hem shal lese or wynne.
And ful demurely they begynne
As by maner of batayle
To diffenden and assayle; (ll. 5845–52)

Lydgate's description of the match highlights the public nature of the play and the power exercised by the crowd.[26] "Folke" come from all over the garden to watch the players' every move on the board, and the poet's sense of excitement is manifest. In order to see "which of hem shal lese or wynne," he makes sure that he, himself, has a prime spot for watching, and he searches "To fynde a place covenable / To sen ther play[e] most notable" so that he can see everything "Fro poynt to poynt of ther pleyng" (ll. 5871–72 and l. 5876). Such attention, however, soon overwhelms him. Although he obeys Cupid and Deduis, who send Sweet Looks to call him to the table— he "ne durste disobey"—he admits that he is "first sore ashamed" (ll. 5958 and 5962).

Figure 4. Miniature from a copy of the *Les Echecs* commentary produced for Louis de Savoie around 1500. Paris Bibliothèque Nationale MS fr. 143, f. 1.

Reason and the Rose

If the Jacobus's *Liber* helped the *Les Echecs* poet shape his chess allegory, what inspired his ideas of reasonable love? On the one hand there can be little doubt that *Les Echecs* is indebted to the thirteenth-century *Roman de la Rose*, which provides the poet with the basic narrative of his work and the shape of his meditation on romantic desire.[27] In both *Les Echecs* and the *Rose* the narrator arrives at a garden surrounded by walls covered with pictures of vice and ruled by the God of Love. In both poems the narrator looks into the fountain of Narcissus and spies the object of his desire. In both poems the narrator, finding himself overwhelmed by his emotions, seeks help from various advisors. (The lady in each work has similar defenders: Shame and Fear, allegorized in the *Roman* as characters in Delight's garden, reappear in *Les Echecs* as chess knights used by the lady to fend off her overeager pursuer.) And finally, both lovers fall prey to their own lust. On the other hand, a fundamental reordering of the narrative events changes the meanings that adhere to the protagonists' actions. Whereas the *Rose* romance ends with the complete collapse of reason and a triumph of desire, the *Les Echecs* poet places the lover's fall midway through the story and devotes the remaining lines to a lesson on individual and civic virtue. Thus rather than showing the futility of reason, or the ways that reason conflicts with romantic desire, *Les Echecs* suggests that love, although a strong emotion, can be governed.

This rewriting of the *Roman*, which like the *Liber* was one of the most popular works of the Middle Ages, is significant. First, as I have already noted, the changes made to the basic narrative underline the poet's commitment to the idea of reasonable love as the foundation for political order. But second and more striking are the ways the poet exchanges the *Roman*'s central allegory (the rose) with another that appears in the *Roman* itself, the allegory of chess. As I will argue, *Les Echecs* does not rely exclusively on the *Liber*'s depiction of the game but also draws on and alters an allegorical chess match that Reason herself uses in her lecture. In short, if the *Les Echecs* poet alters the *Liber*'s political message by yoking civic order to romantic love, so too does he alter the *Roman*'s suspicions of sexual desire by amplifying Reason's own intimations that love can be inherently reasonable and civically useful.

One of the most popular and widely read medieval poems, the *Roman de la Rose* examines the power and pitfalls of carnal desire. In the poem the narrator, Amant, wanders into the Garden of Diversion where he is shot by the God of Love. Once struck, he becomes consumed with passion for a single, red rose. Sensing Amant's lust, the characters Shame, Fear, and Resistance soon appear and shut the rose in a tower. Sure enough, by the end we learn that Amant's love is primarily carnal desire, a fact graphically displayed the moment that Amant's advisors help him win the battle. When he reaches the rose, he "(wishes) to put [his] staff into the aperture, with the sack hanging behind" ["Veil [son] bordon metre en l'archiere / Ou l'escharpe pendoit derriere"], and he assails the opening vigorously.[28] His labor pays off when he finds ingress and, in a few lines whose raciness would rival that of Chaucer, spreads his seed inside.

Standard interpretations of this poem position it as an allegory for the way *cupiditas*, love of an earthly object, and lust distract man from a love of God. Indeed, this is the message of Amant's most vocal opponent, Reason, who endorses friendship as the only acceptable form of love, one that binds men together in communities.[29] As Reason argues, friendship paves the way for fair exchange, and she contrasts proper friendship with romantic love, which she describes as the "simulated desire of loving in hearts sick with the disease of coveting gain" (101) ["fainte volenté d'amer / En cuers malades du mehaing / De convoitise du gaaing"] (ll. 4772–74).[30] Unlike romantic love, friendship is a form of ideal affection that operates on the premise of an equal exchange never enacted; friends would give each other everything, yet friends demand nothing from each other. Whereas sexual/romantic desire expresses itself as carnal lust and as a passion for individual profit, true friends have "such noble hearts" (104) ["les cuers de tex nobleces"] (l. 4925) that they do not love for wealth or gain. Whereas sexual/romantic desire "leads men to death" (101) ["met les gens a mort"] (l. 4768), friendship is "connected to every virtue" (101) ["a toute vertu s'amort"] (l. 4767). Reason belabors this point incessantly. "No amount of riches can equal the value of a friend," she insists, and "riches do not enrich a man who locks them up in treasure" (104).[31]

After her diatribe against romantic love, Reason turns to the subject of Fortune. She offers three examples to illustrate Fortune's fickleness and uses chess as an allegory to narrate the struggle between Charles, Count of Anjou and Provence, and Manfred, the illegitimate son of Emperor Frederick II, for the kingdom of Sicily. Yet her description of the game does not show Fortune's weakness as much as it highlights Reason's faith in her own preeminence.[32] The "game" starts when Charles of Anjou attacks, advancing on his gray horse to declare "eschac" and "mat" (l. 6652). A second game follows this first match, and Charles plays against the team of Conradin and Henry, who begin to fight after Charles's victory:

Ces deus, comme faus garçonnés,
Et rois et fiers et poonés
Et chevaliers au geu perdirent
Et hors de l'eschaquier saillirent,
Tel poor orent d'estre pris
Au geu qu'il orent entrepris.
Car qui la verité regarde,
D'estre mat n'avoient il garde;
Puis que sans roi se combatoient
Eschac et mat riens ne doutoient. (ll. 6663–72)

[These two (Conradin and Henry), like foolish boys, lost rooks, fools (bishops), pawns, and knights in the game and scrambled off the board such fear did they have of being captured in the game that they had undertaken. For if one considers the truth, one sees that they took no precaution against being mated; since they fought without a king they had no fear of check and mate.] (129)

Conradin and Henry do not lose their pieces to Fortune; they lose because they play unreasonably. As Reason points out, the game does not work without a king; no one can win or lose in this situation. Because Conradin and Henry play without a king, they cannot be mated. Nor can they lose the game with a "bare king," an ending that happens when one loses all one's pieces except for the king himself. This is what Reason means when she says, "It must be the king that the player says *have* to. . . . one cannot say 'have' to any other piece" ["Que cis soit rois, que l'en fait have . . . L'en ne puet autrement haver"] (ll. 6683 and 6689).[33] Moreover, anyone who gambles his pieces will face certain disaster. Consequently, the "foolish boys" waste many lives before "scrambling off the board" to avoid the ramifications of their actions. The game ends only when King Charles intercedes and captures the two fugitives.

Reason's faith in her own abilities is further reaffirmed by Charles's mastery of chess, and his own love of Reason becomes manifest in his ability to defeat his opponents at the "game" of war. Reason rewards him for his devotion by giving him control of Sicily, victory over his opponents, and a subsequently stable kingdom. Even if this account of the events is overtly biased —Jean de Meun's praise of Charles reflects the views of a loyal Frenchman—chess in this passage becomes part of an ideological project seeking to show that Charles deserves his conquest and that his rule is legitimate.

In sum, man's ability to reason, like his capacity for friendship, is essential for proper governance. As if to underline this point, in the middle of the allegory Reason includes an etiology of the game that she draws from John of Salisbury: "you will see in the *Polycraticus* that he digressed from his matter, since he should have been writing of numbers, where he found this excellent pretty game which he tested by demonstration" (129). While the story, which attributes the game to the mathematician Athalus, is unremarkable, this reference to John's treatise, a text claiming that "the cultivation of public virtue is the general safeguard of each and every person and of rational nature," is significant.[34] In short this allusion to John's text betrays Reason's investment in civic order, an order that is maintained through and propagated by reasonable love.

This definition of love echoes the *Liber*'s model of a civic polity, which is also founded on principles of fair exchange. Just as Jacobus repeatedly stresses that individuals in a stable society must work toward the common good or common profit, so too does Reason counsel Amant to love everyone generally and abandon any type of particular love ("love them all as much as one, at least with the love of what is common to all").[35] In other words, Reason argues that a stable political order requires men to love each other as friends, the *only* type of reasonable love an individual should pursue. Unlike romantic love, which makes men selfish and undercuts social harmony, friendship leads to a desire for the common good and, in the end, a love for political order itself. Her description of friendship and her encouragement of Amant to love generally form the basis for an ideal order in which men "would never *have* [i.e., say 'have' to] a king or prince" (113) ["jamés roi ne prince n'avroient"] (l. 5558), and where "judges would never hear any clamor (113) ["jamés juges n'avroit clamor"] (l. 5561).

How striking it is, then, when the poem culminates in an unreasonable battle of love, namely the assault on the castle and eventually on the rose itself, an object that represents the lover's cathexis and his departure from reason. The battle, although occurring in the poet's dream and constructed as an allegory, is violent, and his violation of the rose, described graphically at the poem's conclusion, is physical. This narrative structure opposes the notion of reasonable desire, and Amant's obsession reveals that he cannot conceive of his lady in anything but sexual terms—even Evrart, who in his Commentary explicates the general symbolism of roses, notes that the red rose "signifies unreasonable love, in which one desires only carnal delight" (Jones, 347) ["segnefie l'amour desraisonable ou on ne quiert que le charnel delit"] (239). All advice falls flat in the face of Amant's lust.

In contrast to Amant, the *Les Echecs* poet seems to have mastered Reason's lessons well. As I have described above, the *Les Echecs* poet and commentator position chess as an allegory of love and war. But in doing so they do not dismiss the power of reason to regulate strong emotions, assuming instead that romantic love, if not already reasonable, can be shaped by rational thought. Thus an inanimate game, rather than a fickle advisor, facilitates the poet's intellectual development. Unlike the physical objects in the garden of the *Roman*, the *Les Echecs* chess game provides an interactive pastime through which the poet exposes his own conceptions of love, displays his own weaknesses as a lover, and cultivates his potential for improvement. From the poem's opening lines, then, chess is marked as the most significant element in the narrative and as a place of objective, impartial, and rational action.[36] The very titles of the works—the *Rose* poem takes its name from the object of the lover's quest while the modernly titled *Les Echecs* poem, translated by Lydgate as "Reason and Desire," quickly came to be identified with the medium through which love operates—betray this different understanding of love. The contours of reasonable desire are also carefully detailed in the Commentary, which, as noted above, maps the game's symbolism in exquisite detail. According to Evrart, the square board itself by its right nature "signifies the equality of justice and the loyalty that ought to exist in love" (Jones, 973) ["segnifie le equalité de justice et la loyauté qui doit estre en amours"] (605). Or, as one reader observes of Evrart's sentiments, the text shows that mankind's drive to procreate and regenerate "can be handled reasonably by people; part of its beauty is that its human form is not merely biological but controllable by reason."[37]

It is this faith in reasonable love that the *Les Echecs* poet uses to rewrite Reason's chess allegory. Like Reason, the *Les Echecs* poet and commentator see friendship as an important component in civic order. Yet both poet and Evrart also see romantic love as a viable form of the friendship described by Reason. In *Les Echecs* Pallas emphasizes the importance of friendship when she lectures the lover about the nature of marriage. According to Pallas, a man and a woman united in marriage should resemble birds who work together in peaceful accord. "Houses and cities were," she reminds him, "built with the family in view," and the "friendship of marriage includes all possible kinds of love."[38] Pallas's description of the family eventually prompts her to comment on the evils of usury, and the poem breaks off as she begins to discuss the importance of fair exchange. In his Commentary Evrart does not directly address the matter of friendship. Yet he constantly reminds his reader that romantic love and sensual desire must be controlled by reason and that strong passions such as envy will strain the bonds of amity. After all, *la vie active*, or life in a community, is "proper and natural to man," who "naturally wants to live in society" (Jones, 540–41).

Reviving the Body of State

In the previous chapter, I tracked some of the historical forces at play in Jacobus's *Liber*. And while historical context cannot explain why an author writes a particular text, it does help us to understand the cultural pressures that may have contributed to a text's production. If, as I have argued above, the *Les Echecs* poem and its Commentary rewrite two earlier texts, so too do they participate in a contemporary conversation about political organization. It is thus worthwhile to consider the ways their use of their allegory intersects with other ideas about political order that circulated in fourteenth- and fifteenth-century political treatises.

Les Echecs and the Commentary most notably resemble contemporary political writings in the way both texts promote the image of the state as a human body. Indeed, this state-as-body model is implicit in the allegory itself, which positions romantic relationships as products of nature, albeit a nature controlled by man. Thus while the poem borrows heavily from Jacobus's state-as-chess-game model, it does so only to reinscribe the *Liber*'s contractually based (i.e., nonorganic) society within the framework of organic order (lover's body as civic community) and natural structure (cosmos as chess game). Evrart's careful analysis of the body of the lover, the body of state, and the similarities between them works to the same end, and the Commentary constantly moves between the physical and the political. Nor does this return to the state-as-body model appear exclusively in the fabric of the "chess of love" allegory; it also appears in Pallas's lecture as she rhapsodizes about the ideal social order. Like Jacobus, Pallas describes a political community as comprised of individuals from various social classes, but she sees the individuals in these classes as following "natural" patterns of behavior, patterns that are in turn reinforced by man-made laws and traditions. She eventually embraces the state-as-body metaphor outright, stating that the king, who acts as the "soul" of the realm, oversees the functioning of the state as a whole and claiming that "disobedience to a prince is more dangerous than disobedience to a doctor, for the former has the soul in charge."[39]

This use of the state-as-body metaphor, along with its general revival in other works of this time, may reflect the various crises of power in late medieval France and the desire to see the country as a unified kingdom. Unlike late thirteenth-century Italy, fourteenth-century France was not comprised of loosely connected city-states, and the internal struggles for control of the country throughout fourteenth and early fifteenth centuries (exacerbated by

Edward III of England's claim to the French throne in 1337) refocused attention on the king as the key to a unified realm. The country's fairly strong centralized government, manifest in the opening parts of the century by Philip IV's successful resistance to (and eventual cooption of) papal authority, was further strengthened two decades later with the opening sorties of the Hundred Years War, and with a few notable regional exceptions in the southwest, the war with England helped to coalesce the French king's power. The victories of Charles VII in the mid-fifteenth century gave proof to his claim of sovereignty over the lands of France, and the fourteenth and fifteenth centuries ultimately saw "an affective 'pull' towards a sense of French national identity."[40] That the war itself revolved around the rights of royal succession only intensified the importance of the king and his heirs as the primary arbiters of secular power.[41] As French historian Jacques Krynen notes: "All gazes converged on the king, placing him, despite his effacement, at the heart of political debate and indicating the most firm loyalty to the monarchy."[42]

In the literary world the increasing power of the king was reflected in the proliferation of *specula regis*, instantiations of a genre that experienced a small renaissance, and these treatises reflect this increased focus on the king's physical person as the repository of divine authority on earth.[43] Returning to the primary trope used in twelfth- and thirteenth-century political works, writers once again configured the state as a body with the king as its head. Nor did the flurry of political tracts come exclusively from new authors; older works such as the *Policraticus*, which Charles V commissioned in both French and in its original Latin for his own library, were also popular.[44] These older texts may have helped to revive the state-as-body image, and the allegory appeared anew in various works by Jean de Terre-Vermeille, Jean Juvenal des Ursins, Jean Meschinot, Jean Gerson, and Christine de Pizan, who all describe the state as a biological organism with the monarch at the head.[45]

Christine's *Livre du corps de policie* (*Book of the Body Politic*), composed between 1404 and 1407, provides a good example of how these writers borrowed and reshaped the state-as-body allegory. In this text Christine credits her use of the metaphor to the "Letter from Trajan" that John of Salisbury cites in the middle of the *Policraticus*.[46] Like John, Christine uses the metaphor strategically to promote the idea of the natural interdependence that governs the relationship between a community's various members. Christine also divides the state into three major groups, each of which must work with the others for survival: the feet and belly (the common people) sustain the body; the arms (the knights) defend it; and the head (the king) oversees the operation of all. And while her assignment of the clergy to the body's lower ranks may have shocked its fifteenth-century readers, it testifies to the power residing in the secular ruler.[47]

Christine's decision to use the body to represent the state did not stem from an ignorance of the *Liber*. She knew the text well, relying heavily on Jehan de Vignay's translation of Jacobus when she composed her 23,636-line *Livre de la mutacion de fortune*, a poem that predates her *Book of the Body Politic* by several years.[48] In the poem's third part, the inhabitants of Fortune's castle are depicted as occupying a series of seats.[49] At the top of the castle, two men, most likely representing the pope of Rome (Boniface IX) and the pope of Avignon (Benoît XIII), duel over St. Peter's vacant throne.[50] Below them are counselors, advisors, secular and clerical judges, merchants, bankers, and the people of the common trades ("menu peuple"). As Suzanne Solente has observed, their organization bears a striking resemblance to Jacobus's text, and some of the exempla Christine uses in this section are straightforward borrowings from Vignay's translation.[51]

Two things are notable about the way Christine rewrites her source. First, she has dropped the chess metaphor altogether. Whereas the *Liber* shows each piece/profession in its proper role and instructs them to follow a set of rules, the *Mutacion* only loosely groups people by class with no rules binding the "seats" together. This lack of cohesiveness exacerbates the second major change Christine has made to her source: the rewriting of this political community as a place of corruption rather than virtue. The problem does not rest entirely with the squabbling popes at the top. Vice plagues everyone from the counselors, who pursue their own interests at the expense of the common good, to the commoners, many of whom spend their days drinking. For Christine, then, Jacobus's *Liber* has become a means to describe an iniquitous collective of people rather than an ideal political order.

Unlike Christine, the *Les Echecs* poet does not reject the chess metaphor. Yet he too does not seem entirely comfortable with the state-as-chessboard model offered by the *Liber*. While Pallas in her speech may refer to the king as the state's head, the comparison of the lover's body to a collection of chess pieces suggests something quite different, namely that *each individual* at the board (or reading the poem) *naturally* embodies all aspects of the state. Thus rather than a singular body politic, a player/lover embodies an entire kingdom. Or, to use Evrart's terminology, a lover's pieces represent "human polity and community."

In the end this rewriting of the state as something representable by any body, not just the king's, comes out of the tradition of the *Liber*. Yet it is also tempered by a discourse of organic order. As discussed in the previous chapter, the *Liber*'s chess allegory imagined a community's subjects as pieces that move independently of the king. Bound to the state by rules rather than organic bonds, a subject makes a decision to work for the common good out of a sense of moral duty rather than of physical obligation. This new representation of subjects as independent of a central authority does not make them free. Yet unlike the more explicit, physical bonds that subjugate the members of a physical body, the relationships modeled by the chess game carry with them a power that aims at psychological as opposed to physical control. By casting each lover as an embodiment of an entire political community, *Les Echecs* in some respects pushes this point even farther. Not only is the state imagined as a chess game, but each person is imagined as a state unto him- or herself.

This investment in Jacobus's chess allegory is not exclusive to *Les Echecs* or the Commentary; the *Liber* itself had grown in popularity throughout the fourteenth and fifteenth centuries. Jehan de Ferron and Jehan de Vignay turned out two slightly different French versions of the *Liber* (titled *Le Jeu des eschaz moralisé*) in the fourteenth century.[52] Jehan de Ferron's translation, produced for his patron Bertrand d'Aubert, appeared throughout the French-speaking world, while Vignay's translation, dedicated to Jean, duke of Normandy and son of Philippe VI, was aimed more directly at a royal audience.[53] Evrart himself draws attention to his literary debt when he refers to the "the book of *chess moralized*," an aside alerting his readers that he, like the poet, had read Jacobus's treatise (Jones, 16).[54]

Nevertheless, the *Liber* itself underwent changes as it was translated from Latin to French.[55] In her edition of the *Liber*'s French translations, *Le Jeu des eschés, moralisé*, Carol S. Fuller observes that Jehan de Vignay's longest addition (six pages) to Jacobus's original text appears at the beginning of the chapter on the queen and seeks to justify the right of male primogeniture. She quotes Vignay: "C'est avoir touz jours roys par suscession de ligniee sanz ce que femme puisse ne ne doie venir a l'eritage du royaume."[56] His aside reflects a concern with the king not only as a locus of power but as a physical and political body that cannot be penetrated. Perhaps even more significant is the change to the *Liber*'s prologue. Whereas Jacobus specifically states that all men should read his book, Jehan de Vignay's French version was "directed at and dedicated to a prince of France, the future king Jehan le Bon," thus making it, as Fuller points out, a more viable mirror for magistrates.[57] In short, while Jehan de Vignay sought to reduce the *Liber*'s scope, the *Les Echecs* poet was busy recoding the *Liber*'s primary allegory as one of natural virtue and/or individual desire.

At the same time that the *Liber*'s translators reoriented Jacobus's chess allegory, Philippe de Mézières refashioned it altogether, using it to represent the individual emotion and moral choice of the ruler alone. Part propaganda and part advice book, Philippe's *Songe du vieil pèlerin* (ca. 1389) was born of his hopes for a healed papal schism, a peace with England, and a united Europe under French and English leadership.[58] In the final book, the longest of the three, Queen Truth presents Charles, the "Young Moses," with a chessboard "to pass the time and for a lesson in modesty—for kings must not be proud, especially when they go to battle—thus I present you with a square chessboard to play in your royal chariot" ["pour passet temps en pour un esbatement—car le roys ne doyvent pas estre oyseux, et par espicial quant ilz vont en bataille—pource je te present un eschequier quarre, pour jouer aux eschez en ton chariot royal"].[59] As in the *Liber*, the chess game is presented to the ruler, who must understand the game in order to rule correctly.[60]

Yet while Philippe manages to omit the state-as-body metaphor (and thus the idea that the state has its roots in a natural order), his treatise, like those of his contemporaries, focuses on the royal office, and his discussion of the king constitutes the majority of this work.[61] For Philippe, the chessboard's four quadrants are, like the wheels of the royal chariot, representative of "truth, justice, peace, and mercy" ["verite, justice, paix et misericorde"].[62] However, these four quadrants also correspond to the king's person: the first contains the elements of his personal conduct (his "personne royalle"); the second reflects his relationship to the Church; the third encompasses his relationship to his subjects; and the fourth contains "certain moral lessons touching on the common good and welfare of the Christian world and particularly of the kingdom of France" ["certains enseignemens moraulx touchans a la chose publique et bien commun de toute la crestiente et singulierement du royaume de France"].[63] After mapping the board's mechanics, Philippe uses most of the remainder of the book to treat the squares of each quadrant in turn, describing the sixty-four rules that govern a king's actions.

A slightly different reframing of the allegory takes place in *Le Jeu des esches de la dame, moralisé*, a late fifteenth-century poem that exists in a unique manuscript in the British Museum.[64] In this poem the chess pieces are based on those of *Les Echecs amoureux*, yet the allegory is notably more religious. Rather than a game between lovers, the game is played between a lady and the devil, and her soul is at stake. On the devil's side the various pieces represent earthly temptations and sins: his king is pride, his queen is ambition, his bishops are pleasure and ambition, his knights are discord and a lie, and his rooks are grumbling and falseness. On the lady's side are virtues and moral strengths. Her king and queen are, respectively, charity and humility; her bishops are honesty and knowledge of self; her knights are true friendship and truth; and her rooks are patience and loyalty.[65] As in *Les Echecs*, the pieces here represent the general virtues and vices of mankind. Yet as with Engreban d'Arras's "Ch'est li jus des Esques" or the *Quaedam*, the game itself does not function as much as a place of political education as it does a passage to a better place. Once the lady has conquered the devil in the game, she will presumably not have to defeat him again.

The continued popularity of the *Liber* and its rewriting point toward the divergent discourses of civic order in circulation at the time. On the one hand, demographic shifts in fourteenth-century France increased the political power for guildsmen and other lower-class groups. The growing merchant classes, the post-plague migrations, and the increasing ability of the kingdom's subjects to mobilize for social protest (as evinced by the *Jacquerie* of 1358), all attest to a shift in civic organization from kinship bonds governed by hierocratic power to an increasingly affiliative polity held together by professional ties.[66] The *Liber*'s allegory of state, which recognizes the variation in trade and the power of the merchant class, finds a comfortable correlation with this culture. On the other hand, the growing power of the French monarch as well as the debates surrounding royal lineage refocused attention on the king's body. As discussed above, the increasing centralization of political power manifested itself in the continued production of state-as-body allegories.

But the persistence of a hierocratic system can also be charted in the changes made to Jacobus's chess allegory. For Philippe de Mézières the chessboard represents a polity in which the king, whose body subsumes the entire game, wields far more power than the ranks of "pieces" around him.[67] The chess allegory in *Les Echecs* and its Commentary shares some elements with Philippe's *Songe*, most notably the use of pieces to represent virtues, and trades in the more general revival of the state-as-body metaphor. In the poem, Pallas tells the poet, "the good prince governs his people as the soul does the body."[68] In his Commentary Evrart continually reminds us that the state is a physical body with a king at its head. Nevertheless, unlike Philippe and the authors of political treatises that drew on the state-as-body metaphor, Evrart and the *Les Echecs* poet do not use chess to focus on royal power. The only king governing the lover is the king within his body, the heart, over which the laws of nature ultimately rule. Similarly, Pallas's reversion to the state-as-body metaphor paves the way for her to talk about the common citizen, the most important representative of *la vie active*, rather than about the community's monarch.

Wagering on Love

So far I have shown how the conflation of bodies in *Les Echecs* and its Commentary—the layering of the cosmological over the political and the individual—works through and against several different textual traditions. I have still not considered, however, the ways the allegory intersects with the game as it was played in the late Middle Ages. How would a medieval chess player have understood *Les Echecs*? And, more importantly, how does the practice of gambling on the game change the allegory itself? By way of concluding this chapter, I would like to consider the efforts made, both by the poet and by Evrart, to detach the chess allegory from its violent subtext and from its connections to economic exchange. Ultimately their attempts are insufficient. Nevertheless, as I will also argue, the allegory itself anticipates the poem's interest in the world of material exchange, an interest made manifest in Pallas's insistence that romantic love is connected to commerce. It is, in short, no accident that a poem proposing to offer an idealized model of romantic love breaks off in the middle of a discussion of usury.

It should be clear by this point that the chess allegory's logic does not always cohere. That both authors represent ideal love as a tied chess match does little to mask the game's inherent violence. Battles in a lover's heart are not so easily reconciled with the bloodshed of a real war; the metaphor can only go so far. These misalignments also become painfully apparent in the prologue to Evrart's Commentary, where he discusses the ways that the game corresponds to the heavenly bodies, trying to explain the ways *seven* planets correspond to the *six* types of chess pieces. He eventually solves the problem by stating that Mercury, the seventh planet, is "of a mingled nature" ["de nature mellee"] (9). It therefore resembles a promoted pawn who, although moving like the queen, becomes a new type of piece upon reaching the eighth square.[69] Yet Evrart's desire to pass over this comparison "for the sake of brevity" ["pour cause de briefté"] (9) belies an anxiety about the irreducibility of two systems whose relationship might not be as natural as his first comparisons suggest.[70]

While this numerical disparity might be written off as a minor difference between two otherwise analogous structures, other elements of the chess game work to deconstruct the allegory's assumed oppositions between good and bad desire, troubling the poet's attempt to offer an idealized portrait of romantic love. Most notably, the promoted pawn challenges the poem's explicit endorsement of heterosexual unions. When pawns, implicitly male pieces, travel the whole length of the board, they assume the powers of a queen. However, this gender shift proved troubling for players, who created a new name for this piece; s/he was usually called a *fierce* while the original queen was usually called a *reyne*.[71] Nor could a player promote his pawn until the original queen had been taken, a rule that, if applied, matches the chess king with a transgendered male figure. As Evrart's description of Mercury suggests, this piece never fully transforms himself into his newly appropriated female role, and this irresolution troubles the model espoused by the poem. If love between a man and a woman is a "natural" occurrence, what are we to make of the new pairing between a promoted pawn and a king? In short, reading the game strictly as a symbol of heterosexual courtship cannot fully account for the ways that its rules embedded it in larger structures of male-male desire.[72]

While the practice of pawn promotion complicates the poem's endorsement of heterosexual desire, the use of the game for gambling exposes the allegory's investment in pragmatic notions of romantic union. Whereas the *Liber* tries to obscure the game's connections to gambling by avoiding any description of a game in progress, and by reassigning gambling to dice players alone, the *Les Echecs* poet suppresses the disturbing prospect of unequal exchange by casting a tie between two players as the perfect ending. In the idealized match between the lady and Deduis, the two sides reach a state of perfect balance, and the game ends in a draw. One can assume that pieces have been exchanged somewhat equally—if not, the game's conclusion in a tie would be unlikely—and the cordial interaction between the players suggests no bitter feelings. This model of equality and fair exchange contrasts sharply with the second game between the lady and the poet, where the lover is soundly beaten and retreats in shame after losing his pieces. Although his loss at the "chess of love" is figurative, the game's underlying discourses surface in Pallas's speech, where we learn that romantic love itself is driven by material concerns. To return to Duby, marriage lay "at the junction between the material and the spiritual," and medieval culture openly saw the marriage union as a way to "[regulate] the transmission of wealth from one generation to another."[73] Thus while the game may govern the emotions of the two players, it simultaneously served as a medium through which material goods could pass, and its regulatory power extended well beyond the psychological realm into the world of social, economic, and political exchange.

Like the *Les Echecs* poet, Evrart also endorses the model of a tied game, which allows him to rewrite the game's ties to material trade as a form of condoned exchange. Indeed, he spends ample time talking about the ways that the board is balanced, and his criticism of the poet's match stems less from the lost pieces than from the ways these individual losses hurt the harmony of the whole. Unlike the poet, however, Evrart does not avoid the game's seedier subtexts and confronts the practice of gambling directly. He first addresses the topic in his discussion of fortune. To illustrate accidental or "reasonable" fortune, he gives the example of someone who, during his regular occupation, such as digging in the earth, finds some treasure.[74] Natural or "unreasonable" fortune results from "an inclination to the movements of Nature that sometimes moves us to do works without our being moved by reason at all, but only by pure affection of the heart" (Jones, 20) ["une inclinacion ou un mouvement de nature qui nous esmeut aucunesfoiz a faire aucunes oeuvres, sanz ce que nous soions a ce point meu de raison, maiz de la pure affeccion du cuer tant seulement"] (15). This second type of fortune, however, does not necessarily comport evil; some individuals "choose so well in their deeds while following only the inclination of their hearts that advantages come to them and their needs" (Jones, 21) ["sy bien eslisent en leur fait et sont si eureux en enssivant ce que leurs cuers leur en dit seulement qu'il leur vient bien aussi come touzdiz de leurs besoignes"] (16). But Evrart adds that such inclinations more commonly result in less honorable outcomes: "as we see some win in the game of dice, which is entirely and purely played by luck and in pure fortune. And others, on the contrary, always lose it" (Jones, 21) ["sy come nous veons que aucun au gieu des dez communement gaignent, que auques gist tout en pur sort et en pure fortune, et les autres au contraire ausques tousdiz ilz perdent"] (16). Natural fortune not only threatens the division of the players into winners and losers, but it also inspires the "inclination" of a winner's heart toward personal reward.

Initially in his discussion of fortune Evrart associates gambling exclusively with dice, but later in the Commentary he admonishes against those who wager on chess games. He again emphasizes the game's perfection—the board's square shape connotes the ideals of loyalty, equality, and justice, which should guide two lovers—and insists that a player should strive for honest victory not profit: "and so those abuse themselves greatly and err who play it for money, as do those who play it by dice, for this game should not proceed by fortune, but by ingenuity and subtlety, so, also should it be in the chess of love" (Jones, 975) ["pour ce abusent ceulx, et grandement errent, qui pour argent y jouent et ceulx aussi qui y jouent as dés, car ce gieu ne doit pas proceder par fortune, maiz par engin et par soutilleté—tout aussi doit il estre en l'eschiquier d'amours"] (606). Condemning those who gamble on chess or dice, Evrart laments that the players who engage in either game submit to the most sinister form of fortune. Those who gamble aim to better their opponents, thus spoiling the fair and balanced relationship embodied in the tied game.

Nevertheless, Evrart's attempt to detach chess from gambling is undercut by the poet's description of the match between the lover and the lady, which is modeled directly on the chess problems in circulation at this time. In the previous chapter, I briefly described the popularity of problem sets, collections of endgame diagrams that challenged the reader to mate in a certain number of moves. Such collections flourished in the thirteenth and fourteenth centuries and held no little appeal for gamblers. Usually titled and accompanied by a few lines of verse, the problem itself often took the form of a mini-narrative that encrypted clues to completion while at the same time teaching a moral. At no time, however, did a problem ever encourage a player to master the art of a draw.

Game number 20, also titled *Bien trové*, or *Well Found*, in the British Museum King's Library Manuscript 13, A.xviii, one of four Anglo-Norman problem sets that date from the late thirteenth and early fourteenth centuries, provides a fairly typical example of a problem narrative:

Ceste guy si ad noun bien trové.
E si est il sutils & de graunt bealté.
Kar al sime tret matera soun adverser.
A force en my lu del eschecker.
E bien fut trové & bien fust fet.
Kar en li n'ad pur veir nul tret.
Ke ne porte graund force en sey.
En my l'eschecker pur mater le rey.
E sovent en guy venir put.
Kar si vus eyez un roc & un chivaler.
E un altre hom ke put garder
Le poynt ke dl. est només.
Vostre purpose dunkes averés.[75]

[This game is called "Well Found"
Because it is tricky and of great beauty,
For at the sixth move, he mates his adversary
By force in the middle of the chessboard.
And it is well-found and well-made
Because there [in the center] he truly has no move.
Whoever does not carry a large force on his side,
Can mate the king in the middle of the chessboard.
And often in a game this can come about,
For if you have a rook and a knight
And another man who can guard
The square that is called d6,
Your goal is then proven.]

This short passage, which follows the diagram, trades in a language of virtue—the game is "tricky and of great beauty"—yet also gives the reader a hint about how to proceed. At the same time, its championing of a strong centerboard game indicates that the game represents a certain high caliber of play; one who finds the solution has indeed done something well.[76]

While problems like *Bien trové* require a mate in a minimum number of moves, this was not always the case. Some problems required the player to mate in *more* moves than the board seemed to offer. A problem from the *Bonus socius* (*Good Companion*) contains one diagram where the white side has three ways to mate black in a single move. None of these mates, however, is correct; instead the white must mate black in *two* moves.[77] Whatever the goal, all problems highlight a player's skills and ability to defeat an invisible opponent. The successful player of *Bien trové* makes moves that are "soutil," and in *Le Guy de dames & damoyceles*, another problem found in this same collection, ingenious women can protect themselves from certain mate.

Some problems, like several in the British Museum Cotton Manuscript Cleopatra B.ix, explicitly address the practice of gambling. In the very first problem, the compiler narrates the story of a king who has wagered his daughter's hand in marriage against his opponent's life.[78] When the daughter hears about the wager, she comes to chastise her "ami" for his foolhardiness. Nevertheless, the young knight "studied quietly and surveys the board / so that he saw the defense and the mate / which will be taught here now" ["Mult estudia e tant puruit / k'il vit la defense e la mateson / Si cum nus ici le aprendrum"].[79] Although it is doubtful that a reader will find himself in a similar situation, the text's opening lines promise that the problems will help the player "who wants attentively / to learn about the rules of the game / about the subtle moves about mates / about the defenses as they should be taught" ["Kar ki ke voldra ententivement / Des gius aprendere le doctrinement / Des sutils trez, de matesons, / Des defenses cum les aprendrons"].[80] Such skills will help if, like the protagonist of problem number 12 in the Cotton Manuscript, the player has wagered his goods, or if, like the player in problem twenty of the King's Manuscript, he is counterchecked by his opponent. In the latter instance the text warns that the player will "lose his money" ["perdreyt soun argent"].[81]

Returning to *Les Echecs*, we find an endgame that, if not copied directly from a thirteenth- or fourteenth-century problem set, assumes the unmistakable form of a chess problem (Table 3). The lady's pieces can mate the poet in one move, and "it is completely obvious that he who is trapped and held cannot flee so that there are not but five moves necessary to mate

TABLE 3. Endgame in *Les Echecs amoureux* as represented by H. J. R. Murray, *A History of Chess*, 482

a8	b8	c8	d8	**King**	F8	g8	h8
a7	b7	c7	c7	e7	F7	g7	h7
a6	b6	c6	d6	e6	**Pawn**	g6	h6
Pawn	b5	c5	d5	e5	pawn	g5	h5
a4	**Queen**	c4	d4	**Bishop**	F4	g4	h4
a3	b3	c3	d3	e3	F3	g3	h3
a2	b2	c2	d2	e2	F2	**Rook**	h2
king	b1	c1	d1	bishop	**Rook**	g1	h1

The lady's pieces are boldface and capitalized; the lover's pieces are in regular type and not capitalized.

The final moves are	**Pawn**	—	a4	
	king	—	b1	
	Pawn	—	a3	
	king	—	a1	
	Queen	—	c3	
	king	—	b1	
	Pawn	—	a2	
	king	—	a1	
	Queen	—	b2	(Mate)

except for him who wished to draw it out" ["il est tout evident que celui qui est ainsy atrapez et tenuz ne peut fouyr qu'il ne soit a .v. traiz de neccessité mat maiz qu'il vueille atendre"] (763). Instead of swiftly dispatching the poet, the ending is prolonged for the sake of a moral lesson. Using her pawns Sweet Looks and Fair Welcome to trap the poet's king in the corner, the lady advances her queen, Golden Mean, to finish the game.[82] Her choice to finish the game in this manner drives home the point of the poem and the Commentary: mankind's capacity for reason, exemplified by the piece Golden Mean, should dominate in love as it does in all else. At the same time the structure of the endgame and the diagram that accompanied the text in at least one manuscript provide an uncomfortable reminder that most players of the game did not play with this moral in mind. In short, the symbolic iconography at the heart of the "chess of love," a game that claims to idealize evenly matched players with no winner and no loser, comes directly from a tradition that champions individual gain rather than common profit. The endgame throws into relief the economic exigencies surrounding heterosexual relationships, exigencies that, although covered up by the idealized model of lovers' balanced emotions, make themselves felt through the very structure of the allegory itself.

I have spent the first half of this book charting the ways that the chess game circulates various and sometimes conflicting discourses about social organization. In the course of doing so I have created a somewhat artificial division between political order in late thirteenth-century Italy, which I have seen as producing Jacobus's model of a community where power was distributed throughout the social orders, and that of late fourteenth- and early fifteenth-century France, which I have presented as a return to a model of centralized power reinforced by the state-as-body metaphor. In reality, neither region had a monolithic political organization, and tensions between these two different ideals of government were present throughout both regions at both times. While France was indeed becoming increasingly centralized under a strong king, the monarch himself was at one point living as a prisoner of his own family.[83] And while parts of Italy, most notably Florence, prided themselves on being a democratic, associative polity, the Lombard tyrants had coalesced their power early in the fourteenth century and ruled the region with absolutist control.

Nonetheless, it is clear that the discourses circulating through the board had changed between the time of Jacobus's *Liber* and the time of the *Les Echecs* poem. In the second half of this book I will follow the *Liber* and its chess allegory into late medieval England, where, as I will argue, the game became an explicit symbol of economic exchange. For the eponymous hero of the *Tale of Beryn*, chess and dice serve as vehicles for gambling, and he loses his possessions playing both. Similarly, Chaucer's allusions to chess in *Troilus and Criseyde* and the *Book of the Duchess*, while not explicit references to gambling, position the game as one through which things are lost. Yet in all three instances, the game's ties to material trade are not masked but rather form the very substance of its importance. Thus while Beryn, the Black Knight, and Criseyde all view chess with suspicion, none turns away from the game altogether. Instead, these narratives and others see the game as something in need of monitoring rather than of complete dismissal.

Chapter 3
Exchequers and Balances: Anxieties of Exchange in Chaucerian Fictions

[The man of system] seems to imagine that he can arrange the different members of a great society with as much ease as the hand arranges the different pieces upon a chess-board. He does not consider that the pieces upon the chess-board have no other principle of motion besides that which the hand impresses upon them; but that, in the great chess-board of human society, every single piece has a principle of motion of its own, altogether different from that which the legislature might chuse [sic] to impress upon it. If those two principles coincide and act in the same direction, the game of human society will go on easily and harmoniously, and is very likely to be happy and successful. If they are opposite or different, the game will go on miserably, and the society must be at all times in the highest degree of disorder.

—Adam Smith, Theory of Moral Sentiments *(VI.2.17)*

In the second book of Chaucer's *Troilus and Criseyde*, Criseyde catches sight of Troilus from her window, and her vision prompts her to argue "in hire thought" about the pros and cons of returning his love.[1] Although initially swept away by "his excellent prowesse, / And his estat, and also his renown," Criseyde quickly begins to consider the drawbacks to such a union (2.660–61).[2] She is keenly aware that spurning her "'kynges sone'" might endanger her already precarious situation in Troy (2.708). At the same time she worries that loving Troilus will comprise her independence— "Allas! Syn I am free, / Sholde I now love, and put in jupartie / My sikernesse, and thrallen libertee?" (2.771–73)—and she revels in the autonomy conferred on her by her status as a widow:

I am myn owene womman, wel at ese—
I thank it God—as after myn estat,
Right yong, and stonde unteyd in lusty leese,

Withouten jalousie or swich debat:
Shal noon housbonde seyn to me "Chek mat!" (2.750–54)

Criseyde's use of chess in this passage, a continuation of the gaming discourses that dominate the poem, is notable.[3] Serving as a shorthand for the
economics of exchange underlying a marriage contract, the metaphor makes
clear that love, a heady emotion that causes Criseyde to blush when she first
sees Troilus, differs from a relationship between a wife and her husband.
"Unteyd in lusty leese," Criseyde can give her love freely. Married, she cannot. And if a marriage is a chess game where freedom and sexual obligation
are at stake, then Criseyde does not even want to play.

Whereas Crisedye's chess metaphor appears as a brief aside in a lengthy
speech, in the *Book of the Duchess* the game becomes an extended allegory.
Again chess marks a heterosexual relationship. Or at least it seems to function
as such. While spouses do not play against each other—the Black Knight
loses his lady, White, to his opponent, Fortune—the game encodes the same
economic powers and patriarchal structures as it does in Criseyde's brief
aside. In this game the male lover is mated when Fortune, his female opponent, takes his queen. Notably, however, his queen carries with it a double
representation; not only is she his queen on the board, she is also his lady.
Thus, like Criseyde, who fears being "mated" by her husband, White becomes
an object to be won or gained in the process of play, and the Black Knight
uses economic terms to express sorrow about her loss. He mourns his own
"account," sighing that "ther lyeth in rekenyng, / In my sorwe for nothyng"
(*BD* ll. 699–700). As evinced by this reference to "rekenyng," the Black
Knight and Fortune have effectively made a trade: Fortune has remunerated
the Black Knight with "sorwe."

That Chaucer uses chess in *Troilus* and the *Book of the Duchess* to highlight the process and pitfalls of imbalanced material exchange marks a break
with texts like the *Liber* and *Les Echecs amoureux*, where chess embodied
either an abstract system of values or represented (at least in its ideal form)
an equal exchange that ended in a draw. As noted above, Jacobus, in his late
thirteenth-century *Liber de moribus hominum et officiis nobilium ac popularium super ludo scachorum*, uses chess to represent an ideal society. In
order to make his allegory work, he tries to negate the symbolic violence
associated with the game and to detach it from gambling, a practice that cuts
against the ideal of parity he wants to promote. Because playing the game at
all (i.e., creating one winner, one loser, and a trail of "dead" pieces) unsettles the *Liber's* model of peaceful social harmony, Jacobus never describes a

game in progress. Instead, he spends the majority of his time explicating the morals appropriate for each of the twelve different pieces, only offering his list of the rules as an afterthought in his last chapter. Writing a bit later than Jacobus, the author of the fourteenth-century *Les Echecs amoureux* narrates a game as it is played, reveling in the symbolic value of each move. Yet like Jacobus, the *Les Echecs* poet seeks to reduce the game's potential for imbalance, using a tied game to model parity between two players. Thus even as the *Les Echecs* allegory clearly constructs the lovers' relationship as one based on exchange, it also imagines an idealized romantic union where the man and woman assume positions of equal power.

Unlike these earlier allegorists, Chaucer makes no attempt to mask the way chess facilitates material exchange. Instead, he capitalizes on the game's ability to serve as a shorthand for an exchange that either has gone bad or holds the promise of inequality. Criseyde's refusal to be "mated" by a second husband discloses her distrust of a marital union, which she recognizes as an intrinsically lopsided contract. Seeing marriage as a game with a winner and a loser, and realizing she will most likely end up as the latter, her best strategy is to avoid it altogether. In the *Book of the Duchess*, the Black Knight, like Criseyde, also recognizes the inequality of the game and is all too aware that playing produces a winner and a loser. Yet unlike Criseyde, he never rejects the idea of play. His only complaint is that he, himself, did not win the match against Fortune. Had the Black Knight "ykoud and knowe" chess problem sets, collections of endgames used to improve skills, he would "have pleyd the bet at ches / And kept [his] fers the bet therby" (*BD* l. 666 and ll. 668–69). In neither poem does a tied game appear as a possibility or even as a desirable outcome.[4]

In this chapter I will look at this use of chess as a metaphor for economic loss, a use that pushes the game away from its Continental precedents. Although I will be talking about a variety of literary works, including those cited above, I will focus my discussion on the *Tale of Beryn*, a poem published in the early fifteenth century and thought to be a part of the Chaucer canon for many years afterward. As I argue, the games in the *Tale of Beryn* foreground the inequality brought about by playing, and chess itself becomes intertwined with the act of exchange and embedded in a larger, and predominantly negative, discourse of gaming.[5]

Before proceeding any farther, I would like to note that the story features games in two distinct although overlapping ways. *Actual games*, which I will define loosely as recreational pastimes governed by commonly agreed-upon rules, subject to an element of chance, and often played for a stake, are the most easy to identify. In the *Prologue* to the *Tale of Beryn* (now more commonly referred to as the *Canterbury Interlude*) the pilgrims engage in a game of tale-telling; the action is, significantly, set at the "Cheker of the Hope," the word *cheker* referring both to the office of the exchequer and to the game of chess.[6] This allusion to chess foreshadows the appearance of a chess match in the *Tale of Beryn* itself, where this game, along with its seedier counterpart, dice, is played by the protagonist, Beryn. Tale-telling, dice, and chess are all forms of entertainment. But importantly, each of these activities also facilitates an economic exchange—the winner of the tale-telling contest will get a free dinner at the expense of the others, just as the winners of the dice and chess games walk away with Beryn's clothes. In each case, the game leads to tension and conflict. At other moments, however, anxiety about exchange is filtered through a *discourse of gaming*, where a language of games is used to describe a trade gone sour. This type of discourse appears most strikingly in the *Interlude*. Here the tapster, Kitt, and the Pardoner make a straightforward agreement; he gives her money and in return she promises to spend the night with him. Yet this straightforward (even if morally dubious) economic contract is derailed when both parties violate the rules governing the exchange. Rather than waiting for the Pardoner, Kitt buys a goose, which she prepares for her lover. And on his part, the Pardoner never really intended her to keep the money but planned to steal it back that night. These contractual violations end up turning the agreement into a type of game, one that Kitt wins as she collects a free dinner (a prize identical to that for the best tale-teller) at the Pardoner's expense.[7]

This repeated use of games and discourses of gaming in the *Interlude* and *Tale* reflect a rising fifteenth-century concern about the tensions between personal gain and common profit, and also about the rapacity of merchant oligarchs who pursued the former at the expense of the latter. Mercantile wealth was rising across late medieval Europe and especially in England where capitalist entrepreneurs had become very powerful.[8] A rapid yet uneven growth of commerce accompanied an instability in local monetary systems and exchange rates, which, unchecked by consistent government policies, fluctuated wildly.[9] It is thus unsurprising that unlike modern game theorists, who value games as ways to model strategic behavior such as cooperation and deception, the *Beryn* author does not use games as predictive or positive representations of human behavior.[10] Quite on the contrary, the poet uses all games, and chess in particular, as negative examples in order to depict the ways individuals try to negotiate the world of commerce (a world that contains elements of risk and chance), the ways they often fail, and the impact of that failure on the stability of the civic community.[11] Actual games and discourses of gaming thus become ways to represent commerce gone bad, and to emphasize the potential for inequality lurking behind any type of trade. For the *Beryn* poet, the heavy hand of a centralized authority becomes the only way to separate commerce from games and minimize the elements of chance threatening the balance of economic markets.

In some respects these images of chess as a negative example of lost Fortune (*Book of the Duchess*) and fortune (*Tale of Beryn*) echo similar allegories found in earlier works like the *Quaedam*, which uses the game to represent the common fate of all. Nor were Chaucer and his imitator alone in investing chess with this type of symbolic weight. Many of the English versions of the *Gesta romanorum*, a popular collection of moral tales in circulation at this time, contain the narrative of Antonius the Emperor, who, after playing the game for years, suddenly realizes that the king faces the same fate as the other pieces and understands this to be symbolic of his own death. This awareness in turn prompts him to divide his kingdom into three parts, which he divides among the king of Jerusalem, the lords of his realm, and the poor people of the land. In the moral explanation that follows the story, the author explains: "Seth now, good sirs; this emperour, þat lovith so wele play, may be called eche worldly man þat occupieth him in vanytes of the world; but he moste take kepe of the pley of the chesse, as did the emperoure."[12] The author then proceeds to demonstrate the ways each piece falls into error—the rook "betokenyth okerers [usurers] and false merchaunts, þat rennyth aboute over all, for wynnyng and lucre, and rechith not how thei geten, so that thei have hit" and "this quene bytokenyth virgyns and damesels, þat goth fro chastite to synne"—as the game progresses.[13] Like the *Quaedam*, the *Gesta* here highlights the ways in which the world itself is intrinsically fallen.

Whereas the *Book of the Duchess* draws more or less straightforwardly on chess as a negative example of Fortune's power, the *Tale of Beryn*, while showing the unpredictability of games, never tries to eliminate them. Yet significantly, neither poem submits to the idea of Fortune as an all-powerful entity. In the *Book of the Duchess*, the narrator, although overwhelmed at the game by Fortune, recognizes that he himself was unprepared to play.[14] In the *Tale of Beryn* the chaos introduced by the game becomes something to be controlled, rather than eliminated, and it is through this control that the state is brought to order.

In his recent book on fifteenth-century statecraft, Paul Strohm describes this emergent political language as one in which "the idea that Fortune might be mastered, her wheel arrested in its course," and argues that this control of Fortune in turn "opens a space for the practice of statecraft, for a conception of the state as a conscious creation and a product of human exertion."[15] Strohm locates this "pre-Machiavellian moment" in the years between 1450 and 1485, the years in which the battles for power between the Yorks and Lancasterians escalated. However, as demonstrated by the images of statehood in the *Beryn* story, this discourse of manageable Fortune had started to enter the English imagination in the early parts of the fifteenth century.

Markets and Merchants in Late Medieval England

In the wake of the fourteenth century's plague years, the English population enjoyed a significant redistribution of wealth and a commensurate growth of a middle class. More money was flowing within England and more people had purchasing power than had been the case during the late thirteenth and early fourteenth centuries. Italian banking syndicates with representatives in England stretched throughout Europe, allowing merchants to deposit money in one country and withdraw it in another. As noted above, this growth took place in the absence of consistent government policies, and the resulting instabilities often led to the downfall of banks and the ruin of families.[16]

In his study of English markets Richard H. Britnell observes that earlier movements towards commercialization had come in response to population growth, and any improved standards of living had been reserved for the nobility. Between 1330 and 1500, however, this changed, as "the pattern of internal trade altered to supply a better standard of comfort to a declining population."[17] Riding the crest of this increasing market activity were the merchants, who, partially as a consequence of their own rising incomes, found themselves at the center of civic order.[18] Jenny Kermode has looked closely at the records of late medieval merchants in three different English cities, demonstrating how "the combination of commercial and secular power gave merchants a disproportionate prominence in urban affairs."[19] Governmental offices, in which the officeholder himself had to fund civic pageantry and community aid, were expensive and could only be held by the richer members of a community. Thus of the 186 men who served as York's bailiff between 1300 and 1396, sixty-three of them (34 percent) were merchants. The next largest group consisted of the drapers, spicers, or gold-smiths, who account for only twenty-five (13 percent) of the officeholders. Merchants also dominated the offices of sheriff (48 percent for the period between 1396 and 1509) and mayor (79 percent for the period between 1300 and 1509).[20]

Such an imbalance of influence was particularly pronounced in London, where the competition for civic power was often a contest between compet-ing economic interests. Merchant capitalists monopolized civic government, controlling the offices of mayor and alderman and passing laws to benefit their own interests.[21] Masters of small crafts, who comprised a different class of Londoners, made efforts in the last part of the fourteenth century to chal-lenge this power—most notably by trying to enforce an earlier charter, set down by Edward II in 1319, that limited the term of an alderman to one year and made the incumbent ineligible for reelection for the following year. Such efforts, however, ultimately resulted in a system even more favorable to the merchants. Rather than ignoring the 1319 charter, as had been the practice for years, the mayor and parliament responded in 1384 by abolishing it, thus making it easier for elected officials to maintain their offices.[22]

On the one hand, this increased power of the merchant class represented a certain amount of social and political autonomy for many towns, which began to have more direct control over their day-to-day affairs. Yet on the other, the rise of a market economy "brought not the celebration of eco-nomic individualism but an uneasy feeling that private virtue and the social order were under threat."[23] To some extent such fears were justified, as "the political rhetoric of merchant oligarchs promoted a narrowly corporatist view of urban society."[24] And while there is little evidence that burgesses in power used their offices exclusively toward self-interested ends, there are signs that people suspected them of such abuses.[25] Whereas in the fourteenth cen-tury fights about who had the right to power took center stage, in the fif-teenth century complaints were more often about the conduct of those in charge, specifically blaming them for "corruption, incompetent financial management, lavish expenditure and the failure to support the common in-terest."[26] Although exaggerated, Chaucer's Merchant, with his forked beard, his obsession with personal profit, and his sly business dealings—"Wel koude he in eschaunge sheeldes selle" (*General Prologue* l. 278)—represents a common perception of mercantile self-interest.[27] The merchants' hege-mony could in some cases be identified and at least in theory restricted on a local level, yet it was far more difficult to control the impact of different economic markets on the national economy. As Christopher Dyer has argued, the commercial economy by this time "had to some extent developed a life of its own, and was subject to booms and slumps, which caused fluctuations in urban living standards quite distinct from the rise and fall in demand from the countryside."[28] Paul Sweezy has aptly characterized the era between Edward III and Elizabeth I "*neither* feudal *nor* capitalist," but rather a transitional time in which economic markets were subject to unpredictable rises and falls.[29]

While the English government made some efforts to control its merchants and its markets, writers pondered the moral and social consequences of a for-profit economy. Langland was among those more suspicious of the increasing amount of mercantile activity, and he spends the early sections of *Piers Plowman* painting commercial exchange as the foundation for the problems with urban life. The counterpoint to Langland's pessimism was Chaucer, the acknowledged inspiration for the *Beryn* author and a poet whose views on commerce, although admittedly complex, were generally more positive. Yet despite their differences, these poets both linked games and trade in their own works, using the connection either to show the unstable, fallen nature of commerce (Langland) or to suggest that such instability is ultimately solvable by making trade into a process of equal exchange and productive collaboration, in other words, by making it less like a game (Chaucer).

Langland tends to view all commercial transactions with suspicion, and he manifests his distrust of commerce clearly in the confessions of the sins.[30] For Envy, who disparages other men's wares to increase the value of his own, and Covetousness, who swindles men for profit, markets provide a means for personal gain at the expense of others. The accounts of Envy and Covetousness pave the way for Gluttony's confession, a short narrative that shows the problems caused by those who turn exchange into a type of game. Setting out for church, Gluttony is quickly derailed when he stops at an inn and plays "New Fair." In this game each of two players puts up an item for exchange. Appraisers nominated by the whole group then determine the value of the objects, and the player offering the less valuable item must pay cash to the other. As Langland describes it:

Ther were chapmen ychose þis chaffare to preise:
Whoso hadde þe hood sholde han amendes of þe cloke.
Tho risen up in Rape and rouned togideres
And preised þe penyworþes apart by hemselve.
There were oþes an heep, whoso it herde:
Thei kouþe noght, by hir Conscience, acorden togideres

Til Robyn þe Ropere arise þei bisought,
And nempned hym for a nounpere þat no debat nere.[31]

Here the practice of gaming is indistinguishable from that of commerce. Or rather, in New Fair the act of exchange itself becomes a type of game where each participant tries to gain at the expense of the other. Trade becomes an activity dominated by the competing interests of those involved; even the "neutral" evaluators quarrel over the value of the items and threaten to fight. In the end Robin the Roper must intercede and issue a final judgment in order to prevent a fracas.

Although Robin the Roper represents the power of a centralized adjudicator, Langland does not endorse a centralized, supervisory authority as a general solution to the problems created by commercial self-interest. Robin, who like Gluttony leads a sinful life, merely facilitates the perverse trading practices of his friends. Ultimately Langland remains suspicious of all trade, and in the ideal society offered in his poem trade is kept to a minimum and community members work to satisfy need rather than profit. Derek Pearsall has noted that Langland's description of London commerce, both here and earlier in the poem, is "close, detailed, and appalled," and the poet's ideal of life "remains rooted in the traditional world of agricultural labor, the countryside, pilgrimages, and castles."[32] The confession of sins is thus unsurprisingly followed by a return to rural environs, where Piers tries to establish his ideal community. In this agrarian model money does not appear, and the subsistence farm lies far away from the "the merchants and traders who operate the elaborate machinery of the money economy" and who pose the biggest threat to Piers's community.[33]

Like Langland, Chaucer uses both the language and practice of games to describe commerce, the most notable intertwining of the two being the taletelling competition that structures the *Canterbury Tales*. Just as it does in the *Canterbury Interlude*, the contest is often promoted by the participants as a pastime with ludic characteristics that predominate over the promise of financial reward. As the stories progress, however, the competition soon causes discord in the group, and the game itself becomes a vehicle for acts of retribution. Even Harry, who has introduced the tale-telling challenge as a way to "pleye" and to "maken . . . disport," calls for someone to "quite with" or pay back the Knight (*General Prologue* ll. 772 and 775; *Miller's Prologue* l. 3119).[34] The darker potential of "quiting" becomes clear when the Reeve swears that he will "quite" the Miller with a scandalous tale and the Cook insinuates that Harry himself will soon be "quit" by his story (*Reeve's Prologue* l.

3864 and *Clerk's Prologue* l. 4362). The commodification of the tales becomes explicit when the Man of Law characterizes his participation in the contest as paying his "dette" and worries that he cannot tell a "thrifty" (a word that could be best translated as "worthwhile") tale (Introduction to the *Man of Law's Tale* ll. 41 and 46). The game itself threatens to dissolve at one point when Harry gets so angry at the Pardoner's insults that he threatens to cut off the Pardoner's genitals. As he declares to the group at this moment: "I wol no lenger pleye / With thee, ne with noon oother angry man" (*Pardoner's Tale* ll. 958–59). Here the Pardoner has violated one of the game's unstated rules by becoming outraged at Harry's remarks, and the Host declares accordingly that he will no longer play with him or with anyone who demonstrates such rage. Only the interference of the Knight, who steps in momentarily to assume control of the group, prevents Harry's abandonment of the game and the complete collapse of the pilgrim community.[35]

While Chaucer shows the precarious balance of exchanges governing the game of tale-telling, he does not exercise the same equanimity with chess, which he uses as a shorthand for lopsided deal-making.[36] Criseyde's aside in *Troilus* offers one instance where chess represents a loss of economic and/or political power. In the *Book of the Duchess* Chaucer uses chess again in this fashion, although the game's economic exigencies are submerged under the Black Knight's mawkish wooing.[37] Notably, the Black Knight, echoing earlier allegories, initially tries to cast the game as an exercise in reason and to detach it from gambling practices. Labeling Fortune as a "trayteresse fals and ful of gyle," he insinuates that his opponent has tricked him into the game and has cheated while playing it (*BD* l. 620). Fortune, who takes things "now by the fire, now at table," does not seem to recognize the noble character of chess (*BD* l. 646). Yet ultimately the Black Knight acknowledges Fortune's skills and admits that he "wole have drawe the same draughte" had he been more alert to the actions on the board. A few lines later, he embraces the language of economics and mourns the imbalanced trade—his lady in exchange for nothing—that has taken place.

The Black Knight's subsequent remarks are even more telling in this regard and suggest that the knight himself may have gambled away his lady. Upon losing the game, he reveals his knowledge of contemporary gambling practices when he exclaims: "But God wolde I had oones or twyes / Ykoud and knowe the jeupardyes / That kowde the Grek Pictagores" (*BD* ll. 665–67), the term "jeupardyes" referring to the chess problem sets used by chess gamblers to increase their skills and winnings.[38] (The word originates in the Latin expression *jocus partitus* or "divided game.")[39] That the Black Knight has never used them, not even "oones or twyes," could mean that he has never tried to gamble at the game, but rather has played it only as a game of honor. But it could also indicate that the Black Knight has never *lost* a wager, and thus has never needed the help of a practice book. In either case, with his mention of problem sets and of his settled account, the knight reveals his own view of the game as a medium for exchange, one that he now wishes he had mastered.[40]

Although such moments bring to mind the discord of New Fair and appear to reflect a Langlandian distrust of commerce, Chaucer does not condemn commercial practice altogether. To return to the tale-telling contest found in the *Canterbury Tales*, we see a group of pilgrims comprised largely of urbanites with "a lively interest in the world of getting and spending money, the world of commerce."[41] Unlike Langland's New Fair players, the pilgrims are not embodiments of sin but a fellowship of individuals who are, for the most part, identified by their relationship to England's markets. Characters such as the Merchant, Miller, Shipman, Cook, and Wife of Bath are marked by their professional roles, and Chaucer's depiction of them, while not always sympathetic, is never one of complete censure.

In the *Shipman's Tale*, then, Chaucer explores the positive aspects of commercial practice, and gaming (or in this case lack thereof) in this instance becomes a litmus test for responsible trade. For some readers, the *Shipman's Tale* provides a condemnation of commerce.[42] Exchange is so central to the tale that the domestic sphere becomes an extension of the commercial one; because the merchant thinks only in terms of trade, he fails to recognize himself as the dupe of both his spouse (who uses sex to pay off her hundred-franc debt to her husband) and of his friend John (who has borrowed this same one hundred francs from the merchant and has used it to pay for sex with the merchant's wife). Yet if this story highlights the troubling omnipresence of commercial practice, it also shows, as Lee Patterson has convincingly argued, that "this condition is in no sense irremediable."[43] The end of the tale marks, if not exactly a happy ending, then at least a tranquil one. All three parties who have engaged in the transaction come away satisfied; all have, in short, profited.

In the *Shipman's Tale* Chaucer "sees the agents of this recovery as being merchants themselves."[44] Because an act of exchange depends on a collective agreement and a constant reassessment of the fair value of the goods traded, it relies heavily on the character of the parties involved. While these fluctuations in value cause discord for the players of New Fair, the merchant in the *Shipman's Tale*, the one most invested in the commercial system of exchange, displays the strongest moral values and presents "an ideal image of what merchants no doubt wanted themselves to be."[45] It is thus no coincidence that the merchant, while he is off to purchase his wares in Flanders, makes a point of *avoiding* games:

Now gooth this marchant faste and bisily
Aboute his nede, and byeth and creaunceth.
He neither pleyeth at the dees ne daunceth,
But as a marchaunt, shortly for to telle
He let his lyf, and there I lete hym dwelle. (*ShipT* ll. 1492–96)

Here "nede" determines the merchant's activities, not greed or a desire to gain at another's expense. Unlike Beryn, who lands on an island and immediately gambles his wares on a game of chess, this merchant does not "pleyeth at the dees," an activity that, Chaucer suggests, should be held separate and apart from the serious business of trade.[46]

These two poets, who offer very different treatments of exchange, establish a dialectic within which the *Canterbury Interlude* and the *Tale of Beryn* operate. If the Beryn author does not share Langland's abhorrence of a profit-driven economy, he also does not share Chaucer's interest in the merchants' potential to police their own activities. For the *Beryn* author, the problems with commercial practice, and specifically the tendency for one party to swindle another, are best solved by a central authority who acts in the interest of the common good. People are inherently greedy, and thus a person with power over the two parties involved in a trade must make sure that the rules governing a trade are fair and enforced.

Spending the Night at the "Cheker of the Hope"

The concern about mercantile power sketched above circulates openly through the *Tale of Beryn*, a story told by and about a merchant. Not only does Beryn, the ostensible hero of the tale, choose to become a merchant himself, the burgesses who swindle him also make their living through trade. This focus on trading practices allows the poet to expose the problems that come up when individuals try to profit at the expense of others; not only does one party lose his goods, the community as a whole suffers. Imbalanced trade is represented repeatedly through games, which become metaphors for corrupt trading practices. Ultimately, however, the poet's solution to bad trading practices is not a rejection of all commerce but its reconfiguration as a non-gaming activity and its supervision by a centralized authority. This is represented in the *Tale* itself when Beryn eventually abandons his own role as a merchant, becoming the ruler of the island and monitoring the practices of the burgesses on it.

The problems with exchange, the use of a discourse of games to express these problems, and the ultimate regulation of exchange by centralized power are all foreshadowed in the *Interlude*. In this part of the poem, the harmony of the pilgrim community threatens to dissolve under the pressure of personal interest, a destructive force that operates both among the members of the group (as seen in the Miller's incitement of the Friar against the Summoner) and between the group's members and those outside it (as demonstrated by the Pardoner and Kitt's mutual desire to swindle the other). Yet at the same time that the *Interlude* exposes the dangers of exchange, and in particular the dangers of sexual exchange, it, like the *Tale*, ultimately works to contain the disparate forces that threaten to rupture the group's unity.

I will explore the ways discourses of gaming, as well as the game of tale-telling, structure the exchanges that take place during the course of the *Interlude*. In the category of actual games, the contest itself is nearly dissolved by the personal interests of its players; rather than viewing it as a light-hearted pastime, the Friar sees the contest as a way to "pay back" the Summoner for a perceived injustice. Meanwhile, the fairly straightforward exchange between Kitt and the Pardoner becomes reconfigured when discourses of games begin to dominate, leading to a violent altercation. Holding the group together is the Host, "the pilgrims' father, arbiter, and governor," in short the central, governing force of the group.[47] Unlike the *Canterbury Tales*, where power is brokered by different pilgrims at different times and thus remains in perpetual flux, the *Interlude*'s Host works to preserve a community "governed by the stabler standards of scheduled days, balanced accounts, early nights, and a social courtesy that suggests moral clarity as well."[48]

Before looking at the events narrated in the *Interlude*, I would like to consider the story's primary setting, the "Cheker of the Hope," since it offers the first clue to the poet's interest in the connections between chess and exchange.[49] The English form of the words "chek" and "cheker" derives from the Latin word *scaccarium*, which had circulated earlier in England with two meanings.[50] The twelfth-century *Dialogus de scaccario* laid out the basic responsibilities of the government office overseeing the country's financial health, the office of the exchequer, one meaning of the word. And, in this same century, a short history on the game of chess appeared in a manuscript under the heading *De scaccis*, a second meaning of "chek."[51]

The overlap between the two meanings was not lost on Richard Fitz Nigel, the author of the *Dialogus*, who exploits the symbolic power of the shared etymology.[52] Early in the treatise, which is modeled as a conversation between the *magister* (most likely Richard in his capacity as treasurer under Henry II) and a *discipulus*, the young scholar wonders how the Exchequer acquired its name. The master explains:

Master. I can think, for the moment, of no better reason than that it resembles a chess-board.
Scholar. Was its shape the only reason why our wise forefathers gave it that name? For they might have equally called it a draught-board.[53]
Master. I was justified in calling you "precise." There is another less obvious reason. For as on the chessboard the men are arranged in ranks, and move or stand by definite rules and restrictions, some [the barons] pieces in the foremost rank and others in the foremost position; here, too, some preside, others assist *ex officio*, and nobody is free to overstep the appointed laws, as will appear later. Again, just as on a chessboard [*sic*], battle is joined between the kings; here too the struggle takes place, and battle is joined, mainly between two persons, to wit the Treasurer and the Sheriff who sits at his account, while the rest sit by as judges to see and decide.[54]

According to Fitz Nigel the *magister* has good reason to make his comparison between games and accounts, although the cloth's division into twenty-eight squares (as opposed to the chessboard's sixty-four) is *not* the key resemblance. Instead, according to the *magister*, the game and table are linked by the accounting sessions, usually held at Easter and Michaelmas.[55] In these sessions a sheriff, having previously deposited his income into the treasury, would come to the Exchequer's table with a series of markers representing the amounts received. At the same time the officials who received the payments would keep track of them with counter tallies. Officials placed the counter tallies on the board in columns according to their value while the sheriff placed his tallies near the board to counterbalance the treasurer's reckonings. In a swift series of moves the accounts were balanced. Under certain circumstances the sheriff might "win" any surplus, although he was more commonly required to remit it to the crown. By contrast if he "lost" the accounting match, he was accountable for any shortfall. An even balance would result in a "draw." Surrounding the board in specifically demarked places were the "spectators," various officials of the Exchequer who supervised the transactions that took place.

It is thus no surprise to find that the Cheker of the Hope provides a context for a variety of games and financial exchanges, and that the discourses of both often battle for supremacy. The vacillation between the two appears most obviously in the tale-telling contest, alternately conceived of as a game and as a financial transaction, revealing an uneasy blurring between these two categories as well as a desire to keep them distinct. Reminding the pilgrims that the tales are designed for "shorting of the way" (l. 700), the Host sees the trip as a contest, one that he, as the "rewler of hem al, of las and eke of more" (l. 16), will judge. Yet while the Host's claim aims to suppress the contest's game-like qualities, other moments in the *Interlude* foreground the potential for chance and risk still at play in the inn. The Host himself, like the *General Prologue*'s Harry Bailly, introduces the idea of drawing straws to determine the order of the tale-tellers only to reject his own suggestion as too risky. What if the straw went to a fasting man who did not feel "jocounde" (l. 709)? And what would happen if it fell "On som unlusty persone that were nat wele awaked" (l. 705)? In the end, selecting lots, a random act that will determine the order of the tales, makes this activity *too* game-like and throws into relief the element of chance inherent in a contest where the "winner" will be chosen at random, the "moves" made by one player will affect the others, and one individual will earn the right to tell his tale first. In eliminating the element of chance, the Host is able to assert more power over at least one aspect of the competition—he has placed himself in a position to select the next storyteller.

Chance is not the only factor that can contribute to the unfair nature of games. If a player cheats or decides to change the rules without informing the others, the structure of the game is invalidated and a new game with a different stake formed. In the *Canterbury Tales* even a perceived change in the nature of the contest, such as the Miller's "attack" on the Reeve, not only disrupts Harry's illusion of control but also threatens to destabilize the community of players—whether only two or, in the case of the contest, many—as individuals begin to doubt everyone's willingness to play and/ or their ability to follow the rules. The Reeve's decision to tell a story about bad millers becomes a side game, where a tale is judged not by *sentence* and *solas* but by how much it ridicules its target. This assault is violent and disrupts the group's harmony.[56] It is also repeated when the Friar and Summoner use their tales as platforms for attacks on each other and when Harry himself gets angry at the Pardoner for selling his relics.

In the *Interlude* we see this potential to destabilize the social order clearly in the Summoner's attack on the Friar. For the Summoner, the nature of the tale-telling competition changes right after the group visits Becket's shrine. While there, the Miller has grabbed a handful of "Caunterbury broches," and as they walk back to the Cheker of the Hope, the Summoner orders the

Miller to share half of the stolen trinkets with him (ll. 175, 179). Rather than responding to the Summoner's request, the Miller tries to divert the Summoner from the pilfered booty by pointing to the shifty Friar and warning him that the Friar can see them. Sure enough, the easily distracted Summoner forgets his demand and begins to plot his revenge for the Friar's tale of bad summoners:

So cursed a tale he told of me, the devil of hell hym spede—
And me!—but yf I *pay* hym wele and *quyte* wele his mede,
Yf it hap homward that ech man tell his tale,
As we did hiderward, thoughe I shuld *set at sale*
Al the shrewdnes that I can, I wold hym nothing spare.
(ll. 185–89; emphasis mine)

Here any undesirable elements of chance are eliminated as the Summoner renarrates the tale-telling game as a type of exchange. Vowing to "pay" the Friar with a tale of his own, the Summoner envisions his own tale-telling skills as something to be "set at sale." Even as he recognizes that the best tale is the likeliest to earn a free meal, he nonetheless claims to "nothing spare" in his pursuit of revenge. A chance at winning the game is, in his opinion, much less satisfying than a guaranteed outcome, in this case the humiliation of the Friar. The Summoner's sudden interest in gain at any cost is not without cause. Having just witnessed the Miller's thieving, an act that will allow the Miller to profit when he returns to London and sells his souvenirs, his thoughts are already preoccupied with winning even if he needs to rewrite the rules of the game.

In this case it is not only the Friar who will suffer from the Summoner's retaliation; it is also the integrity of the original game and, by extension, the community that has decided to play it that is damaged. If two players cheat, or drop out, or decide to play by their own rules, what is to prevent others from doing the same? While such an unraveling of the social fabric is somewhat expected in the *Canterbury Tales*, where the pilgrims' differences are highlighted, it is less so in the *Interlude*, where the pilgrims at times form a fairly cohesive unit. The group visits Becket's tomb together, after which it breaks into smaller, yet still harmonious, subgroups. The Knight takes the Squire to inspect the town walls, "Devising ententiflich the strengthes al about" and pointing out to his son "the perell" that could face the city (ll. 239–40). The Merchant, Manciple, Miller, and Reeve go into town together, ostensibly to trade. The Monk invites the Parson and Friar to meet a Canterbury citizen he has known for three years. That the Host—who has promised "To set [them] in governaunce by rightful jugement"—takes on the role of ruler highlights the structural similarities between the pilgrim band and a civic body (l. 213). If, as David Wallace has argued, Chaucer's *General Prologue* works to construct "a functional associative polity," albeit one that Chaucer himself sees as "a difficult, precarious, practical, affair," the *Beryn* author, by placing this group within the walls of a city and depicting the pilgrims as participants in its affairs, has sharpened Chaucer's focus on the civic underpinnings of the *felawshipe*.[57]

This social cohesion has not escaped most of the *Interlude*'s readers, and many see the group as a harmonious whole.[58] Yet in analyzing the pilgrim collective, scholars have overlooked the problems of exchange lying at the heart of the group's internal divisions. On his part Peter Brown sees the threat of communal collapse as an external one posed by Kitt and company.[59] But though the ruffians surely endanger the fellowship, Brown's reading overlooks the internal fissures that divide various factions and individuals in the group itself, as evinced by the quarrel provoked by the "broches" at Becket's shrine. And while Kitt may provide temptation, it is in fact the Pardoner who pursues the Tapster, not the other way around. Glending Olson and Stephen Medcalf, who locate all social discord in the character of the Pardoner, offer more compelling analyses. However, both underestimate the allure of profit, the root of discord for the group. The Pardoner, who pays money for a sexual encounter with the intent to steal it back, bears a strong resemblance to his *Canterbury Tales* counterpart, who peddles false trinkets.[60] There is nothing to indicate, as Olson suggests, that he has reformed as he leaves town concealed by the company of his fellow travelers. Moreover, the same thirst for gain grips the Miller, who, in order to hoard his stolen goods, pits the Summoner against the Friar with little care for how his actions may or may not disrupt the group's cohesion.

In short, the Summoner's threat to vitiate his contract necessarily becomes more than a simple attack on the Friar; it exemplifies the tenuousness of civic community and the perpetual potential for its disruption, a potential that persists through the course of the *Interlude*. If all the pilgrims begin to "pay back" the others, the game will become a type of exchange (or, following the model of the Summoner, a series of mini-exchanges) where individuals acting autonomously will try to gain at each other's expense.

While the tale-telling contest can barely contain its own undercurrents of exchange, the *Interlude*'s main narrative, the Pardoner's attempted seduction of Kitt, is openly configured as an economic transaction. Or at least this is how it starts. A reversal of the dynamic found in the pilgrims' competition, in which a game turns in to an exchange, Kitt's prank shows how easily a straightforward contract can quickly become a game with hidden rules, a high stake, and, as opposed to the ideal of equitable trade, only one winner rather than two.

Significantly, her deal with the Pardoner also exposes the ability of sex to be placed on a market of exchange and the dangers such a transaction poses. Under the terms of the Pardoner's contract with Kitt, he will give her money and she will give him an "after hours" dinner for the two of them. But we soon learn that neither party actually intends to maintain his/her side of the contract. The Pardoner has already plotted "to pike hir purs and wyn (his) coste ageyn" when he comes to her room (l. 376). Meanwhile Kitt, instead of preparing dinner for the Pardoner, uses his money to purchase the best goose found in town, which she eats with her lover and the Innkeeper. At the moment where the original contract has become impossible to recuperate, the whole incident is transferred from an exchange to a game. It is Kitt, the winner, who makes the semantic switch when she tells her lover to answer the Pardoner's scratching at her door:

> Ye must wake a while,
> For trewlich I am siker that within this myle
> The Pardoner wol be comyng, his hete to aswage.
> But loke ye *pay hym redelich* to kele his corage;
> And therfor, love, dischauce yewe nat til this *chek* be do.
> (ll. 467–71; emphasis mine)

Much like the Summoner who plans to "pay [the Friar] wele," Kitt initially thinks of her contract as an exchange. But rather than give the Pardoner what he has purchased (or what he thinks he has purchased), Kitt and her lover will "pay him redelich" with something else. By the end of her speech, she has recoded her actions as part of as a game. As Furnivall glosses it, "chek" in this passage means "trick" or "mischief," which in this case would seem to apply to the joke Kitt has played on the Pardoner.[61] In his edition, Bowers has opted for the word "feat." However, as noted above, the word could refer to a chessboard or game, and also to the treasury. When used in the former sense, the word was also frequently paired with the accompanying "mate," as in "chek mate," a phrase that will appear in the *Tale of Beryn* the moment that Beryn loses the chess game to the burgess.[62]

Returning to the moment of Kitt's "chek" we see again the problems that ensue when gaming begins to dominate commerce in the narrative. Like the Summoner, Kitt has sought, in reneging on her offer, to maximize her personal profit; she is playing to win. Her actions lead to social upheaval that, although entertaining, is violent and destructive. The Pardoner is hit with a staff; Kitt's lover get whacked with a pan; and Jack the Innkeeper steps on a brand from the fire and smashes his shin into the pan that the Pardoner has dropped during his flight from the scene.

In the end Kitt's game with the Pardoner leads directly to the larger "game," namely, the physical battle among the three men. In this game the contest is not for monetary gain, but rather to make the other players suffer the same losses and to penalize the Pardoner for his inappropriate sexual advances. Indeed, the ensuing mêlée highlights the importance of the sexual stake and the ways that wealth can pass through it; in a triangle that bears some similarity to that found in the *Miller's Tale,* two men try to enforce their rights to a woman's body while a third (who as the Innkeeper is Kitt's boss) attempts to regain authority over events that spiral out of control. Like Alison, Kitt escapes unscathed, the offer of her body having facilitated the transmission of wealth from one man, the Pardoner, to two others, who enjoy a meal at his expense.

Playing to Win in *The Tale of Beryn*

Whereas the *Interlude*'s connections between commerce and gaming are implicit and playful, the *Tale of Beryn* makes an explicit and serious tie between the two activities. Games are everywhere, all facilitating significant redistributions of property and wealth. Beryn's habit of playing dice leads directly to an agreement with his father to trade his inheritance for a set of five merchant ships filled with goods. Later Beryn loses the cargo in these ships over a game of chess, precipitating a series of bogus lawsuits wherein most of the claimants insist that Beryn has swindled them. Beryn does not lose penny antes; he gambles away his fortune. And in doing so, he exposes the social fragmentation present in two different cities. In short the *Interlude*'s comic blurring between games and economic transactions becomes more serious, and the poet presents a society of near anarchy where order comes about only after Beryn abandons games, takes control of the island, and begins to monitor the community's commerce.

The increased panic about the ludic nature of exchange is connected to the importance of two communities represented in the story. In the *Interlude* the civic body is only loosely conceived. The pilgrim *felawshipe,* although representing a cross-section of social classes, functions more as a metaphor for community than as a viable political group. By contrast the *Tale*, which situates its action within the cities of Rome and "Falsetown," dwells at length on the problem of social deterioration, tracing its roots to the propensity of the citizens in each place to conceive of trade as a game and thus a chance to win goods openly.[63] Facilitating this type of imbalanced exchange are two different games—dice in Rome and chess in Falsetown—that encourage individuals to pursue their own good at the expense of the community.

The story opens in Rome, and the Merchant begins by rhapsodizing about the city's golden age:

When rightfullich by reson governed were the lawes,
And principally in the ceté of Rome that was so rich,
And worthiest in his dayes and noon to hym ilich
Of worshipp ne of wele, ne of governaunce. (ll. 734–37)

This fantasy encompasses more than order, stability, and social cohesion; it is also one of wealth. Rome is "rich" and its riches flow in ways governed by "reson." This is, the Merchant notes, a contrast to modern times, which are marked by greed, gluttony, and lawlessness: "No mervell is thoughe Rome be somwhat variabill / Fro honour and fro wele, sith his frendes passed, / As many another town is payred and i-lassed" (ll. 752–54).

Yet the Merchant quickly undercuts this image of Rome as a golden city when he introduces Faunus, one of the senators of Rome, and Faunus's recalcitrant son Beryn. Unlike the realm that is managed "rightfullich by reson," Faunus's household follows a path of slow deterioration. Rather than staying at home to learn the art of statecraft from his father, Beryn goes out each day to gamble, often coming home "al naked" after losing his clothes in a game of dice (l. 928). Even after his mother, Agea, becomes ill, he refuses to leave his gaming pursuits to sit by her side. The seriousness with which Beryn takes his gaming is highlighted rather shockingly when, as Agea reaches the last hours of her life, Beryn refuses to abandon his dice game to be with her. "I had lever my moder and also thowe were dede / Then I shuld lese the game that I am now in!" he tells the family servant who has come to fetch him (ll. 1020–21). Agea's illness is never explained, and we learn only that she "fil in grete sekenes" (l. 947). Yet the fact that her "sekenes" arrives shortly after Beryn begins to gamble implies a link between the two and, as the illness turns fatal, suggests that Beryn's dice playing may have led directly to her death. Rame, who marries Faunus after Agea's death, recognizes that Beryn's predilection for gaming is a weakness that she can exploit, and she complains loudly about Beryn's addiction: "For and he pley so long, halff our lyvlode / Wold scarsly suffise hymselff oon" (ll. 1218–19). Eventually Faunus confronts Beryn, admonishing his son to give up "tables and merelles and the hazardry" (l. 1250). Still Beryn refuses to abandon his "disepleying," insisting that he would rather lose his inheritance, a boast that his father eventually accommodates.

Dice playing proves especially troubling for the Merchant, a narrator whose profession dictates that goods must be traded and not put up for a possible loss:

When Beryn passed was seven yeer and grewe in more age
He wrought ful many an evill chek, for such was his corage
That there he wist or myghte do eny evill dede,
He wold never sese for aught that men hym seyde. (ll. 913–16)

Again the word "chek" surfaces, this time as something the Merchant finds unequivocally "evill." And again the word is not misplaced, for at the heart of Beryn's "evill deed[s]" is his weakness for games, specifically for "hazard." The Merchant's distrust of dice is apparent in his description of the game as one of "losery," or rather a type of game where the chance of loss is high (l. 925). (Notably the Merchant does not care about the fact that there is always a chance at winning.) Shortly after he offers this horrified description of Beryn's addiction to dicing, he attributes the boy's foolishness to youth. Yet this excuse soon becomes unsustainable, as Faunus, who perpetually settles his son's debts, chastises Beryn for having reached the age of twenty without abandoning his recklessness. Thus while age might be a factor, the Merchant must eventually resign himself to the fact that game playing has become Beryn's "besynes" (l. 1072).

Unlike the Pardoner, whose loss at the "game" with Kitt leads to a localized punishment, Beryn's dice games have ramifications for his family, which, due to Faunus's status as a senator, becomes representative of the Roman government. If a senator cannot manage his son, what hope is left for the rest of the populace? The larger problems in the community are hinted at by the fact that Beryn comes home each night without his clothes: what kind of citizens swindle each other out of shirts and shoes? The Merchant highlights this social fragmentation by referring ironically to Beryn's gaming partners as his "feleshipp" (l. 1070), a term evocative of the fellowship of the pilgrims. Also highlighting the parody is Beryn himself, who after returning home naked insists angrily to his father: "My felawes loketh after me; I woot wele they do so. / I woll nat leve my feleshipp ne my rekelages [wild ways], / Ne my dise-pleying for all yeur hostages [properties]!" (ll. 1266–68). Like the *felawshipe* of the pilgrims, which threatens to unravel as its members each seek to profit at the expense of the others, Beryn's "felawes" unite only for individual gain.

With this background Beryn leaves to start his career as a merchant. His travels take him to a new city with a different set of financial challenges and a different game. Instead of Rome Beryn finds himself in Falsetown, where citizens eagerly swindle all strangers who land on their shores. Instead of dice Beryn gambles over the game of chess. And instead of simply losing his clothes, Beryn loses all his possessions.[64] His lost chess game also opens the door to a series of four subsequent swindles, which happen over the course of a single day. Soon after Beryn loses his ships, another burgess, Hanybald, cheats him out of his cargo. A woman claims that Beryn is her husband and must pay for the years he has abandoned her. A blind man accuses Beryn of stealing his eyes. And finally, a man named Macaign produces a knife that he claims to have found in Beryn's sleeve, arguing that it was used to murder his, Macaign's, father.

Richard Firth Green has demonstrated that the five lawsuits initiated by the town's citizens offer a scathing critique of the corruption of England's merchant courts, which were known to extort money, especially from foreigners who had little knowledge of the legal system.[65] Yet the first court case, which is brought by the burgess after the fateful chess match in order to validate his claim to Beryn's ships, differs qualitatively from the other swindles. The last three charges—eye stealing, wife abandonment, and homicide—are outright lies. Beryn has never met his accusers and has no way of disproving their false claims. The second court case is a bit closer to the first. Like the chess game it has been generated to validate an exchange, namely Beryn's willingness to trade all the cargo in his ships in return for all the possessions he can find in the house of one of the burgesses. (He loses when the burgess, after taking Beryn's wares, removes all the possessions from the house and hides them elsewhere. Because Beryn cannot "find" anything, the burgess owes him nothing.) In the second trade Beryn seems to think he is making a fair exchange. Still, this second swindle differs from the initial loss of his ships. In this first game there is no pretense of fairness but instead a return to Beryn's earlier gaming pursuits. The Merchant drives home the similarities between the chess match and Beryn's dice playing when he observes that after the checkmate Beryn would be "Likly to lese his marchandise, and go hymselff al naked" (l. 1792). Just as in Rome, where lost clothing signified the risks of gaming and Beryn's foolishness with his money, so too in Falsetown will Beryn's misplaced faith in games again be exposed and shown "naked" to everyone.

Like the dice games in the *Interlude*, chess facilitates an unequal economic exchange, and this aspect of the game is emphasized in the Merchant's description of the match.[66] The game takes place in plain view of witnesses who, like the officials of the Exchequer, surround the board and watch as the pieces change sides, one at a time. Even before the game commences we are alerted to the fact that these merchants might run their business a bit like Beryn's *felawshipe* when the Merchant describes one burgess "pleying atte ches" with his neighbor, also a burgess (l. 1646). The location of the board between these two men emphasizes the game's ties to commerce. Read this way, the burgess's many pieces—he has so many that he can mate with whichever piece he wants—become account markers and the burgess's winning a representation of his surplus.[67]

This emphasis on exposure brings the game in line with earlier chess matches discussed in this book's previous chapters. As in Jacobus's *Liber* and *Les Echecs amoureux*, the chess players are put on display and their moves evaluated. Yet shame here works differently than it did in these earlier examples, as it does not cause Beryn to mind his actions off the board. Instead, the public display of the match leads directly to the community's monitoring of Beryn's actions. An hour into their last game, the burgess, knowing that Beryn will protest the bet, summons the town's law officers and asks them to watch the final moves. If the laws governing the island were just, the community's surveillance would be appropriate. Indeed, by the story's end, Beryn becomes the one who monitors the burgesses. Here, however, the community monitors a transaction that the poet sees as flawed; trade should not be played like a game.

The Merchant's description of the final chess match introduces yet another danger inherent in the consensual rules that govern a game. In the Cheker of the Hope individuals cheat at games by changing the rules, thus their actions become shady and covert. The Pardoner and Kitt each maneuver secretly to alter the terms of their contract, while the Summoner plots in private to pay back to Friar. In this case, however, the burgess has not changed the game's rules. Instead, he has been disingenuous about his own abilities, and by deliberately throwing the first several matches has misled his opponent about his own skills. The problem of misinformation, already unfair in games with low or no stakes, has serious repercussions in the realm of exchange, where an individual makes a choice based on what he or she perceives to be accurate information. (Such is the case in the exchange that follows the chess game, where the information Beryn has about the full house of goods is suddenly outdated and wrong.) The burgess knows he can win but makes Beryn believe "that he coude pley better then [the burgess]" (l. 1770). Like a change in rules, which must be done in secret, this withholding relies on some amount of secrecy. Yet at the moment the information comes to light, the burgess depends on his witnesses to legitimize his "fair" winning. "Com-eth nere," he beckons to the spectators, "Ye shul se this man, / How he shall be mated with what man me list" (ll. 1820–21).

It is the public and communal nature of the transaction that ultimately proves so troubling for the Merchant—"howe shuld o sely lombe among wolves weld / And scape un-i-harmed?"—and reveals the extent of the social fragmentation in Falsetown (ll. 1803–4). In the *Interlude* the consequences of games (or of economic transactions that become games) are either minimal (i.e., the uncertainties in tale-telling contest) or localized (i.e., Kitt's game with the Pardoner). In the *Tale* the consequences of games are severe: Beryn loses his clothes, trades away his inheritance, and eventually arrives in False-town, where unfair exchange is normalized as a legitimate practice. Reading Falsetown, as Green does, as a representation of fifteenth-century England, the poem becomes a scathing critique of a system of trade that is ludic in its riskiness, its ideal of one winner and one loser, and its complete disregard for common good.

While an attempt to control the uncertainties of the market may have failed in England, the story narrates a different ending: Falsetown changes its false laws and becomes a stable community. Yet in presenting these changes the story does not condemn the Falsetown merchants alone; Beryn, who ini-tially holds both the town and the burgess responsible for the deception, eventually realizes that his troubles are partly his own fault. At the point in the story when he seems to have lost everything, Beryn offers a long solilo-quy about his failings. At the beginning of his speech he muses:

For yit in al my lyve sith I ought understode,
Had I never will for to lern good.
Foly—I haunted it ever, there myght no man me let;
And now he hath i-paid me; he is cleen out of my dett. (ll. 2317–20)

In accordance with a narrative preoccupied with the mechanics of commerce, Beryn's speech rewrites his failing as a type of trade. After having had Folly in his "debt," Beryn has now balanced his accounts and is free to restart his life.

Beryn's new awareness of his own culpability in turn dovetails with his sense of exposure. Or rather, the moment Beryn recognizes the larger implications

Chapter 4
"The Kynge Must Be Thus Maad":
Playing with Power in
Fifteenth-Century England

Wherfore bycause thys sayd book is ful of holsom wysedom and requysyte unto every astate and degree, I have purposed to enprynte it, shewing therin the figures of such persons as longen to the playe, in whom al astates and degrees ben comprysed.

—Caxton's 1483 preface to The Game and Playe of the Chesse

In the early fifteenth century the poet Thomas Hoccleve, trapped
[...]aying post at the Office of the Privy Seal and missing his yearly
[...]tempted to compensate for his financial hardship by writing a
[...]*egis* for the young prince Henry, later to become King Henry V.
[...]ng poem, *The Regement of Princes*, falls roughly into two parts. In
[...]lf the character Hoccleve meets a beggar, who urges the poet to
[...]is desire for material wealth. In the second half, considered by
[...]e the *speculum* proper, Hoccleve shifts from dialogue to mono-
[...]counsels the king to uphold a variety of virtues that include hon-
[...]e, and, most important, generosity toward his subjects.[1]
[...]nost medieval writers, Hoccleve did not write the *Regement* ex nihilo
[...]on a variety of texts and genres to craft his work. Literary forms
[...]r in the first half of the poem range from serious Boethian com-
[...]omic self-presentation bordering on fabliau. At some points he
[...]ows the language of devotional texts, as is the case in his opening,
[...]ssumes the posture of a suppliant Mary.[2] In the second half of the
[...]Hoccleve does not leave us wondering about his sources, which
[...]tright. They are: the pseudo-Aristotelian *Secretum secretorum*, or
[...]*ecrets*; the "Regiment / Of Princes" by Aegidius Romanus; and "a

of his bad behavior is also the moment that he recognizes that his individual actions can be seen and thus judged by others. Although Beryn has felt wronged during the chess game, he never acknowledges that his problems are of his own making. Nor is he bothered by his literal nakedness. Only now does he admit that he "wold nat be governed" in his youth and that he never before had "will for to lern good" (ll. 2322 and 2318). This sudden understanding of his own folly causes him to scrutinize his own actions, and for the first time Beryn feels "sorow and shame" for what he has done. Like Jacobus's imagined reader, who suddenly sees his "self" represented on the board, Beryn obtains an external perspective, one which prompts him to renarrate the events that have occurred up to this point. Like the Merchant telling the tale, he has a view from outside the text, and while it pains him to do so, he does not hold back from recounting his poor choices, which as he admits were "right wele deserved" (l. 2331).

Beryn's recognition of his own past mistakes eventually leads him to get rid of the "fals lawe" that dictates commerce in Falsetown. He soon meets Geffrey, a sage old man whose manipulation of the court cases both saves Beryn from jail and doubles Beryn's fortune. From that point on Geffrey serves as Beryn's advisor: " . . . thereof he lered, / And of other thinges, howe he hym shuld govern" (ll. 3960–61). Marriage is soon arranged between Beryn and the daughter of Duke Isope, the lord of the land, thus making the (now wise) Beryn the ruler of Falsetown. Everyone is happy except for the burgesses, who find themselves stripped of their power:

But they were ever hold so lowe under foot
That they myghte nat regne, but atte last were fawe
To leve hir condicioune and hir fals lawe.
Beryn and Geffrey made hem so tame
That they amended ech day and gate a better name. (ll. 4014–18)

In the end, trade is not suppressed altogether but tamed and brought under control. The merchants with their corrupt forms of commerce no longer "regne" with "hir fals lawe"; it is Beryn who now regulates the exchanges in the kingdom, ensuring that swindles (and by implication, high-stakes chess games) no longer take place.

Beryn's ability to stay marks more than an adoption of indigenous ways. Simple assimilation would have led Beryn to become the town's chief swindler rather than its reformer. Instead, Beryn's position as ruler marks a changed social order. Unlike Rome, which is left in a suspended state and never mentioned again, "Falsetown" becomes a solid, stable, and unified city through the restriction of the burgesses, who had mistakenly seen trade as a game of self-interest and one-sided profit, and not, as they ought to have seen it, as a regulated and fair exchange. By the end they too have changed.

In the context of the work as a whole, then, we can see the desire to control economic exchange in the *Tale* as a rewriting of the end of the *Interlude*, where the terms of trade and the traffic in women are brought under supervision and used to stabilize a community. Just as the Host wishes to regulate the tale-telling contest and limit contingencies that might profit one member of the group at the expense of another, so too does Beryn take away the burgesses' laws to replace them with his own. In both cases these rules are enforced by a single authority speaking from a position of centralized power. In both cases, the game-like qualities of the transactions—the potential for unequal trade, for a winner and a loser, and for random chance, all of which are inherent in games—are extinguished. And finally, in both cases the elimination of these attributes leads to a more or less (more in the case of Falsetown, less in the case of the pilgrims) stable community.

In endorsing centralized regulation as a solution to the inequalities inherent in exchange and commerce, the *Beryn* poet distances himself from those who distrusted commerce as intrinsically sinful and aligns himself with those who saw commerce as an acceptable activity, even if subject to abuses. On the one hand, he is perhaps less optimistic than Chaucer about the ability and desire of any individual, especially a merchant, to act in accord with good will and trust. As he suggests, without adequate information or someone to enforce the rules of trade people can and will make injurious exchanges. And without a regulatory power, people who have something to sell will inevitably withhold information, change the terms of the trade, or do both. Yet on the other hand, the *Canterbury Interlude* and the *Tale of Beryn* show a Chaucerian acceptance of the increasingly commercial nature of their culture. Only a few years after *Beryn*, an anonymous poet composed the *Libelle of Englyshe Polycye*, a poem that advocates a national protection of maritime trading routes and advises the king to "cheryshe marchandyse."[68] In the end, the *Beryn* poet's endorsement of trade regulation only foreshadows the increasing interest of national governments in protecting, promoting, and controlling their own economic markets.

If my discussion of the *Tale of Beryn* has wandered from the subject of the chess, it is only because the game in this story loses it status as a noble pastime or idealized model of social order. Embedded in a discourse of uneven exchange, the game becomes little more than a way to gamble, a practice

that in the *Canterbury Interlude* and th
of the communities therein. Nor does
of the *Beryn* poet's acknowledged pred
chapter, the games in *Troilus* and in t
brief asides that betoken the same t
player will get nothing, the other, all. In
cause authors like the *Beryn* poet seek t
munity while others like Chaucer rew
many, and a suspect one at that. It is li
of the Duchess opts to read rather than

This is, however, not medieval Er
Jacobus's *Liber* circulated in fourteentl
an audience in fifteenth-century Englar
model of civic order. For Thomas Ho
Liber in his *Regement of Princes*, chess sti
he, like the *Beryn* author, used the game
ment draws on the *Liber*'s various stor
scribe royal power. And although his fo
Beryn-like interest in centralized author
readers that such authority is constrained
later in this same century, William Cax
treatise, the first in English, as working t
ton dedicated his first translation of the
his second edition to all men, thus rei
currency it had at its origin and once ag
one among the many in the community.

in a low
annuity.
speculu
The res
the first
abando
many t
logue a
esty, ju
Li
but dr
that ap
plaint
even b
where
Regem
he list
Secret

book Jacob de Cessolis / Of the ordre of prechours maad, a worthy man, / That the Ches Moralysed clepid is," the last of which furnishes him with nearly forty examples of virtues essential for a monarch.[3]

As Hoccleve begins to discuss the "Ches Moralysed," his name for Jacobus de Cessolis's thirteenth-century *Liber*, he foregrounds the ways the game works as both allegory of social order and metaphor for financial exchange. Yet rather than talk openly about chess as a model of civic community or as a representation of economic transactions, Hoccleve couches the game's symbolic valences in a discussion of his own chess-playing abilities:

And al be it that in that place sqwaar
Of the listes—I meene th'eschequeer—
A man may lerne to be wys and waar,
I that have aventured many a yeer
My wit therein, but lyte am I the neer,
Sauf that I sumwhat knowe a kynges draght;
Of othir draghtes lerned have I naght. (ll. 2115–21)

Here Hoccleve engages in a bit of word play. Having already referred to the "Exchequer" as the place responsible for his annuity (ll. 820–21), and also as the place that still owes him money (l. 1877), he once again mourns the Exchequer's failure to allow him "neer" any type of profit. Such punning brings Hoccleve in line with the pilgrims of the *Canterbury Interlude*, whose arrival at the Cheker of the Hope coincides with the commencement of several different financial transactions.[4] Yet in this stanza's final lines Hoccleve implicitly reinvests the chess game with the symbolic value it had in Jacobus's text. Just as his retitling of the *Liber* as the "Ches Moralysed" recalls the game's seedy origins, so too does it indicate a return to the game's earlier symbolic register: that chess can be "moralysed" means that it can have some positive value. By referring to the king's move, Hoccleve conceives of the board as a representation of a political community. Like Evilmerodach, the tyrannical ruler who mastered the game in the *Liber*, Prince Henry must learn the rules governing his own chess piece, which, as Hoccleve notes, are those most "needful unto [his] persone" (l. 2124). Only after assimilating these rules will the prince become virtuous. Thus by the end of the verse Hoccleve's "place sqwaar" takes on a different meaning, becoming both a literal chessboard and a figurative one. When he claims to know the ways a king can move, Hoccleve is not boasting of his chess skills—he himself insists that he is ignorant "of othir draghtes"—but of his ability to advise the king on matters of conduct.

In the previous chapter I considered the ways the chess game in late fourteenth- and early fifteenth-century England, at least in the works of Chaucer and the *Beryn* poet, had become openly entwined with discourses of financial exchange and mercantilism. As illustrated by Hoccleve's puns on the double meaning of the word "eschequeer," which he uses to remind the prince of his missing paychecks, this connection of chess to economic interest continued in the fifteenth century.[5] In this chapter, however, I will look at the resurfacing in England of chess as a symbol for the civic body. This reappearance is evident in Hoccleve's *Regement*, which, even as it discards a piece-by-piece allegorization as a larger organizational tool, preserves the idea that a civic community can resemble a game of chess. In reading the *Regement* this way, I challenge Paul Strohm's understanding of Hoccleve as one who "abandons the stance of admonitory critic, assuming instead that of wholehearted ally determined in no respect to offend."[6] As I demonstrate, Hoccleve capitalizes on the political implications of this allegory for the monarchy, using it strategically as a counternarrative to his otherwise full-throated endorsement of Lancastrian kingship.

While the *Regement* only hesitantly introduces the game's potential to allegorize civic order, William Caxton's *Game and Playe of the Chesse* openly embraces the chess allegory and its political implications. A translation of a French copy of Jacobus's *Liber*, the *Game and Playe* was one of the few items Caxton printed in Bruges—he printed the text for the first time in 1474—and was also the first English version of the text. It was also one of Caxton's first English texts, second only to his *Historyes of Troyes*. That Caxton opted to produce this translation so early in his career as a printer suggests that he envisioned it as an easy-to-market volume. And indeed it seems to have succeeded as such, for claiming to have sold all the copies of his initial print run, Caxton printed it a second time in England in 1483.[7]

Caxton's decision to print the *Liber* a second time may indicate his business acumen; it is, after all, marginally cheaper and less risky to reprint a popular text than to translate a new work.[8] Yet Caxton also made two notable changes to this second printing: he rewrote the prologue—he had dedicated the first version to King Edward IV's brother George, Duke of Clarence, whereas he directs the second to all men—and added a series of woodcuts. Thus even if these changes stemmed from Caxton's ideas about what he could sell, his alteration to this second printing suggest commensurate changes in Caxton's readership. Both the prologue and the woodcuts help to refocus the text, which becomes, as it was when Jacobus wrote it, a work aimed at an audience larger and more diverse than a single member of the king's household. The volume's appearance in 1483, the same year that Richard III seized the throne, thus reflects a complex picture of royal authority, and the book's subsequent popularity indicates a shifting political climate.[9] Again, this is not to say that Caxton had a sudden change of heart about rule by monarch. But his two prologues to *The Game and Playe of the Chesse* reflect an ambivalent attitude about governmental power, an ambivalence reflected in the instability of the politics and of the socio-political and literary discourse of the time. In a country torn apart by the Wars of the Roses and still recovering from the fiscal drain of the Hundred Years War, the idea of a civic body with multiple and self-regulating nodes of power held particular appeal.

Hoccleve's *Regement* and Caxton's *Game and Playe* are thus linked not only by their references to (and use of) Jacobus's treatise, but also by the simple fact that both authors see the *Liber*'s allegory as applicable to their personal and political milieus.[10] In this fashion Hoccleve's puns on the "Exchequer" and his jokes about a "kynges draght" resemble Caxton's urgings (first to Clarence and then to all men) to his audience to read his book. At the same time both works also reveal a particular concern about the ways their reader will interpret the chess allegory itself. Or to put this in a slightly different way, while Hoccleve and Caxton rely on the *Liber*, each feels a need to modify or redirect its full force. For Hoccleve, this means reducing the chess allegory to an aside and recoding it as a joke about his missing paycheck. For Caxton, this means retitling the *Liber*—hence *The Book of Morals of Men and Duties of Nobles* becomes *The Game and Playe of the Chess*—and prefacing it with two different prologues, each of which attempts to control who should read the volume and to clarify his relationship to his own translation. Nevertheless, for both authors the *Liber* remains an unshakeable presence, becoming once again a text that advances complicated ideas about political organization and power under the guise of moral allegory.

To "Knowe a Kynges Draght": Lancastrian Rulers and Social Administration

Composed around 1411, Hoccleve's *Regement* responded directly to the complex network of powers that upheld and undercut the monarch.[11] This is not to say that monarchial power formed a new topic of interest, but rather that in an era marked by marked by political upheavals, most notably the struggle between the Lancastrians and the Yorkists, governmental authority and legitimacy became a central concern.[12] Any dynastic struggle prompts questions of royal authority, and the Wars of the Roses were no different.

The sometimes tenuous nature of the Lancastrian claim to power was manifest in the struggles for control that took place between the Lancastrians and their detractors, and also among the family members themselves. On the one hand Henry IV took power easily from the somewhat hapless Richard II, and the subsequent Lancastrian monarchs worked to fortify their authority.[13] They quelled rebellions, seized property, and burned heretics, acts that served to reaffirm the absolutist nature of their authority. Yet on the other hand, the family perpetually faced challenges to its legitimacy. As described by Paul Strohm, these kings represented "a shifting body of ambitions, grudging acceptances, and unrealized dreams" and were only "erratically capable of imposing ideas, rallying support, and affecting historical consequences."[14] Strohm also notes that "despite the advantages of incumbency and despite the supplementary assistance of an ingenious symbolic program, oppositional imagination remained vitally alive throughout the Lancastrian decades."[15]

In addition to external challenges to Lancastrian control, internal struggles for power took place in 1406 when the king's council took over the management of the government's finances.[16] The groundwork for the council's power had been laid during Richard II's reign in 1390, the year the young king came of age to rule. After Richard ascended to the throne, parliament passed an ordinance that required the approval of several councillors before the king could make any grant or gift. Richard took over the council in 1397, but Henry IV, who assumed power in 1399, initially ignored it. Still, after a long parliament in 1406 the council once again assumed control and placed Henry IV's son, prince Henry, as the head of the office that oversaw government spending. The king's financial power at this point was thus weakened in that he could not make grants alone. Nevertheless, the prince's usurpation did not strip the king of all authority; the council still acted in the king's name, thus preserving the idea that Henry IV retained control of his purse.[17]

These internal and external struggles for control helped to contribute to an increasingly active discussion of monarchial power. Whereas poets of the mid-fourteenth century had not hesitated to produce social commentary, poets from the late fourteenth and early fifteenth centuries seem to focus ever more attention on questions of royal authority.[18] The *speculum regis* enjoyed yet another resurgence, and the three most prominent poets of the early decades, Gower, Hoccleve, and Lydgate, placed kingship at the center of their most significant works.[19] Along with a flurry of new works came reissues of older ones, such as John Trevisa's late fourteenth-century translation of *De regimine principum*, a text that would function as an authoritative source for early fifteenth-century writers such as Hoccleve.

For Strohm, the advice texts like Hoccleve's, produced under Lancastrian kings, demonstrate "a quality of unease, a kind of nervous reciprocity in which the adviser at once experiences a closer identification with his monarch, and a heightened uncertainty about the spirit in which even the most complicitous reassurances will be received."[20] Yet this analysis does not capture the tensions inherent in *Regement*, a work that reflects a complicated relationship to Lancastrian power as well as the fraught nature of monarchial authority itself. The simple fact that Hoccleve does not address his *Regement* to the monarch but to the prince provides the first indication of the poet's desire to affirm authority and at the same time to relocate its center elsewhere. Henry IV is still England's king, yet he does not seem to control Hoccleve's paycheck. Even the Beggar, Hoccleve's interlocutor during the poem's first half, advises Hoccleve to address himself to the prince rather than the king: "Syn my lord the Prince is, God holde his lyf, / To thee good lord, good servant thow thee qwyte / To him, and treewe, and it shal thee profyte" (ll. 1944–46). In short, while the *Regement*'s second half works to uphold the ideal of monarchial supremacy, Hoccleve in the first half looks to the young Henry to restore his missing annuity. In crafting the *Regement*, then, Hoccleve writes to the young Henry as a king, not as a prince, and he projects his advice into an imagined future when Henry will wield political control.

This tension between a support for and a limitation of royal power makes itself felt even more strongly in Hoccleve's use of sources, in particular his borrowings from Jacobus's *Liber*, a text that becomes for Hoccleve a way to simultaneously uphold and challenge royal authority. Hoccleve's list-like disclosure implies a similar focus among the three texts he names; it seems that *De regimine*, the *Secretum*, and the *Liber* are simply the best princely advice books to be found. However, the *Liber* conceives of royal power in a way that differs from the other two texts, and a close look at Hoccleve's introduction of each work reveals his awareness of such differences.

Hoccleve opens his list of sources with the anonymously authored *Secretum*, a work that takes the form of a letter from Aristotle to Alexander the Great and was one of the most popular political commentaries in the late Middle Ages.[21] When introducing it, Hoccleve emphasizes its focus on royal power, stating that Aristotle's advice, "wel bet than gold in cofre," will keep the prince from harm (l. 2040). The *Secretum* itself positions the ruler as the only authority in the kingdom and is directed to him alone. With chapters that range from "How a kynge ought to kepe his body" to "Of the governayle of helth," it repeatedly stresses the importance of the king's *corpus*, and its chapters lovingly detail what a ruler should eat, wear, and do.[22] This attention to the ruler's physical condition highlights the ways the ruler himself is seen as the lone embodiment of the nation: *sanus rex, sanus civitatus* seems to be the author's operative ideology. Only in its final section, "Of physonomye," does the author address other bodies in the realm. But even here the *Secretum* merely characterizes a king's subjects by physical type, a guide that will help the ruler identify the personalities of those around him. This section, a collection of short descriptors such as "Small eeres betokeneth foly, and lechery," removes all autonomy from the members of the realm, who become mere types for the king to monitor.[23]

Hoccleve next mentions Aegidius Romanus's *De regimine principum*, another text preoccupied with a monarchial body. When introducing this second source Hoccleve emphasizes the parallels between his own book and that of Aegidius. Not only are they both "Regiments," but both also describe a monarchial power set in an imagined future; like Prince Henry, Philip has yet to become the king.[24] Divided into three books, *De regimine* is, like the *Secretum*, focused on the ruler, in this case, the prince and future King Philip IV of France, and Aegidius instructs Philip on the proper ways to manage himself (book 1), his household (book 2), and his kingdom (book 3). Unlike the author of the *Secretum*, Aegedius does not spend the majority of his book on issues of the king's personal health and toilet. Nevertheless, like the *Secretum*, *De regimine* is addressed to a specific ruler, and Aegidius emphasizes the connection of the prince's well-being to the well-being of the realm: "he þat desireþ to make his principate perpetual in hymself and in his children and successours schal study with gret bysynesse þat is governans be kyndelich."[25]

The third source to be named is the *Liber*, a work does not contain the same focus on royal authority found in the other two texts. Having introduced the *Regimine* and the *Secretum* in rapid succession, and having used both to talk about the monarch's physical being, he pauses to deliver six stanzas of self-deprecation in which he praises Chaucer, draws attention to his own dull wit, and concludes with a fervid: "O maistir, maistir, God thy soule reste!" (l. 2107). Only at this point does he return to his "mateere," which now lies several stanzas away from the other two works.

The effect of this physical separation is compounded by the self-deprecation that comes between the first two sources and the third; not only is the *Liber* isolated from *De regimine* and the *Secretum*, it apparently makes Hoccleve feel dumb. Yet accepting David Lawton's proposal that claims to dullness often masked incisive or even dangerous moments of truth-telling, Hoccleve's insistence that he himself "was dul and lerned lyte or naght" (l. 2079) tips us off to the possibility that something controversial might follow.[26] Thus the fact that the poet spends upward of seven stanzas excusing the "dul conceit" (l. 2057), "smal konnynge" (l. 2066), and little "letterure" (l. 2073) that make his own works pale in contrast to those of "fadir, Chaucer" (l. 2078) augurs something important.[27] By the end of the seventh stanza Hoccleve reaches a fever of abjection, and only at this point does he mention his third and final source, the "Ches Moralysed." And even after he introduces the text, he has trouble treating it seriously, as indicated by his repeated punning. Although Charles Blyth finds this word game evidence that "suggests an author and work less daunting than his other two sources," it seems more likely that Hoccleve's joking was at least partially designed to mask the political implications of his source.[28]

In fact, such a masking might be crucial, given the degree to which Hoccleve relies on the *Liber* as a source. To use Nicholas Perkins's words: "If the only criterion for influence on the *Regiment* were the volume of borrowings from each source, any argument could quickly be settled in favour of *De ludo scaccorum* [i.e., the *Liber*]."[29] Yet the nature of the source itself is even more significant than the volume of information borrowed from it. Unlike *De regimine* and the *Secretum*, treatises aimed at a specific ruler that provide a model for Hoccleve to follow, the *Liber* addresses all men and does not dwell on the king's body alone. In using chess as a metaphor for the body politic, the *Liber* (as I have argued at various point in this book) minimizes the importance of kingly self-governance by offering a model of civic community that relies less on subordination than it does on the active participation of all people in a network of social relations. If a knight is essential for the kingdom's well-being, the "blacksmith" pawn, who is found in front of the knight and who makes the knight's armor, is equally important.

This type of civic reimagining does not necessarily make the *Liber* an overtly subversive text. In the game of chess, as in the allegory it engenders, the king remains the most important piece on the board. However, as discussed in the opening chapter to this book, Jacobus's allegory poses a challenge to the notion of royal absolutism in the way it conceives of a civic order where the king, one of many pieces on the board, is contractually bound to the pieces around him. Moreover, each piece has the capacity to move independently, an ability that represents each citizen's facility for moral choice.

This emphasis on shared responsibility—everyone has the power to affect the good of the whole—is further highlighted by the fact that Jacobus addresses his book to all men and not to a single ruler. Designed to teach the members of the realm how to fulfill their professional roles, the book encourages everyone, not just a monarch, to learn the rules of the game.[30]

Nevertheless, although Hoccleve relies on Jacobus for the matter of his own work, he drops the *Liber*'s overarching allegory, a change that in turn leads to differences in the two texts' organization. Whereas the *Liber* is divided into social groups (king, queen, judges, knights, legates, and the various individuated trades of the pawns), Hoccleve organizes his book by virtues, listing the fifteen essential qualities for a king.

What should one make of Hoccleve's decision to use the *Liber* most heavily as a source yet at the same time drop its structure? One might see this choice as a willful dismissal of the *Liber*'s allegory for civic organization. Such an argument positions Hoccleve as uninterested in the moral decisions made by a community's members, dismissive of (or nervous about) the *Liber*'s overarching chess allegory, and eager to use the *Liber*'s exempla to instruct the king.[31] Indeed, the king's virtues are purportedly the ones at stake, and Hoccleve, like Aegidius and the *Secretum* author, places the monarch at the center of both his work and the realm.

Yet Hoccleve's use of the *Liber* is much cannier than this, and his punning about the text reveals a poet who sees this source as something more than an encyclopedia of good stories. Indeed, it is through his rewriting of the *Liber*, specifically through his use of stories from all over the *Liber*, that Hoccleve can conceive of a kingship that is both powerful yet simultaneously embedded in a network of affiliations, restrictions, and rules. Moreover, by reminding the prince of Jacobus's original text at the same time that he jokes about the symbolic value of the allegory therein, Hoccleve is able to smuggle a challenge to royal authority into the entire project. In short, while Hoccleve downplays the implications of Jacobus's allegory, he does not completely dismiss the *Liber*'s ideas about an associative social order.

It is perhaps in his willingness to use exempla from different parts of the *Liber* that Hoccleve poses the greatest challenge to other conceptions of royal authority. Rather than borrowing stories only from Jacobus's chapter on the king, Hoccleve incorporates into his *Regement* many exempla and *sententiae* that Jacobus has used to counsel other members of the civic community, including figures that are of a much lower status than the monarch. Of the thirty-nine exempla he borrows from the *Liber*, seventeen come from Jacobus's chapter on the rooks (which in the *Liber* serve as the king's legates), far more than the eight taken from the *Liber*'s chapter on the king (Table 4).[32] Hoccleve also uses material from the *Liber*'s chapters on the two knights, the two bishops, and the queen. Nor are his borrowings confined to the Jacobus's second *tractatus*, which describes the board's back row, since he draws a few stories from the *Liber*'s third *tractatus*, which contains chapters on notaries, tavern keepers and game players. In other words, the majority of the material Hoccleve uses to advise the prince comes from the sections of the *Liber* addressed to the most powerful people around the king and not to the king himself. And even though Hoccleve's introduction to Jacobus's text suggests that the *Liber* is applicable to the king alone, his manipulation of the text itself and his wide-ranging borrowing of examples points toward his conception of the royal body as one similar to the other citizens in the community. In fact, this structural change *reverses* the flow of advice found in Aegidius's *De regimine*; rather than seeing princely conduct as behavior that others might follow, Hoccleve's use of the *Liber* implies that the king might want to model himself on the virtues appropriate to other men.

If Hoccleve's decision to draw from all parts of the *Liber* points toward the limits placed on the royal office, the exempla themselves depict monarchial power as tenuous and preserved only through the will of a ruler's subjects. Perkins, who refers to the *Liber* as "a potentially significant, yet dangerous source for Hoccleve's poem," has done a good job of fleshing out the ways Hoccleve's rewriting of Jacobus's stories works to "[set] subjects on a plane of discourse with the ruler."[33] But I would like to look for a moment at a more basic way two of Hoccleve's early exempla, ones he has taken from Jacobus, drive home the fraught nature of royal authority.

Indeed, it is notable that Hoccleve opens the first part of his *speculum* by telling Henry that kingship is an office of "peril." To illustrate this point, he recounts the story of Fabius, who, upon becoming king, hesitates before wearing the crown, commenting that any smart person would never put it on.[34] Shortly after this tale of Fabius, Hoccleve narrates the story of King Pyrrhus's physician, who tries to betray Pyrrhus to Fabricius, the king's enemy.[35] The plan fails only because Fabricius has too much pride to fight in such a deceitful manner and hands the physician back to Pyrrhus.[36] Although Hoccleve includes this story as an example of kingly integrity, it offers yet a striking reminder of a ruler's physical vulnerability. As the second story demonstrates, the very person who should be the keeper of Pyrrhus's body also has the power to destroy it.[37]

While Hoccleve's revisiting of the chess allegory tempers his endorsement of royal power, the *Regement*'s narrative frame further emphasizes the

TABLE 4. Stories in Hoccleve's *Regement* and their antecedents in Jacobus's *Liber*. The top portion indicates the social group described in each chapter of the *Liber* and the number of stories borrowed from it. The bottom portion lists the titles of Hoccleve's chapters in the *Regement* along with the numbers and locations of stories he imported from the *Liber*.

Liber de ludo scachorum

Book 1

Under which king the game was invented
Who discovered chess—1
Reasons the game was invented—1

Book 2 (back row)

The king—8
The queen—1
The bishops (judges)—4
The knights—1
The rooks (vicars/legates)—17

Book 3 (front row)

First pawn (farmers)
Second pawn (smiths and carpenters)
Third pawn (notaries and wool workers)—4
Fourth pawn (merchants and money changers)
Fifth pawn (doctors and apothecaries)
Sixth pawn (tavern keepers)—1
Seventh pawn (toll keepers and custodians of the city)
Eighth pawn (wastrels, players, and messengers)—1

Book 4

On chess
On the moves of the king
On the moves of the queen
On the moves of the judge
On the moves of the knight
On the moves of the rook
On the moves of the pawns
The epilogue

Regement of Princes

Prologue   Two from rooks
                                        One from king

Regement

On the keeping of faith	Two from rooks Two from king
On justice	Three from rooks Two from judges One from knights One from book one
On pity	Five from rooks One from king One from third pawn
On mercy	One from rooks Two from king
On patience	Four from rooks One from king
On chastity	Three from third pawn One from king One from queen One from sixth pawn
On the magnanimity of the king	
	Two bishops One from book 1
The king must not place his happiness in riches	
	One from eighth pawn
On the virtue of generosity and vice of prodigality	
On the vice of avarice	
On the king's wisdom	
On taking council in all actions	
On peace	

poet's worry about a royal authority unbound by limits. Early in the *Regement*'s prologue Hoccleve makes an oblique reference to the deposition of Richard II, which he offers as an example of bad fortune:

Me fil to mynde how that nat longe agoo
Fortunes strook doun thraste estat rial
Into mescheef, and I took heede also
Of many anothir lord that hadde a fal
In mene estat eek sikirnesse at al

Ne saw I noon, but I sy atte laste
Wher seuretee for to abyde hir caste. (ll. 22–28)

Here Hoccleve stresses the precious nature of kingship, which comes with
no "seuretee."[38] For Blyth, the *Regement*'s most recent editor, this moment
"forces a connection between the Prologue and the *Regiment* proper, and in
so doing implies that the entire work needs to be seen as a series of interac-
tions—between prologue and *Regiment*, between poet's mirror (self-portrayal)
and prince's mirror (as in *Fürstenspiegel*), between private and public."[39]
Fortune, which "doun thraste estat rial / Into mescheef" during Richard's reign,
has now come to torment Hoccleve, who similarly finds himself "in mene
estat." Missing in Blyth's account, however, is the way this reference to Richard's deposition also alludes to the *Liber*, which opens with the illegitimate
overthrow of Nebuchadnezzar by his son, Evilmerodach. In both cases, a king
is killed by a relative who subsequently claims the throne. Yet Hoccleve, like
Jacobus, does not see regicide as the simple replacement of one royal body
with another. Instead, he uses this historical fact to remind the prince that a
king, like his advisors, must follow a certain set of rules and that following
such rules will help him to escape the vagaries of Fortune.[40]

This fretting about monarchial authority ultimately explains Hoccleve's
emphasis on a king's mastery of his own piece. After acknowledging that he
"sumwhat knowe a kynges draght" (and also admitting, "Of othir draghtes
lerned have I naght"), Hoccleve stresses the importance of the king's ability
to play the game:

And for that among the draghtes echone
That unto the ches apparteene may,
Is noon so needful unto your persone
To knowe as that of the cheertee verray
That I have had unto your noblesse ay,
And shal, if your plesaunce it be to heere,
A kynges draght reporte I shal now heere. (ll. 2122–28)

If in the stanza previous to this one Hoccleve claimed to only "sumwhat
knowe" the moves appropriate to kingship, here he dispels all doubts. Not
only does he promise to report "a kygnes draght," he also states that this
move is most "needful unto [the king's] persone." By the logic of the allegory, then, Hoccleve appears to be both *above* the game and the king—only
he can see how, where, and when a king must move—and at the same time
in the game. Hoccleve insists that a king's most important virtue is "cheertee,"

since he, like a pawn on the board, depends on the king for his livelihood. Yet in returning to the *Liber*'s primary metaphor, Hoccleve also reminds his reader that other pieces on the board have their own moves. Although he, himself, may only know a "kynges draght," the one most "needful" to the prince, each piece has its own set of rules essential for the good of the entire community.

In sum, whereas Jacobus's *Liber* reimagines a community's political power as a network of contractual associations, Hoccleve's *Regement* makes reference to this network in order to imagine the king's place within it. Or, to borrow from the imagery of the chessboard, whereas the *Liber* uses a game symbolic of all people in a civic body, the *Regement* takes the moral stories assigned to game's various pieces and uses them exclusively to instruct the king. In doing so Hoccleve prioritizes the monarch; unlike Jacobus he places the king at the center of his work. If the stories of Fabius and Fabricius warn of the dangers inherent in royal authority, so too do they point to the ways Hoccleve is able, in Larry Scanlon's words, "to reduce an aggregate of individuals to a single entity, imagined in one way or another as a single person, or a single body."[41] Echoing the sentiment found in the *Secretorum*, Hoccleve's exempla highlight the importance of the king's *corpus* as a repository of power and as a metaphor for the civic community as a whole. As these stories imply, the king's health needs to be preserved at all costs; his death would not only lead to chaos but also to the invasion (and thus metaphorical death) of the state itself. At the same time, by flagging the *Liber* as his source, one that Henry has "red," Hoccleve draws the prince's attention to the restrictions on royal power (l. 2130). That the king both reigns supreme but can also be a recipient of the same advice given to a tavern keeper or a bishop indicates both an absorption of other civic identities—Hoccleve's imagined ruler has taken on the virtues necessary to Jacobus's entire community—and a leveling among them. In this way Hoccleve is not merely "legitimating . . . Prince Henry, and through him the Lancastrian kings," but also informing the prince that the monarchial body, like the subjects it subsumes, is itself subject to certain restrictions.[42]

Publishing Authority: Caxton's Early Prologues

Roughly seventy years after Hoccleve finished his *Regement of Princes*, Caxton translated Jacobus's *Liber* into English as the *Game and Playe of the Chesse* and in doing so validated a new (or at least newly accessible for English readers who did not know French) model of political order. Why did Caxton choose the *Liber* as one of his first books to print? And why did he reprint it nearly a decade later in England with woodcuts added to the front of each chapter? While one can only guess Caxton's motivations, his two editions of the *Game and Playe* ultimately reflect a continuation of the complex discourses surrounding fifteenth-century political organization. His dedication of the 1474 *Game and Playe* to George, Duke of Clarence, and his prologue to this printing are aimed at repackaging the text as a straightforward *speculum regis*, a textual frame that sustains royal authority. In 1483, however, Caxton rewrote his original prologue, and his new version, in which he directs the work to all people, complicates monarchial authority at the same time that it emphasizes the increasing importance of all classes and professions as arbiters of power. In addition to redirecting the *Game and Playe* to all readers, Caxton added a series of woodcuts that dramatically illustrate the need to place restrictions on the king's power.

When considered on their own, the changes Caxton made to this particular prologue might imply either a radical reformulation of political power or a sudden shift of sentiment on the part of Caxton or on the part of his readers, or even a more general change that affected both the printer and his audience. Such a reading would be misleading at a time when there were many different models of royal authority available and in circulation, and when monarchial authority was still strong.[43] More to the point, this particular dedicatee, Clarence, had been executed in the interim, which in itself would furnish a reason to rewrite the volume's prefatory matter. Nevertheless, Caxton's decision to direct his 1483 prologue to all men rather than toward a specific person poses a challenge to monarchial power by suggesting that a stable realm requires virtue on the part of all citizens, not simply on the part of a king. Or put another way, by emphasizing the need for all men to act virtuously, Caxton, like Jacobus, recognizes that a community consists of multiple nodes of power, and he foregrounds this fact in his prologue. To further emphasize the *Liber*'s model of associative political order, Caxton also added woodcuts to his second edition. Made especially for this text, these woodcuts offer an explicit challenge to royal absolutism; the first image (see Figure 1, p. 18) features a decapitated king, whose body is being chopped to bits.[44] In short, even if Caxton himself was not openly hostile to royal authority, his decision to reprint the *Liber*, and the way he chose to reprint it, indicate a public eager for a book that offered a different model of political order.

Before discussing the *Game and Playe* itself, I will look at Caxton's own experience as a printer, at the posture he adopts in his early prologues, and at the ways he positions himself as a contributor to the literary landscape of the late fifteenth century. This last point is perhaps the most important, as scholars have traditionally praised Caxton only for his business acumen, identifying in his various prologues and epilogues "clear evidence of a mass-marketing strategy."[45] Although successfully dismissing earlier characterizations of Caxton as dependent on patrons, as mindlessly translating earlier works, or as both, such praise has had the unfortunate effect of downplaying Caxton's impact on the culture of late medieval England. More recently, William Kuskin, whose work focuses on the importance of Caxton's editorial choices both in terms of the texts he published and how he presented them, has started to recuperate Caxton as an important literary figure in his own right. Kuskin argues that Caxton's strategy as a printer "merges the material *reproduction* of his sources with the ideological *production* of fifteenth-century culture."[46] Like Kuskin, I will consider the ways Caxton, his books, and the market he envisions reflect the tensions between a more absolutist form of government with static social distinctions and a more participatory society organized around "a latticework of temporary positions defined by the subject's immediate relation to authority."[47]

Before becoming a printer, Caxton worked as a mercer with a trading circuit that kept him traveling between the Low Countries, Calais, and London.[48] By the mid-1450s, Caxton had become one of England's main importers of luxury goods, including cloth, silk, ermine, fur, and saffron, and his success as a merchant and financier provided entree into powerful circles. Although no one has established the year Caxton began to serve as an envoy for the Crown, a 1458 charter referring to him as a person "of the Staple at Calais" provides the first record of this type of service, and subsequent documents point to his ever-expanding role as a diplomat. By 1462, he was elected by Edward IV as "Governor of the English Nation," and in this role he functioned on several occasions as the king's representative for trade negotiations with the dukes of Burgundy and the Hanseatic League.

When Caxton turned to printing in the early 1470s, he was embedded in a matrix of commercial and political power, and his social position stood him in good stead. Although at least one scholar has recently downplayed his reliance on patronage and connections, there is no doubt that the young printer capitalized in the early stages of his business on regular trading allies and on royal support.[49] Caxton himself writes in his prologue to his first book, the *Recuyell of the Historyes of Troyes*, that his translation of the text was partially funded by the king's sister, Margaret of York, who gave Caxton a "yerly fee and other many goode and grete benefetes."[50] Admittedly, Caxton does not always provide accurate information about his channels of commercial and social support. That he dedicated the first edition of the *Game and Playe of the Chesse* to the king's brother, George, Duke of Clarence, a man he had most likely never met, suggests a tie between the two men that in reality probably never existed. However, even if this particular attempt at forging a connection failed, it nonetheless bespeaks Caxton's attempts to promote himself as a printer who catered to royal tastes, produced his texts for a courtly audience, and endorsed the traditional authority of a patron over a producer, which in the case of Caxton functions an extension of royal authority over lay power. Not just anyone bought Caxton's books; he sold them to members of the king's household.

Or at least this is the impression Caxton strives to create in his prologues and prefaces, which he uses in order to position his patron as both a literary and political authority. In the preface to the *Troye* book, for example, he repeatedly affirms Margaret's political supremacy and draws a parallel between his own translation project and that of Raoul Lefèvre, who first translated the Troy story from Latin to French for Philip, the duke of Burgundy. Just as Philip, a "ryght noble gloryous and myghty prynce in his tyme," sponsored Lefèvre, so too has Caxton, at the "comaundement of the right hye myghty and vertuouse Pryncesse" Margaret, translated the work from French to English (3). Caxton then follows the preface with a prologue in which he offers two more reasons for Margaret's superiority: her education and her social class. According to Caxton, Margaret's facility with language far exceeds his own "brode and rude Englissh," and upon learning of his partially completed translation project, she corrects his errors before funding the rest of his work (4).

Margaret's intellectual and financial control over his project cannot be detached from her political status, and in the middle of his prologue Caxton carefully lists each one of her titles that he has elsewhere abbreviated. It is thus "mylady Margarete by the grace of god suster unto the kynge of englond and of france, my soverayn lord Duchesse of Bourgoine of lotryk, of brabant, of lymburgh, and of luxenburgh, Countes of fflandres of artoys & of bourgoine Palatynee of heynawd of holand of zeland and of namur Marquesse of the holy empire, lady of ffryse of salius and of mechlyn," who is able to correct the humble printer's translation and fund its completion (5). In a tautologically closed system, Margaret is portrayed as Caxton's educational and moral superior, a condition that both produces and is produced by her noble status.

This is not to say that Caxton, in listing these titles, breaks from a traditional prologue form: he doesn't. Not only was it common practice to list a
patron's titles, it was also common for Caxton simply to translate the French
original or recycle pat turns of phrase. Such is the case with the prologue to
the *Doctrinal of Sapience*, which Caxton has merely adapted to his own purposes, and the epilogue to the *Life of Our Lady*, which commences with the
formulaic "Goo, lytle book."[51] Even Kuskin, who tends to romanticize Caxton's place outside the court, argues that Caxton ultimately uses a type of
"fourme" shifting "to go—financially, diplomatically, and commercially—
where the nobility cannot."[52] Or, as he observes elsewhere: "What matters to
Caxton is less an actual patronage relationship—truly, patronage is not
really discussed in the *Game of Chesse*—than the elaboration of a system of
public legitimation through which Caxton can stage himself as counselor to
kings and dukes."[53]

Kuskin's formulation highlights the tradition behind Caxton's form
and also points to the ways Caxton's early prologues were called upon to
reinforce royal authority. In short, Caxton's early prefaces and prologues
underscore his willingness, or even need, to use preexisting social structures
in order to validate his translation. And while Caxton may have modeled
this particular preface on his French copy text, he has, as N. F. Blake observes,
expanded it "considerably."[54] The French preface to the *Historyes of Troyes* reads
simply: "Icy commence le volume intitulé *Le Recueil des Histoires de Troyes*
composé par venerable homme Raoul Lefevre, prestre chappellain de mon
tres redoubté seigneur. Monseigneur le Duc Phelippe de Bourgoingne, en
l'an de grace mil cccclxiiii."[55] What for Lefèvre served as a single sentence
explaining the when, what, and why of his text—and notably Lefèvre gives
the title of the book, his own name, and his own title before he names
his patron—becomes for Caxton an occasion for extensive praise and for a
narrative of the translation's origin. Thus even if we read Caxton's use of
Margaret as one of expediency or rhetoric, Caxton's depiction of himself as
dependent on a member of the noble class to fund his translation and, implicitly, to buy his book makes him appear beholden to royal authority, and
he uses his preface and his prologue to imagine his relationship to her as
one of servitude.[56]

Caxton does not confine his homage to royal authority to the *Recuyell*'s
prologue; the work itself sanctions the legitimacy and authority of the Yorkists. As Caxton reminds us in the epilogue to the *Recuyell*'s second book, the
poem had already been translated into English verse by John Lydgate at the
request of Prince Henry, later to be King Henry V. (Started in 1412, Lydgate's

Troy Book was completed in 1420, well after the prince had assumed the throne.) A free adaptation of Guido delle Colonne's *Historia destructionis Troiae*, a Latin prose account of the Troy story written in 1287, Lydgate's poem emphasizes the martial prowess of the ancient leaders and their chivalry during a time of war. Commissioning this particular translation was a strategic move by the soon-to-be king, who sought to provide Englishmen an example "of verray knyghthod" and "to remembre ageyn . . . the prowesse of olde chivalrie."[57] It was also part of a larger translation agenda, and Henry promoted a national literary tradition "as a deliberate policy intended to engage the support of Parliament and the English citizenry for a questionable usurpation of the throne."[58] By making the "matter of Troy" into the "matter of England," or rather by tying the history of England to the history of Troy as Lydgate does in the prologue, both poet and king, in an echo of the Romans' use of the *Aeneid*, could recast the English campaigns against the French as an extension of an epic historic struggle. It is the "worthy prynce of Walys" who will eventually rule over "Brutys Albyoun."[59]

In choosing this particular work as his first to print, then, Caxton recognizes his own potential as a contributor to a national literary tradition and, simultaneously, as a supporter of Yorkist claims to power.[60] If the book has been, as Caxton notes, "newe and late maad and drawen in to frenshe," then why not translate it into English "to thende that hyt myght be had as well in the royame of Englond as in other landes?" (4). It is at this very moment that Caxton frets about his prose and turns to Margaret, the sister of the king of France, to validate it, thus attaching the Yorkists to the same type of literary project that the Lancastrians had engaged in years previous. In this fashion, the story of Troy is rewritten once again to reflect, as Caxton notes in his epilogue to the second book, "the troublous world and of the grete devysions beyng and reygnyng as well in the royames of englond and fraunce" (502). This time, however, a Yorkist king is in charge.

Kuskin is right, however, to complicate the conventional views of Caxton as entirely beholden to a traditional system of patronage or, for that matter, of royal power. While Caxton's early prologues serve as a testament to the superiority of the noble class, he also poses subtle challenges to this type of categorization. As noted above, the prologue to the *Recuyell* foregrounds his indebtedness to his patron Margaret of York, whose authority over him is affirmed not only by her ability to fund his project but also by an education that far surpasses his own. At the same time a frontispiece that accompanied the work, which features a monkey standing between Caxton and Margaret and holding up its hands in a gesture either to give or receive a book, casts a different light on Caxton's gestures of subservience. If, as Kuskin has argued, the monkey represents Caxton, it can be read as a sign of the printer's own masquerade and willingness "to play the monkey because it locates him within the Burgundian court."[61] But the position of the monkey, who stands right next to Margaret as if waiting to receive its own gift from Caxton, also forms (perhaps inadvertently) an uncomfortable parallel to Margaret herself, and such a reading effectively upends the hierarchy Caxton has so carefully constructed.[62]

A similarly complicated portrait of royal patronage also appears in Caxton's third English publication, the *Dictes or Sayengis of the Philosophers* of 1477.[63] For this text the patron was the politically powerful Earl Rivers, the governor of King Edward's Ludlow household and the brother to Edward's wife, Elizabeth Woodville. Rivers had translated the work and, as explained in the epilogue, had given it to Caxton to correct and print. Insisting that he can find no faults with the translation, Caxton returns it to his patron, who thereupon shows Caxton "dyverce thinges whiche as him semed myght be left out."[64] It is thus Rivers, "Lord of Scales and of the Ile of Wyght, Defendour and directour of the siege apostolique for our holy fader the pope in this royame of Englond and governour of my lord prynce of wales" authorizing Caxton's printing. Here it seems that Rivers, who has given Caxton "good reward" for his work, knows best (73r, 75v).

Yet again Caxton provides a counterpoint to these gestures of humility and obedience. Whereas the *Recuyell*'s frontispiece disrupts the patron-printer relationship articulated in its prologue, later parts of the epilogue to *Dictes or Sayengis* seem to contradict the hierarchy established in its opening lines. Immediately after proclaiming his inability to correct Earl Rivers's "right wel and connyngly made" translation and his willingness to obey the earl's "comaundement" to print it, Caxton admits that he does find a very serious omission in the text where the lord "hath left out certayn and dyverce conclusions towchyng women" (73r–73v). Caxton proceeds to offer several excuses for this error, none of which is particularly flattering to his patron. Perhaps, Caxton muses, a woman asked Rivers to drop this section. Perhaps he was "amerous on somme noble lady" and did not want to offend her (73v). Perhaps Rivers was worried about offending all people, although he himself should know that Socrates wrote about Greek women, who are, Caxton insists, much different than women of England, who are "right good, wyse, playsant, humble, discrete, sobre, chast, obedient to their husbondis, trewe, secrete, stedfast, ever besy, and never ydle, attemperat in speking, and vertuous in alle their werkis—or atte leste sholde be soo" (74r).

Or perhaps Rivers had a bad copy of the text. Or maybe he had a good copy, but a leaf of the manuscript had blown over as he was translating. Caxton's excuses are facetious, or at least they are no more "trewe" or "sobre" than the women of England, and after having fun at the earl's expense, he goes on to add the section in question.

Caxton's insouciance should not be mistaken for open hostility or for an attack on the hierarchy that separates patron from printer. On the contrary, Caxton makes clear at the end of the epilogue to *Dictes or Sayengis* that he has added Socrates' dialogues to the end of the book rather than placing them in their original context so as not to offend his patron, who has requested their omission altogether. Although he may feel strongly that they should be there, "as it is acordaunt that his dyctes and sayengis shold be had as wel as others," his primary interest is "in satisfyeng of all parties," the most important of which is his benefactor (75r). In short, while Caxton may at times poke fun at the social and political hierarchies governing his book production, such gestures, in addition to creating an image of familiarity and thus hinting favorably at Caxton's proximity to the royal household, are only possible when the hierarchy itself faces few challenges to its hegemony. Nor does Caxton need or want to dismantle a social structure that he has used successfully to authorize his books.

Between the *Recuyell* and the *Dictes or Sayengis* Caxton published Jacobus's *Liber*, the second English work he printed, and to it he added a preface that echoes the hierarchical models established in the other two prologues.[65] As noted above, Caxton dedicated the volume to the duke of Clarence in a gesture typically interpreted as a bid for patronage but which may well have been a warning to Edward IV's brother.[66] Regardless of the intended audience, Caxton uses his prologue to frame the *Liber* as a work that confirms royal authority.[67] The epilogue differs from the prologue "only in that the focus shifts slightly from Clarence to his brother the king, though as both are considered guardians of the kingdom and the praise is so general the shift is not very marked."[68]

This foregrounding of royal authority appears early in the preface; Caxton opens by listing his patron's titles and connections to the king:

To the right noble, right excellent & vertuous prince George duc of Clarence, Erle of warwyck and of salisburye, grete chamberlayn of Englond and leutenant of Irelond, oldest broder of kynge Edward, by the grace of god kynge of England and of fraunce, your most humble servant william Caxton, amonge other of your servantes, sendes unto yow peas, helthe, Joye and victorye upon your Enemyes, Right highe puyssant and redoubted prynce. For as moche as I have understand and knowe, that ye are enclined unto the comyn wele of the kynge, our sayd saveryn lord, his nobles, lordes and comyn peple of his noble royame of Englond, and that ye sawe gladly the Inhabitants of the same enformed in good, vertuous, prouffitable and honeste maners, In whiche your noble persone wyth guydyng of your hows haboundeth, gyvyng light and ensample unto all other. Therfore I have put me in devour to translate a lityll book late comen into myn handes out of frensh in to englishe.[69]

Here Caxton packages the *Liber* as a type of advice-to-princes text, or perhaps more accurately as an advice-to-the-prince's-brother text. After reminding the reader of his "patron's" many titles, Caxton uses a trickle-down theory of virtue to suggest that Clarence's good actions give light to the common man. The masses, Caxton explains, need strong leaders, without which they will have trouble learning "good, virtuous, profitable, and honest conduct." Addressed to a royal body, either explicitly to Clarence or implicitly to Edward IV, the dedication foregrounds the importance of royal power even as it gestures toward a larger audience.

As with his other prologues from this time, Caxton occasionally punctures his prefatory homage. At several points in his dedication he suggests that the *Game and Playe* should be read by all men, observing that the original author collected these stories in order to apply them "unto the moralite of the publique wele as well of the nobles as of the comyn peple" (2). And while Caxton has translated the book to honor Clarence, he also claims that he has made it "to thentent that other of what estate or degre he or they stande in may see in this sayd lityll book if they governed themself as they ought to doo" (2). In other words, Caxton here recognizes that many people will read his book and advises all who do so to use it for self-betterment.[70]

In the body of his translation the printer makes even stronger suggestions about the importance of individual morality and of a shared responsibility for the common good.[71] In a passage appearing nowhere in the French translations, Caxton entertains a reverie of communal property, which, as he sees it, is the form of life most acceptable to God:

And also hit is to be supposyd that suche as have theyr goodes comune & not propre is most acceptable to god. For ellys wold not thise religious men as monkes freris chanons obseruantes & all other avowe hem & kepe the wilfull poverte that they ben professid too. For in trouth I haue my self ben conversant in a religious hous of white freris at gaunt Which have all thynge in comyn amonge them, and not one richer than an other, in so moche that yf a man gaf to a frere 3d. or 4d. to praye for hym in his masse, as sone as the masse is doon he deliuerith hit to his ouerest or procuratour in whyche hows ben many vertuous and deuoute freris. And yf that lyf were not the beste and the most holiest, holy church wold never suffre hit in religion. (88)

Seeing this addition as an indication of Caxton's "communism" or as "an anti-clerical tirade of his own invention in which he praises egalitarianism as a better social arrangement than feudalism" is to push past reasonable interpretive limits, especially given the printer's own success as a business-man.[72] The White Friars that Caxton has met do not avoid profit; they sell their prayers and share the take. And it is not that they are not rich, but rather that there is "not one richer than an other."[73] Nevertheless, Caxton's praise of common property gestures toward a fantasy of communal responsibility just as it acknowledges a more general dispersal of power already present. That private property forms a locus of concern means that these property owners had some degree of economic and political power. This is the reason that Caxton must address "the moralite of the publique wele as well of the nobles as of the comyn peple"; the nobles are not the only ones in power.

At the end of the volume, however, Caxton refocuses his attention on the king and the nobles of the realm. Whereas Jacobus concludes the *Liber* by encouraging every man to live a moral life and enjoining all men to return to God, Caxton finishes the *Game and Playe* by urging those in power to rule wisely. "In conquerynge his [Edward's own] rightfull enheritaunce," Caxton hopes "that verray peas and charite may endure in bothe his roy-ames" (187). This hand-wringing about princely virtue even creeps into the text itself. "Alas how kepe the prynces their promisses in thise dayes, not only her promises but their othes her sealis and wrytynges and signes of their propre handes," he says in the chapter on the chess king, an addition to the original text that underscores the importance of a just monarch (22). With these changes—a dedication addressed to Clarence, an ending aimed at the noble class, and some embellishments to the chapter on the king— Caxton alters the text's compass, effectively reassigning the moral thrust of the its multifarious exempla to one man, the monarch's brother. In doing so he draws Jacobus into the orbit of his other early publications such as the *Historyes of Troye*, works that, through their prefaces, or their content, or both, serve to reaffirm royal power.

"Persons as longen to the playe": Caxton's 1483 Preface

When Caxton returned to England, he continued to cultivate his connec-tions to the royal household and the court. His most powerful patrons were members of the Woodville family, and foremost among them was Earl Rivers, for whom Caxton printed Rivers's own translations of Christine de

Pizan's *Moral Proverbs* (1478) and of *Cordial* (1479), the latter of which Caxton had printed earlier in French in Bruges.[74] For Elizabeth Woodville, wife of King Edward IV, Caxton translated and printed *Jason*, a continuation of the Troy story, which he presented to her son, the Prince of Wales, in 1477.[75] Although it is impossible to gauge his degree of intimacy with the royal family, Caxton obviously still cultivated these ties and continued to use their names in his prologues and epilogues, evidence that he needed or at least wanted such endorsements to publish his books.

In April of 1483, however, Edward IV died, and the political landscape began to change. After a struggle with the Woodvilles, Edward's brother Richard, Duke of Gloucester, claimed the throne in June. Southern England never acknowledged Richard's legitimacy, and various dissidents planned a series of rebellions for October. While the principal figures included such high-placed people as Elizabeth Woodville and Henry Tudor, it was primarily a mutiny of Edward IV's household nobles, and it failed.[76]

How did Caxton respond to this new political climate? At least one critic has postulated that Caxton's decrease of dedications around this time offers evidence of his increased independence from patrons.[77] Blake, observing the same phenomenon, has argued that the change was one of political necessity and sees *Caton*, which was finished in December of 1483, as Caxton's attempt to change his approach to patronage. "Up till now," Blake writes, "books had been produced without dedication or under the patronage of a nobleman. . . . *Caton* marks a break with the past for it is dedicated to the City of London. Not only did he dedicate it to London, but he stated his own allegiance to that city in no uncertain way; the prologue opens: 'I, William Caxton, cytezeyn & coniurye of the same [i.e., liveryman of London], & of the fraternyte & felauship of the Mercerye.'"[78] Rather than continue to foreground his affiliations with the nobility, as this argument goes, Caxton now addressed his fellow merchants and effectively severed his allegiance with the Woodville camp.

Yet while I agree that Caxton's embracing of the merchant class may have been a prudent business decision on the part of the printer, his writings also reveal a more complicated portrait of royal absolutism. This shift in Caxton's presentation of monarchial power appears clearly in the changing nature of Caxton's 1483 prologues and prefaces. In the first half of that year, Caxton printed both the *Pilgrimage of the Soul* (June 6) and *Festial* (June 30). In the *Pilgrimage of the Soul*, a translation of Guillaume de Deguileville's dream vision, Caxton omits a formal prologue, noting only in a short *incipit* that the final text was been "fynysshed the sixth day of Juyn the yere of Our Lord MCCCClxxxiii and the first yere of the regne of Kynge Edward the Fyfthe."[79] The reference to Edward IV's young son as the monarch, however, became invalid two days later when Edward V's name ceased to appear on privy seal writs. Soon after this, Edward's coronation was rescheduled for later in the year, although by the end of the month Richard III had been crowned king.[80] In September Caxton printed the *Confessio amantis*, the first book that he acknowledges as being published "the fyrst yere of the regne of Kyng Richard the Thyrd."[81] Like that of the *Pilgrimage* and *Festial*, however, the prologue was pared back, and it includes only three sentences: one that names the king, one that describes Gower's poem, and one that points the reader to a table showing the poem's various exempla.

While these prefaces notably sidestep any direct discussion of royal power—in each Caxton omits any dedication, offering the reader information of a purely mechanical sort—other prefaces also published in this year replace praise of patrons with praise of textual accessibility. Caxton's fairly lengthy prologue to the *Canterbury Tales* opens by lauding the philosophers, clerks, and poets who have recorded valuable learning for the education of people in the present time. Caxton then situates Chaucer in this tradition, hailing him as the father of English poetry, and reminds his readers of their own national heritage.[82] Chaucer, Caxton argues, deserves the title of poet laureate for having taken the "rude speche" of the realm and "by hys labour enbelysshyd, ornated and made faire" the English language.[83] "Fair" language, as Caxton soon proposes, means accessible language. Chaucer thus deserves fame because he assembled stories, recast them into both rhyme and prose, "and them so craftyly made that he comprehended hys maters in short, quyck and hye sentences, eschewyng prolyxyte, castyng away the chaf of superfluyte, and shewyng the pyked grayn of sentence utteryd by crafty and sugred eloquence."[84]

Whether or not one agrees with Caxton that Chaucer's language casts away "the chaf of superfluyte" (an argument that does not hold up well with a tale like the *Squire's*), the *idea* of a condensed, easy-to-read Chaucer is important for Caxton, as it reinforces the printer's insistence that the *Canterbury Tales* are about people from every class and thus intended for everyone. In Chaucer, Caxton finds "many a noble hystorye of every astate and degre," and he sees the pilgrims as sources for virtuous stories even if they do not always serve examples of virtue in their own right.[85] These stories should in turn improve the reader, and Caxton implores everyone to "take and understonde the good and vertuous tales that it may so prouffyte unto the helthe of our sowles."[86] That Caxton does not dedicate the text to a particular person further underscores its ecumenical aims.

If Caxton's prologue to the *Canterbury Tales* emphasizes the idea of community as both a diverse and inclusive entity, then the text itself pushes this point even farther. Written by an author who, like Caxton, came from mercantile background, Chaucer's poem imagines civic order as a self-governing group of people of different classes and genders held together by common interests.[87] Caxton had published Chaucer previously, and the *Canterbury Tales* volume was most likely one of the earliest works off his Westminster press.[88] Yet to this second edition, which as Caxton tells us has been corrected from his first, he adds a series of twenty-three woodcuts that illustrate Chaucer, the individual pilgrims, and the pilgrim collective seated at a table, a picture that reemphasizes once again the egalitarian nature of the group. In sum, Caxton has, in his choice of texts, his introductory remarks, and his use of woodcuts, designed a book that emphasizes a horizontally ordered social order.

Caxton had, to be sure, framed some of his earlier publications in a similar fashion. To his translation of Boethius's *Boke of Consolacion of Philosophie*, published around 1478, Caxton had added an epilogue in which he expresses his hope for his readers to "see what this transitorie and mutable worlde is and whereto every mann livyng in hit ought to entende."[89] Obviously, such language is as inclusive as that found in the prologue to the *Canterbury Tales*. Yet it is notable that his Boethius epilogue, although encouraging all men to be virtuous, spends most of its energy lionizing Boethius and Chaucer, the former for his resistance to tyranny and the later for his glorification (and *not* simplification) of the English language. The epilogue ends with Stephanus Surigonus's epitaph for the poet who, as Caxton informs us, was buried at Westminster. Thus rather than praising Chaucer's ability to write for the common man, Caxton elevates him as a poet of ornate language, whose burial site reaffirms his close relationship to the ruling class.

While the second edition of the *Canterbury Tales* points toward changes in Caxton's designated audience, or at least to the printer's changed perceptions of his book buyers, his second edition of Jacobus's *Liber* gestures more specifically toward the types of political discourses in circulation among his readership.[90] Unlike the first printing of *The Game and Playe of the Chesse*, which had been dedicated to Edward's brother, the now deceased duke of Clarence, this edition claims no royal patron, nor does it address a royal audience. Instead, Caxton opens with a citation from Romans 15:4. "Alle that is wryten is wryten unto our doctryne and for our lernyng."[91] In case his readers miss the inclusiveness of this gesture, Caxton insists later in the prologue that "thys sayd book is ful of holsom wysedom and requysyte unto every astate and degree."[92] It is for this reason, Caxton claims, that he has decided to print it again, this time with pictures "of suche persons as longen to the playe."[93]

Like the woodcuts in the second edition of the *Canterbury Tales*, the pictorial schema in the *Liber*, a series that features the different chess pieces on the board, highlights a diverse society of people that constitute civic community. Unlike the *Canterbury Tales*, however, the pictures also offer a narrative of limits on monarchial power. In my opening chapter I briefly discussed Caxton's first woodcut, an image that shows King Nebuchadnezzar's murder by his son Evilmerodach, and talked about the ways it serves as a warning against unlimited monarchial power. But I would like to return to this image to consider its fifteenth-century resonance and its relationship to the woodcuts that follow it.[94]

I have already noted that Nebuchadnezzar's decapitated body offers a striking commentary on royal authority (see Figure 1, p. 18). The king, reduced to a crowned head with closed eyes, lies on the ground in front of a chopping block as his executioner looks on. Four carrion birds swarm within the frame, each holding a body part it has seized from the corpse. One would be hard-pressed to make any claims about the identity of the king, nor does this story depicted in the picture exactly match the narrative of Richard III's rise to power, which took place after his brother Edward IV had died of natural causes. Nevertheless, this representation of regicide would have had strong cultural reverberations in the context of Richard's assumption of the throne, an act that resulted in the execution of several people with royal connections, including Edward IV's two sons, who disappeared into the Tower never to be seen again. Even if the picture does not offer a specific reprimand of Richard's actions, it presents a graphic reminder of the destructibility of the royal body.

At the same time, the subsequent woodcuts, like the chapters they introduce, do not wholly condemn such destruction. Although never sanctioning regicide, the image series positions this act as the fulcrum for the game's creation, which subsequently refashions the king's relationship both to his own body and to the body of state. This refashioning begins to take place over the next three images. In the second woodcut we see Philometer playing chess (see Figure 2, p. 19). Here the chaos and disorder of the swirling birds has given way to a single figure, who sits calmly in a room carefully studying the board. The picture's symmetrical design and the frame around the image, which features thick pillars on both sides, highlight the logic and reason of his pastime and reinforce the idea of stability and permanence. By matching the checkered pattern of the floor with the checkered pattern of the board, the illustrator reminds us that the game should model real life.

In the third woodcut Philometer and the king, ostensibly Evilmerodach, sit at a chessboard (Figure 5). Again, the board is located in a room and framed by pillars, although in this picture the differences between the two players disrupt the symmetry of the image. The king sits on a throne to the left, while the philosopher sits on the board's right, perched, it seems, on an invisible stool. The king's throne, crown, and fur-lined robe help us to identify him and also confer on him his political power. Yet the limits of his power are emphasized by Philometer, who holds a piece and shows the king the proper rules of play. Positioned to the right side of the board, the side that connotes his moral and intellectual authority, the philosopher prepares to explain to Evilmerodach the king's position on the board and the ways the game represents the king's relationship to the other subjects in his realm.[95]

In the fourth woodcut we finally see the king alone (Figure 6). Once again, sturdy pillars frame the image, and an arch with two windows reinforces the scene's symmetry. The king sits on the throne facing the reader yet with his eyes closed, and he holds an apple of gold and a scepter. As the text nearby explains, the apple indicates the king's ability to think about the administration of justice while the scepter represents the ruler's ability to punish any rebels.

These first four woodcuts thus move from an image of a king's fragmented body to a picture of a king intact. Between the two lies the process of reconstitution, namely the creation of the chess game, which allows Philometer to rebuild the king's body as a piece and as the fourth figure in the series. "The kynge must be thus maad," explains the first sentence in the chapter, a formulation that even further highlights the idea of the king's body as a manufactured entity over which the writer and illustrator have control. The piece itself is portrayed as a composite of the two "real" kings from the first two woodcuts; his robe, his smooth face, and his throne match those of Evilmerodach, while his closed eyes recall Nebuchadnezzar's corpse. The fifth woodcut, which shows the king seated next to the queen of the kingdom, pushes this point even further by adding a beard to the king's face while at the same time carrying over the scepter from the previous drawing (Figure 7). Although the beard can be taken as a sign of the king's maturity and readiness to marry, a contrast with his unshaved and youthful face in the previous woodcut, it also firmly links the picture back to the initial image of Nebuchadnezzar's decapitated head.

By showing the destruction and subsequent rebuilding of the king's body, Caxton offers a graphic reminder of the limits of monarchial authority. The opening picture of Nebuchadnezzor's dismemberment illustrates the destructibility of the royal body, an act that leads in turn to a refashioning of the civic body in the form of a chess game. This new metaphor for social order reimagines the king as a member of the kingdom; the realm is no longer a reflection of royal will but rather a complicated matrix of different affiliations in which the king is one piece among many. The importance of all the pieces is depicted by the woodcuts that follow, each of which illustrates a different piece/profession and emphasizes its contributions to the community as a whole. Just as the farmer's plow represents his identity as the provider of food for the kingdom, so too do the king's apple and scepter symbolize his job. As the manager of the realm, he has a responsibility to dispense justice. And if he fails to do his job correctly, he can be held accountable by the people he governs. The chess king, already a composite of both Evilmerodach and Nebuchadnezzar, is representative of all kings, including the one currently occupying the English throne.

Figure 5. Third woodcut from Caxton's 1483 edition of *The Game and Playe of the Chesse* (book 1, chap. 3). Newberry Library folio inc. 9643.

Thus when read against his earlier works, Caxton's 1483 and early 1484 prefaces, prologues, epilogues, and woodcuts (which themselves were a relatively new addition his volumes), offer complicated views of royal power.[96] And while his later volumes likely ended up in upper-class hands, gone are the laudatory paragraphs about his noble patrons. In their place stands a foregrounding of "the fraternyte and felauship of the mercerye," a group in which Caxton proudly counts himself a member. This is not to say Caxton never again dedicated a book to a monarch. The *Order of Chivalry*, published in 1484, is dedicated to "Kyng Rychard, Kyng of Englond and of Fraunce," who, according to Caxton, commissioned the printer to translate the work from its French original.[97] And *Blanchardin and Eglantine*, published in 1489, is presented to Margaret, the duchess of Somerset and the mother of Henry VII. Yet in both cases, Caxton is much more reserved in

Figure 6. Fourth woodcut from Caxton's 1483 edition of *The Game and Playe of the Chesse* (book 2, chap. 1). Newberry Library folio inc. 9643.

his praise of these royal patrons than he was of his patrons in his previous works. Although excusing his "rude and comyn Englyshe" in *Blanchardin,* he is not, as he was with Margaret of York, overwhelmed by the expertise of his patron, and he quickly adds that his foremost concern is that "it shall be understonden of the redars and herers—and that shall suffyse."[98] In the *Order of Chivalry* Caxton omits a prologue altogether. Instead, he ends the work with a long epilogue in which he offers a long diatribe about the shoddiness of England's knights. "O ye knyghtes of Englond," Caxton laments, "where is the custome and usage of noble chyvalry that was used in tho dayes? What do ye now but go to the baynes and playe atte dyse?"[99] Here Caxton acknowledges noble power only to dismiss England's knights as lacking in self-control, evidence of which he finds, interestingly, in their penchant for playing dice. Only in the final portion of the epilogue does Caxton

Figure 7. Fifth woodcut from Caxton's 1483 edition of *The Game and Playe of the Chesse* (book 2, chap. 2). Newberry Library folio inc. 9643.

encourage the monarch to give this book to "other yong lordes, knyghtes and gentylmen" so that they can improve themselves.[100] At no point does Caxton position his patron as a moral or intellectual superior.

It is also notable that Caxton's *Game and Playe* was not the only work he published that drew on Jacobus's model of civic order. In the same year that he re-released the *Liber* Caxton also printed the *Court of Sapience*, yet another work influenced by the *Liber*'s ideas of associative polity.[101] Written in the middle of the fourteenth century by an unknown author, the poem opens with a seventy-line *Prohemium* in which the narrator states his goal—he wants to learn Wisdom—and prays for help writing. Immediately after this introduction, the narrator goes to bed and, in his mind, plays a game of chess against the World and Dame Fortune. When he loses, Reason chides him, after which he falls asleep. In his dream he soon meets Sapience. She and her companions, Intelligence and Science, escort him home (across the River Quiet) to their castle, the description of which occupies the bulk of the poem.

That the dreamer's lost chess match inspires him to seek Wisdom is less significant than his careful explication of the game itself, which the dreamer accepts as a metaphor for political order and his place in it. When he first introduces the game, he acknowledges that a player usually seeks his own end:

The chesplayer, or he a man have drawen,
Hath only thought to make good purveaunce
For kyng and quene, aulfyn, knyght, roke and pawne;
Echone of these he hath in remembraunce.
So eche estate and wordly governaunce
In one eschekker in my mynd I sawe,
But I ne wyst what draught was best to drawe.[102]

In this passage the player, an Everyman figure, seeks to control his own fortune by making good "purveaunce," or providence, for his own future. Eager to follow the chess player's model, the dreamer then envisions "eche estate and worldly governaunce" yet cannot figure out which "draught was best to drawe."

His meditation on the board continues in the subsequent stanza, and he details more specifically the ways in which the game reflects political order:

Fyrst, my desyre was to have drawen my kyng,
At hertes lust, in sure prosperyte;
But in the chesse I had espyed a thyng:
The kyng to purpoos may not passe his see,
To make hym way, or some pawne drawen bee;
Than bothe to guyde the kyng and pawnes eke
And al other, my wyttes were to seke. (ll. 85–91)

Here the dreamer's contemplation of the board inspires his desire to move the king, a move he sees as a sure way to win. Yet almost immediately he realizes that this move is not possible unless "some pawne drawen bee." This prompts him to use his wits to figure out ways to move "the kyng and pawnes . . . and all other" pieces on the board. In short, the narrator learns that the king is not the linchpin to the game. Instead, he must take account of the entire board and all the pieces on it; one cannot move the king alone.[103]

The dreamer uses the next stanza to expand on this idea of a realm that contains interdependent subjects, and his consternation at his inability to move prompts him to meditate on the ways chess contains a "moral phylosophye" and teaches men their place in the world:

I thought how by moral phylosophye
The chesse was founde, and set in dyversite
Of draught for a myrrour of polocye;
The whiche vertu departed is in thre:
Fyrst must man conne hymself reule in degre,
Efte his houshold, and than in unyverse,
Cyte and reygne; these ben the thre dyverse. (92–98)

Outlining the three lessons he finds in chess, the dreamer sees the master of the "self" as the first item to be learned, a lesson that stems directly from the game's mimetic power. That every man must "hymself reule" further highlights the same idea of individual moral responsibility that appears in Jacobus's treatise. Here again, the emphasis is on "the kyng and pawnes eke / And al other," rather than on the ruler alone. After learning to rule himself, an individual must learn to rule his household, and subsequently his place in the city and kingdom; as the dreamer notes in the following stanza, these lessons are spelled out in Aristotle's "Poletyk Book" (99). If chess is a "myrrour of polocye," then it necessarily reflects each person in the realm. It is not, in other words, a mirror of the prince; it is a mirror of the entire body politic.

Thus when, after this four-stanza analysis of the game, the dreamer decides to play against the World and Fortune, he does not lose on account of the game's unpredictability. Rather, as Reason points out, his initial mistake lies in taking on "moble Fortune and fals Worldlynesse" (l. 114). These two opponents do not play fairly, and "in theyr draught al deceyte is in-clude" (l. 118). In the end Wisdom is not a matter of avoiding the World; it is a matter of not being unprepared in the game of life.[104] When the *Court's* dreamer eventually reaches Wisdom's castle, he encounters the doctrinal figures of Hope and Faith. Yet also present in Wisdom's inner sanctum are the seven liberal arts, their handmaidens, and their many "admirers," or historical figures commonly associated with them. These are the figures that will allow the dreamer/player to master his role on earth.

This returns us to Caxton's decision to print the *Game and Playe of the Chesse*. Catherine Batt has argued that this work represents an exercise in "'safe' and conservative social comment."[105] However, this formulation does not seem wholly accurate. Instead, it seems more likely that Caxton's choice to reprint this particular text with graphic woodcuts, to reprint the *Canterbury Tales*, to print the *Court of Sapience*, and to change his standard format for dedications appears as part of a larger shift in fifteenth-century ideas of political authority and civic organization.[106] Lest we think that such changes bypassed Caxton's own readers, we need look no farther than Caxton's request for a pardon, which he obtained in 1484 shortly after the October 1483 rebellion against Richard III.[107] Caxton was not alone in his request; from February 1 to July 31 of that year, roughly 1,100 people petitioned for a pardon from the crown. Although we cannot trace Caxton's need for a pardon directly to his publications, it is impossible to see the two as entirely unrelated. His 1483 prologues offer tangible evidence of the fluctuating discourses of royal power and also of Caxton's willingness to draw on all of them in order to shape his readership, and it was on the heels of *Caton* that he sued "to indemnify himself as a perceived threat to the new regime." Such a "threat" is raised most tangibly by the woodcuts. But coupled with a text that seeks to redistribute power across a political community, it is not difficult to imagine why the royal household felt apprehensive.

It is in this fashion that the *Liber*, a work created in late thirteenth-century Lombardy and translated throughout Europe, finally appeared in English. The political context for the text had changed dramatically—the city managers ruling the Genoa of Jacobus's era bore little resemblance to the English monarchs who governed Caxton's England. But indeed, this is perhaps the very reason for the *Liber*'s reappearance. Whereas Jacobus's original work seems to reflect his own social order, Caxton's choice to translate and, more importantly, to reissue the text with woodcuts signifies something deeper: the possibility for change.

Epilogue

*[Kings] have power to exalt low things, and abase high things, and
make of their subjects like men at the Chesse; A pawne to take a Bishop
of a Knight, and to cry up, or downe any of their subjects, as they do
their money.*

—King James VI and I, speech to Parliament, March 21, 1610

*The story is told of an automaton constructed in such a way that it
could play a winning game of chess, answering each move of an
opponent with a countermove. A puppet in Turkish attire and with a
hookah in its mouth sat before a chessboard placed on a large table. A
system of mirrors created the illusion that this table was transparent
from all sides. Actually, a little hunchback who was an expert chess
player sat inside and guided the puppet's hand by means of strings.
One can imagine a philosophical counterpart to this device. The puppet
called "historical materialism" is to win all the time. It can easily be a
match for anyone if it enlists the services of theology, which today, as we
know, is wizened and has to keep out of sight.*

—Opening to Walter Benjamin, Theses on the Philosophy of History

Finishing a book is, in many ways, more difficult than starting
one. My own reluctance to end comes from two main sources, the first and
more minor being my frustration about the texts I did not have space to
discuss. For if I have read and taken account of many references to chess in
medieval literature, I have also remained silent on even more. I could have
expanded my analysis to include *Aspremont*, a twelfth-century chanson de
geste about Charlemagne and his knights that mentions chess in passing
several times.[1] I probably could have also discussed *Le Bâtard de Bouillon*,
in which one character kills another with a chessboard.[2] These stories and
others are compelling, and I appreciate the ways so many authors push
chess symbolism in slightly different directions.

Yet to the extent that the chess symbolism in most of these poems does not change my overall argument, I opted not to include such references merely for the sake of coverage. In the context of a project already scattered geographically and chronologically, such additions would inevitably feel appended or list-like, making my project into a catalogue rather than an argument. I thus leave it to those who have a greater investment in these stories and others to investigate the ways such works may (or may not) contribute to the chess allegory's cultural significance.

My second difficulty in ending this project is one of narrative. As I have argued, chess in the late Middle Ages served as a vehicle for political and economic ideology and as a way for individuals to imagine their own civic identities. Upon the game's arrival in Europe in the late tenth century, medieval cultures deliberately turned it into a representation of their own social milieu(s). By the late thirteenth century chess had become so popular and so well known that Jacobus de Cessolis had little difficulty harnessing its allegorical power, and he drew on the game's mimetic qualities in order to model the workings of a contractually based political order. In doing so he provided a way for people to think about their identities as individuals and as citizens. If the *Liber*'s allegory allowed a player the fantasy of ultimate power over the game, its exempla reminded individuals of their responsibility to the political community.[3]

In the opening of this book I demonstrated that this dual representation of citizens as both players and pieces is not one of a free social order based on an individual's independent self-determination. In fact, it is arguably just the opposite, offering a totalizing vision of a state in which all citizens are marked primarily by their professional obligations. Jacobus's preoccupation with commercial production might even strike some as offering an illusion of choice in a system of rigid rules or symbolizing individual disenfranchisement, much in the way Benjamin uses the automaton player as a metaphor for our helplessness in the face of "historical materialism."[4] Seen in this most menacing light, the state-as-chessboard becomes an inflexible structure that forces its members to occupy rigidly determined categories.

Yet as I hope I have also shown, this allegory does not have to be dismissed as merely another technology of constraint. The *Liber*'s emphasis on ethical responsibility, while not empowering subjects with completely autonomous choice, does not have to be seen as completely *dis*empowering in its vision of social order. Under the dictates of the allegory, players may be bound by rules. However, they are also able to move their own pieces, pieces that represent their trades rather than merely their social class. The state itself is dependent on the individuals who inhabit these professions; it is, in fact, produced by the individual professions just as much as it produces them. Although still socially stratified, the *Liber*'s model depicts smiths, innkeepers, notaries, farmers, and other "commoners" as crucial members of the larger whole that will flourish only by collective collaboration. Seen this way, Jacobus's vision of social harmony is one based on a communalistic ideal of voluntary interdependence and collaboration.[5]

There is much evidence to suggest that medieval readers themselves received the *Liber*'s allegory in a variety of ways. For some, Jacobus's model of state may have provided a welcome relief from the tired state-as-body model and its outdated notions of social roles. The very fact that his treatise circulated so widely is evidence of its warm reception. Yet as demonstrated by literary responses to the *Liber*, other readers were more apprehensive about Jacobus's emphasis on individual autonomy and about his proposal that civic bonds are artificial and expedient rather than organic and divinely patterned. The fourteenth-century *Les Echecs amoureux* and the later Commentary on the *Les Echecs* poem are both telling in this regard. On the one hand, the poet and commentator acknowledge that chess offers a viable vision of state order, and both make open allusions to Jacobus's text. Yet on the other hand, the *Les Echecs* poet takes care to graft Jacobus's allegory onto two other symbolic systems, portraying the pieces as representative not only of professional identities but also of internal emotions and cosmological bodies. The commentator reemphasizes these links between the different symbolic systems, and his text, like the poem it glosses, rewrites the *Liber*'s allegory as one produced by a natural order.

Naturalizing Jacobus's state-as-chess model was not the only way to handle its more threatening implications, and other writers overlooked the state-as-chess allegory altogether in order to highlight other aspects of the game, namely its use as a vehicle for wagering. In late fourteenth- and early fifteenth-century England in particular, chess often appears as a gambling game little better than dice. No longer a metaphor for an idealized body politic, it represents both the act of exchange and the problems attendant on trade. Linked in this manner to other games and discourses of gaming, chess becomes a way for writers, like the anonymous author of the *Tale of Beryn*, to address rising fifteenth-century concerns about the tensions between personal gain and common profit, and also about the members of a civic community who pursue the former at the expense of the latter.

Yet not all English writers were eager to abandon Jacobus's model, and other works from the fifteenth century reveal an ambivalence about the game and the allegory it engendered. Thomas Hoccleve's *Regement of Princes*, written in the early part of the century, is perhaps the most telling in this regard. In this work Hoccleve capitalizes on the game's links to economic exchange and profit at the same time that he hints at its potential to model a viable political state. Later in the same century William Caxton demonstrated his own uncertainty about the role of the *Liber*'s chess allegory. In 1474, the year he first translated and printed Jacobus's *Liber* as the *Game and the Playe of the Chesse*, Caxton presented the work as a *speculum regis*, and his prologue positions the text as most applicable to the noble classes. In his 1483 reprint, however, Caxton changed his prologue to echo the *Liber*'s closing injunction to all men to live a moral life, and he promotes the treatise as a work to be read by all members of the political community.

What happened to Jacobus's state-as-chess model in England after Caxton? While it would be a mistake to say that the allegory disappeared altogether, it clearly did not have the same impact that it enjoyed during the first two centuries after its composition. Writers still drew on chess, often using it as shorthand for an idealized political order or as a way to represent the chaos that ensues when political order is destroyed. Nevertheless, the game never again appears as a fleshed-out model of an ideal citizenry in which members are both bound by rules and granted autonomy of action. Chess as an allegory is found only rarely in poetic works, and with the exception of Thomas Middleton's infamous play *A Game at Chess*, chess scenes on the Renaissance stage are comparatively rare, appearing most often as minor glosses to a play's larger thematic concerns.[6] Even *A Game at Chess*, which contains the most extensive allegorical use of the game in Renaissance drama, turns on a specific threat to English national unity. In this instance the black pieces represent the Spanish, the white the English, and the play as a whole came as part of a rash of anti-Spanish propaganda that celebrated the failed marriage contract between King James I's son, Prince Charles, and the sister of King Philip IV of Spain. In order to make sure the audience would see the Black Knight as the Spanish ambassador, Don Diego Sarmiento de Acuña (by this time also the Conde de Gondomar), the company either obtained or built a replica of the ambassador's famous sedan chair, which had a seat designed to accommodate his fistula.[7] As suggested by this attention to detail, the game's meaning derives more from the figures that occupy the roles than from our expectations of the pieces themselves.

Middleton's use of chess emblematizes a broader shift in the ways the Renaissance stage figured political issues. Whereas drama in earlier eras concerned itself primarily with man's spiritual state, English drama in the late sixteenth and early seventeenth centuries addresses the concerns formerly circulating through the game. A genre that featured kings, queens, bishops, and all other members of the civic order, drama became the most powerful way to represent the social order and to envision its potential for (in)stability. As Michael Hattaway has noted, theater is *re*presentation; "kings become 'subjects' in the sense that the monarchy and many other institutions become the subjects of the playwrights' analytic endeavours."[8] Where once the chessboard had served as a place to represent the negotiations between different members of a civic order, the stage now provided a space where "a changing, troubled, and divided society" could articulate its political conflicts.[9]

If a displacement of political symbolism from board to stage provides one possible explanation for the waning of the *Liber*'s metaphor, the changes in the game itself may provide another. The increased power of the queen and bishop in the fifteenth century made the game into a more challenging and fast-paced contest, and these new rules spread quickly throughout Europe.[10] H. J. R. Murray argues that in Italy and Spain by 1510, "the old game was obsolete in all places in the main stream of life."[11] In France and England, change came soon after, with the last evidence of the earlier rules coming in the form of old problems (1530–40 in France and 1529 in England). This change in rules led to a commensurate change in the game's literature. Production of Jacobus's *Liber*, which was not printed in English after Caxton's 1483 edition, soon ceased altogether.[12] Meanwhile, chess rule books became extremely popular. To quote Murray yet again: "Henceforward [i.e., after the late fifteenth century] *analysis*—the investigation into the effectiveness of different methods of commencing the game—becomes the ruling motive in the literature of chess."[13] A late sixteenth-century manuscript currently housed in Göttingen is emblematic of this change. The first part of the manuscript describes openings, while the second contains thirty problems, each with a diagram and a solution. Rather than allegorizing the game, this manuscript and many others that followed instead dwelled on strategy.[14]

A few of these texts try to preserve the game's allegorical valences while offering instructions for artful play. *Chesse-play*, a 1597 English edition of Pedro Damiano's *Questo libro e da imparare giocare a scachi et de li partiti*, a collection of problems and openings, opens by telling its readers that chess,

breedeth in the players, a certain study, wit, pollicie, forecast and memorie, not onely in the play thereof, but also in actions of publike governement, both in peace and warre: wherein both Counsellors at home, and Captaines abroad may picke out of these wodden peeces some pretty pollicy, both how to governe their subjects in peace, and howe to leade or conduct lively men in the field in warre.[15]

Here, in a nearly verbatim repetition of the *Liber's* overall lesson, *Chesse-play* links the game to a properly working political system. Nor does the allegory stop here. The opening parts of the book give a metaphorical purpose to the moves of the pieces. A player who wants to learn "the actions of publike governement" must know that the rooks are designed "for the succour of their king" and that the "best pawns" are "next unto the king."[16]

Yet despite this nod to the game's moral valences, the majority of *Chesse-play* covers strategies for playing rather than exempla for living a virtuous life. Perhaps even more telling is John Donne's reaction to this volume. When Donne, as a young man about town, wrote to his friend Henry Wotton, he described this allegorizing impulse as outdated: "Then let us at these mimic antiques jest, / Whose deepest projects, and egregious jests / Are but dull Moralls of a game at Chests" (ll. 22–24).[17] Here Donne casually dismisses the "Moralls" associated with chess and a product of antiquated thought; they belong to an earlier age, not to the seventeenth century.

The relationship between chess's change in rules, the increase in the number of rule books, and the decreasing interest in the game's political valences is, I should add, ultimately unclear. Did the rapid adoption of the new rules and the flurry of rule books that followed lead to a rethinking of the game and its metaphorical uses? Or did the increase in the queen's power suggest that larger social changes, ones that would have affected *any* version of the chess game, were already afoot? It is not possible to answer this with any certainty. Yet whatever the cause, it is clear that the change in the game's rules coincided with its altered cultural role. Moreover, the shifted emphasis in chess literature from repeated scenes of playing and extended allegories to lengthy rule books—it is telling in this regard that I have had to omit so many medieval stories that feature the game yet did not feel so restricted with early modern instances of chess play—suggests that the game itself was in the process of acquiring a new meaning in Western culture.

This is not to say that chess completely lost its metaphorical power; the game continued to appear in a variety of texts and contexts. In her *Way of Perfection* Teresa of Avila uses the game to describe the way a nun should use her humility as a queen to checkmate the "divine king" on the board.[18] In Francesco Colonna's *Hypnerotomachia poliphili* and in Rablais's *Cinquiesme livre de Pantagruel*, chess appears as a ballet of thirty-two players, sixteen in gold and sixteen in silver, who dance three games, each successive match increasing in tempo, in order to teach the protagonist a lesson in reason.[19]

Nor did the chessboard cease to model an idealized state: in Shakespeare's *The Tempest* and Middleton's *A Game at Chess*, chess performs ideological work similar to that found in the *Liber*. In *The Tempest*, the overarching narrative poses general questions about the license and limits of governance. How should a ruler act? How should power be distributed? When Ferdinand and Miranda play chess in the play's final act, they do so because as the future rulers of Milan and Naples they need to learn how to organize and negotiate secular power.[20] *The Game of Chess* is no less forthright its use of chess to represent civic order, only this time the order itself has gone awry. The plot opens with the thwarted rape of the White Queen's Pawn by the Black Bishop's Pawn, an action that mirrors the Black King's plans to capture the White Queen and defeat the entire White kingdom.

An even more explicit emphasis on the capacity for chess to act in an equalizing manner appears in Nicholas Breton's "The Chesse Play," a 72-line poem included in a collection titled *The Phoenix Nest*, by Richard Stapleton. In this short poem Breton describes each piece as emblematic of a specific quality. At first, it seems that the king is the most important figure, who "overlooketh all his men" and only "steps among them now and then" when it is time for the check.[21] Yet near the poem's end, Breton warns at the end that even the pawns, which he describes as "sillie swaines" can "lay their traines, / To catch a great man in a trap."[22] And in William Cartwright's short 1643 treatise *The Game at Chesse: A Metaphoricall Discourse Shewing the Present Estate of this Kingdome*, the state is once again compared to the chessboard, with the white pieces representing the parliamentary armies and the black ones the cavaliers.[23]

Yet despite the proliferation of references, the game never seemed to regain the figurative capital it had in earlier eras. Breton's remarks about the pawn's power are motivated by his interest in the game's strategy more than its allegorical uses; as the poem's last two lines warn, "loose not the Queene, for ten to one, / If she be lost, the game is gone."[24] And Cartwright's use of the chess, like Middleton's in *A Game at Chess*, is a way of talking about a specific historical moment rather than of presenting a universal theory of political order. It is, I think, telling that in Shakespeare's vast corpus, no character ever utters the word "chess" or makes a direct reference to the game.[25] At the same time, "check" and "pawn," terms that were formerly associated with chess, appear in his plays most often in non-gaming context; honor, life, blood, and ducats are pawned, or deposited as a pledge, while emotions and actions are held in check.

The fact that Shakespeare does not continually feature chess is in itself no indication of the game's devaluation as an allegory. After all, as I noted in an earlier chapter, Chaucer's references to the game are minimal. What *is* notable is the way Shakespeare uses terms formerly associated almost exclusively with the chessboard that have acquired meanings independent of the game. That someone can "pawn" one's honor or hold one's emotions in "check" suggests that words once commonly associated with the game were now valued for their other meanings, meanings that were connected to the discourses of personal action and power.[26]

This detachment of these terms from the game points to one final reason chess in early modern England might have lost the symbolic weight it had in Jacobus's *Liber*, namely that its argument for associative polity was no longer needed. Much has been made of the ways the Tudor and Stuart monarchs worked to centralize power. As one standard historical narrative goes, English society from the late fifteenth through the early eighteenth centuries experienced the rise of an absolutist polity that worked to curtail individual rights.[27] This emphasis on royal-prerogative absolutism might also have contributed to the promotion of the state-as-body metaphor, with the king firmly situated at the head, or even in the rewriting of the chess metaphor altogether. In the speech to Parliament that heads this chapter, James I, whose claim that "[Kings] have power to exalt low things, and abase high things, and make of their subjects like men at the Chesse" reveals a desire for unmediated power over his people, a lesson that one does not find in the *Liber*.

However, this historical narrative takes the idea of early modern absolutism too far. Rulers such as Elizabeth and James may have worked to consolidate power and to promote themselves as the ultimate authorities on earth. But even as they trumpeted the divine right of kings, they also worked to court favor, please their supporters, and foster the kingdom's economic stability; they also faced resistance to their attempts at social control.[28] In short, while sixteenth- and early seventeenth-century English subjects may have found themselves confronted by various and repressive tools of monarchial governance, these same subjects also had increasing power to affect the social order.[29] James himself inadvertently reveals his own dependence on the members of "his" civic body in the second part of his quote, where the metaphor he has chosen resists the new meanings he attempts to attach to it. The king may indeed be able to move a pawn in order "to take a Bishop of a Knight, and to cry up, or downe any of their subjects, as they do their money." Yet as his own words make clear, he must rely on his pawn to make his move; he cannot do it alone. In short, the game itself builds in a limit to his action. Not only must he follow a set of rules that governs the movement of many pieces, but the king does not have complete control of the board.

James's remarks point toward more than loss of the game's allegorical power; they demonstrate the increasing ways the game's allegorical and "moral" values were becoming detached from its pieces, which to this day remain frozen into their medieval roles. By the time Benjamin Franklin wrote "The Morals of Chess," a short article, published in 1779, in which he sees the game as a way for individuals to learn "foresight," "circumspection," and "caution," chess had ceased to mirror any sort of political fantasy. The game itself still had pieces that represented a monarchy with its attendant social categories. Yet Franklin does not seem troubled by the possible implications posed by this, viewing the game only as a means of personal betterment.[30] A similar detachment allows contemporary Western cultures to use chess, a game still populated by kings, queens, and knights, to represent a variety of things from terrorist attacks to "sweeps week" on television, from the canniness of "historical materialism" to, as Ferdinand de Saussure uses it, the ways language systems work.[31] Thus ultimately, while we continue to read the game as symbolic of political or social power, this power is now disassociated from the game itself. Or, to regard this from another vantage point, while we continue to rewrite the chess allegory, we do not see a need to rewrite the rules, which have not changed since the late fifteenth century. Chess has become thus ultimately flexible, a game that can be used in multiple symbolic systems yet perhaps because of this malleability, now both full of meaning and simultaneously meaningless.

Notes

Introduction

1. "He who wished might play as he pleased. / And so for the nonce it stood there / Yet not one of those / high-placed lords dared to approach it" [Hi mochte gaen spelen dies begh*aer*de / Dus laghet d*aer* uptie wile doe / D*aer* ne ghinc niemen of no toe / Van allen gonen hoghen lieden]. *Roman van Walewein*, ed. and trans. David F. Johnson, Garland Library of Medieval Literature 81, ser. A (New York: Garland, 1992), ll. 50–53. The italicized letters are used by Johnson to indicate the words he has expanded from their abbreviated forms found in the original manuscript.

2. Several readers have noticed the parallels between this poem and the Middle English *Sir Gawain and the Green Knight*. Bart Besamusca compares the two poems in order to chart the changes made to Gawain's personality in later works ("Gauvain as Lover in the Middle Dutch Verse Romance *Walewein*," in *The Arthurian Yearbook II*, ed. Keith Busby (New York: Garland, 1992), 3–12. Felicity Riddy argues that the two poems' similarities stem from "common sources in French romance" ("Giving and Receiving: Exchange in the *Roman van Walewein* and *Sir Gawain and the Green Knight*," *Tijdschrift voor Nederlandse Taal-en Letterkunde* (*TNTL*), 112, 1 (1996): 18–29, at 21. For a good study on the crossovers between the English and Dutch literary traditions, see *England and the Low Countries in the Late Middle Ages*, ed. Caroline Barron and Nigel Saul (New York: St. Martin's Press, 1995). That the *Gawain* poem itself resembles a chess match has been noted by Thomas Rendall, who argues that "the game of chess provided the poet with a strikingly appropriate metaphor for his story's central actions." "Gawain and the Game of Chess," *Chaucer Review* 27, 2 (1992): 186–99, at 197.

3. A writer named Penninc composed the majority of the poem; a second writer named Pieter Vostaert finished it.

4. In the introduction to his edition of *Walewein*, Johnson offers a comprehensive overview of scholarship on the *Walewein* poem and summarizes the contrasting arguments of J. D. Janssens and J. H. Winkelman thus: According to Janssens, the appearance of the mysterious chess set at Arthur's court, Cardoel (alternately called Carlion), "lays bare a fundamental polarity: the courtly Arthurian world versus the uncourtly Otherworld; *ordo*, the Arthurian ideal, versus *inordinatio*, the reality of the Otherworld" (xxviii). For Janssens, the Otherworld calls into question the ability of Arthur's court to maintain its *ordo*. But, as he argues, Walewein's travels ultimately ensure its dissemination and dominance over the *inordinatio* of the Otherworld. J. H. Winkelman dismisses Janssens's characterization of the Otherworld as a space distinct from Arthur's realm because it elides the problem

of the *inordinatio* found within Arthur's court itself. Pointing to the cowardice of Arthur's knights, Winkelman argues that the chess set's appearance reveals the court's weaknesses rather than its strengths: "The purpose of the quest is to make good the inner failing [of the court], and the outer loss of face, brought to light by the appearance of the chess-set" (xxxi). For both of these readers, then, chess marks a conspicuous lack of political order in Arthur's court.

5. "Beter dan al Aerturs rike" (*Roman van Walewein*, l. 62).

6. As Walewein rides off, Kay mocks him for his failure to grab the chessboard—"Haddi ghenomen enen draet / Ende hadde den ant scaec ghestrect / So mochtijt nu hebben ghetrect / Dat u niet ne ware ontvaren" [If you had taken a cord / and had tied it to the chessboard, / you might now be able to reel it in / so that it would not have escaped you] (ll. 176–79). Kay's criticisms are echoed several scenes later when the rightful owner of the chess set, King Wonder, makes essentially the same assertion.

7. For a more detailed reading of this story, see my "Pieces of Power: Medieval Chess and Male Homosocial Desire," *Journal of English and Germanic Philology* 103, 2 (April 2004): 197–214.

8. H. J. R. Murray observes that, based on philological evidence, the knowledge of chess reached Europe "outside the Iberian peninsula certainly at an earlier date than 1000 A.D., and probably earlier than 900 also." *A History of Chess* (Oxford: Oxford University Press, 1913), 402. It is unclear whether chess reached Europe through Italy or through Spain, although it seems likely that it was a combination of both.

9. Murray writes: "During the latter part of the Middle Ages, and especially from the thirteenth to the fifteenth century, chess attained to a popularity in Western Europe which has never been excelled, and probably never equalled at any later date" (*A History of Chess*, 428).

10. Ibid., 452. Although other historians have given broad overviews of the early rules of chess, my description of the medieval game comes from ibid., 452–85.

11. Pawns in the medieval game, like those in modern chess, could advance one square vertically, although they had no power to advance two squares on their opening move.

12. In some regions the names *femina, virgo,* and *mulier* were used for the queen, while *domina* was often used to describe a promoted pawn (Murray, *A History of Chess*, 425–27).

13. European players also began to experiment with new rules. As early at 1100 the use of a checkered board became common, and by 1485 the bishop and queen had, in most regions, increased their powers. Nevertheless, it is important to remember that chess rules varied regionally. Thus while some Italian players could advance the king diagonally three squares or more on his first move, Spanish players around the same time could only move the king one square at a time. In her *Birth of the Chess Queen* (New York: HarperCollins, 2004), Marilyn Yalom traces the transformation of the queen from the weakest piece to the strongest, a transition that she sees as probably occurring in fifteenth-century Spain under the rule of Isabella of Castile. Mark N. Taylor has argued for a more general and uneven transformation of the rule. "How Did the Queen Go Mad?" paper presented at the Thirty-Ninth International Congress on Medieval Studies, Kalamazoo, Mich., May 2004.

14. The Lewis chessmen date from the twelfth century and were discovered in the nineteenth century on the Isle of Lewis, an island off the coast of Scotland. The "Charlemagne chessmen" date from either the eleventh or twelfth century, long after Charlemagne's rule, and were housed for a long time at the abbey at St. Denis. In an appendix to one of his chapters, Murray notes that he has "collected many references to chess-sets in inventories, wills, and accounts of the period from 1100–1600" (*A History of Chess*, 447). Unfortunately, he does not offer a complete list of these, nor does he indicate exactly how many he had found. Among the earliest wills and inventories that he does list, however, are: Count Siboto II of Falkenstein (1180), King Edward I (1299–1300), Roger de Mortimer (1322), Count William of Holland (1343), Hugh Despenser (1397), King Martin of Aragon (1410), Prince Carlos of Viana (1461), and Charles the Bold, Duke of Burgundy (ca. 1467).

15. Murray notes that he collected more than fifty references to the game from the twelfth century. He then adds: "From thirteenth-century works I have collected well over a hundred allusions to the game which establish its popularity from Italy to Iceland and from Portugal to Livonia" (428).

16. Literary examples of low-born players include the steward who plays chess with Guy in *Guy of Warwick*, the grooms who play in *Elie de St. Gille*, the sergeants who play in *Durmart*, and the jailer who plays with Floire in *Floire et Blancheflor*. Examples of female players include Guilliadun, who is being taught to play in Marie de France's *Eliduc*; Yvorin's daughter, who has beaten many men at the game and who nearly defeats Huon in the Charlemagne romance, *Huon de Bordeaux*; the unnamed lady who plays in *Les Echecs amoureux*; and the lady Fesonas in Jacques de Longuyon's *Vœux du Paon*. Although we cannot assume that such depictions were realistic, it seems logical that a game of the nobility eventually "extended to the other members of a castle household" (ibid., 439).

17. Ibid., 428. For Maimonides on chess, see 446–47. Both Maimonides and the fourteenth-century rabbi Kalonymos b. Kalonymos disapproved of the game but "failed to influence the general attitude towards chess" (446).

18. That various texts, in particular romances, represent the game as simultaneously popular and noble does not necessarily mean that everyone played it; one only has to think of well-respected books that sit unopened on coffee tables in our own time to know that popularity does not always indicate active interaction. Yet regardless of the number of actual players, the fact that chess surfaces and resurfaces in literary and nonliterary texts indicates its dominant role in medieval culture.

19. "E por que el acedrex es más assessegado juego e onrra(n)do que los dados nin las tablas, fabla en este libro primeramientre de él." Alfonso X El Sabio, *Libros del ajedrez, dados y tablas*, facsimile reproduction by Vincent García Editores, S. A. Valencial—Ediciones Poniente, 2 vols. (Madrid, 1987). The translation has been provided by Karen Upchurch. Similar references to the game as a noble one appears in other problem sets of the time such as the *Bonus Socius* (Good Companion), which credits the invention of the game to a Trojan knight and his lady who played during the siege of Troy. The author of the pseudo-Ovidian *De vetula*, who similarly locates the game's origins at Troy (although in this case the credit goes to Ulysses, who creates it to stave off his soldiers' boredom) insists: "Cest gieu est noble et honourable, / Non suspect et non dommagable" [This game is noble and honorable, / not suspicious

and harmful]. He goes on to chastise those who play chess for money. This citation comes from a thirteenth-century French translation of *De vetula*, titled *La Vieille; ou, Les Derniers amours d'Ovide (Poëme français du XIVe siècle traduit du Latin de Richard de Fournival)*, ed. Hippolyte Cocheris (Paris: August Aubry, 1861), ll. 1647–48.

20. Although one might legitimately wonder if medieval audiences would see a romance and a problem set, both secular texts designed for entertainment, as fundamentally dissimilar.

21. The title of Jacobus's book varies in both medieval manuscripts and modern scholarship. Some readers refer to the text as the *Libellus* (Marie Anita Burt, Raymond D. Di Lorenzo, Thomas Kaeppeli, Carol S. Fuller), others use the word *Liber* (H. J. R. Murray, Alain Collet, Jean-Michel Mehl, William E. A. Axon), while library catalogs most often drop the first word altogether, listing this text as *De ludo scachorum*. The word *scachorum* is itself subject to contention, with some readers preferring *scachorum* (Burt, Yalom), some *scaccorum* (Kaeppeli, Mehl), and at least one *schachorum* (Di Lorenzo) and another *scacchorum* (Collet). In the interest of ease, I refer throughout *Power Play* to Jacobus's treatise as the *Liber*.

22. Such manuscript versions include the Bibliothèque Nationale Latin MS 10286, a fourteenth-century Latin manuscript that contains 290 problems followed by the *Liber*, and Dresden 059, a late fourteenth-century manuscript ruined during the Second World War that contained a collection of problems and a French translation of Jacobus. See Murray, *A History of Chess*, 607, 621. A copy of the Dresden manuscript is available in the John G. White collection of the Cleveland Public Library.

23. Murray's *A History of Chess* contains a long discussion of chess literature. Yet Murray, whose penchant for listing is hard to match, simply divides various works into "moralities" and "romances" without saying how one might affect the other, or how both might relate to similar cultural factors or philosophical movements. And while literary scholars have produced insightful readings of chess games in particular romances or poems, few have carried their conversations beyond a single work.

24. I have taken this phrase from David Wallace's *Chaucerian Polity: Absolutist Lineages and Associational Forms in England and Italy* (Stanford, Calif.: Stanford University Press, 1997).

25. While Wallace moves synchronically, looking at the dialectic between Italian and English modes of secular order, Lee Patterson, who also takes Chaucer as his primary subject, is concerned with the ways that "the pilgrims become individuals who have been assigned those functions, men and women enacting externally imposed roles toward which each has his or her own kind of relationship." Patterson, *Chaucer and the Subject of History* (Madison:University of Wisconsin Press, 1991), 27.

26. Michel Zink, "Time and Representation of the Self in Thirteenth-Century Poetry," *Poetics Today* 5, 3 (1984): 627. While Zink is talking in particular about medieval French literature, his observations are equally applicable to other parts of western Europe.

27. Johan Huizinga, *Homo Ludens: A Study of the Play-Element in Culture* (New York: Roy Publishers, 1950). This edition was prepared from the 1944 German edition (published in Switzerland) and from the author's own English translation of the text. The original book was written in 1937 and published in 1938. A similar theory of civilized advancement through play also dominates Herman Hesse's 1943

novel *Das Glasperlenspiel,* or *The Glass Bead Game,* translated into English as *Magister Ludi.* In this novel Hesse imagines a sophisticated society in which the intellectual elite play a sophisticated game synthesizing aesthetic and scientific knowledge. The act of playing this game leads to further enlightenment.

28. *Man, Play, and Games,* trans. Meyer Barash (New York: Free Press of Glencoe, 1961), 6, 5. Caillois's original volume, *Les Jeux et les hommes,* was published in 1958.

29. Ibid., 54.

30. Ibid., 67.

31. "Deep Play: A Few Notes on a Balinese Cockfight," in Clifford Geertz, *The Interpretation of Cultures: Selected Essays* (New York: Basic Books, 1973), 412–53, at 448.

32. Ibid., 436, 449.

33. I should add that Geertz's project is necessarily different from my own. In addition to the large gap of time and culture that separates twentieth-century Bali from thirteenth-century Europe, Geertz had the benefits (and drawbacks) of firsthand spectatorship. By contrast, my sole access to the medieval chess game comes through written, and often incomplete, texts.

34. As the rules changed and the queen's power increased, copies of problem sets had to be updated. Given the relative uniformity of these texts, it seems that most rules were standard throughout Europe by the end of the fifteenth century.

35. The full text of this section reads: "But all these moves he made in vain. / For God made such a Virgin Queen / That he was mated and undone. / When gracious God saw near game's end / That he had neither rook nor bishop / And that the devil in his ravaging / Knights, rooks, queen nor king / Nor even pawns wanted to spare / To the game He deigned to stoop and share / And made a masterful and merciful move / By which He saved all His men" ["Mais toz ces trais fist il en vain. / Car Diex une tele fierce fist / Qui le mata et desconfist. / Quant li douz Diex vit vers le fin / Qu'il n'avoit ne ros ne daufin / Et qu'anemis par son desroi / Chevalier, roc, fierce ne roi / Nes poon n'i voloit laissier, / Au giu se daigna abaisier / Et fist un trait soutil et gent / Par coi rescoust toute sa gent"] (Steven M. Taylor, "God's Queen: Chess Imagery in the Poetry of Gautier de Coinci," *Fifteenth Century Studies* 17 (1990): 403–19, at 413, ll. 216–26. Taylor has taken this from the first volume of the second edition of *Les Miracles de Nostre Dame,* ed. V. Frederic Koenig (Geneva: Libraire Droz, 1966 [vols. 1 and 3], 1961 [vol. 2], 1970 [vol. 4]).

36. "Thenne þe kyng asshet a chekkere, / And cald a damesel dere; / Downe þay sette hom in fere / Opon þe bed syde. / Torches was þer mony light, / And laumpus brennyng full bryghte / Butte notte so hardy was þat knyghte / His hede onus to hide. / Butte fro þay began to play, / Quyle on þe morun þat hit was day, / Euyr he lokette as he lay / Baudewynne to byde. / And erly in the dawyng / Come þay home from huntyng, / And hertis conne þay home bring, / And buckes of pride." *The Avowing of King Arthur,* ed. Roger Dahood (New York: Garland, 1984], ll. 861–76.

37. "De touz bons trais seit la maniere / Et s'est de traire si maniere / Ses amis trait de tous maus poins" (Taylor, "God's Queen," ll. 305–7).

38. Mary Carruthers, *The Book of Memory: A Study of Memory in Medieval Culture,* Cambridge Studies in Medieval Culture Series (Cambridge: Cambridge University Press, 1990), 14.

39. Wallace, *Chaucerian Polity,* 1.

40. Steven Epstein, *Genoa and the Genoese, 958–1528* (Chapel Hill: University of North Carolina Press, 1996), 65–66.

41. Lauro Martines, "Political Violence in the Thirteenth Century," in *Violence and Civil Disorder in Italian Cities, 1200–1500*, ed. Lauro Martines (Berkeley: University of California Press, 1972), 331–53, at 331.

42. Caxton first published the *Game and Playe of the Chesse*, his translation of Jacobus's *Liber*, in Bruges in 1474, although as I will argue in my final chapter, his reprinting of the text in England in 1483 more fully captures the text's symbolic power.

43. Richard Firth Green traces the emergence of a contractually-based English polity in *A Crisis of Truth: Literature and Law in Ricardian England* (Philadelphia: University of Pennsylvania Press, 1999). Green's focus—he looks specifically at the concept of "trouthe," a word that changed in meaning from "something like 'integrity' or 'dependability'" to "its modern sense of 'conformity to fact'" (xiv)—is much tighter than my own. Nonetheless, his argument that "the beginnings of a modern law of contract in the late thirteenth and fourteenth centuries, so far from marking an advance toward greater social order . . . reflect a breakdown of the established conventions governing personal obligations" (49–50) mirrors (to some extent) my own thinking about the impersonality of a polity based on contractual bonds. It is also telling that Green, when describing this shift, resorts to chess as a metaphor for the mechanistic nature of legal machinery as it was transformed from an oral folk tradition to centralized, written legal codes: "What J. A. [*sic*] Baker has aptly called 'the possible moves in the recondite games of legal chess' became so numerous that play might be spun out almost indefinitely, the attacker's hopes of pinning down an elusive opponent constantly frustrated by a defender only too happy to settle for a stalemate." Green, 139, citing John H. Baker, *An Introduction to English Legal History*, 3rd ed. (London: Butterworths, 1990), 205.

44. *Le Livre des eschez amoureux moralisés*, ed. Françoise Guichard-Tesson and Bruno Roy (Montreal: Éditions CERES, 1993).

45. Ideas about equal exchange were shaped by canon law, which defined interest on loans as usurious and thus sinful. Predictably, lawyers and moral philosophers developed systems to work around such restrictions. Yet this did not stop the church from cracking down on what it saw as a violation of its teaching. By the close of the twelfth century, popular preachers were campaigning against those who charged interest, and Gregory IX's thirteenth-century *Decretals* articulated prohibitions against usury even more stridently. For lengthier treatments of this subject, see J. Gilchrist, *The Church and Economic Activity in the Middle Ages* (London: Macmillan, 1969), and Robert B. Ekelund, Jr., Robert F. Hébert, Robert D. Tollison, Gary M. Anderson, and Audrey B. Davidson, *Sacred Trust: The Medieval Church as an Economic Firm* (Oxford: Oxford University Press, 1996).

46. Larry Scanlon characterizes this type of kingship as "a corporate fiction" in his essay "The King's Two Voices: Narrative and Power in Hoccleve's *Regement of Princes*," in *Literary Practice and Social Change in Britain, 1380–1530*, ed. Lee Patterson (Berkeley: University of California Press, 1990), 216–47, esp. 221.

47. *The Regiment of Princes*, ed. Charles R. Blyth, TEAMS Series (Kalamazoo, Mich.: Medieval Institute Publications, 1999), ll. 2120–21, 2116.

48. Ibid., l. 2139.

49. It should be noted that the first dedicatee, George, Duke of Clarence (and also King Edward IV's brother), had been executed by the time Caxton printed the text in 1483. Yet the death of the first dedicatee does not alone account for Caxton's subsequent decision to address the people of London rather than find another noble patron.

Chapter 1

Epigraph: Louis Althusser, "Ideology and Ideological State Apparatuses (Notes Towards an Investigation)," in *"Lenin and Philosophy," and Other Essays*, trans. Ben Brewster (New York: Monthly Review Press, 1971), 174.

1. A scriptural mention of Evilmerodach appears in 2 Kings 25:27 "And in the thirty-seventh year of the exile of Jehoiachin king of Judah, in the twelfth month, on the twenty-seventh day of the month, Evil-merodach king of Babylon, in the year that he began to reign graciously freed Jehoiachin king of Judah from prison." D. J. Wiseman describes Evilmerodach (Amel-Marduk) as the son of Nebuchadnezzar, who took over his father's throne in 562. *Nebuchadnezzar and Babylon*, Schwich Lectures of the British Academy (Oxford: Oxford University Press, 1985), 9. Wiseman adds that Amel-Marduk's "reign was marred by intrigues, some possibly directed against his father." The historical Nebuchadnezzar, who was the king of Babylon in the sixth century B.C., is famous for his immense building in the city. For a history of the city, an overview of Nebuchadnezzar's contributions to its construction, and several diagrams that highlight its gridlike nature, see ibid., 42–80.

2. Jacobus initially refers to Philometer as "Xerxes" but then reverts to his "Greek" name for most of the rest of the *Liber*. This historical Xerxes was king of Persia and the son of Darius of Persia. In book 7 of his *Histories* Herodotus describes Xerxes' attacks on Egypt and Greece.

3. "O, domine, mi rex, tuam gloriosam vitam desidero, quam videre non possum nisi iustitia et bonis moribus insignitus a populo diligaris" [Oh, lord, my king, I desire that you have a glorious life, but I am not able to see that unless you have justice and good morals and are loved by the people]. Marie Anita Burt, "Jacobus de Cessolis: *Libellus de moribus hominum et officiis nobilium ac popularium super ludo scachorum*," Ph.D. dissertation., University of Texas, Austin, 1957, 9–10. Burt's dissertation is an edition of Jacobus's *Liber* based on four extant Latin manuscripts of the text. It remains the best and most readily available edition of this work, the only other edition I know of being Ernst Köpke's *Mittheilungen aus den Handschriften der Ritter-Akademie zu Brandenburg* (Brandenburg, 1879). All subsequent references to this edition appear in parentheses in the text.

4. Although it was popular in ancient texts such as Plato's *Republic* and *Timaeus*, John of Salisbury was the medieval writer perhaps most responsible for promulgating the state-as-body metaphor. His extended comparison of civil order to a human body lies at the heart of his twelfth-century *Policraticus* (discussed below), and later writers frequently recycled John's treatment of this topic.

5. I realize that the idea of the "self" remains a thorny issue for scholars of medieval and early modern literature, with the latter tending to identify the "self" as

a Renaissance concept unavailable at earlier times and the former mustering considerable ammunition to demonstrate the multifarious "selves" available to medieval individuals. In raising this issue, I am less interested in engaging an argument
about whether individuals in the medieval world had a sense of self—they did—
than I am in showing the ways Jacobus's text complicates this category. On the one
hand, Jacobus conceives of a civic polity where individuals are identified by social
class and/or trade, which runs counter to modern notions of individualism. On the
other hand, Jacobus encourages all men to play, and his allegory suggests that an individual player will be able to locate his own piece, his "self at that particular moment,"
on the board. In short, I am interested in the way that the *Liber's* allegory tries to
regulate an individual self at the same time that it ushers people into collective bodies
via larger categories of identity. For a good outline of this debate, see Lee Patterson's
introduction to *Chaucer and the Subject of History* (Madison: University of Wisconsin
Press, 1991), 3–46. For a response to theorists who see premodern concepts of interiority as either flawed or incomplete, see Katharine Eisaman Maus, *Inwardness and
Theater in the English Renaissance* (Chicago: University of Chicago Press, 1995), 1–35.

6. On bans against the game, see H. J. R. Murray, *A History of Chess* (Oxford:
Oxford University Press, 1913), 441, n. 66.

7. Obviously, Jacobus's text did not cause this shift. Material conditions such
as the growing emphasis on secular governmental affiliations in the late thirteenth
and early fourteenth centuries and changes in economic markets were also con-
tributing factors that had an impact on an individual's public identity. Writing about
the commercialization of the thirteenth-century Italian city-states, Robert S. Lopez
observes that the rise of the tradesman and the new distribution of wealth fueled "a
much closer economic and political collaboration than that between noblemen and
serfs in the manors and many towns outside Italy." *The Commercial Revolution of the
Middle Ages, 950–1350* (Englewood Cliffs, N.J.: Prentice-Hall, 1971), 67. I would argue
that Jacobus's text, written in the context of the Italian commercial growth Lopez
describes, was only embraced in the northern parts of Europe as those areas developed their own commercial centers of trade and experienced commensurate dis-
ruptions in their political and civic organization.

8. The most significant work on this subject is Jean Delumeau's monumental
Sin and Fear (originally *Le Péché et la peur*, 1983), which traces the rising importance
of guilt and shame in Western Europe from the thirteenth through the eighteenth
centuries. See *Sin and Fear: The Emergence of a Western Guilt Culture, 13th–18th Centuries*,
trans. Eric Nicholson (New York: St. Martin's Press, 1990). As Delumeau observes,
the idea of "self-recognition as a sinner" became the dominant way of thinking in
the thirteenth century, a self-recognition that was promoted and reinforced by a flurry
of penance manuals and handbooks written during this time (197). Jacobus's *Liber*
represents a secular appropriation of this fundamentally clerical discourse.

9. Louis Althusser, "Ideology and Ideological State Apparatuses (Notes Towards an Investigation)," in *"Lenin and Philosophy," and Other Essays*, trans. Ben
Brewster (New York: Monthly Review Press, 1971), 174.

10. Burt, "Jacobus de Cessolis," xxix–xxxvii, and Murray, *A History of Chess*,
545–50.

11. Murray, *A History of Chess*, 537.

12. Thanks to an allusion to a statue of Frederick II on a marble gate at Capua, a possible *terminus a quo* for the original manuscript is 1240, the year that Frederick had the statue erected. Murray, who has made this observation, also notes that this reference to the statue was used by the author of the *Gesta romanorum*. He also cites Tassilo von Heydebrand und der Lasa (*Zur Geschichte und Literatur des Schachspiels* (Leipzig: Veit, 1897), who mentions that Jacobus's preference for hereditary succession might have been produced by the interregnum of 1254–73, although given Genoa's relatively isolated status, I find this theory a difficult one to accept (Murray, *A History of Chess*, 539). In a University of Chicago master's thesis, Judith Kolata notes that "Jean-Thiébaut Welter suggests that Cessolis must have written his sermons before 1325 because he speaks favorably of tournaments which were specifically prohibited that year by Pope John XXII's *Extravagantes*." Welter, *L'Exemplum dans la littérature religiuese et didactique du Moyen Age* (Paris: Occitania, 1927), 351, cited by Kolata, "Livre des Echecs Moralisés," master's thesis, University of Chicago, 1987, 5. As for a *terminus ad quem*, Burt notes that the earliest extant metrical translations of the text appeared in German in the 1320s and 1330s. These include the undated *Das Schachgedichte*, *Das Schachbuch des Pfarrers zu dem Hechte*, and Kunrats von Ammenhausen's *Schachzabelbuch* (Burt, xxx–xxxi).

13. My history of Italy at this time comes primarily from W. F. Butler, *The Lombard Communes* (London: T. Fisher Unwin, 1906); Dorothy Muir, *A History of Milan Under the Visconti* (London: Methuen, 1924); Daniel Waley, *The Italian City-Republics* (New York: McGraw-Hill, 1969); Lauro Martines, ed., *Violence and Civil Disorder in Italian Cities, 1200–1500* (Berkeley: University of California Press, 1972); and Steven A. Epstein, *Genoa and the Genoese, 958–1528* (Chapel Hill: University of North Carolina Press, 1996).

14. Thomas Kaeppeli, "Pour la biographie de Jacques de Cessole," *Archivum Fratrum Praedicatorum* 30 (1960): 149–62. As Kaeppeli observes, earlier scholars placed Cessolis in France, specifically at the convent of Rheims, an idea that he traces to a catalogue of Dominican writers composed in the mid-thirteenth century by a certain Laurent Pignon, who lists "Fr. Ioannes de Teryace, de conventu Remensi" as the author of "moralitates super ludum scacorum." Kaeppeli also notes that eighteenth-century historians saw Cessolis as a native of Cessières, a village in the Picard region. For more on Cessolis, in particular his use of Lombard rules, see Murray, *A History of Chess*, 537–38. Part of the difficulty in tracing Cessolis lies in the variants in his name, which include Sessolis, Cessulis, Casulis, Cessoles, Chessolis, Czessalis, Cessalioz, Cassal, Cazzalis, Gazalis, Thessalis, Thessalonia, and Tessalonia (Burt, "Jacobus de Cessolis," xxiv).

15. *Hunc autem libellum ad honorem et solatium nobelium et maxime ludum sciendum, ego frater Jacobus de Cessolis ordinis praedicatorum composui.* This is recorded in MS Vat. lat. 1042, a fourteenth-century manuscript at the Vatican Library. This introduction is cited in Raymond D. Di Lorenzo, "The Collection Form and the Art of Memory in the *Libellus Super Ludo Schachorum* of Jacobus de Cessolis," *Mediaeval Studies* 35 (1973): 205, n. 1.

16. In addition to Kaeppeli and Murray, see Joan Morton Jones, *The Chess of Love* (Old French Text with Commentary), Ph.D. dissertation, University of Nebraska, 1968, xxiv–xxviii.

17. See Kaeppeli, "Pour la biographie de Jacques de Cessole," 154. Kaeppeli further speculates that a second mention of Jacobus as "de Ast" confirms that the author was from the province of Asti in which the town of Cessole is located (155).

18. Although the *podestà's* power was usually concentrated in the cities, his control often extended into the countryside.

19. Milan, primarily a Guelf city in the first half of the thirteenth century, had become Ghibelline by the end of the second half.

20. Butler, *The Lombard Communes*, 346.

21. Although Genoa is currently in the Liguria region, medieval Liguria encompassed a larger expanse of land, including "parts of the Lombard plain now in Lombardy or Piedmont" (Epstein, *Genoa and the Genoese*, 10).

22. Ibid., 20–21.

23. Ibid., 115. The faction was led by Guglielmo de Mari, who led his followers to the heart of the city and occupied its primary buildings.

24. Ibid., 116.

25. If Jacobus did indeed write his treatise in Genoa, he did so during a flourishing of literary production that might also have come out of Genoa's political and social changes. Among the works that date from the last part of the thirteenth century are: Giovanni Balbi's *Catholicon*, an encyclopedic work composed in 1286 and modeled on Isidore of Seville's *Etymologiae*; Jacobus Doria's chronicle of the city's history, completed in 1294; and Jacobus de Voragine's *Legenda aurea* (Golden Legend), which was composed in the early 1260s. Of these, the *Legenda* enjoyed the greatest popularity throughout Europe, and William Caxton's fifteenth-century English translation alone was printed nine times between 1483 and 1527. What Jacobus de Cessolis did for the genre of the *speculum regis*, Jacobus de Voragine did for the genre of saints' lives, expanding the canon of traditional stories to include newer saints who came from lay origins and/or from the lower classes of society. For more on this particular aspect of the *Legenda*, see Sherry L. Reames, *The* Legenda Aurea: *A Reexamination of Its Paradoxical History* (Madison: University of Wisconsin Press, 1985), 197–209. For a brief discussion of Genoese culture and authors at the end of the thirteenth century, see Epstein, *Genoa and the Genoese*, 160–74.

26. Epstein, *Genoa and the Genoese*, 149. As Epstein describes it, Boccanegra, the first "captain" of the city, helped the city's finances by creating what was in effect a system of public bond whereby creditors would receive a set amount of interest for the life of their loan to the city. This capped the rate at which the wealthy could collect on the work of the merchants who underwent the risk of trade. Or rather, trade loans became state sponsored rather than privately sponsored. Boccanegra used the profits from this to build public buildings for government, which "symbolized the rise of public power in Genoa; as the new palace rose, so too did the *popolo*" (149).

27. Ibid., 149.

28. This struggle could be said to have originated with Pope Gregory's (1073–85) reform movement, which tried to expand papal power.

29. In a good synopsis of this conflict, Antony Black notes that the rift between Philip and Boniface "gave rise to a flurry of theoretical writings" (Black, *Political Thought in Europe, 1250–1450* [Cambridge: Cambridge University Press, 1992], 49).

For a more extended discussion, see R. W. Dyson's introduction to his translation of James of Viterbo's *On Christian Government (De regimine Christiano)* (Woodbridge: Boydell Press, 1995), iv-xvi.

30. Similarly supportive of the pope's leadership, James's *De regimine Christiano*, most likely written a year or two after *De ecclesiastica potestate*, is at once less shrill and less vehement than its predecessor. Although unwilling to call a ruler unsanctioned by the pope illegitimate, James views pontifical power as more perfect and thus higher than its secular counterpart. Kings, he insists, must follow popes in order to achieve the highest form of perfection before God. This assertion comes at the very end of several tortuous arguments about the nature of power. He finally concludes: "the highest spiritual power, of which kind is the power of the Supreme Pontiff, has primacy over all the pontiffs of all churches, and is also superior in dignity and causality to every temporal power, it can therefore rightly be concluded that in the Supreme Pontiff there pre-exists all fulness of pontifical and royal power" (*De regimine Christiano*, 128). James and Aegidius wrote from positions outside of northern Italy, removed from the orbit of Ghibelline power and the day-to-day violence that plagued the Italian city-states, and sheltered by the protection of the papacy. Such factors inevitably contributed to their support of papal authority. James's *De regimine Christiano* almost undoubtedly earned him his position in Naples, and Aegidius's *De ecclesiastica potestate* is the product of a loyal functionary. Dyson speculates that Boniface "made James of Viterbo an archbishop as a reward for the loyalty attested by the appearance of the treatise" (xvi). But he also adds that *De regimine Christiano* could have come as an expression of gratitude for preferment.

31. Dante's investment in a single ruler finds roots in the author's experience in his native Florence, where he became a victim of papal meddling. Although the city at this time no longer had a huge conflict between the Guelfs and Ghibellines, the Ghibellines having ceased to be a factor in the mid-thirteenth century, the Florentine Guelfs had divided into White and Black factions. Dante was a White Guelf and thus part of the ruling group. Yet in 1301 while he was in Rome trying to mediate between the pope and the Florentine citizens, Charles of Valois entered the city and under orders from Boniface supported the Black Guelf faction. When the Black Guelfs took charge of the city, Dante and many other prominent White Guelfs were exiled. While Dante's support of secular power might have been strengthened by his bitterness at his exile, harder to explain is Marsiglio of Padua's systematic attack on the papacy. Unlike Dante, Marsiglio, who was working as a rector at the University of Paris the same year that *De monarchia* appeared, would have benefited from papal support. Moreover, criticism of the clergy carried with it a certain amount of danger, and it is little surprise that after the publication of his 1324 *Defensor pacis*, Marsiglio had to seek refuge with King Ludwig of Bavaria.

32. Dante Alighieri, *De monarchia*, trans. Richard Kay (Toronto: Pontifical Institute of Mediaeval Studies, 1998), 7. For the Latin version of this text, see page 6 of this edition.

33. While *De monarchia* tears down arguments in favor of papal power, Marsiglio's *Defensor pacis* uses the Italian communes as specific examples of civil "discord" with which "the worst fruits and troubles will befall any civil regime or state." Before the Church overreached its power, Marsiglio writes, "the inhabitants of Italy

lived peacefully together, [and] they experienced those sweet fruits of peace which have been mentioned above, and from and in those fruits they made such great progress that they brought the whole habitable world under sway." See Marsilius of Padua, *Defensor pacis*, ed. and trans. Alan Gewirth (New York: Columbia University Press, 1956); reprint Medieval Academy Reprints for Teaching (Toronto: University of Toronto Press, 1980), 4. His repeated references to clerical control as a "pernicious pestilence" infecting the health of his homeland and his lengthy refutation of key clerical positions make Dante's *De monarchia* seem like a collection of sotto voce suggestions for change. The Church responded accordingly, excommunicating Marsiglio in 1326.

34. In his 1302 *Unam sanctam* Boniface drew on a metaphor of corporeality, arguing that the Church was "one mystical body, the head of which is Christ, and the head of Christ is God" (Leonard Barkan, *Nature's Work of Art: The Human Body as Image of the World* [New Haven, Conn.: Yale University Press, 1975], 74. The representation of the Church as a somatic body stretches back to early Christianity; I will discuss this in more detail later in the chapter.

35. *Defensor pacis*, 63.

36. *De regimine Christiano*, 17.

37. Barkan, *Nature's Work of Art*, 63. For an overview of classical and late antique writers who fleshed out the body metaphor (these included Plato, Aristotle, Cicero, Seneca, and Paul), see pages 61–80 of Barkan's volume.

38. Paul Edward Dutton has argued that the popularity of this image in the twelfth century was brought about by a renewed reading of the third book of Plato's *Timaeus*. As glossed by Calcidius, a writer most likely from the fourth century, Plato's tripartite scheme for society broke down easily into a tripartite bodily division of head (the nobles, who command), the chest (the fighters, who act), and the feet (the lower classes, who are governed). As Dutton observes: "The implications of this scheme for an understanding of the state are important, since a static, hierarchical, and elitist conception of the state could be justified by recourse to the nature of the human body." "*Illustre Civitatis et Populi Exemplum*: Plato's *Timaeus* and the Transmission from Calcidius to the End of the Twelfth Century of a Tripartite Scheme of Society," *Mediaeval Studies* 45 (1983): 79–119, at 85.

39. 1 Corinthians 12:12 (unless otherwise noted, all citations of the Bible are from the RSV).

40. 1 Corinthians 12:14–25.

41. What counts as a *speculum regis* is still being debated. Jean-Philippe Genet, in an attempt to narrow earlier definitions of the *Fürstenspiegel* (*speculum regis* in Latin, *miroir au prince* in French) genre, identifies four "chief characteristics" of a *speculum regis*: the text must be written by a friar, concerned with pedagogy, engaged in questions of ethics and morals, and built on an Aristotelian foundation. He therefore does not include Jacobus as part of this tradition (*Four English Political Tracts, of the Late Middle Ages*, ed. Jean-Philippe Genet [London: Offices of the Royal Historical Society, 1977], xiii–xiv). By contrast, in his introduction to *Caxton's Game and Playe of the Chesse, 1474: A Verbatim Reprint of the First Edition* (London: Elliott Stock, 1893), William E. A. Axon refers to the *Liber* as a mirror and hypothesizes that Jacobus used Aegidius's *De regimine principum* as his model. See ibid., xxviii. Also

see David Hooper and Kenneth Whyld, *The Oxford Companion to Chess* (Oxford: Oxford University Press, 1984), 60. Raymond D. Di Lorenzo calls the *Liber* a part of "the type of medieval didactic literature known as *regimen principem*" in his "The Collection Form and the Art of Memory," 206.

42. Patricia J. Eberle, "Mirror of Princes," *Dictionary of the Middle Ages* **vol. 8**, ed. Joseph S. Strayer (New York: Scribner's 1987), 435. Eberle is my source for many of the texts I discuss in this paragraph. See also Genet, *Four English Political Tracts*, xii. The popularity of this genre is evinced in the 350 (or so) extant manuscripts of Aegidius's *De regimine*, a book that, like Jacobus's *Liber de ludo scachorum*, enjoyed a wide circulation throughout Europe.

43. Antony Black's introduction to his *Political Thought in Europe* (1–13) contains a good, brief description of this explosion of political writings in the late Middle Ages.

44. Some writers positioned the monarch as the heart of the kingdom, although in these cases the heart, in keeping with medieval custom, contained the attributes we normally assign to the head or brain.

45. Cary Nederman offers a brief outline of John's career in his introduction to his *Policraticus: Of the Frivolities of Courtiers and the Footprints of Philosophers*, ed. and trans. Cary J. Nederman, Cambridge Texts in the History of Political Thought, (Cambridge: Cambridge University Press, 1990), xvi–xviii. For a more detailed account of John's very complicated relationship to Henry and to the major Church leaders at this time, see Christopher Brooke, "John of Salisbury and His World," in *The World of John of Salisbury*, ed. Michael Wilks (Oxford: Blackwell, 1984), 1–20.

46. As Nederman notes: "Books Five and Six, comprising some one hundred and seventy five pages in the critical edition of the *Policraticus*, are in fact wholly devoted to a microscopic dissection of the 'parts' of the polity employing terminology drawn from the model of the human organism." Nederman, "The Physiological Significance of the Organic Metaphor in John of Salisbury's *Policraticus*," *History of Political Thought* 8, 2 (Summer 1987): 211–23, at 212.

47. *Policraticus*, ed. and trans. Nederman, 66. Although I cite from Nederman's abridged edition of the *Policraticus*, I have also consulted John Dickenson's translation of books 4, 5, and 6 (and portions of 7 and 8) in *The Statesman's Book* (New York: Russell and Russell, 1963), and Joseph B. Pike's translation of books 1, 2, and 3 (and portions of 7 and 8) in *The Frivolities of Courtiers and the Footprints of Philosophers* (Minneapolis: University of Minnesota Press, 1938), which together contain nearly the complete text.

48. *Policraticus*, ed. and trans. Nederman, 67.

49. Ibid., 76.

50. John puts pressure on his metaphor to justify his support of tyrannicide in the event that a king rules unjustly. As he explains, the health of the whole body is more important that the well being of one part, even if that one part is the ruler.

51. *Policraticus*, ed. and trans. Nederman, 25.

52. Black, *Political Thought in Europe*, 17.

53. *Policraticus*, ed. and trans. Nederman, 175–80.

54. Antony Black, *Guilds and Civil Society in European Political Thought from the Twelfth Century to the Present* (Ithaca, N.Y.: Cornell University Press, 1984), 4.

The *Policraticus* continued to influence the authors of even later *specula*. Christine de Pizan used John as the primary source for her comparison of the state to a human body in *Le Livre du corps de policie*, composed between 1406 and 1407. Christine does not cite John directly, although she attributes her body analogy to the (fictitious) letter from Plutach to Trajan that appears in the *Policraticus*. The emphasis on corporeality that appears in the title of this work carried over into the English translation of Christine's work, *The Body of Polycye*, which most likely appeared in the mid- to late-fifteenth century. See *The Middle English Translation of Christine de Pisan's Livre du Corps de Policie*, ed. Diane Bornstein (Heidelburg: Carl Winter, 1977), 40.

55. Black argues that *De regno* was, with the exception of the first chapter, probably not written by Aquinas (*Political Thought*, 22). By contrast, John Finnis thinks that *De regno*, although "written in a style unlike Aquinas' academic works in philosophy and theology," was "probably authentic" (*Aquinas: Moral, Political, and Legal Theory* [Oxford: Oxford University Press, 1998], 228). Although I have used the edition of *De regno* found in *Aquinas: Selected Political Writings*, ed. A. P. D'Entrèves, trans. J. G. Dawson (Oxford: Blackwell, 1948), for both the original text and the translation, I should note that Paul Sigmund's translation of this chapter in *St. Thomas Aquinas on Politics and Ethics* (New York: Norton, 1988), 14–17, is very similar.

56. "Naturale autem est homini ut sit animal sociale et politicum" (*De regno*, in *Aquinas*, ed. D'Entrèves and trans. Dawson, 2–3).

57. Ibid., 10–13.

58. "Hoc igitur officium rex suscepisse cognoscat, ut sit in regno sicut in corpore anima, et sicut Deus in mundo" (ibid., 66–67).

59. Ibid.

60. Ibid., 80–81.

61. "Unde impossibile est quod bonum commune civitatis bene se habeat, nisi cives sint virtuosi" (*Summa theologica* 2.93.3; *Aquinas*, ed. D'Entrèves and trans. Dawson, 118–19).

62. *Summa theologica* 2.96.2; 134–35.

63. Writing of the type of governance outlined by Aquinas, Finnis notes that that "law needs to be present in the minds not only of those who make it but also of those to whom it is addressed—present if not actually, at least habitually—as the traffic laws are in the minds of careful drivers who conform to them without actually thinking about them. The subjects of the law share (willingly or unwillingly) in at least the conclusions of the rulers' practical thinking and in the plan which the rulers propose (reasonably and truthfully or unreasonably and falsely) as a plan for promoting and/or protecting common good" (*Aquinas: Moral, Political, and Legal Theory*, 256–57).

64. From the Norman Anonymous, *De consecratione pontificum et regnum*, ca. 1100, cited by Ernst Kantorowicz, *The King's Two Bodies: A Study in Mediaeval Political Theology* (Princeton, N.J.: Princeton University Press, 1957), 46.

65. Kantorowicz cites John of Paris's thirteenth-century *De potestate regia et papali* (*The King's Two Bodies*, 103).

66. Kantorowicz offers a good general summary of this shift in *The King's Two Bodies*, 96–97.

67. Early modern scholars have made similar arguments against Kantorowicz's

tendency to read the king's political body as a representation of centralized, royal power. Lorna Hutson, who has looked specifically at his reading of Edmund Plowden's 1571 *Commentaries*, argues that Kantorowicz's narrow view of this work "led him to ignore the extent to which the vision of the 'weale publique' that emerges from the text actually marginalizes, rather than makes central the symbolic power of the monarch. "Not the King's Two Bodies: Reading the 'Body Politic' in Shakespeare's *Henry IV*, Parts 1 and 2," in *Rhetoric and Law in Early Modern Europe*, ed. Victoria Kahn and Lorna Hutson (New Haven, Conn.: Yale University Press, 2001), 166–98, at 176. David Norbrook also criticizes similar aspects of *The King's Two Bodies* in "The Emperor's New Body? *Richard II*, Ernst Kantorowicz, and the Politics of Shakespeare Criticism," *Textual Practice* 10.2 (1996): 329–57.

68. In his introduction to *Caxton's Game and Playe of the Chesse*, William E. A. Axon sees Aegidius's *De regimine principum* as Jacobus's primary influence (Axon, xxviii). By contrast Murray claims that Axon's suggestion is "impossible," citing the composition dates of the works as roughly contemporaneous. Instead, Murray argues that "the whole style of Cessolis's sermon is modelled upon [the latter] part of the *Polycraticus*" (Murray, *A History of Chess*, 541, n. 27).

69. To my knowledge, there is no critical Latin edition of this text. I have thus used John Trevisa's Middle English translation of the work. In that version this passage reads: "Therfore in moral matir the processe mote be by evydens and figures and liknes. For theigh this book be itytled of the lore of princes, yut al the puple schal be itaught þerby; and theigh nought eueriche man may be kyng oþer prince, yit everich man schulde desire besiliche to make / himself worthi to be a kyng oþer a prince." *The Governance of Kings and Princes: John Trevisa's Middle English Translation of the* De Regimine Principum *of Aegidius Romanus*, ed. David C. Fowler, Charles F. Briggs, and Paul G. Remley (New York: Garland, 1997), 7.

70. Ibid.

71. Ibid., 58 and 118.

72. Ibid., 295, 300, 411, 59.

73. That Philip successfully imposed a kingdom-wide sales tax without the help of a standing army or large police force testifies both to his power and to the increasing belief in the French realm as a unified body politic worth preserving. Philip and his ministers worked hard to promote this idea, and they used various types of propaganda to depict the *regnum* as a type of sovereign state. For a complete history of Philip's administrative power, see Joseph R. Strayer's *The Reign of Philip the Fair* (Princeton, N.J.: Princeton University Press, 1980). Synopsizing such changes in the nature of governmental power, Strayer observes: "The reign of Philip the Fair marked the point when the balance of loyalty definitely swung toward the secular sovereign state" (xii-xiii).

74. "Eche citeseyn schulde kunne rewle his owne hous and maynye not onlich for suche reulyng is his owne profit but also for such reulyng is iordeyned to þe comyn profit as to þe profit of regne and of citee" (*The Governance of Kings and Princes*, 168).

75. The full Latin text reads: "Multorum fratrum ordinis et diversorum saecularium precibus persuasus, dudum munus requisitum negavi ut transcriberem solatiosum ludum" (3).

76. Jacobus did not create his exempla but borrowed them from numerous authors including Cicero, Ovid, Seneca, and most significantly, Valerius Maximus, from whom he takes at least forty-eight items. For a list of his sources, see Burt, "Jacobus de Cessolis," xix–xxi.

77. I am thinking here of Bernard Williams's account of shame as a feeling that plays on "a sense of who one is and of what one hopes to be." Unlike guilt, shame operates visually, which is to say it turns on the publicness of one's actions and the subsequent loss of power that comes from unprotected external scrutiny. Moreover, shame, unlike guilt, incorporates the potential for self-correction and can lead directly to attempts to improve one's behavior. *Shame and Necessity* (Berkeley: University of California Press, 1993), 102. My short summary cannot do justice to Williams's very complex ideas about shame and shame culture that he sketches in the chapter titled "Shame and Autonomy," 75–102, and in his first endnote, 219–23.

78. In an unpublished conference paper, "Space and the Body: The *Jeu des Echecs Moralisee*," Michael Camille argues that "the eight pawns and their neatly-packed collection of trades and activities are misrepresentations of the historical situation" (11). The board thus oversimplifies an increasingly disparate number of crafts—Camille identifies 130 regulated trades in Paris in 1292—each of which competed with the others for political status and economic power. Yet while I agree with Camille that the game serves as an inaccurate gauge of actual practice, my argument turns on the *possibility* for a reader to identify himself as a piece and also on the ways the board reflects the emerging power of a bourgeois class. (The same argument could be made about Barbie and her "trades." Like Jacobus's description of the pawns, Barbie dolls misrepresent historical reality. Although seeking to include all possible female identities, the dolls inevitably invite young girls to imagine themselves as living within a limited number of preset lifestyles, and also within the confines of an anatomically impossible body.) As Camille himself notes in a later section of the same paper, the 1358 Jacquerie occurred shortly after the *Liber* was translated into French (12). Many thanks to Michael for passing this paper along to me while I was in his class.

79. While expensive sets did use human shapes for the *nobilis* (e.g., the famous twelfth-century Lewis Chessmen), most sets differentiated all figures only by general shape. Murray has a good chart outlining the illustrations of chess pieces from five different manuscripts (Murray, *A History of Chess*, 769).

80. "Fideles et legales eos esse necesse est. Quanta namque eis committuntur, non solum metalla, verum etiam navigantibus humana corpora et pecunia fabris committitur" [It is also necessary that they are true and just. For surely much is entrusted to them, not only metals, but human bodies are entrusted to sailors and craftsmen] (80).

81. The story appears on pages 103–4 of Burt's edition.

82. This story is found on pages 91–92 of Burt's edition. In calling friendliness a "virtue" I am following Jacobus, who sees this as an asset equal to other *virtutes* like *sapientia, liberalitas, prudentis militis, miseracordia, fortitudo*, and *custodia populi*.

83. This story, taken from Valerius Maximus's *Factorum et dictorum memoabilium*, is found on pages 45–46 of Burt's edition.

84. The verb Jacobus uses is *illudere*, which means "to make sport with" but also "to violate or destroy" (30).

85. This story also reinforces the message that a woman's "professional" responsibility is to bear the future rulers of the community. Rosimond's crime is in her lust, and her willingness to indulge it points to the perpetual potential for illegitimacy, which in turn threatens "natural" succession. Her behavior is contrasted sharply with that of her daughters, who take pains to guard their chastity and are in turn rewarded with their mother's own title—they become queens. Also reinforcing the female role of childbearing is the fifth pawn, a doctor, who must tend to the queen's body, the vehicle by which the patriarchy is perpetuated.

86. Murray, *A History of Chess*, 530.

87. Ibid. (Murray includes Latin text on page 561). In his "All the World's a Chess-Board [*sic*]," *Speculum* 6 (1931): 461–65, Lynn Thorndike reproduces a Latin text of the *Quaedam* not consulted by Murray. The differences between Thorndike's and Murray's versions consist only of minor word choices and do not affect the overall meaning of the allegory.

88. Murray, *A History of Chess*, 561 (translation my own). Murray's brackets indicate differences in other manuscripts that he consulted.

89. See Jenny Swanson, *John of Wales: A Study of the Works and Ideas of a Thirteenth-Century Friar* (Cambridge: Cambridge University Press, 1989), 65, and Murray, *A History of Chess*, 530–31.

90. Valerius, the most heavily cited author in the *Liber*, is the third most cited author in part 1 of the *Communiloquium*. Seneca, whom Jacobus cites seventeen times, is cited seventy-one times by John. See Burt's introduction to her edition of the *Liber*, xx, and Swanson, *John of Wales*, 104.

91. Swanson, *John of Wales*, 81.

92. John's *Breviloquium de virtutibus antiquorum principum et philosophorum*, a collection of exempla illustrating the virtuous behavior of ancient princes and philosophers, places a similar emphasis on proper rule. "Respublica" is a term Swanson uses.

93. Swanson, *John of Wales*, 72 (the italics are Swanson's).

94. "Istius autem ioci conditio talis est, ut unus alterum capiat; et cum ludum compleverint, sicut de uno sacculo exierunt, ita iterum reponuntur. Nec est differencia inter regem et peditem pauperum, quia simul in unum dives et pauper" (Murray, *A History of Chess*, 560).

95. The volume in question is MS 669. All information about Galvano is from Charles Kohler, "Traité du recouvrement de la Terre Sainte adressé, vers l'an 1295, à Philippe le Bel par Galvano de Levanto, Médecin Génois," *Revue de l'Orient Latin* 6 (1898): 343–69.

96. This allegory may or may not come before Jacobus's, although Félix Lecoy has dated it to the last years of the thirteenth century ("Le Jeu de Echecs d'Engreban d'Arras," in *Mélanges de philologie romane et de littèrature médiévale offerts à Ernest Hœpffner* [Paris: Les Belles Lettres, 1949], 307–12, at 308).

97. "Or vous puis je bien dire a vor, / Quant li juer ki le ju mainent / Ont mis les esciés ou il mainent / Et il sont u sac rebouté / Que plus i ont li debouté / Et d'avantage et de soulas / Ke n'ont li grant, ki desous, las!" (ibid., ll. 138–44). Lecoy's article contains the full text of the poem.

98. Murray, *A History of Chess*, 408.

99. Ibid., 414. I have also used Murray's translation, which is on page 408.

100. Ibid., 408. The Latin reads: "aliud scachum esse, aliud aleam" (414).

101. There is evidence of players using dice in connection with chess as early as the eleventh century (Murray, *A History of Chess,* 409–10). The thirteenth-century Alfonso MS gives explicit instructions about how to use dice when playing. Namely, the king moves when a six is thrown, the queen when a five is thrown, and so on. (Murray, *A History of Chess,* 458, n. 12). For the use of dice with backgammon, see Richard Eales, *Chess: The History of a Game* (New York: Facts on File Publications, 1985), 48–49.

102. Murray, *A History of Chess,* 410.

103. For information about Damian's life, see Patricia McNulty's introduction to her book, *St. Peter Damian: Selected Writings on the Spiritual Life* (London: Faber and Faber, 1959), 11–52.

104. Murray, *A History of Chess,* 411, n. 52.

105. In the York pageant of *The Crucifixion,* the "miles" draw lots to see who can have Christ's "kirtill" (cloak). The first soldier draws the shortest lot and thus claims "þis mantell is myne." See *York (The Pinners): The Crucifixion,* in *Medieval Drama: An Anthology,* ed. Greg Walker (Oxford: Blackwell, 2000), ll. 291–300.

106. Murray, *A History of Chess,* 410.

107. In "Chess and Courty Culture in Medieval Castile: An Analysis of the *Libro de Ajedrez* of Alfonso X, el Sabio" (unpublished paper, 2005), Olivia Remie Constable considers the ways the *Libro de ajedrez* represents the "social relations at Alfonso's court."

108. From James F. Magee's introduction to *Bonus Socius (Good Companion): XIIIth Century Manuscript Collection of Chess Problems* (Florence: Tipografia Giuntina, 1910), 17.

109. Murray, *A History of Chess,* 474.

110. This translation appears without the original Latin in Murray, *A History of Chess,* 653.

111. Alfonso X El Sabio, *Libros del ajedrez, dados y tablas,* facsimile reproduction (Madrid: Vincent García Editores, S. A. Valencial–Ediciones Poniente, 1987), 2 vols.

112. *La Vieille; ou, Les Derniers Amours d'Ovide (Poëme français du XIVe siècle traduit du Latin de Richard de Fournival),* ed. Hippolyte Cocheris (Paris: August Aubry, 1861), 82, ll. 1647 and 1656.

113. William L. Tronzo, "Moral Hieroglyphs: Chess and Dice at San Savino in Piacenza," *Gesta* 16.2 (1977): 15–26.

114. In the *Pardoner's Tale* Chaucer offers a similar warning about mixing gambling with governance. As the Pardoner warns: "If that a prynce useth hasardrye, / In alle governaunce and policye / He is, as by commune opinioun, / Yholde the lasse in reputacioun," *The Riverside Chaucer,* 3rd ed., gen. ed. Larry D. Benson, (Boston: Houghton Mifflin, 1987), ll. 599–602.

115. The story is found on pages 129–30 of Burt's edition of the *Liber.* This story will also appear in Hoccleve's *Regement of Princes,* which I will discuss in Chapter 4 of this book.

116. John's story resembles the types of law cases described in Richard Firth Green's discussion of "maintenance contracts by which late medieval peasants sought to bind their children to care for them in their old age." Green, *A Crisis of*

Truth: Literature and Law in Ricardian England (Philadelphia: University of Pennsylvania Press, 1999), 161. The increasingly technical nature of such contracts highlights a "weakening village cohesiveness in the face of a growing spirit of particularism." Green, 163, who is in turn citing Edwin Brezette Dewindt, *Land and People in Holywell-cum-Needingworth: Structures of Tenure and Patterns of Social Organization in an East Midlands Village, 1252–1457* (Toronto: Pontifical Institute of Mediaeval Studies, 1972), 263.

117. Although Jacobus states that this pawn also represents couriers, the bulk of his exempla are addressed to gamblers. Only at the very end of the chapter does he address the couriers.

118. Roberto Alejandro, *Hermeneutics, Citizenship, and the Public Sphere* (Albany: State University of New York Press, 1993), 14. In his essay "Secular Criticism," Edward Said makes a somewhat similar distinction between bonds of "filiation" and "affiliation." For Said, the latter of these are formed by "institutions, associations, and communities whose social existence was not in fact guaranteed by biology" (although at a later point in his essay, Said argues that nationality and professionalism are products of filiative relationships). See *The World, the Text, and the Critic* (Cambridge, Mass.: Harvard University Press, 1983), 17. Although confining himself to the examination of modern states, David Held covers some of the same ground in his *Political Theory and the Modern State: Essays on State, Power, and Democracy* (Stanford, Calif.: Stanford University Press, 1989).

119. Alejandro, *Hermeneutics, Citizenship, and the Public Sphere*, 10.

Chapter 2

Epigraphs: Georges Duby, *The Knight, the Lady, and the Priest: The Making of Modern Marriage in Medieval France*, trans. Barbara Bray (New York: Pantheon, 1983), 19; C. S. Lewis, *The Allegory of Love: A Study in Medieval Tradition* (London: Oxford University Press, 1936), 30 (emphasis Lewis's)

1. *Les Echecs amoureux* was most likely composed between 1370 and 1380. Ideally, this chapter would take the entire poem into account, but unfortunately no complete manuscript has survived. The longer of the two extant manuscript fragments, Dresden O66 of the Royal Library, suffered irreparable damage in that city's fire-bombing of 1945, leaving readers with one usable manuscript of half its length in Venice. Reginald Hyatte and Maryse Ponchard-Hyatte, introduction to *L'Harmonie des sphères: Encyclopédie d'astronomie et de musique extraite du commentaire sur* Les Echecs amoureux *(XVᵉ s.) attribué à Evrart de Conty. Edition critique d'après les mss de la Bibliothèque Nationale de Paris* (New York: Peter Lang, 1985), ix. Only a few fragments of the Dresden text were transcribed and published in the earlier part of the twentieth century, and the one other source for this poem, John Lydgate's *Reson and Sensuallyte*, breaks off midway through the description of the lady's chess pieces. Thus, while readers have a fairly complete knowledge of the poem *en toto* from Lydgate, from Christine Kraft's *Die Liebesgarten-Allegorie der* Echecs amoureux: *Kritische Ausgabe und Kommentar* (Frankfurt-am-Main: Peter Lang, 1977), and from

Stanley L. Galpin's very thorough "*Les Eschez Amoureux*: A Complete Synopsis, with Unpublished Extracts," *Romanic Review* 11, 4 (1920): 283–307, one can only hazard a guess as to the final state of the complete work. Yet while the manuscript as a whole has been lost, the chess match has been better preserved. Joseph Mettlich transcribed folios 127–38 of the Dresden Manuscript, which describe the chess match between the lady and the lover, in his *Die Schachpartie in der Prosabearbeitung der allegorisch-didaktischen Dichtung* Les Eschez amoureux (Münster: Aschendorffschen Buchdruckerei, 1907), 9–30. Ernst Sieper transcribed the poem's description of the chess pieces in his *Les Echecs amoureux: Eine altfranzösische Nachahmung des Rosenromans und ihre Englische Übertragung* (Weimar: Emil Felber, 1898), 46–51. Sieper also offers a short synopsis of *Les Echecs amoureux* in the notes to his edition of John Lydgate's *Reson and Sensuallyte*, vol. 2 (studies and notes), EETS e.s. 89 (Oxford: Oxford University Press, 1903), 59–64, although his summary is far less extensive than Galpin's.

2. Galpin describes Pallas's lecture as "advice and information on miscellaneous subjects—love, manner of living, Paris and its university, the various professions of life and how they should be pursued, the duties of husband and wife, the rearing of children, music, the music of the spheres, the value of physical exercise, the management of servants, the kind of house it is best to live in, its situation, the kind of water it is best to drink, five ways to get rich . . . end of MS" ("*Les Eschez Amoureux*: A Complete Synopsis," 283–84).

3. For the sake of clarity, I will refer to the commentary on *Les Echecs amoureux* as the "Commentary." When citing this text, I have used the most recent critical edition, namely Evrart de Conty, *Le Livre des eschez amoureux moralisés*, ed. Françoise Guichard-Tesson and Bruno Roy (Montreal: Éditions CERES, 1993). References to this text are noted parenthetically by page number. I have produced many of the English translations of these citations. For the more complicated passages I have consulted an English edition of the text produced by Joan Morton Jones as "*The Chess of Love* (Old French Text with Commentary)," Ph.D. dissertation, University of Nebraska, 1968. Passages translated by Jones will also be noted parenthetically by page number, following the English text.

4. Françoise Guichard-Tesson has suggested that Evrart de Conty, a doctor who treated both King Charles V and his wife, Queen Blanche de Navarre, was the author of the Commentary. Evrart, who was at the court of Charles V in the late fourteenth century, became involved in a number of translation and editing projects at this time. See Guichard-Tesson, "La Glose des *Echecs amoureux*: Un Savoir à tendance laïque, Comment l'interpréter?" *Fifteenth-Century Studies* 10 (1984) 229–60, at 229; and *Le Livre des eschez amoureux moralisés*, ed. Guichard-Tesson and Roy, liii–liv. As noted above, the Commentary was used as an educational text, serving most notably as the source for much of the *Champ Fleury* (1529), one of the primary encyclopedic works in early modern France. On the use of the Commentary as an educational text and its relationship to the *Champ Fleury*, see Reginald Hyatte and Maryse Ponchard-Hyatte's introduction to *L'Harmonie des sphères*, v. For more information on the state of the original manuscripts of the Commentary, see ibid., vi.

5. That Evrart amplifies the game does not mean, however, that the original poem marginalizes it. In the original poem, the account of the game occupied

roughly 580 of the 30,060 lines. H. J. R. Murray, *A History of Chess* (Oxford: Oxford University Press, 1913, 476.

6. The Commentary uses a variety of terms—"author of the poem," "author," "lady," "young girl," and "young maiden"—to describe the two players. For the sake of clarity, I will use the term "lover" to describe the male player and will refer to the female player as "lady."

7. Although this term was not in circulation at this time, I have chosen the word "taxonomy" deliberately. A science that groups plants and animals according to their perceived relationships, taxonomy uses the concept of nature to support a structure devised by human invention and designed to reaffirm mankind's supremacy. Its claim for universality—and indeed, what could be more universal than a science that pinions all living things into one system—obscures the artificiality and subjectivity inherent in its methods. As suggested by its etymological root "tangere," to touch, and its explicit ties to "tax," a word related to the estimation of value (and concomitant charge), taxonomy is not innocent; it touches, evaluates, and sometimes extracts a payment from the life forms that it classifies. Above all, to taxonomize something is to politicize it, to embed it in a larger social structure and then to use it to support this structure itself.

8. Evrart offers a lengthy explication of the ruby in his Commentary (654–55; Jones, 1070–73). In this section he notes that the *Les Echecs* poet "pretends that the queen was made of a fine ruby, precious above all, to signify to us the dignity and great excellence manners have above all the other amorous graces and virtues" (Jones, 1070). Of the diamond, Evrart observes that the diamond, which is "of a nature so firm and solid that it cannot be broken or shaken by iron, fire, or in any other way, except only by the blood of a ram, all hot and new," denotes the purity and fidelity of true love (Jones, 1125). His full explication of the diamond can be found on pages 680–82; Jones, 1125–27.) Evrart most likely drew on medieval lapidaries for his descriptions of the properties of these stones. The diamond was described throughout the Middle Ages as a symbol of eternal love and fidelity. Valerie Gonero, *Parures d'Or et de Gemmes: L'Orfèvrerie dans les romans antiques du XII* siècle (Aix-en-Provence: Publications de l'Université de Provence, 2002), 150–52. Yet this particular stone also carried with it the types of religious overtones that Philippe uses in his work. As one early twelfth-century alphabetical lapidary notes, the stone symbolizes the purity of Christ's love for man. Paul Studer and Joan Evans, eds., *Anglo-Norman Lapidaries* (Paris: Edouard Champion, 1924), 204. The ruby appears less often in lapidary texts and is often confused with the "escharboncle," or carbuncle, a garnet cut in a way that best showed its color. According to the late fifteenth-century Peterborough Lapidary, the carbuncle's most notable feature is that "it schineþ in derk places, & it semeþ as it were a feyr. " Joan Evans and Mary S. Serjeantson, eds., *English Mediaeval Lapidaries*, EETS o.s. 190 (London: Oxford University Press, 1933), 82.

9. Joan B. Williamson, "Allegory in the Work of Philippe de Mézières," *Analecta Husserliana: Yearbook of Phenomenological Research* 41 (1994): 107–21, at 109–10. Philippe drew on Albertus Magnus's *Book of Minerals* (letter 27) for the meanings he attaches to his stones. In some places he describes the ruby as the greatest stone because it can illuminate the darkness. In other places he gives equal importance to the diamond, which he depicts as a type of lodestone. Joan B.

Williamson, "Jewels in the Work of Philippe de Mézières," in *Autour d'Eustache Deschamps: Actes du Colloque du Centre d'études médiEvales de l'Université de Picardie-Jules Verne, Amiens, 5–8 novembre 1998*, ed. Danielle Buschinger (Amiens: Centre d'études Médiévales, 1999), 261–76, at 263, 268–70. I will discuss Philippe's chess allegory, which appears in his *Songe du vieil pèlerin*, near the end of this chapter.

10. The pun on "fierce" and "fers," the name for the promoted pawn, was likely deliberate and should not go unnoticed.

11. The board's darker squares (made of adamant) betoken the natural attraction of the lovers, while the lighter squares (made of amber) contain a pleasing brightness and correspond to "the joy of love and delight" ["la joye d'amours et le delit"] (628).

12. In his fifteenth-century translation of these lines, John Lydgate uses an even meter to reinforce the symmetry between the two lovers: "Whan the play I-ended was / Atwex hem two, thus stood the cas: / Without a maat on outher syde" (ll. 5901–3) (*Reson and Sensuallyte*, ed. Sieper, vol. 1, 155). Subsequent references to this edition will be cited parenthetically by line number.

13. Galpin, "*Les Eschez Amoureux*: A Complete Synopsis," 293, 296.

14. Here Galpin quotes *Les Echecs* directly (ibid., 298).

15. The character Reason in the *Roman de la rose* promotes a similar notion of friendship, although unlike Pallas she sees friendship as irreconcilable with romantic love.

16. Galpin, "*Les Eschez Amoureux*: A Complete Synopsis," 301.

17. Ibid., 302.

18. Ibid.

19. After showing the ways that chess represents stable political order, Evrart introduces a slightly different semiotic system, that of battle. In this system, most of the pieces retain their primary identities—the king, for example, is still a king or at least the leader of the battle, and the queen, knights, and councillors are virtually unchanged. The rooks and the commoners show the greatest change. In this symbolic order the former represent messengers rather than legates; the latter are now uniform foot soldiers. Yet despite their different roles, these pieces still represent social groups that work together toward a common goal, namely the preservation of political order.

20. Evrart's interest in the parallels between the cosmological, political, and psychological orders, and in particular the effects of the cosmos on individual people, extends past his prologue into the remainder of the Commentary. His description of Nature, the poet's first advisor, opens the treatise, and this prompts him to consider again the ways planetary bodies affect human ones. Man is, as Evrart explains, the microcosm and a direct reflection of the universe, or macrocosm. The macrocosm is dependent on God, "just as the members of the human body are, in respect of its first and principal member, the heart, on which all life depends" (Jones, 89) ["tout aussi tout les membres du corps humain sont ramené au cuer come au premier et au plus principal membre de tout le corps, duquel toute la vie humaine se despend"] (59). Just as the sun is in the center of the sky, "so the heart is situated and seated in the center of the body" ["aussi le cuer est ou milieu du corps situés et assiz"] (59). At the same time, the sun "signifies princes and kings, and vast kingdoms

and lands" ["seignifie les princes et les roys, et les grans royaulmes et les grans seignouries"] (51), in a worldly realm.

21. This multilayered accretion most likely comes from the fourteenth-century poem *La Vieille*, a translation and expansion of an earlier Latin poem titled *De vetula*, attributed by medieval scribes (incorrectly) to Ovid. In his prologue Evrart himself names *La Vieille* as his source. In *La Vieille*, the movement of the pieces is similar to the "movements" of their human counterparts; the king, for example, remains behind the other pieces "because it is necessary to defend him" ["Qu'il lui est besoing de défendre"]. *La Vieille; ou, Les Dernières Amour d'Ovide [Poëme français du XIVe siècle traduit du Latin de Richard de Fournival]*, ed. Hippolyte Concheris (Paris: August Aubry, 1861), l. 1551. Yet this comparison to political offices takes a back seat to the larger connection that the pseudo-Ovidian writer makes between the pieces and the heavenly bodies, and most of his discussion of the game revolves around his comparison of each piece to a planet. The king "is like the beautiful sun" ["Au beau souleil est comparé"], because he dominates his entire realm just as the sun's light illuminates the world (l. 1588). The rook is like the moon who "is corrupt and badly formed" ["Corrompant est et mal estable"]," while the queen is Venus, "Aimable est et amoureux" ["lovable and loving"] (ll. 1593, 1601). The movements of the pieces represent "the warring and sparing movements of the whole heavenly assembly" ["meuvent guerres et discors / Tout à l'assemblance des corps / Celestielz"] (ll. 1579–81). Rather than an individual body, this chessboard almost exclusively represents the celestial "corps." For a good edition of the Latin poem, see Dorothy M. Robathan, ed., *The Pseudo-Ovidian De Vetula* (Amsterdam: A. M. Hakkert, 1968).

22. For a careful analysis of the ways the game reflects the lover's lack of reason and loss of intellect, see Kristin E. Juel, "Loving the Creator and His Creations: Ethical Reflections on the Nature of Love in the Fourteenth-Century *Echecs Amoureux*," Ph.D. dissertation, Indiana University, 2002, 231–52.

23. From Mettlich, *Die Schachpartie in der Prosabearbeitung der allegorisch-didaktischen Dichtung* "Les Eschez amoureux," 12. The lines from the Dresden Manuscript read: "Le dieu, qui ne se pot plus taire, / M'escrie que je me deffende / Et que je traye, or je me rende."

24. For Evrart even material objects contain secrets to be exposed. Thus at the same time that bad lovers "are secretly signified to us by Narcissus, who loved his shadow madly" (Jones, 363) ["sont secretement segnefies par Narcisus qui folement son umbre jusques a la mort ama"] (249), so too the string of an instrument "secretly contains in itself all kinds of musical instruments imaginable" (Jones, 233) ["contient en soy secretement toutes manieres de instrumens ymaginables"] (157).

25. Some things, as we discover, do not need as much explanation as others. Describing the daughters of Venus, named Beauty, Fine Speech, and Touching respectively, he takes care to emphasize that their nakedness is symbolic of the fact that love "shows itself easily to everyone" ["se moustrent a tous assez legierement"] (245). At this moment he doubles the image of exposure: Beauty, Fine Speech, and Touching are already naked for us to see. Yet by explaining the reason for their nakedness, he ties their physical state to a mental condition, a link that effectively points to the lover's own unclothed emotions.

26. Although Lydgate did not usually make substantial alterations to his sources,

there is no way to know how much he may have amplified or cut the original poem. Thus while Lydgate's *Reson and Sensuallyte* is most likely a faithful rendition of *Les Echecs amoureux*, it should be kept in mind that it is a separate work.

27. In his translation of *Les Echecs* Lydgate calls attention to this literary debt when he begins to describe Cupid's garden, which "Is remembred, in soothnesse, / Of many clerkes as be writyng" (ll. 4812–4813). "Most specialy of everychon," however, is the *Roman de la Rose*. Lydgate proceeds to describe the plot of the *Roman* in some detail, after which he vows to consider the points where his "dremyng" will "be lyke" the *Rose* poem (l. 4816, l. 4915, and l. 4918). Lydgate's odd syntax at this point makes his intentions difficult to decipher. His exact comments are:

Now shal ye here, and ye take hede,
Al the processe of my spede,
Both the gynnyng and the fyn,
And how I kam to that gardyn,
And the maner of myn entre,
Wonder desirous for to se;
And first gan in my self recorde,
Wher the beaute dyde acorde
By any maner Resemblaunce,
Touching my drem in substaunce,
Wher yt be lyke in any thing,
I mene as thus, wher my dremyng,
Which in this book I shal disclose,
Be lyke tke Romaunce of the Rose
Oonly, in conclusyon,
Touching our bothe avysion. (ll. 4905–20)

The editor's decision to place a comma after "Oonly" suggests that the poet wishes to compare his dream solely to the *Rose* romance. Without the comma, "oonly" indicates the idea of exception: the dreamer's poem resembles the *Roman de la rose* except for its "conclusyon." In either case, however, it seems that Lydgate sees the *Roman* as the closest counterpart to *Les Echecs*. Moreover, his choice of the title *Reson and Sensuallyte* highlights the balance that can be achieved between rational thought and romantic love.

28. The English translation of the poem comes from Guillaume de Lorris and Jean de Meun, *The Romance of the Rose*, trans. Charles Dahlberg (Princeton, N.J.: Princeton University Press, 1971), 352. The original French text comes from Guillaume de Lorris and Jean de Meun, *Le Roman de la rose*, ed. Daniel Poiron (Paris: Garnier-Flammarion, 1974), ll. 21605–6. Subsequent references to these editions will appear parenthetically.

29. In the Commentary on *Les Echecs* Nature shares some characteristics with Boethius's Lady Philosophy, and her tall stature—her head is in the sky and her crown is made of the planets—gives her an authority nearly as great as that of Pallas. In the introduction to her translation of the Commentary, Jones sees Nature as a counterpart to the *Roman*'s Reason: "Nature is treated in much the way Alanus de

Insulis treats her, a tradition deriving from Lady Philosophy in Boethius' *Consolation* and, ultimately, from the woman crowned with stars in Revelation. In the gloss, Nature includes the qualities of Reason and those of Nature in *The Romance of the Rose*; Reason is not separately personified except in citations from that poem" (Jones, ed., *The Chess of Love*, iv). The replacement of Reason with Nature further highlights the ways Evrart rehabilitates (and endorses) the power of natural desire. Yet Reason's speeches are difficult to interpret not only because of her tendency to meander but also because it is hard to know how seriously we are meant to take them. At times Reason gives the narrator viable pieces of advice, offering him sage warnings about the fickle nature of Fortune. But she is also inconsistent, sometimes describing all love as untrustworthy and sometimes arguing for the merits of love in the case of friendship. Her position as the Lover's first advisor might indicate the high regard Jean de Meun has for her capabilities. Then again, it might also indicate the author's distrust of her as a final judge in all worldly matters.

      30. Reason's slippery nature has baffled many readers, and at least two opposing camps have emerged with very different understandings of her character. Per the D. W. Robertson-John Fleming school, Reason is "the single voice within the *Roman de la Rose* that consistently articulates the moral and intellectual standards against which Amant's erotic drama is to be understood and finally judged." John V. Fleming, *Reason and the Lover* (Princeton, N.J.: Princeton University Press, 1984), 64. Robertson's view is articulated most clearly in his *Preface to Chaucer* where he observes: "The themes to be elaborated are set for by Raison (ll. 4221 ff.) whose Boethian discourse affords the positive ideas against which the subsequent materials in the poem are set." D. W. Robertson, Jr., *A Preface to Chaucer: Studies in Medieval Perspectives* (Princeton, N.J.: Princeton University Press, 1962), 198. Opponents of this position, who include Donald Rowe and Michael Cherniss, argue that "no figure emerges to provide an authoritative, valid definition of *amor*, because none can be drawn from this context, from the realm of post-lapsarian nature." Michael Cherniss, "Irony and Authority: The Ending of the *Roman de la Rose*," *Modern Language Quarterly* 36 (1975): 227–38, at 230. For his part, Rowe argues that Reason, while aware of her own importance for man, does not recognize her own limitations. See Donald W. Rowe, "*Reson* in Jean's *Roman de la Rose*: Modes of Characterization and Dimensions of Meaning," *Mediaevalia* 10 (1984): 97–126. Daniel Poirion, who sees Reason as a viable voice yet one that comes too early to have any effect on the Lover, could also be included here. See Poirion's introduction to *Le Roman de la Rose*, 18. In many ways the critical controversy surrounding this poem replicates the medieval quarrels about its modes of representation. Specifically, the debate revolved around the character of Reason and her use of the word *coilles* (testicles) (l. 6966) to describe male genitalia. Christine de Pizan's opening salvo on the poem, composed as a letter to Jean de Montreuil, incited further criticism from Jean Gerson, whose *Tractatus contra romantium de rosa* appeared shortly thereafter. Defending the various charges against the poem was Pierre Col. For a good summary of the *querelle du Rose*, see Robertson, *A Preface to Chaucer*, 361–64, and Charles Frederick Ward, *The Epistles on the* Romance of the Rose *and Other Documents in the Debate* (Chicago: University of Chicago Press, 1911).

31. The French reads: "Et por ce que nulle richece / A valor d'ami ne s'adrece" and "Si ne fait pas richece riche / Celi qui en tresor la fiche" (ll. 4943–44, 4975–76).

32. The chess match between Charles and Manfred is also significant as the poem's first of two references to contemporary, thirteenth-century events. Charles of Anjou killed Manfred at the Battle of Benevento on February 26, 1266, and then accepted the throne of Sicily from Pope Clement IV. Conradin, Manfred's nephew, continued the fight against Charles and Henry of Castille. Although Henry soon turned on Charles, Charles eventually defeated both men. See Dahlberg, *The Romance of the Rose*, 381, notes on ll. 6631–6740; introduction, 1–2.

33. Dahlberg's translation here is confusing. He writes: "it must be the king that one puts in check . . . one cannot check or mate any other man" (129). But in this instance Reason is not talking about a check but about a "have," or a bare king ending. For details on this ending, see Murray, *A History of Chess*, 467–68 and 750–51.

34. John of Salisbury, *Policraticus: Of the Frivolities of Courtiers and the Footprints of Philosophers*, ed. and trans. Cary J. Nederman, Cambridge Texts in the History of Political Thought (Cambridge: Cambridge University Press, 1990), 16.

35. Dalhberg, *The Romance of the Rose*, 111. The French reads: "Aime les touz autant cum un / Au moins de l'amor du commun" (ll. 5449–50).

36. Galpin, "*Les Eschez Amoureux*: A Complete Synopsis," 284.

37. Jones, *The Chess of Love*, xi–xii.

38. Galpin, "*Les Echez Amoureux*: A Complete Synopsis," 301.

39. All of these references come from Galpin's summary in "*Les Echez Amoureux*: A Complete Synopsis," 299. Galpin writes in his synopsis that the original poem, at least the copy found in Dresden MS O66, promotes the idea that "the good prince governs his people as the soul the body."

40. Kathleen Daly, "'Centre,' 'Power' and 'Periphery' in Late Medieval French Historiography: Some Reflections," in *War, Government and Power in Late Medieval France*, ed. Christopher Allmand (Liverpool: Liverpool University Press, 2000), 124–44, at 128. On Charles VII's battles, see P. S. Lewis, *Later Medieval France: The Polity* (New York: St. Martin's Press, 1968), 60.

41. One of the fifteenth-century French responses to the English claims for power highlights even more crisply the primacy of a ruler's physical body. Turning to the Salic Law, a code written in the fifth century and subsequently overlooked for many years, Jean de Montreuil argued in 1410 that the throne could not pass to female claimants. For an overview of the Salic Law and its use in this context, see Katherine Fischer Drew, Introduction to *The Laws of the Salian Franks*, trans. Drew (Philadelphia: University of Pennsylvania Press, 1991), 1–55.

42. "Tous les regards, en effet, convergent vers le roi, le placent, en dépit de son effacement, au cœur du débat politique, et lui manifestent le plus solide loyalisme monarchique." Jacques Krynen, *Idéal du prince et pouvoir royal en France à la fin du Moyen Age (1380–1440): Étude de la littérature politique du temps* (Paris: Editions A. et J. Picard, 1981), 42–43.

43. "Sous Charles VI et durant la première moitié du règne de Charles VII, la production d'œuvres politiques, loin de tarir, s'intensife considérablement" (ibid., 42).

44. Kate Langdon Forhan, introduction to Christine de Pizan, *The Book of the*

Body Politic, ed. and trans. Kate Langdon Forhan, Cambridge Texts in the History of Political Thought (Cambridge: Cambridge University Press, 1994), xx.

45. Lewis, *Later Medieval France*, 87–101.

46. The *Book of the Body Politic* opens by showing how a civic body is like a human body in which "the prince and princes hold the place of the head in as much as they are or should be sovereign and from them ought to come particular institutions just as from the mind of a person springs forth the external deeds that the limbs achieve. The knights and nobles take the place of the hands and arms. Just as a person's arms have to be strong in order to endure labor, so they have the burden of defending the law of the prince and the polity. They are also the hands because, just as the hands push aside harmful things, so they ought push all harmful and useless things aside. The other kinds of people are like the belly, the feet, and the legs. Just as the belly receives all that the head and limbs prepare for it, so, too, the activity of the prince and nobles ought to return to the public good, as will be better explained later. Just as the legs and feet sustain the human body, so, too, the laborers sustain all the other estates" (Christine de Pizan, *The Book of the Body Politic*, 4). The French reads: "le prince ou les princes tiennent le lieu du chief, en tant qu'ilz sont out doivent estre souverains, et du eulx doivent venir les singuliers establissemens, tout ainsi comme [de] l'entendement de l'omme sourdent et viennent les foraines œuvres que les membres achevent. Les chevaliers et les nobles tiennent le lieu des mains et des bras, car tout ainsi que les bras de l'omme qui son fors pour soustenir labeur et peine, doivent-[ilz] avoir le charge de deffendre le droit du prince et la chose publique. Et sont aussi comparez aux mains, car si que les mains deboutent les choses nuisibles doivent-ilz mettre arriere et degetter toutes choses malfaisans et inutiles. Les autres gens de peuple sont comme le ventre et les piez les jambes, car si comme le ventre reçoit tout en soy ce que prepare le chief et les membres, ainsi le fait de l'exercite du prince et des nobles doit revertir ou bien et en l'amour publique, si comme cy aprés sera plus declairié. Et ainsi comme les jambes et piez soustiennent le fais du corps humain, semblablement les laboureurs soustiennent tous le autres estas." Christine de Pizan, *Le Livre du corps de policie*, ed. Angus J. Kennedy (Paris: Honoré Champion, 1998), 1–2.

47. Christine de Pizan, *The Book of the Body Politic*, xxii. Jean Gerson presents a more cautionary image of the state-as-body in his late fourteenth-century sermon *Adorabunt eum*, which he addresses to the king. Gerson writes, "Sire, if the arms of your kingdom, by which I mean the noble knights who defend the common welfare by their arms and swords, hate and persecute the eyes, that is to say the clergy, they will blind your kingdom. If the arms and eyes have a distain for and destroy the feet, that is to say the minor people, your kingdom will not be able to support itself. . . . For why is civic order established if not for one to help the other each according to his condition" ["Sire, se le bras de vostre royaulme par lesquelz je entens le nobles chevaliers qui deffendent la chose publique par leurs bras et a l'espee, hayoient et persecutioent les yeux, c'est assavoir le clergie, ilz aveugleroient votre (*sic*) royaulme. Se les bras et les yeulx avoient en desdaing et destruisoient lez piez, c'est assavoir le menu peuple, vostre royaulme ne avroit qui les portast. . . . Pour quoy est ordonnee police, se ce n'est pour aider l'ung l'autre et chascun selon son estat"] (Krynen, *Idéal*

du prince et pouvoir royal, 158–59). Focusing on the vulnerability of the kingdom's various "organs," Gerson uses the state-as-body metaphor to warn of the dangers of a sick kingdom. If any one part does not work to help the others, the body will fail. Nevertheless, the most important task for each of the body's members is the protection of the body's head, for otherwise: "l'ordre du corps mystique de la chose publique seroit tout subverti" ["the order of the kingdom's mystical body is overthrown"] (Kantorowicz, *The King's Two Bodies*, 219). Lewis notes that Jean de Terre-Vermeille, who was also writing in the early fifteenth century, used the body metaphor "to argue for almost a Hobbesian degree of obedience by the members of the body politic to the head and single will: rebellion was unnatural" (Lewis, *Late Medieval France*, 88).

48. The poem was started before 1399 and finished in 1403. It was presented to the dukes of Bourgogne and Berry in 1404. Christine de Pisan, *Le Livre de la mutacion de fortune*, ed. Suzanne Solente (Paris: Éditions A. and J. Picard, 1959), vol. 1, ix–xi. For the specific stories that Christine borrows, see Solente, "Le *Jeu des échecs moralisés*, source de la *Mutacion de fortune*," in *Recueil de travaux offert à M. Clovis Brunel* vol. 2 (Paris: Société de l'Ecole des Chartres, 1955), 556–65. These stories include: Anaximenes' tricking of Alexander, the laws of Anacharsis, the words of Caesar, and some aphorisms about gluttony.

49. The poem contains seven parts. Part 3 begins at line 4273 and ends at line 7052 (*Le Livre de la mutacion de fortune*, ed. Suzanne Solente, vol. 2).

50. Solente persuasively argues that this section is a deliberate allusion to the contemporary papal schism ("Le *Jeu des échecs moralisés*," 556).

51. This is the inter-title used between l. 6412 and l. 6413.

52. In the late fourteenth century Guillaume de Saint-André also produced a metrical version of Jacobus's text. For excerpts of this version, see Félix Lecoy, "Guillaume de Saint-André et son *Jeu des échecs moralisés*," *Romania* 67 (1942): 491–503. It is notable that this version served as a conclusion to the much longer *Libvre du Bon Jehan, duc de Bretaigne*, a work addressed directly to a royal patron (see ibid., 491–94).

53. See Alain Collet's introduction to his edition of Jacques de Cessoles, *Le Jeu des éschaz moralisé: Traduction de Jean Ferron, 1347* (Paris: Honoré Champion, 1999), 85–91.

54. Like Jacobus, Evrart also says that the chessboard is square so that it "represente la cité de la grant Babiloine" (604) ["represents the city of Babylon the Great"] (Jones, 971).

55. Oliver Plessow and Pamela Kalning at the Westfälische Wilhelms-Universität in Münster are currently working on Jacobus's German and Swedish translations and the *Liber*'s reception in medieval central Europe. Kalning has looked in particular at the changes made by Konrad von Ammenhausen in his 1337 German verse translation, which he revitalizes with "neue Exempel und Sentenzan [new exampla and sententiae]" (Kalning, "Der Ritter auf dem Schachbrett: Ritterliche Tugenden im Schachbuch Konrads von Ammenhausen," forthcoming).

56. "This is in order to have at all times the king's succession without a woman being able to come into the inheritance of the kingdom." The French can be found in Carol S. Fuller, ed., "A Critical Edition of *Le Jeu des Eschés, Moralisé*, Translated by Jehan de Vignay," Ph.D. dissertation, Catholic University of America, 1974, 78.

57. Ibid., 77. Fuller also notes that "Jehan [de Vignay] tended to interpret and paraphrase the Latin work rather than to translate it precisely. His French text contains many additional *exempla* and digressions, as well as numerous proverbs, quotations, and personal interpolations; it is the nature of these additions which places the *Jeu des eschés* in the *regimen principum* literature more firmly than the original Latin work" (4).

58. For a good background on Philippe, see G. W. Coopland's introduction to his edition of *Le Songe du vieil pèlerin*, 2 vols. (Cambridge: Cambridge University Press, 1969), vol. 1, 1–80. As one of my readers has noted, Philippe was purchasing European unity through the promotion of another crusade against Islamic forces in the Holy Land.

59. Ibid., vol. 2, 176. The allegory of the "royal chariot," with its wheels of Truth, Mercy, Peace, and Justice, precedes that of the chessboard.

60. In his introduction to his edition of the *Songe*, Coopland argues that Philippe uses the board "in quite a different fashion" than Jacobus does in his *Liber*: "He [Philippe] allots the four corner squares to the virtues of truth, mercy, peace and justice and then proceeds to use the remaining sixty squares" to point out the various virtues appropriate to the king. Unlike, the *Liber*, Philippe's *Songe* had "little mention of the chessmen" and "shows reflection and careful planning." Setting aside Coopland's artistic bias, his analysis fails to account for the fact that Jacobus, like Philippe: opens his treatise with the story of a chess set presented to a king; takes care to order his virtues; and is not as interested in showing a game in progress as in the way the board itself serves to organize virtue. I do, however, agree with Coopland's observation that the *Songe* differs from the *Liber* "in essence," although for me this essence is its focus on the king and (consequently) its minimization of the importance of a community's other members. Coopland's discussion of the *Liber* is in his edition to the *Songe*, vol. 1, 22–23.

61. Philippe's first book introduces the main character of the pilgrim and charts his travels over the earth. The second book discusses the problems with the various hierarchies in France. These hierarchies are: the Church (prelates, canons, religious), the nobility (the king and princes, the nobles, the army chiefs), the law (members of parliament, judges, lawyers), and the people (merchants, artisans, laborers). Philippe's third and final book is devoted to the king alone, whose virtue is most important to the community's stability.

62. *Le Songe du vieil pèlerin*, vol. 2, 177.

63. Ibid., 204. Even if this shift in emphasis is produced by Philippe's envisioned audience—he writes for a king and not for a general public—it reveals the way a writer could rework the chess allegory into one that turned less on affiliation and more on sustaining a traditional hierarchy.

64. According to Murray, the manuscript number is MS Add 15820 (*A History of Chess*, 558). I have not consulted the original manuscript and have relied only on Murray's summary of the work. There is also a short (190-line) French poem titled "Comment l'estat du monde puet estre comparu au Jeu des eschecz," which occurs in a MS of the poems of Alain Chartier (MS Paris, Arsenal 3521, f. 263b). Because so little is known about this poem, I have not discussed it here. For information on this poem, see Murray, *A History of Chess*, 557–58.

65. For a complete list of the pieces and their symbolism, see Murray, *A History of Chess*, 558. The lady mates the devil in nine moves.

66. The Jacquerie was one of several peasant rebellions that took place in France in the late fourteenth century. The Jacquerie is known as such since the common name for a peasant at this time was a "Jacques."

67. That Philippe knew of the *Liber*'s model is evident in Queen Truth's explanation of the game's origins, a story that offers an abbreviated version of the Evilmerodach's conversion. Yet at the same time, Philippe, like the *Les Echecs* poet, emphasizes the idea that natural law, in addition to man-made law, governs the ruler's actions. As Truth tells Charles: "Ung saige philosophe fit et composa le gracieux livre des eschez, ou quel il descript quelx traiz le roy et la royne, les rocs et les offins, les chevaliers et les pions en l'eschequier doivant faire, or est assavoir moralisant la forme juste de gourvernement du roy et de tous les dessusdiz et quelz ilz doivent estre selon droyt et rayson; et comment le roy, selon la loy de nature et moralle policie, se doit porter envers ses subgiez et le subgiez envers lui. Or advint que le dit philosophe presenta au dit roy cruel les eschez et l'eschequier comme une chose estrange et nouvelle, en lui moustrant les trays du roy et des autres ou dit eschequier par maniere d'esbatement, le quel present fu assez plaisant au roy, et, jouant aux eschez a grant plaisance, devint ung pou plus debonnayre et y print amour ou dit philosophe" ["A wise philosopher invented and composed the elegant book of chess in which he described the moves that the king and queen, the rooks and bishops, the knights and pawns must make, that is to say moralizing the just form of government by the king and all those mentioned above and how they should rightfully and reasonably behave, as well as how the king, according to natural law and moral policy must behave towards his subject and his subjects towards him. Now it happened that the said philosopher presented the chess set to the cruel king as something unfamiliar and new, showing him the moves of the king and the other pieces on that chessboard as a form of entertainment. The king was delighted with that gift, and playing chess with great pleasure, he became a bit more good natured and took a liking to the aforementioned philosopher"] (*Le Songe*, vol. 2, 200). Many thanks to Donald Maddox for help with this translation.

68. Galpin, "*Les Eschez Amoureux*: A Complete Synopsis," 299.

69. Under medieval rules, as with modern chess, pawns that reached the eighth square obtained the power of queens (which at that time usually meant a single square move in a diagonal direction). Yet unlike modern rules, these pawns were usually given a different name to distinguish them from the original queen. For a discussion of the implications of this switch, see Marilyn Yalom, *The Birth of the Chess Queen* (New York: HarperCollins, 2004), 95–99, and Murray, *A History of Chess*, 423–28.

70. After matching the planets and the pieces (sun as king, Venus as queen, Jupiter as bishops, Mars as knights, moon as rooks, and Saturn as pawns), Evrart explains: "But I pass over this for the sake of brevity. For this would be too long to explain at length and in detail, because there are six sorts of chess pieces and no more, and there are seven different planets in the sky. Therefore those who make this comparison say that Mercury, who is the seventh planet, because he is by nature

a mingler, converts to the nature of the planet with which he is in conjunction and sometimes shows himself mingled" (10).

71. As Yalom notes, early rules often prohibited pawn promotion "while the original queen was still on the board (in) an attempt to preserve the uniqueness of the king's wife, his only permissible conjugal mate according to Christian doctrine" (*Birth of the Chess Queen*, 18).

72. For a more extensive discussion of the homosocial aspects of chess games, particularly those in medieval romance, see my "Pieces of Power: Medieval Chess and Male Homosocial Desire," *Journal of English and Germanic Philology* 103, 2 (April 2004): 197–214.

73. Duby, *Knight, the Lady, and the Priest*, 19.

74. This concept of fortune comes from Boethius's *Consolation of Philosophy*, 5.1.13–19.

75. Murray, *A History of Chess*, 593. Murray also offers a description of the other three manuscripts (579–82). Murray does not cite this passage in stanza form, although I have included line breaks to indicate the poetic nature of the original. Many thanks to Karen Duys for help with this translation.

76. Murray notes that some writers saw a centerboard mate as a sign of skilled player. In addition to the mate in the *Les Echecs* poem, which occurs in the "quatre poins" (or the center four squares), the mates in *Le Roman de la Rose* and in Chaucer's *Book of the Duchess* take place in the middle of the board (*A History of Chess*, 474 and note 54).

77. David Hooper and Kenneth Whyld, "Medieval Problems," in *The Oxford Companion to Chess* (Oxford: Oxford University Press, 1984), 210.

78. *Garin de Montglane* and *Huon de Bordeaux*, two late medieval chansons de geste, contain a similar scenario. In *Garin* the eponymous hero arrives at Charlemagne's court, and his reputation as a chess player becomes immediately known. Desiring to test him, Charlemagne proposes a match. If Garin wins, Charlemagne will give him the realm of France and Charlemagne's own wife; if Garin loses the game, he will lose his head. Although Garin wins the game, he wisely declines to accept his prize, settling instead for the town of Montglane (modern-day Lyons) as his reward. In *Huon de Bordeaux* the hero plays against the Emperor Yvorin's daughter. The emperor himself has determined the stakes. If Huon wins, he may sleep with the princess; if he loses, he will die.

79. Murray, *A History of Chess*, 583. (Murray does not give line numbers with the problems.)

80. Ibid., 583. The King's Library manuscript follows this proclamation almost exactly: "Kar ky voudra ententivement / Des guispartiez aprendre le doctrinement, / Les sutiles trayt & les mateysounes, / Les defenses cum les aprenderounes / En une cours sisseurement / juer porra le plus afeitement" ["For he who wishes to learn well the rules of play of the games covers the shrewd moves and winning endgames, and defensive strategies just as effectively at we learn them at court"] (588). Many thanks to Donald Maddox for help with this translation.

81. Ibid., 581, n. 24.

82. The endgame is narrated by Murray in *A History of Chess*, 482.

83. Christine de Pizan, *The Book of the Body Politic*, xv.

Chapter 3

Epigraph: Adam Smith, *The Theory of Moral Sentiments*, ed. Knud Haakonssen (Cambridge: Cambridge University Press, 2002), 275.

1. *The Riverside Chaucer*, 3rd ed., gen. ed. Larry D. Benson (Boston: Houghton Mifflin, 1987), bk. 2, l. 694. All Chaucer quotations are from this edition and will be cited parenthetically by the work's title (or abbreviation thereofe) and line number.

2. Much has been written about this scene. Sarah Stanbury, examining the power of voyeurism in the poem, sees Criseyde at this moment as a "female spectator caught between desire and the taboo on looking." Stanbury, "The Voyeur and the Private Life in *Troilus and Criseyde*," *Studies in the Age of Chaucer* 13 (1991): 141–58, at 148–49. Donald R. Howard argues that Criseyde's inner monologue "explores . . . the relationship between experience (what we do) and consciousness (what we think)." Howard, "Experience, Language, and Consciousness: *Troilus and Criseyde*, II, 596–931," in *Medieval Literature and Folklore Studies: Essays in Honor of Francis Lee Utley*, ed. Jerome Mandel and Bruce A. Rosenberg (New Brunswick, N.J.: Rutgers University Press, 1970), 173–92, at 174. Chauncey Wood, observing that by the time Criseyde begins her inner debate, her arguments "will more often be about practical than ethical considerations," charts the progress of the heroine's thoughts. *The Elements of Chaucer's* Troilus (Durham, N.C.: Duke University Press, 1984), 136.

3. The narrative is thick with references to gaming. Upon discovering Troilus's love for Criseyde, Pandarus remarks: "A ha! . . . Here bygynneth game" (1.868). When Pandarus eventually informs Criseyde of Troilus's affection, she continues this discourse of gaming and observes: "It nedeth me ful sleighly for to pleie" (2.462). And finally, after seeing Troilus's dismay at Criseyde's departure, Pandarus counsels his friend to pursue other women and "sette the world on six and sevene" ["gamble the world on a throw of a dice"] (4.623). Critics have not failed to note this discourse of gaming. Wood notes that Criseyde "starts by refusing to play the game, then tries to play by her own rules, and at last she just plays" (*The Elements of Chaucer's* Troilus, 137). In his "Chaucerian Comedy and Criseyde," Alfred David notes that "Criseyde regards life as a most enjoyable game. . . . She is well aware that she is the prize in a game Pandarus is playing, and she will let herself be won, so she believes, in her own time and on her own terms," in *Essays on Troilus and Criseyde*, ed. Mary Salu (Cambridge: D.S. Brewer, 1979), 90–104, at 92.

4. Some may argue that allegorical characters such as Fortune and the Black Knight cannot be compared to those like Criseyde. But even after setting aside the fact that all characters are equally fictional—Criseyde is no more real than a chess-playing Lady Fortune—the imagined relationships of the characters to the game are similar. Just as the Black Knight quite literally plays chess with his lady White, so too does Criseyde imagine herself locked in battle with a spouse, with a mate on the board as emblematic of a greater loss of power and freedom. For a discussion of the connections between chess problem sets and gambling, please see the previous chapter.

5. Although I will be focusing on texts that come from the late fourteenth and early fifteenth centuries, I should note that in his early fourteenth-century

preaching manual, *Handlyng Synne*, Robert Mannyng of Brunne cautions that those who "evere wyþ iogelour, / Wyþ hasardour oþer wyþ rotour, / Hauntyst taverne or were to any pere / To pleye at þe ches or at þe tablere" on holy days is going "agens þe comaundement / And holy cherchys asent." *Handlyng Synne*, ed. Idelle Sullens (Binghamton, N.Y.: Medieval and Renaissance Texts and Studies, 1983), ll. 1041–44, 1046–47).

6. This new name is used in "The *Canterbury Interlude* and the Merchant's *Tale of Beryn*," in *The Canterbury Tales: Fifteenth-Century Continuations and Additions*, ed. John M. Bowers (Kalamazoo, Mich.: Medieval Institute Publications, 1992). In an essay subsequent to his edition Bowers explains that he coined this term because it "better acknowledges the ludic quality of the continuation and its central positioning within the Northumberland manuscript where the unique copy of the work survives." "Controversy and Criticism: Lydgate's *Thebes* and the Prologue to *Beryn*," *Chaucer Yearbook* 5 (1998): 91–115, at 92, n. 3. Bowers's new title is apt as it recognizes both the material conditions of the tale and the departure this text takes from the pilgrims' prologues in the *Canterbury Tales*. All references to the *Interlude* and *Tale of Beryn* come from Bowers's edition and are noted in parentheses by line number.

7. My understanding of actual games and discourses of games differs from Glending Olson's more general concept of games as recreational pastimes in *Literature as Recreation in the Later Middle Ages* (Ithaca, N.Y.: Cornell University Press, 1982), and also from Laura Kendrick's ideas about play in *Chaucerian Play: Comedy and Control in the* Canterbury Tales (Berkeley: University of California Press, 1988). Olson's primary interest is in medieval attitudes about the relationship between texts and pleasure. For the medievals, Olson argues, literature could be gamelike in its ability to bring pleasure to the reader and thus promote his or her physical well-being. Kendrick sees games as part of a larger project of play, an act that "enables man to sublimate and channel his dangerous desires and to master his anxieties as he expresses these or sees them expressed in the safe, ordered 'other world' of the game via transforming, controlling fictions" (3). Either as a means to create pleasure or to help negotiate the realm of desire, games for both Olson and Kendrick are not only positive but also psychologically significant. By contrast, I argue that the games that appear in *The Tale of Beryn* are portrayed as negative pastimes with a social and economic, rather than psychological, impact on those who play them.

8. See Henri Pirenne, *Economic and Social History of Medieval Europe*, trans. I. E. Clegg (New York: Harcourt, Brace, 1936); M. M. Postan, *The Medieval Economy and Society: An Economic History of Britain, 1100–1500* (Berkeley: University of California Press, 1972); Raymond de Roover, *Business, Banking, and Economic Thought in Late Medieval and Early Modern Europe: Selected Studies of Raymond de Roover*, ed. Julius Kirshner (Chicago: University of Chicago Press, 1974); Robert S. Lopez, *The Commercial Revolution of the Middle Ages, 950–1350* (Englewood Cliffs, N.J.: Prentice-Hall, 1971); and John Day, *The Medieval Market Economy* (Oxford: Blackwell, 1987). For recent scholarship on medieval markets specifically in England, see J. L. Bolton, *The Medieval English Economy, 1150–1500* (London: J.M. Dent, 1980); Christopher Dyer, *Standards of Living in the Later Middle Ages: Social Change in England, c. 1200–1520* (Cambridge: Cambridge University Press, 1989), and *Making a Living in the Middle Ages: The People of Britain, 850–1520* (New Haven, Conn.: Yale University

Press, 2002); R. H. Britnell, *The Commercialisation of English Society, 1000–1500,* 2nd ed. (Manchester: Manchester University Press, 1996); Jenny Kermode, *Medieval Merchants: York, Beverley and Hull in the Later Middle Ages* (Cambridge: Cambridge University Press, 1998).

9. Roover talks about the hazards of banking and the unpredictability of exchange rates in his essay "What Is Dry Exchange?" See *Business, Banking, and Economic Thought,* 183–99.

10. Modern game theory was launched by John von Neumann and Oskar Morgenstern, who published *Theory of Games and Economic Behavior* in 1944 (Princeton, N.J.: Princeton University Press, 1944). In the early 1950s John Nash expanded on von Neumann and Morgenstern's theories by creating models of bargaining between rivals.

11. Although the words "trade," "commerce," and "exchange" have overlapping meanings, I have tried to use "trade" and "commerce" to designate large-scale economic transactions and "exchange" to refer to small-scale trades between individuals.

12. Sidney J. H. Herrtage, *The Early English Versions of the* Gesta Romanorum, EETS e.s. 33 (London: Trübner, 1879), 71. It is telling that another chapter in the *Gesta* (chapter 178) uses Jacobus's descriptions of the pieces to describe the perfect kingdom, yet, as if nervous about using the game as a metaphor, drops the allegory altogether. This chapter is omitted in the early English versions of the *Gesta* and can be found in *Gesta romamorum,* ed. Hermann Oesterley (Berlin: Weidmann, 1872; reprint Hildescheim: Georg Olms, 1963), 579. The story of Antonius is chapter 275 in Oesterley's edition.

13. Ibid., 71.

14. The Black Knight's game against Fortune in the *Book of the Duchess* is one of the few instances where Fortune is portrayed allegorically as a chess player. Despite the widespread notion that chess served as a popular medieval allegory for Fortune, there is little evidence that this was the case.

15. Paul Strohm, *Politique: Languages of Statecraft Between Chaucer and Shakespeare* (Notre Dame, Ind.: University of Notre Dame Press, 2005), 4.

16. See Roover, "What Is Dry Exchange?"

17. Britnell, *The Commercialisation of English Society, 1000–1500,* 164. Although Christopher Dyer cautions against seeing post-1350 England as a "golden age" of laborers, he also confirms that standards of living were generally higher in this century than they were in the previous century (*Standards of Living in the Middle Ages,* 6).

18. The merchants themselves contributed to the increase in demand, and their "consumption of material goods was conspicuously greater than that of their craftsmen neighbours" (Kermode, *Medieval Merchants,* 19).

19. Ibid., 2. Kermode's main sources are freemen's rolls, memorandum books, house books (which followed memorandum books), and chamberlains' account rolls (11).

20. All of these figures come from ibid., 39.

21. Ruth Bird, *The Turbulent London of Richard II* (New York: Longmans, Green, 1949), 1.

22. Ibid., 30–33. For a good analysis of the violence surrounding the mayoral elections of 1384, the factions behind this violence, and the ways that the social

drama of factional violence are narrated, see Paul Strohm, *Hochon's Arrow: The Social Imagination of Fourteenth-Century Texts* (Princeton, N.J.: Princeton University Press, 1992), 11–31.

23. Britnell, *The Commercialisation of English Society, 1000–1500*, 172. Britnell in turn cites R. H. Hilton, "Medieval Market Towns and Simple Commodity Production," *Past and Present* 109 (1985): 22.

24. Kermode, *Medieval Merchants*, 2.

25. Ibid., 68. Kermode in turn cites a fourteenth-century Letter Book from the London Guildhall which records that three aldermen were accused of exploitation.

26. Ibid., 54.

27. The depiction of merchants as greedy and self-interested was fairly commonplace in medieval estates satire. Such portraits appear in places like John Gower's *Miroir de l'omme* in the form of characters named Trickery, Avarice, and Avarice's third daughter, Usury. For a discussion of these and other satirical portraits of merchants, see Jill Mann, *Chaucer and Medieval Estates Satire: The Literature of Social Classes and the* General Prologue *to the* Canterbury Tales (Cambridge: Cambridge University Press, 1973), 99–103. Part of this concern about merchants and other tradesmen undoubtedly stemmed from a more general anxiety about social cohesion in an era where professional differentiation was on the rise. Such a worry about social fragmentation, professional specialization, and individual profit can be seen in the staging of Corpus Christi plays, which began in the early fourteenth century. As Mervyn James has argued, the plays provided a place where "the diachronic rise and fall of occupational communities could be confronted and worked out." See his "Ritual, Drama, and Social Body in the Late Medieval English Town," *Past and Present* 98 (February 1983): 3–29, at 15. Britnell echoes James's connection between the production of Corpus Christi plays and the cultural emphasis on civic unity, noting that the ritual "implied that without charity the effect of occupational specialisation would be to tear society apart," and observing that guild groups were fined if they failed to take part in the festivities (*The Commercialisation of English Society, 1000–1500*, 173). By contrast, Sarah Beckwith has argued that the Corpus Christi cycle was a ritualized activity and as such was made up of various sets of tensions which do not build toward a cohesive whole. She finds that James's model is not "capable of engaging in any explicit way with the theatrical practices of the plays themselves." "Ritual, Theater, and Social Space in the York Corpus Christi Cycle," in *Bodies and Disciplines: Intersections of Literature and History in Fifteenth-Century England*, ed. Barbara A. Hanawalt and David Wallace (Minneapolis: University of Minnesota Press, 1996), 63–86, at 65.

28. Dyer, *Standards of Living in the Middle Ages*, 7.

29. Paul Sweezy, "A Critique," in *The Transition from Feudalism to Capitalism*, ed. Paul Sweezy (London: N.L.B., 1976), 33–56, at 49. The italics are Sweezy's. In his introduction to this volume, Rodney Hilton argues that "during the course of the relatively unfettered commodity production in the 15th century, the necessary preconditions were created for later capitalist development" (*The Transition from Feudalism to Capitalism*, 9–29, at 25–26). John Hatcher and Mark Bailey cover some of the same ground in *Modelling the Middle Ages: The History and Theory of England's*

Economic Development (Oxford: Oxford University Press, 2001), although their study looks primarily at modern economic models proposed for (or as they would probably argue, imposed on) late medieval England rather than the conditions of living at that time.

30. While Langland's worry about profit also lies at the heart of Lady Mede's trip to court, his concern in that section of the poem is specifically about illicit exchanges such a bribes, payoff, influence peddling, and corruptions of penance.

31. *Piers Plowman: The B Version*, ed. George Kane and E. Talbot Donaldson (London: Athlone Press, 1975), passus 5, ll. 323–30.

32. Derek Pearsall, "Langland's London," in *Written Work: Langland, Labor, and Authorship*, ed. Steven Justice and Kathryn Kerby-Fulton (Philadelphia: University of Pennsylvania Press, 1997), 185–207, at 199.

33. Ibid., 193. James Simpson has persuasively argued that Langland undermines his own hostility to a profit economy by using commercial economic terms to describe man's relationship with God. By coopting such terms to describe spiritual reward, Langland ends up "countenancing new forms of economic relations on earth." "Spirituality and Economics in Passus 1–7 of the B-Text," *Yearbook of Langland Studies* 1 (1987): 83–103, at 85. It is difficult, however, to maintain this analogy, which ignores the qualitative differences between the material and spiritual world. It is notable that when we turn to the countryside, the merchants are mentioned only in the margin of the pardon in B, passus 7, underscoring Langland's distrust of contemporary mercantile practice.

34. As R. A. Shoaf aptly puts it: "The Canterbury pilgrims repeatedly fail [in mutual and just exchange], fail in community, because they are forever opposing or 'quiting' someone or something." *Dante, Chaucer, and the Currency of the Word: Money, Images, and Reference in Late Medieval Poetry* (Norman, Okla.: Pilgrim Books, 1983), 167.

35. The Knight's concern with reconciling the Host and the Pardoner draws the pilgrim fellowship further closer to the practices of parish guilds, which emphasized solidarity among their members. Writing of fourteenth-century parish guilds, Carl Lindahl lists five characteristics that bring these organizations in line with Chaucer's pilgrims: the parish guild was primarily a middle-class institution; its members came from varied economic statuses; its members came from varied occupations; most guilds admitted women and members of the clergy; and most guilds aimed at providing religious edification and entertainment for their members. Lindahl adds: "Growing from the decay of the noble class and a set of newfound opportunities in urban life, the two groups represent a new middle world presaging the social realignments of subsequent centuries." *Earnest Games: Folkloric Patterns in the Canterbury Tales* (Bloomington: Indiana University Press, 1987), 31. Such a comparison between the Chaucer's "compaignye" and the English guilds of the late fourteenth century has also been made more recently by David Wallace in *Chaucerian Polity: Absolutist Lineages and Associational Forms in England and Italy* (Stanford, Calif.: Stanford University Press, 1997), 83–103.

36. Margaret Connolly argues that the allegory's application is "limited" and does not accurately represent John of Gaunt's misfortune. She concludes that the game "may be an indication that Chaucer himself was confused, and probably also not very interested in the idea of chess itself." "Chaucer and Chess," *Chaucer Review*

29, 1 (1994): 40–44, at 43. Guillemette Bolens and Paul Beekman Taylor agree that the chess metaphor is "confused." However, they relocate the source of the confusion from Chaucer to the Black Knight, arguing that "the poet, his dreamed persona, and the Black Knight he interrogates have distinct conceptions of the game, and that much of the force and sense of the poem depends upon a collaborative correction of the knight's confused chess metaphor in the duration of time before the castle bell toll [*sic*] ends of the game, hunt, and dream." "The Game of Chess in Chaucer's *Book of the Duchess*," *Chaucer Review* 32, 4 (1998): 325–34, at 325. Bolens and Taylor also discuss this same chess scene in "Chess, Clocks, and Counsellors in Chaucer's *Book of the Duchess*," *Chaucer Review* 35, 3 (2001): 281–93. This interpretation holds that Chaucer has *deliberately* confused the metaphor; thus, the chess allegory succeeds through its very failure. This line of criticism, however, rests on the assumption of a transparent correspondence between characters and pieces, characters and historical figures, a real game and an allegorical one. It also overlooks the way the game also facilitates a fairly straightforward exchange between the two players. As noted above, the Black Knight himself understands the match as a reckoning of accounts, his Whit being exchanged for sorrow. Much as the young Beryn will do, he has gambled on the game to his own detriment. For a longer response to Connolly, Bolens, and Taylor, see my "Pawn Takes Knight's Queen: Playing with Chess in the *Book of the Duchess*," *Chaucer Review* 34, 2 (1999): 125–38.

37. Mark N. Taylor argues that Chaucer has used the chess metaphor "to express, in the conventional terms of the day, the depths of the Knight's love for his late wife" and that "the poet's knowledge of chess was adequate to this purpose." "Chaucer's Knowledge of Chess," *Chaucer Review* 38, 4 (2004): 299–313, at 299. While I completely agree with Taylor's assertion that Chaucer had an adequate knowledge of chess (and indeed have argued as much myself in the same journal), I remain less convinced that Chaucer in this poem is trying to paint a vivid picture of woe. The poem's narrator, a figure of no little comic relief, continually ruins the Black Knight's attempts at bathos. Moreover, the Black Knight himself, although apparently gloomy throughout the poem, ends up returning to his castle as a king. If indeed he has wagered his happiness with Fortune, as Taylor also argues, he has definitely gained something else in return.

38. Notably, this is the same word that Criseyde uses right before she uses her chess metaphor.

39. H. J. R. Murray, *A History of Chess* (Oxford: Oxford University Press, 1913), 566.

40. That the *Book of the Duchess* narrates the story of John of Gaunt and his first wife, Blanche, is widely accepted. A few exceptions include Edward I. Condren, "This Historical Context of the *Book of the Duchess*: A New Hypothesis," *Chaucer Review* 5, 3 (1970): 195–212, and "On Deaths and Duchesses and Scholars Coughing Ink," *Chaucer Review* 10, 1 (1975): 87–95; and D. W. Robertson, Jr., "The *Book of the Duchess*," in *A Companion to Chaucer Studies*, rev. ed., ed. Beryl Rowland (New York: Oxford University Press, 1979), 403–13). The poem's closing reference to a "long castle" with white walls by "Seynt Johan, on a ryche hil" works as a clever pun on the names of John of Richmond and Blanche of Lancaster, providing the means for readers (at least those in the know) to identify the subject matter at hand. In fact, a

few contemporary readers have taken this identification so literally that they have assumed that the Black Knight's mawkish wooing provides a historical account of John's courtship of Blanche. In her biography of John of Gaunt, for example, Anil de Silva-Vigier cites large portions of the Knight's heartfelt lament in her description of Gaunt's sentiments without using any other source to substantiate her "history." *The Moste Highe Prince . . . John of Gaunt, 1340–1399* (Edinburgh: Pentland Press, 1992), 84–88. D. W. Robertson has argued that the poem was used in connection with the annual service held by the duke in memory of his deceased wife, and Lisa J. Kiser writes that John commissioned Chaucer to write the poem after Blanche's death. See Robertson, "The *Book of the Duchess*," 403, and Kiser, *Truth and Textuality in Chaucer's Poetry* (Hanover, N.H.: University Press of New England, 1991), 24. At the beginning of her discussion of the poem, Kiser also muses: "can a poet speak with authority about how it is for John of Gaunt, who loved Blanche, to miss her?" (12). Yet the critical desire to read the poem as a firsthand account of John of Gaunt's mourning for Blanche of Lancaster tends to obscure the fundamentally contractual nature of his relationship with his first wife. That John may indeed have loved Blanche does not negate the fact that the marriage was arranged by their families and needed special papal dispensation to bypass laws of consanguinity: they were third cousins. Moreover, their marriage came eight years after a failed attempt to arrange a more politically expedient marriage between John and the daughter of the Count of Flanders. And while John may have been grief-stricken after the death his of first wife, negotiations for his second marriage were underway within three months of Blanche's death. Though John's first marriage had made him one of the richest men in England, his second, to Constanza of Castile, made him royalty by giving him the kingship of Leon and Castille. So invested was John in his new status that he refused to bring Constanza officially into London until King Edward and Parliament recognized his new titles. Moreover, none of this takes into account the fact that John by the early 1370s had a mistress, Katherine Swynford, whom he eventually married after the death of his second wife. If Chaucer wrote the poem in 1372, the *terminus ad quem* of composition, the Black Knight's rather insipid speech rings a bit false, a way to mask a lucrative marriage contract as a version of *amor courtois*. If Chaucer wrote the poem as early as 1368, the year of Blanche's death, the swooning, pale-faced knight seems more worthy of ridicule than respect, less flattering than fumbling. Even the dreamer, who interrupts the Knight's speech several times, seems bored by the story of love. The chess game against Fortune, however, embodies a fairly realistic, even cynical, representation of what was, after all, an arranged marriage. The game does not deny the possibility of love or sentiment; there is little reason to doubt that the Black Knight's lost "fers" upsets him. But like upper-class marriages, the medieval chess game bound players in contracts, furnishing the opportunity for financial loss or gain.

41. Patricia J. Eberle, "Commercial Language and the Commercial Outlook in the *General Prologue*," *Chaucer Review* 18, 2 (1983): 161–74, at 163. Although Eberle here is describing Chaucer's audience, her description also captures the temperaments of the pilgrims.

42. Those who have written about exchange practices in the *Shipman's Tale* include Paul S. Schneider, " 'Taillynge Ynough': The Function of Money in the *Shipman's*

Tale," *Chaucer Review* 11, 3 (1977): 201–9; David H. Abraham, "*Cosyn* and *Cosynage*: Pun and Structure in the *Shipman's Tale*," *Chaucer Review* 11, 4 (1977): 319–27; and Robert Adams, "The Concept of Debt in the *Shipman's Tale*," *Studies in the Age of Chaucer* 6 (1984): 85–102.

43. Lee Patterson, *Chaucer and the Subject of History* (Madison: University of Wisconsin Press, 1991), 352.

44. Ibid.

45. Ibid., 357.

46. It is notable that Patterson, when describing the anxieties that surrounded England's increasingly commercial economy, also begins to draw on the language of games. Noting that money worried aristocrats, Patterson states that the nobility tried to recoup cash loses through "the highly unreliable lottery of warfare." Meanwhile, the peasantry was becoming an increasingly powerful class "that took advantage of the many opportunities for self-improvement available in the changing world of late-medieval agriculture to develop into the most dynamic players in the economic game" (328, 329).

47. Elizabeth Allen, "The Pardoner in the 'Dogges Boure,'" *Chaucer Review* 36, 2 (2001): 91–127, at 103.

48. Ibid., 107.

49. Writing about the choice of location, Peter Brown observes that the Cheker was erected in the late fourteenth century by a prior named Chillenden in an effort to facilitate the pilgrim trade. Brown goes on to argue that "if the *Beryn* author had been writing after 1438 it is likely that he would have sited the action of the prologue at The Sun by virtue of its closeness to the cathedral and its novelty as a building." Peter Brown, "Journey's End: The Prologue to *The Tale of Beryn*," in *Chaucer and Fifteenth-Century Poetry*, ed. Julia Boffey and Janet Cowen (London: King's College, 1991), 143–74, at 151. Yet closeness and novelty do not necessarily dictate name choice, especially when this particular name has such resonance.

50. See "chek" in Hans Kurath and Sherman Kuhn, eds., *Middle English Dictionary* (Ann Arbor: University of Michigan Press, 1979). Also see "check" and "exchequer" in the *Oxford English Dictionary*.

51. Murray, *A History of Chess*, 511. Although Murray attributes this passage to Alexander of Neckham, there is no proof that Neckham was the author.

52. Richard Fitz Nigel, *Dialogus de Scaccario: The Course of the Exchequer*, ed. and trans. Charles Johnson, with corrections by F. E. L. Carter and D. E. Greenway (Oxford: Clarendon Press, 1983). Although written in the twelfth century, the *Dialogus* laid out the basic practices of the Exchequer's office that "persisted till the sixteenth century in spite of the general adoption of Arabian arithmetic" (introduction to the *Dialogus de Scaccario: The Course of the Exchequer*, xxxvi).

53. According to David Hooper and Kenneth Whyld, draughts (or "checkers") was invented in France in the twelfth century and was the most popular game in Europe after chess. *The Oxford Companion to Chess* (Oxford: Oxford University Press, 1984), 95.

54. *Magister*. Nulla mihi verior ad presens occurrit quam quia scaccarii lusilis similem habet formam. *Discipulus*. Numquid antiquorum prudentia pro sola forma sic nominauit? Cum et simili ratione posset tabularium appellari. *Magister*. Merito

te scrupulosum dixi. Est et alia set occultior: sicut enim in scaccario lusili quidam ordines sunt pugnatorum et certis legibus vel limitibus procedunt vel subsistent, presidentibus aliis et aliis precedentibus, sic in hoc quidam president quidam assident ex officio, et non est cuiquam liberum leges constitutas excedere, quod erit ex consequentibus manifestum. Item, sicut in lusili pugna committitur inter reges, sic in hoc inter duos principaliter conflictus est et pugna committitur, thesaurarium scilicet et vicecomitem qui assidet ad compotum residentibus aliis tanquam iudicibus ut videant et iudicent (*Dialogus de Scaccario: The Course of the Exchequer, 7*).

55. The most comprehensive history of the medieval English Exchequer is still Thomas Madox's *History and Antiquities of the Exchequer of the Kings of England*, first published in 1769 and reprinted by Augustus M. Kelley in 1969. Madox, however, ends his study with Edward II, leaving out the changes to the office that took place in the early fifteenth century, the most notable of which is the first appointment of a layman as chancellor of the Exchequer in 1410. For a brief mention of this appointment, see Henry Roseveare, *The Treasury: The Evolution of a British Institution* (London: Allen Lane, 1969), 35.

56. Most scholars see the *Miller's Tale* as a response to the Knight rather than an attempt to rile up Oswald the Reeve. It is only Oswald who sees the story as a personal attack on him.

57. Wallace, *Chaucerian Polity*, 66, 79. My conception of Chaucer's fellowship blends the ideas of Carl Lindahl (*Earnest Games*, 19–31), who maps resemblances between Chaucer's pilgrim group and late fourteenth-century parish guilds, with those of Richard Firth Green, who notes that the words "fellowship" and "compagnie" were "loaded terms" at this time, as they implied "the existence of oaths of mutual loyalty taken in defiance of established authority." *A Crisis of Truth: Literature and Law in Ricardian England* (Philadelphia: University of Pennsylvania Press, 1999), 190.

58. Peter Brown argues that the central theme of the *Interlude* "concerns the question of fellowship, adopted from *The Canterbury Tales*, as an ideal with an alarming propensity to disintegration" (Brown, "Journey's End," 164). Glending Olson sees Chaucer's Pardoner as the most subversive member of the *Canterbury Tales* and posits that the *Interlude* brings this "churl" back in line. Although Olson uses the phrase "social conformity" rather than "community" or "fellowship" to describe the taming of the Pardoner, his emphasis on social order gets at the same phenomenon. "The Misreadings of the *Beryn* Prologue," *Mediaevalia* 17 (1994): 201–19, at 211. And finally Stephen Medcalf argues that interaction with the shrine inspires a feeling of "communitas" among the pilgrims with the exception of the Pardoner, who cannot situate himself within the group. "Motives for Pilgrimage," in *England in the Fourteenth Century: Proceedings of the 1991 Harlaxton Symposium*, ed. Nicholas Rogers (Stamford, Conn.: Paul Watkins, 1993), 77–108, at 104.

59. "False fellowship," he argues, "is particularly associated with the alliance formed by Kitt, her lover, and Jak the hosteller" (Brown, "Journey's End," 165).

60. In showing how the Pardoner is "normalized," Olson argues that the Beryn poet rewrites this character "into heterosexual romance" ("The Misreadings of the *Beryn* Prologue," 211). But while the *Beryn* Pardoner's lust for Kitt may be a rewriting of Chaucer's Pardoner's (debatably) queer sexual orientation, the fact that he spends the night under the stairs, attempting to get closer to a dog that bites whenever he

comes near it, unsettles this easy reformation and suggests that Pardoner is an opportunist or possibly more sexually ambiguous than previously depicted.

61. See Furnivall's glossary at the end of his edition of *The Tale of Beryn, with a Prologue of the Merry Adventure of the Pardoner with a Tapster at Canterbury*, ed. F. J. Furnivall and W. G. Stone, EETS e.s. 105 (London: Kegan Paul, Trench, Trübner, 1909), 206.

62. "Chek" is also used in the Chaucer canon exclusively in the context of a chess game. In *Troilus*, Criseyde vehemently dismisses the possibility of marrying a second husband, insisting that she will never remarry: "Shal noon housbonde seyn to me 'Chek mat!'" (2.754). Similarly, in the *Book of the Duchess* the Black Knight loses his White Queen when Fortune mates him during an extended chess game. In both instances the word "chek" encapsulates a monetary and/or social diminution of power. For instances of Chaucer's uses of "check," see John S. P. Tatlock and Arthur G. Kennedy, *A Concordance to the Complete Works of Geoffrey Chaucer and to the* Romaunt of the Rose (Washington, D.C.: Carnegie Institute of Washington, 1927), 134.

63. The town's name was created by Furnivall, who introduced it in the side notes to his edition (see note to l. 1631). I have used it, since it offers a convenient shorthand for the poet's lengthier formations of the same idea.

64. The late thirteenth- or early fourteenth-century poem *Sir Tristrem* contains a similar moment of gambling. In this instance Tristan plays the game with some mariners, and he bets twenty shillings against one of their hawks. As Alan Lupack notes, the fact that Tristrem is said to "gave has he gan winne / In raf [winnings]" (ll. 327–28) suggests that Tristrem deliberately throws several rounds in order to keep raising the stakes. In the end Tristrem wins "an hundred pounde," (l. 341), and his victory inspires the mariners to seize and take him on board with them. Lancelot of the Laik *and* Sir Tristrem, ed. Alan Lupack, TEAMS editions (Kalamazoo, Mich.: Medieval Institute Publications, 1994), 151, 165. It is notable that in early versions of the legend chess marks the hero's nobility rather than his sneakiness. In the early thirteenth-century prose *Tristan*, the game appears during Tristan's journey with Iseult, and the lovers drink the magic potion while they play the game. In Gottfried von Strassburg's version, as in *Sir Tristrem*, Tristan plays chess with sailors, and is abducted as a result. Many thanks to Ann Higgins for helping me with the Tristan legend.

65. Richard Firth Green, "Legal Satire in *The Tale of Beryn*," *Studies in the Age of Chaucer* 11 (1989): 43–62, esp. 54–62.

66. A similar connection of checkmating to financial loss also appears in an early fifteenth-century poem called "A Remembrance of Fifty-two Follies." Here the poet scolds an imaginary figure named "Flaundres" for her mistakes. She was "þe richest land, and meriest to mynne" but her princes mismanaged her into poverty. In the penultimate stanza the poet warns: "Who so wil not knowe his awen astat, / Ne delivere chekkys, er þat he be mat / He shal have worldis wondryng, / And his sould hyndryng, / And ay in paynes pondryng; / To mende þanne, is to late [Whoever thus will not know his own estate / Nor to cover his check before he is mated / He shall have a worldly wondering / And hindering his soul / And always pondering in pain / To mend then; it is too late]." See *Twenty-Six Political and Other Poems*, part 1, ed. J. Kail, EETS o.s. 124 (London: Kegan Paul, Trench, Trübner, 1904), ll. 57, 107–12.

67. Although Green has convincingly shown that the *lex mercantoria* is the

legal system at work in the tale, it should be noted that the Exchequer had numerous judicial activities, functioning as "a revenue court, a court of common law and a court of equity" (Roseveare, *The Treasury: The Evolution of a British Institution*, 34). It thus might serve as another possible target of the satire.

68. *Libelle of Englyshe Polycye: A Poem on the Use of Sea-Power, 1436*, ed. Sir George Warner (Oxford:Clarendon Press, 1926), l. 6.

Chapter 4

1. So dramatically different are these two halves that some fifteenth-century scribes labeled the whole work as the *Regement* while others inserted this title only above the last three thousand lines. Ethan Knapp discusses both medieval and modern vexations over the different parts in *The Bureaucratic Muse: Thomas Hoccleve and the Literature of Late Medieval England* (University Park: Pennsylvania State University Press, 2001), 82.

2. For a good examination of the ways Hoccleve "follows Boethius in rejecting the monologic lyricism of the complaint" yet never allows his dialogue "to pass into consolation, that higher form of monologue," see ibid., 94–104, at 98. Jennifer E. Bryan has convincingly argued that Hoccleve's language of complaint recycles contemporary devotional discourse. Although Bryan looks primarily at Hoccleve's "Complaint of the Virgin," she also sees the *Regement* as a place where "Hoccleve commodifies his interiority, spectacularizing singularity, excess, and failure in the service of an audience that desires the pleasure of intimacy" ("Hoccleve, the Virgin, and the Politics of Complaint," *PMLA: Publications of the Modern Language Association* 117.5 [2002]: 1172–87, at 1181).

3. *The Regiment of Princes*, ed. Charles R. Blyth, TEAMS series (Kalamazoo, Mich.: Medieval Institute Publications, 1999), ll. 2052–53 and ll. 2109–11. Subsequent references from this edition will be noted parenthetically by line number. As noted in the opening chapter, the full title for Cessolis's work is the *Liber de moribus hominum et officiis nobilium ac popularium super ludo scachorum* (The Book of the Morals of Men and the Duties of Nobles and Commoners, on the Game of Chess; henceforth the *Liber*). The *Regement* contains numerous exempla and aphorisms from Scripture, from authorities like Gregory the Great and Bernard of Clairvaux, and even from Hoccleve's fellow English poets, Chaucer and Gower. Importantly, though, Hoccleve only explicitly credits these three sources.

4. For a full discussion of this, see Chapter 3.

5. Hoccleve uses chess in only one other place in his poetry, and in this case the economic discourses are explicit. In the fourth part of Hoccleve's *Series*, the *Ars utilissima sciendi mori* (or, as it's more commonly called, "Lerne to Dye"), the disciple loses patience after listening to the (seemingly endless) laments of a dying man. After one of the man's self-directed eulogies, the disciple responds by insisting that while death itself may be difficult, it at least deals with people equally: "Evene to all is dethes iugement. / Thurghout the world strecchith hir paiement" (ll. 153–54). He then adds: "Deeth favorable is to no maner wight. / To all hirself shee delith equally. / Shee dredith hem nat þat been of greet might, / Ne of the olde and yonge hath no

mercy. / The ryche and poore folk eek certainly / Shee sesith. Shee sparith right nooon estaat. / *Al þat lyf berith with hir chek is maat*" (ll. 155–61; emphasis mine). Figured as a merchant, Death "hirself delith equally" to all her customers regardless of their social status, age, or income. Hoccleve uses the final line to drive home this point; when Death calls for a checkmate, one does not just lose one's body but all that life produces. In the next stanza, the mercantile discourse continues, and the disciple chides the dying man for thinking himself immune: "Wendist thow han been at swich avantage / þat shee nat durste han paied the thy wage / But oonly han thee spared and forborn . . . ?" (ll. 165–67). No longer a merchant who distributes her wares (i.e., herself) equally among her customers, Death is now a lord who deals out the same wages to all. In short, if chess and death resemble each other, it is only because the first represents the same economic culture the second destroys. All quotations of "Lerne to Dye" come from *"My Compleinte" and Other Poems*, ed. Roger Ellis (Exeter: University of Exeter Press, 2001).

6. Paul Strohm, *England's Empty Throne: Usurpation and the Language of Legitimation, 1399–1422* (New Haven, Conn.: Yale University Press, 1998), 179.

7. The *Liber* also appears in a unique Middle Scots version in the Asloan Manuscript, a Middle Scots miscellany that dates from roughly 1515, *The Buke of the Chess: Edited from the Asloan Manuscript*, ed. Catherine van Buuren (Edinburgh: Scottish Text Society, 1997), xii.

8. As N. F. Blake notes, "the greatest expense in printing books was the capital investment of buying the paper." *Caxton: England's First Publisher* (New York: Harper and Row, 1976), 29. Nonetheless, Blake also observes that Caxton could not translate books as quickly as his workmen could print them; see *Caxton and His World* (London: Andre Deutsch, 1969), 60–62.

9. Blake claims that it is not possible to know "how many copies of any first edition were printed," yet also adds that "we must assume that he thought they would be sufficient to satisfy the expected demand" (Blake, *Caxton: England's First Publisher*, 184). It is thus significant that of the many translations Caxton printed, he reprinted only four: *Dictes or Sayengis of the Philosophres* (reprinted twice), the *Game and Playe of the Chesse, Mirrour of the World*, and the *Historye of Reynard the Foxe*. Moreover, the fact that eight copies of the 1474 text and twelve of the 1483 text are extant suggests that the number of copies of the *Game and Playe* produced was high.

10. William Kuskin has compared the *Regement* and the *Game and Playe* in order to map "the specific historical articulation of the social relations by which capital and labor produce the individual as a subject" ("The Erasure of Labor: Hoccleve, Caxton, and the Information Age," in *The Middle Ages at Work*, ed. Kellie Robertson and Michael Uebel [New York: Palgrave Macmillan, 2004], 229–60, at 230). For Kuskin, Caxton tries quite deliberately to erase the presence of Hoccleve from his own work in an effort to demonstrate a "technological effortlessness," and this recasting of leisure for labor allows him in the *Game of Chesse* to translate "Lancastrian poetics to a Yorkist literary culture in which the theme of paternity has changed" (ibid., 240 and 243–44). While I agree that Caxton may have responded to Hoccleve, I am less interested in their larger ideological contrasts than in the ways they position themselves in relation to this particular text. I am grateful to Professor Kuskin for allowing me to look at a copy of this article before its publication.

11. Writing about poetic posturing in the fifteenth century, David Lawton has

observed that public discussion of royal power contributed to the "construction of the king as a subject" at the same time that it created a "reification of kingship" and a centralization of monarchial power. "Dullness and the Fifteenth Century," *English Literary History* 54, 4 (1987): 761–99, at 789. These ideas are echoed by Larry Scanlon, who draws on Perry Anderson's genealogy of absolutism to argue that the centralization of power in the fifteenth century accompanied a shift away from the individual king and toward a corporate identity. With the phrase "corporate identity," Scanlon indicates a system of governance that promotes a single leader as the repository of power and in doing so masks the networks that have established him as the ultimate authority. Thus as the secular government increased its control over the various aspects of daily life, the fifteenth-century king had become more powerful. At the same time, this increased authority came with contingencies and was shared by the nobility, who "had a greater stake in defining how royal power was to be exercised." Scanlon, "The King's Two Voices: Narrative and Power in Hoccleve's *Regement of Princes*," in *Literary Practice and Social Change in Britain, 1380–1530*, ed. Lee Patterson (Berkeley: University of California Press, 1990), 216–47, at 223). See also Perry Anderson, *Lineages of the Absolutist State* (London: N.L.B., 1974).

12. In her introduction to a collection of essays on the *Long Fifteenth Century*, Helen Cooper notes: "the murder of Richard II in 1399 set the pattern for the murders of Henry VI in 1471 and Edward V in 1483, and the genealogical turbulence it created lasted beyond the death of Richard III at Bosworth to the carnage of the battle of Stoke in 1487." Nor was political upheaval confined to England. Regicide also plagued the kings of Scotland, where James I was murdered in 1437, and where James III was killed in 1488 during a rebellion against him; see *The Long Fifteenth Century: Essays for Douglas Gray*, ed. Helen Cooper and Sally Mapstone (Oxford: Clarendon Press, 1997), 5.

13. Michael Bennett offers an overview of Richard's reign in his *Richard II and the Revolution of 1399* (Stroud: Sutton Publishing, 1999).

14. Strohm, *England's Empty Throne*, xi-xii.

15. Ibid., 31.

16. Judith Ferster, *Fictions of Advice: The Literature and Politics of Counsel in Late Medieval England* (Philadelphia: University of Pennsylvania Press, 1996), 144.

17. Although largely cast as advice to the king, the 1406 ordinances of Parliament essentially placed all power of governing in the hands of the prince of Wales. Henry IV did not regain power until 1411. Ferster narrates the battles over the monarchial power in ibid., 142–45.

18. Janet Coleman reminds us that such treatises fall more generally into "literature of social unrest" and that such literature was often formed in reaction to spiritual and social abuses (*Medieval Readers and Writers, 1350–1400* [New York: Columbia University Press, 1981], esp. 58–156).

19. Lydgate's most explicit commentary on kingship is his last and most famous work, *The Fall of Princes*, a translation of Boccaccio's *De casibus virorum illustrium*. Yet as Strohm argues, Lydgate's *Troy Book*, which claims the prince as its patron, and *Siege of Thebes*, seemingly a paean to the Henry's conquest in France, also engage this topic (*England's Empty Throne*, 186–95). Similarly, Gower uses book 4 of his *Confessio amantis* to address the subject of kingship, and this entire section

of his poem reads as a *speculum regis*. That Gower changed his dedication of this volume from Richard II to Henry of Derby (later Henry Bolingbroke, and later still King Henry IV) bespeaks Gower's vision of his own work as one with a royal audience, if not practical application. Gower's *Vox clamantis* and his *Chronica tripertita* also touch on political matters and contain moments of princely advice. Writers who preceded Gower and Lydgate might have been more circumspect in administering their advice. Nevertheless, Langland's *Piers Plowman* contains passages that draw directly on the language of the *speculum regis*, while Chaucer's *Tale of Melibee* could be labeled a *Fürstenspiegel* proper. Ann W. Astell also argues that Chaucer's *Parliament of Fowles, Monk's Tale,* and *Nun's Priest's Tale* all function as political allegories in which "the king is a material cause for the poet." *Political Allegory in Late Medieval England* (Ithaca, N.Y.: Cornell University Press, 1999), 94.

    20. Strohm, *England's Empty Throne,* 174.

    21. The *Secretum secretorum,* a translation of the Arabic *Kitāb sirr al-asrār* (The Book of the Secret of Secrets), exists in roughly five hundred manuscripts dating from the twelfth century onward. Its full title can be translated as *The Book of the Science of Government, on the Good Ordering of Statecraft;* see *Secretum Secretorum: Nine English Versions,* ed. M. A. Manzalaoui, EETS o.s. 276 (Oxford: Oxford University Press, 1977), ix.

    22. *Secretum secretorum,* Robert Copland's 1528 edition, ed. Manzalaoui, 329, 333.

    23. Ibid., 381.

    24. Hoccleve highlights this parallel by referring to Prince Henry in the same breath as he does Aegidius's *Regimine.* After describing Aristotle's project, Hoccleve adds: "Of which, and of Gyles of Regiment / Of Princes, plotmeel thynke I to translate. / And thogh that symple be my sentement, / O worthy Prince, I yow byseeche algate, / Considereth how endytynge hath in hate / My dul conceit" (ll. 2052–57). His use of the word "Prince" twice in quick succession drives home the similarities between his own project and that of Aegidius. As I have observed earlier in this book, Aegidius at times looks to a larger audience beyond the prince and claims that his treatise works for all men: "For theigh this book be itytled of the lore of princes, yut al the puple schal be itaugt þerby; and theigh nougt everiche man may be kyng oþer prince, yit everiche man schulde desire besiliche to make himself worthi to be a kyng oþer a prince." *The Governance of Kings and Princes: John Trevisa's Middle English Translation of the* De Regimine Principum *of Aegidius Romanus,* ed. David C. Fowler, Charles F. Briggs, and Paul G. Remley (New York: Garland, 1997), 7. This glance beyond the throne, however, remains merely a gesture in the context of a work that upholds royal authority. And although Aegidius may see his advice as applicable to all men (or at least to all nobles), his treatise is designed specifically for Philip. I have found no critical Latin edition of this text and have thus used John Trevisa's Middle English translation of the work, which may have been the copy that Hoccleve used.

    25. Ibid., 3.

    26. Lawton, "Dullness and the Fifteenth Century," 761–99.

    27. I would argue that Hoccleve's complicated relationship to Chaucer as an authority mirrors his complicated relationship to royal authority. Just as Hoccleve praises and undermines Chaucer's art, so too does he praise and undermine the king's control of his subjects. Writing about the two poets' relationship, Knapp argues

that Hoccleve's relationship with "fadir Chaucer" was vexed and that, along with praising Chaucer, Hoccleve's references to the earlier writer "present a strategy for poetic usurpation" (*The Bureaucratic Muse*, 109). Roger Ellis sees Hoccleve as similar to Chaucer and observes that "like Chaucer, and in common with many other writers at the close of the Middle Ages, Hoccleve is engagingly self-conscious about his own status as writer, in ways that anticipate the English Renaissance and hark back to the Italian Renaissance in the previous century" (*"My Compleinte" and Other Poems*, 4). John M. Bowers feels that Hoccleve "worked the hardest to install Geoffrey Chaucer as the Father of English Poetry and to claim his own position as direct lineal heir in this literary genealogy" yet ultimately failed to become part of the trinity that included Chaucer, Gower, and Lydgate. "Thomas Hoccleve and the Politics of Tradition," *Chaucer Review* 36, 4 (2002): 352–69, at 352. On her part, Bryan sees Hoccleve as attached to Chaucer through his interest in devotional tradition. Yet she also demonstrates the ways that Hoccleve's strategic use of complaint, his way of publicizing an "elaborate spectacle of singular inwardness—of introspection and excess," separates him from other writers ("Hoccleve, the Virgin, and the Politics of Complaint," 1185).

28. *The Regiment of Princes*, ed. Blyth, 9.

29. Nicholas Perkins, *Hoccleve's* Regiment of Princes: *Counsel and Constraint* (Cambridge: D.S. Brewer, 2001), 94.

30. As discussed in Chapter 1, learning the rules meant more than learning how to move one's own pieces or even how to play the game as a whole. For Jacobus, mastery of the game meant knowledge of the virtues appropriate to one's own profession.

31. Perkins, who has studied the *Regement*'s structure, does not find any significance in such changes. He notes that "Jacobus de Cessolis pursues the same themes of justice, mercy and chastity that Hoccleve's other sources present," and this organization "makes it possible for Hoccleve to include in the *Regiment* several exempla one after another, straight from Jacobus" (*Counsel and Constraint*, 97). However, this assessment overlooks the fact that the *Liber*, by virtue of its structure alone, addresses itself to the various members of a kingdom that do not occupy the throne. Thus while these two authors may be pursuing similar themes, Hoccleve's decision to change the framework for his text imbues such themes with a different significance.

32. One early nineteenth-century scholar purportedly traced twenty-one of the *Regement*'s thirty-nine references to the *Liber*'s chapter on the rooks. I have not been able to look at his article directly, although I suspect that he has lumped the stories from the knights' and bishops' chapters into one general category of "advisors." Perkins cites Friedrich Aster on this point on page 97 of *Counsel and Constraint*.

33. Ibid., 99 and 108. Ultimately, Perkins argues (I think rightly) that the *Liber*'s ultimate aim is not "merely to extend the King's power, but to bind it into a system of governance—an ideology—that is generated and regulated by people such as philosophers and councillors" (101).

34. The actual Fabius, who was elected consul of the Roman republic in 233 and 228 B.C.E. and was probably dictator in 221, was known for his caution and earned the nickname "Cunctator," or "the Hesitator," for his reluctance to fight in pitched battles. See the *Oxford Classical Dictionary*, 3rd ed. (Oxford University Press, 1996), 583.

35. This is found in the *Regement*'s chapter "De Justitia," ll. 2654–74.

36. That Fabricius was also known for his dedication to poverty—as censor in 275 he ordered a patrician exconsul expelled for possession of too much silver table-ware—further emphasizes Hoccleve's lessons on royal humility (*Oxford Classical Dictionary*, 585). Many thanks to Stephen Harris for searching out this information for me.

37. In his section on justice, Hoccleve tells the story of a senator who refuses to shirk a law that he, himself, has set down, a refusal that results in the loss of one of his own eyes. And in his section about loyalty and honesty, he narrates the tale of Marcus Regulus, who is captured by the Carthaginians in battle but who refuses to allow himself to be exchanged for their prisoners, since he knows it would not be profitable for the Roman army. Both of these stories, which emphasize the physical and psychological restrictions placed on the virtuous man, come from the *Liber*.

38. In the next stanza Hoccleve notes that only those in a poor estate remain immune to bad Fortune.

39. Blyth's introduction to *The Regiment of Princes*, 11.

40. Again, this anticipates the pre-Machiavellian moment that Paul Strohm locates later in the century. In *Politique: Languages of Statecraft Between Chaucer and Shakespeare* (Notre Dame, Ind.: University of Notre Dame Press, 2005), Strohm opens his discussion of statecraft with a close reading of a 1460s image of Edward IV sitting on top of Fortune's wheel. Instead of showing the wheel's inevitable turn (and Edward's inevitable tumble off it), the image depicts Ratio, who sits near the wheel's base ready to "spike" it and stop its motion. Thus, as Strohm argues: "Within Fortune's own traditional ambit, other forces now prevail" (3).

41. Scanlon, "The King's Two Voices," 220.

42. Ferster, *Fictions of Advice*, 158.

43. Gerald L. Harriss has shown that the emergence of a political society in which all ranks "came to be involved in the activity of governing" grew out of economic, social, and political changes that took place from the thirteenth to the fifteenth centuries, and that the changes in political order and descriptions thereof did not take place as a singular, rapid occurrence. "Political Society and the Growth of Government in Late Medieval England," *Past and Present* 138 (February 1993): 28–57, at 33).

44. In her study of early book illustration, Martha W. Driver aptly notes: "When we look at book illustration in particular, the movement from manuscript to print can be traced as a political act, with the print medium empowering newly literate readers, both women and men, to read and think for themselves." *The Image in Print: Book Illustration in Late Medieval England and Its Sources* (London: British Library, 2004), 3.

45. Russell Rutter, "William Caxton and Literary Patronage," *Studies in Philology* 84, 4 (1987): 440–70, at 444. Behind this point of view is N. F. Blake, whose work has set the tone for much of late twentieth-century Caxton scholarship. Blake repeatedly promotes this idea of Caxton-as-businessman, although as Rutter himself notes, at several moments Blake characterizes Caxton as dependent on patrons (Blake, *Caxton and His World*, and Rutter, "William Caxton and Literary Patronage," 442). For another characterization of Caxton as market-savvy, see Marilynn Desmond's

discussion of Caxton's *Eneydos* in *Reading Dido: Gender, Textuality, and the Medieval Aeneid* (Minneapolis: University of Minnesota Press, 1994), 167–76. Desmond stresses that "Caxton produced his *Eneydos* to meet a particular demand for texts in English" (170).

46. William Kuskin, "Caxton's Worthies Series: The Production of Literary Culture," *English Literary History* 66, 3 (1999): 511–51, at 512.

47. Ibid., 516.

48. Details of Caxton's life before he began his career as a printer can be found in William Blades, *The Life and Typography of William Caxton, England's First Printer*, vol. 1 (London: J. Lilly, 1861–63; reprint New York: Burt Franklin, 1966), 1–22; Blake, *Caxton and His World*, 13–45; George D. Painter, *William Caxton: A Biography* (New York: G. P. Putnam's Sons, 1977), 1–42; and Louise Gill, "William Caxton and the Rebellion of 1483," *English Historical Review* 114, 445 (1997): 105–18. The subsequent historical information has been taken primarily from Gill and Blake.

49. Looking at authors of manuscripts, Russell Rutter has argued that "the sustenance Caxton received from patrons was by comparison thin and inconsequential" ("William Caxton and Literary Patronage," 444). Yet later in this same article Rutter argues that the printer did rely on patronage in the early parts of his career, and that it was only "once Caxton begun to reach a larger public" that "patrons became less important to him" (463).

50. Raoul Lefèvre, *The Recuyell of the Historyes of Troyes*, vol. 1, reproduced with a critical introduction by H. Oskar Sommer (London: D. Nutt, 1894), 5. I have modernized aspects of Sommer's edition, such as his long *s*, and have also expanded his abbreviations. Subsequent references to this edition are cited parenthetically by page number.

51. Blake, *Caxton's Own Prose*, 156.

52. William Kuskin, "Reading Caxton: Transformations in Capital, Authority, Print, and Persona in the Late Fifteenth Century," *New Medieval Literatures* 3 (2000): 149–83, at 170.

53. Kuskin, "The Erasure of Labor," 242.

54. Blake, *Caxton: England's First Publisher*, 108.

55. Ibid.

56. Writing of the prologues and miniatures that appear in presentation manuscripts, Dhira Mahoney argues that "the offering is always presented in a context of power," with the recipient standing or seated on a throne and the author kneeling, both positions that emphasize status. Mahoney goes on to show "the way that a writer can exploit the conventions of the discourse, using both text and image for self-authorization, or to further a particular agenda." See Dhira B. Mahoney, "Courtly Presentation and Authorial Self-Fashioning: Frontispiece Miniatures in Late Medieval French and English Manuscripts," *Mediaevalia* 21 (1996): 97–160, at 101, 104. Caxton, who seems to have used the presentation copy as a model for his own prologues, writes to a similar end. In other words, even if Caxton was not entirely dependent on Margaret for financial support, it becomes expedient for him to conceive of his relationship to her in these terms.

57. John Lydgate, *Troy Book*, ed. Henry Bergen, EETS e.s. 97 (London: Kegan Paul, Trench, Trübner, 1906), prologue, ll. 76–78.

58. John H. Fisher, "A Language Policy for Lancastrian England," *PMLA* 107, 5 (1992): 1168–80, at 1170. Fisher's arguments are expanded by Derek Pearsall, who draws on Fisher's thesis to support his argument that Prince Henry may have had an active involvement in Hoccleve's composition of the *Regement of Princes*. "Hoccleve's *Regement of Princes*: The Poetics of Royal Self-Representation," *Speculum* 69 (1994): 386–410. On his part Lee Patterson demonstrates that the Lancastrian language policy consisted of more than translating texts and included a promotion of the English language as unified and direct in opposition to French, which was at the same time portrayed as devious and guileful. "Making Identities in Fifteenth-Century England: Henry V and John Lydgate," in *New Historical Literary Study: Essays on Reproducing Texts, Representing History*, ed. Jeffrey N. Cox and Larry J. Reynolds (Princeton, N.J.: Princeton University Press, 1993), 69–107.

59. *Troy Book*, ed. Bergen, ll. 102 and 104. Geoffrey of Monmouth's twelfth-century *History of the Kings of England*, credits the founding of Britain to Brutus, the great-grandson of the Trojan Aeneas.

60. Critical debate about the ways Caxton chose his texts ranges greatly. Jennifer Summit and R. F. Yeager both see Caxton as an active shaper of literary taste who helped define a market. While Summit argues that "Caxton's prologues and epilogues represent an important early theoretical formulation of English literary culture at a major stage in its construction," Yeager observes that printers like Caxton "had to have read more than they printed" and their choices demonstrate they "had literary ideas which governed their activities in the manner of a critical theory." See Summit, "William Caxton, Margaret Beaufort and the Romance of Female Patronage," in *Women, the Book and the Worldly: Selected Proceedings of the St. Hilda's Conference, 1993*, vol. 2, ed. Lesley Smith and Jane H. M. Taylor (Cambridge: D.S. Brewer, 1995), 151–65, at 153; and Yeager, "Literary Theory at the Close of the Middle Ages: William Caxton and William Thynne," *Studies in the Age of Chaucer* 6 (1984): 135–64, at 139 and 136. Blake, however, sees Caxton's choices as dictated by a preexisting market demand and requests by the nobility for specific books. Or, as Blake put it: "There is thus a very close connexion between the choice of books and the establishment of the press at Westminster," the type of books in this case being popular ones (*Caxton and His World*, 81). My own position seems somewhat closer to the one underlying Kuskin's arguments, namely that Caxton's publishing program was the product of constant negotiation between the printer and his various reading publics.

61. Kuskin, "Reading Caxton," 170. Kuskin sees the monkey as representative of Caxton alone.

62. Blake claims that although the picture and text are contemporaneous, there is "no indication that the kneeling figure is meant to be Caxton or even that the engraving was designed for this book" (*Caxton: England's First Publisher*, 133). Nevertheless, its inclusion indicates that the manuscript compiler found this image an appropriate representation.

63. The *Dictes or Sayengis* (reprinted by modern editors as *Dictes and Sayings*) is the first dated book from Caxton's Westminster press, although there is record of an indulgence that he printed in December 1476 (Blake, *Caxton: England's First Publisher*, 192).

64. *The Dictes and Sayings of the Philosophers: A Facsimile Reproduction of the*

First Book Printed in England by William Caxton in 1477 (London: E. Stock, 1877), 73r. As I did with the *Recuyell,* I have modernized aspects of this text. Because there are no page numbers printed in this edition, subsequent references to this edition will be cited parenthetically by page number with an "r" or "v" to indicate "recto" and "verso."

65. Blake argues that Caxton's French manuscript copy most likely did not contain a prologue, thus forcing Caxton to return to the *Recuyell* for a model. As in the *Recuyell* he uses this space to launch into "a rather extravagant praise of [his patron] which is expressed in laudatory platitudes." "Continuity and Change in Caxton's Prologues and Epilogues: The Bruges Period," *Gutenberg-Jahrbuch* (1979): 72–77, at 75, 76. In the introduction to his reprint, Axon posits that Caxton borrowed from Jehan de Vignay's preface, in which the writer dedicates his French translation to Prince John of France: "A Tres noble & excellent prince Jehan de france duc de normendie & auisne filz de philipe par le grace de dieu Roy de france. Frere Jehan de vignay vostre petit Religieux entre les autres de vostre seignorie/ paix sante Joie & victoire sur vos ennemis. Treschier & redoube seign'r/ pour ce que Jay entendu et scay que vous veez & ouez volentiers choses proffitables & honestes et qui tendent al informacion de bonne meur ay Je mis vn petit liuret de latin en francois le quel mest venuz a la main nouuellement/ ou quel plussieurs auctoritez et dis de docteurs & de philosophes & de poetes & des anciens sages/ sont Racontez & sont appliquiez a la moralite des nobles hommes et des gens de peuple selon le gieu des eschez le quel livre Tres puissant et tres redoube seigneur jay fait ou nom & soubz umbre de vous pour laquelle chose treschr seign'r Je vous suppli & requier de bonne voulente de cuer que il vostre daigne plaire a receuuoir ce livre en gre aussi bien que de un greign'r maistre de moy/ car la tres bonne voulente que Jay de mielx faire se je pouoie me doit estre reputee pour le fait / Et po'r plus clerement proceder en ceste ouvre / Jay ordene que les chappitres du liure soient escrips & mis au commencement afin de veoir plus plainement la matiere de quoy le dit liure pole" ["To the very noble and excellent Prince John of France, duke of Normandy and oldest son of Philippe, by the grace of God, king of France. Brother John de Vignay, an unworthy monk amongst the others in your realm, [wishes you] peace, health, joy, and victory over your enemies. Very dear and feared sir, because I heard and know that you see and listen willingly to things [that are] profitable and honest and lend themselves to the formation of good morals, I have translated a little book out of Latin into French that recently came into my possession in which several true stories and saying of doctors, philosophers, poets, and wise men of old are narrated and applied to the morals of noble men and of commoners according to the game of chess. Very powerful and feared sir, I have completed this book in your name and under your shadow. Very dear sir, I beg and pray with all my heart that you deign to receive this book as willingly as if [it came] from a greater scholar than me, for the very great desire that I have to do better if I could must outweigh the deed. In order to proceed more clearly with this work, I have commanded that the book's chapters be written and set at the beginning in order to see more clearly the matter or which this said book speaks"]." William E. A. Axon, Introduction to Jacobus de Cessolis, *Caxton's Game and Playe of the Chesse, 1474: A Verbatim Reprint of the First Edition* (London: Elliot Stock, 1893), xxiii–xxiv. The parallels between this passage and Caxton's prologue are striking. Yet it is not clear that Caxton had access to one of Jehan de

Vignay's manuscripts for his edition. It is also worthwhile to note that Jehan de Ferron's translation of the *Liber* is prefaced by remarks that resemble Caxton's 1483 prologue. Ferron writes: "Le Sainte Escripture dit que Dieux a fait a chascun commandement de pourchassier a tous nos prochains leur sauvement. Or est-il ainsi que nos prochains ne sont pas tout un, ains sont de diverses condicions, estas et manieres, sy comme il appert. Car les uns sont nobles; les aultres non: les aultres sont de cler engin; les aultres, non: les aultres sont enclins a devocion; les aultres, non" ["Holy Scripture says that God gave each [of us] the commandment to obtain the salvation of all our neighbors. Now our neighbors are not all one, but are of diverse conditions, estates, and classes, as it appears. For some are noble, others not. Some are of honest intent, others not. Some are bent to devotion, others not"]" (ibid., xx). Many thanks to Meriem Pages for help with both of these translations.

66. It is possible that Caxton, rather than soliciting Clarence's support, used the text to appeal directly to Edward himself. There are few better ways to secure the king's favor than by translating a text that reproves violent usurpation and then dedicating it to a brother who had, three years previous, aided in a rebellion against the king; see Gill, "Caxton and the Rebellion of 1483," 111; Blake, *William Caxton and English Literary Culture* (London: Hambledon Press, 1991), 176. Kuskin has argued that Caxton used this prologue to put Clarence in his place, underscoring the weakness of Clarence's position as Edward's brother yet also offering him a way to save face in his position: "Caxton's prologue thus frames Clarence's power in terms of his continued allegiance to the king; in short, it makes necessity a virtue" ("The Erasure of Labor," 242). Kuskin's argument opposes that of George D. Painter, who reads "the inner secret" of the Caxton's preface as a chastisement of Edward IV for his bad councillors and an endorsement of Clarence as the next king of England. Painter uses this claim in turn to explain Caxton's departure from the office of governor in 1470 and his application for a pardon in March 1472. He does not, however, explain how these events could come from a dedication that appeared two years later (*William Caxton: A Biography*, 65–67). Yet despite their antithetical views, Kuskin and Painter both draw attention to the fact that Caxton's main focus is on royal authority rather than on the need for all men to read the book.

67. In this way Caxton anticipates later advice texts such as the sixteenth-century *Mirror for Magistrates*, a revision of Lydgate's *Fall of Princes* that William Baldwin, the *Mirror*'s primary printer, offers up to his "lords and gods." In this same prologue Baldwin also insists that "the goodnes or badnes of any realme lyeth in the goodnes or badnes of the rulers." *The Mirror for Magistrates*, ed. Lily B. Campbell (Cambridge: Cambridge University Press, 1938; reprint New York: Barnes and Noble, 1960), 67, 64.

68. Blake, "Continuity and Change," 76.

69. Axon, *Caxton's Game and Playe of the Chesse*, 1–2. Axon includes both the 1474 dedication and the 1483 preface in his edition. Both of these can also be found in Blake, *Caxton's Own Prose*, 85. As with Sommer's edition of the *Historyes of Troyes*, I have modernized the long *s* and expanded some of the abbreviations. For the sake of clarity, I have also added some commas. Subsequent references to this edition will be noted parenthetically in the text.

70. Obviously, such additions speak to Caxton's marketing concerns; he wanted

as many people as possible to buy his book. Nevertheless, this suggestion that the *Game and Playe*'s morals can apply to all men is vastly overshadowed by the prologue's praise of Clarence. In short, such a marketing technique would probably not have been all that effective.

71. Other than a few asides (discussed below), Caxton's translation of his French sources is faithful. Robert H. Wilson has argued that the manuscript closest to Caxton's version is the "Cockerell" manuscript, or the University of Chicago Library's MS 392. Although he admits to numerous small differences between the French manuscript and Caxton's translation, he also argues that "on the basis of the fundamental correspondence, one must believe that Caxton derived his combination of Faron and Vignay from a MS related to the Cockerell." "Caxton's Chess Book," *Modern Language Notes* 62 (1947): 93–102, at 96. Christine Knowles supports this claim: "a comparison of the English version with a microfilm of the Chicago manuscript shows an exact correspondence between the two, including the change-over to Jean de Vignay's translation towards the end of the chapter on the Rooks" ("Caxton and His Two French Sources: The *Game and Playe of the Chesse* and the Composite Manuscripts of the Two French Translations of the *Ludus Scaccorum*," *Modern Language Review* 49.4 (1954): 417–23, at 423. Knowles also observes that Caxton "seems to have made very careful and detailed use of the Latin [text]" (420).

72. For a reference to this moment as one of communism, see Wilson, "Caxton's Chess Book," 97. For the idea that Caxton promotes "egalitarianism," see William Poole, "False Play: Shakespeare and Chess," *Shakespeare Quarterly* 55.1 (2004): 50–70, at 53. Poole's idea that Caxton is responding to feudalism ignores the generally capitalist nature of late fifteenth-century London.

73. Notably, this passage does not appear in the chapter about the judges but in the one dedicated to the blacksmiths.

74. Blake, *Caxton and His World*, 86–87.

75. Ibid.

76. Gill, "William Caxton and the Rebellion of 1483," 112.

77. "Once Caxton had begun to reach a larger public, patrons became less important to him. This explains why so many of his prologues and epilogues, unlike their manuscript counterparts, refer both to patrons and to one or more segments of the reading public" (Rutter, "William Caxton and Literary Patronage," 463).

78. Blake, *Caxton and His World*, 92. Noting that "the book was designed to improve the morals of merchants rather than to amuse the nobility," Blake goes on to argue that Caxton "had previously printed books for the merchant market without stating his allegiance to the merchant community" and thus reads the change as an attempt by the printer to distance himself from the Woodvilles (92). But immediately after asserting this, Blake observes that Caxton still produced items for the Woodvilles, such as the *Knight of the Tower* (1484), which was most likely completed for Elizabeth Woodville, who by this point was living at Westminster Abbey (92). Sure enough, the Woodvilles came sailing back into the political scene when, in January 1486, Henry VII married Elizabeth, daughter of Elizabeth Woodville and Edward IV. Yet despite their return, Caxton never readopts the same glowing and florid style of his earlier prologues.

79. Ibid., 128.

80. The initially unstable nature of Richard's rule seems to be reflected in Caxton's printing of John Mirk's collection of homilies, *Festial,* which dispenses with any introductory material at all.

81. Blake, *Caxton's Own Prose,* 70. Caxton also opens the book by noting that Gower wrote the Confessio "in the tyme of Kyng Richard the Second," thus implying a link between the two kings (69).

82. Blake dates both the second edition of the *Canterbury Tales* and the second edition of the *Game and Playe of the Chesse* before the *Golden Legend,* published in November 1483, and *Aesop,* published in March 1484 (*Caxton: England's First Publisher,* 149). At one point Blake hypothesizes that *The Game of the Chesse* might have appeared as early at 1482, although for the reasons implicit in my argument, I find 1483 more plausible.

83. Blake, *Caxton's Own Prose,* 61.

84. Ibid., 61–62.

85. Ibid., 62.

86. Ibid., 63.

87. Although the Host is the purported leader of the group, his only power is that of judging the best tale, a power granted to him "by oon assent" (i.e., by a unanimous agreement, *General Prologue* l.817). As David Wallace observes, "The most powerful instantiation of associational ideology in Chaucer comes through the formation of the pilgrim *compagnye* at the opening of the *Canterbury Tales.* This process of group formation, where the right to exist *as* a group is simply assumed from within rather than conferred from without, represents a singular moment of political confidence that will not be repeated on English territory." *Chaucerian Polity: Absolutist Lineages and Associational Forms in England and Italy* (Stanford, Calif.: Stanford University Press, 1997), 2.

88. For publication dates of all Caxton's works, see Blake, *Caxton: England's First Publisher,* 192–96.

89. Blake, *Caxton's Own Prose,* 59.

90. This second printing is virtually identical to the first with the only notable differences being the two prologues and the tables of contents. For a careful examination of the latter, see Wilson, "Caxton's Chess Book," 100.

91. *The Game of the Chesse,* facsimile reprint by Vincent Figgins (London: Trübner, 1866). William Kretzschmar has argued that Caxton sometimes used this particular citation, which appears in many of Caxton's prologues and epilogues, "as an explicitly historical justification" of his texts, in particular the *Morte Darthur.* "Caxton's Sense of History," *Journal of English and Germanic Philology* 91, 4 (1992): 510–28, at 527. However, as Kretzschmar admits, such a justification was not necessary for a book like the *Game and Playe,* which had already claimed status as collection of historical exempla. Thus Caxton's decision to use this particular phrase may be understood to emphasize the text's universal application as much as it is a reminder of its historical status.

92. *The Game of the Chesse,* ed. Figgins, 1.

93. Ibid., 1–2.

94. According to Blake, the woodcuts for this volume were done by a single artist who also did the woodcuts for the *Canterbury Tales,* and most of the woodcuts

for *Aesop* and for the *Golden Legend*. Blake also notes that the *Chess* book was one of only four translations that Caxton printed a second time (*Caxton: England's First Publisher*, 142 and 184). Wynkyn de Worde reused the several woodcuts from the *Game and Playe of the Chesse* for his 1498 edition of the *Canterbury Tales*. I thank Maidie Hilmo for first alerting me to this fact.

95. Although it is tempting to identify the piece in Philometer's hand as the chess king, it is most likely the rook. Not only does the board feature a rook identical to the piece he holds, earlier diagrams such as Alfonso El Sabio's *Libros del axedrez, dados et tablas* depict the rook with a roughly similar shape. If this is the case, the picture offers a blunt reminder that the king derives much of his power through his counselors, who represent him in his kingdom.

96. Other than the frontispiece to the *Recuyell*, which as discussed above may or may not have been produced for Caxton, none of the printer's early works contain elaborate ornamentation. The earliest works to have woodcuts are the *Mirror of the World* (1st ed.), a poem by Benedict Burgh titled *Cato* (3rd ed.), the *Canterbury Tales* (2nd ed.), and the *Game and Playe of the Chesse* (2nd ed.). See Blake, *Caxton: England's First Publisher*, 139.

97. Blake, *Caxton's Own Prose*, 127.

98. Ibid., 58.

99. Ibid., 126.

100. Ibid., 127.

101. In *England's First Publisher*, N. F. Blake dates this printing to about 1480 (111). However, in her edition of this work E. Ruth Harvey dates Caxton's printing to 1483 based on Blades' analysis of print type. *The Court of Sapience*, ed. E. Ruth Harvey (Toronto: University of Toronto Press, 1984), xiii-xiv.

102. *The Court of Sapience*, ed. Harvey, ll. 78–84. Subsequent references to this edition will be noted parenthetically in the body of the text.

103. In her notes to her edition of this poem, Harvey describes the narrator's bewilderment at the chessboard as a manifestation of his youthful and undisciplined ways: "Allegorically, the poet seems to mean that, having decided to 'give youth his head' and seek for enjoyment in life, he is in the position of the chess-player who wants to move his king without taking care of the pawns that block his way" (84). This failure at the board in turn prompts him to realize that worldly happiness is controlled only by Fortune, and he prays for wisdom to help him negotiate the sublunary realm. I do not wish to dispute Harvey's claim about the poem, which indeed starts with a foregrounding of the poet's youth. Yet even if the game does capture the narrator's juvenile beliefs about the world, it is notable that a game representing "a myrrour of polocye" acts as the fulcrum for his quest for wisdom. The passages themselves reveal the contours of the narrator's initial misunderstanding and the assumptions that initially arise out of the "fruteles worldly medytacyon" that has driven him to bed in the first place. In short, trying to move the king first might be a juvenile act, although it is also a logical mistake for an inexperienced player who had not yet learned the rules of the game/state. Moreover, that the dreamer emphasizes the importance of moving all the pieces further highlights the interdependence of members of the body politic.

104. Such an understanding of chess's symbolic power diverges sharply from that found in the *Quaedam*, which sees the game as symbolic of fallen nature.

105. See Catherine Batt, "Recreation, the Exemplary, and the Body in Caxton's *Game and Playe of the Chesse*," *Ludica* 2 (1996): 27–43, at 40.

106. In his entry "William Caxton," Seth Lerer makes a similar argument: "[Caxton's] projects, in short, need to be seen not as the miraculous inventions of a native artisan but as responses to long-standing traditions and new cultural challenges. Poet, printer, reader and dedicatee functioned in a literary system that, for all its seemingly transitional appearance and the paradoxes of its retrogressions and advances, articulated early Tudor notions of the public place of English writing and the social function of the writer and the press," in *The Cambridge History of Medieval English Literature*, ed. David Wallace (Cambridge: Cambridge University Press, 1999), 720–38, at 723.

107. Gill, "William Caxton and the Rebellion of 1483," 105. All of the information about Caxton's request for a pardon comes from Gill's article, which, I should note, also reproduces the pardon itself.

Epilogue

Epigraphs: King James VI and I, *Political Writings*, ed. Johann P. Sommerville, Cambridge Texts in the History of Political Thought (Cambridge: Cambridge University Press, 1994), 181; Opening to "Theses on the Philosophy of History," in Walter Benjamin, *Illuminations*, ed. Hannah Arendt and trans. Harry Zohn (New York: Schocken Books, 1969), 253–64, at 253.

1. The knight Gorhon is said to be "valiant, brave, with courtly skills endowed; / At chess and draughtes he wins bout after bout [pros et hardis et molt cevalerous, / D'esciés, de tables fu molt bon joëors]" (ll. 2214–15). Later in the story Agolant plays chess with King Abilant (l. 6161–62) while Aumont fights a battle. Still later in the story Charlemagne's court is described as sumptuous, and the game contributes to the image of wealth: "You could sit down at ease to dine and wine / Or play a game of chess or draughts alike / Without the need for any candle's light [Em poriés aseoir au disner / Et as escés et as tables joër; / Ja n'i estuet candelles alumer]" (ll. 7022–24). And finally, near the end, Agolant's dead body is brought back to the palace where chess games have taken place: "The Paynim's corpse he placed upon a bier / And bore inside the palace for all to see; / Where it was usual for the young folk to meet, / At chess and draughts to play and to compete [En une biere en fist le cors lever / Et en mi liu del palais aporter. / La jovene jent i soloient anter / Et as escés et as tables joër]" (ll. 10579–82). All quotations come from *The Song of Aspremont (La Chanson d'Aspremont)*, trans. Michael A. Newth (New York: Garland Publishing, 1989), and *La Chanson d'Aspremont: Chanson de geste du XIIᵉ siècle*, vols. 1 and 2, ed. Louis Brandin (Paris: H. Champion, 1919–20).

2. Other versions of this violent act occur in the *Four Sons of Aymon*, *Ogier of*

Denmark, and *Fouke Fitz Warin,* and the resemblance among them merits closer inspection. The editions of these texts that I have consulted are: *The Right Plesaunt and Goodly Historie of the Foure Sonnes of Aymon, Englisht from the French by William Caxton and Printed by him about 1489,* ed. Octavia Richardson, EETS e.s. 45 (London: Trübner, 1885); *Le Chevalier, Ogier le Dannoys: Roman en prose du XVᵉ siè-cle,* facsimile reproduction by Knud Togeby (Munksgaard: Det danske Sprog-og Litteraturselskab, 1967); and *Fouke le Fitz Waryn,* ed. E. J. Hathaway, P. T. Ricketts, C. A. Robson, and A. D. Wilshere (Oxford: Blackwell, 1975). Chess is also used as a weapon by Gawain in Chrétien de Troyes's *Perceval; or, The Story of the Grail.* In this instance Gawain throws oversized pieces out of a window when he and a lady are attacked. For editions of this text see *Le Roman de Perceval; ou, Le Conte du graal,* ed. William Roach (Geneva: Droz, 1959), and *Perceval; or, The Story of the Grail,* trans. Ruth Harwood Cline (Athens: University of Georgia Press, 1985).

3. Again, this does not mean that individuals at this time had no sense of interiority or private life, but merely that Jacobus's text does not concern itself with the shape this private life might take under these circumstances. As Katharine Eisaman Maus observes, theorists often resist the notion of a "self" in early cultures due to an anxiety about imposing modern (and thus universalizing) paradigms on past eras. In responding to these theorists, Maus differentiates between philosophical arguments and historicist ones: "The difference [between these two types of arguments] is worth keeping in mind, because philosophical claims about the necessarily social constitution of *any* subjectivity, Renaissance or modern, sometimes seem to get confused with historicist claims about an early modern form of subjectivity supposedly less inward-looking than our own." *Inwardness and Theater in the English Renaissance* (Chicago: University of Chicago Press, 1995), 27.

4. Benjamin's Turk was a fake "automaton" that toured Europe and America in the eighteenth and nineteenth centuries until it was destroyed by a fire in the mid-1900s. But contrary to Benjamin's description of the machine, it was not operated by a dwarf; the owners hired top notch players from cafes in Paris. Nor did it always win. See Tom Standage, *The Turk: The Life and Times of the Famous Eighteenth-Century Chess-Playing Machine* (New York: Walker, 2002).

5. As Jonathan Dollimore notes, the difference in these two perspectives is "between those who concentrate on culture as this making of history, and those who concentrate on the unchosen conditions which constrain and inform that process of making. The former allows much to human agency and tends to privilege human experience; the latter concentrates on the formative power of social and ideological structures which are both prior to experience and in some sense determining of it, and so opens up the whole question of autonomy." "Introduction: Shakespeare, Cultural Materialism, and the New Historicism," in *Political Shakespeare: Essays in Cultural Materialism,* 2nd ed., ed. Jonathan Dollimore and Alan Sinfield (Ithaca, N.Y.: Cornell University Press, 1994), 2–17, at 3.

6. *A Game at Chess* enjoyed an incredible nine-day run, one of the longest at time when reparatory performances were the norm, before it was shut down. Chess also appears briefly in Middleton's *Women Beware Women* (where Livia plays a game against Mother) and in Shakespeare's *The Tempest* (where Ferdinand plays against Miranda).

7. Thomas Middleton, *A Game at Chess*, ed. T. H. Howard-Hill (Manchester: Manchester University Press, 1993), 24. The Black Knight also refers to himself as "the fistula of Europe" (2.2.46), and "the early version of the beginning of v.i was rewritten to accommodate the Black Knight's entrance in [his chair]" (24).

8. Michael Hattaway, "Drama and Society," in *The Cambridge Companion to English Renaissance Drama*, ed. A. R. Braunmuller and Michael Hattaway (Cambridge: Cambridge University Press, 1990), 91–126, at 92. Hattaway in turn cites David Scott Kastan's "Proud Majesty Made a Subject: Shakespeare and the Spectacle of Rule," *Shakespeare Quarterly* 37 (1986), 459–75.

9. Margot Heinemann, "Political Drama," in *The Cambridge Companion to English Renaissance Drama*, 161–205, at 161.

10. Formerly restricted to one-square moves, the bishops now had unlimited diagonal motion while the queens could move an unlimited number of spaces in any direction. In his forthcoming book, *The Immortal Game: A History of Chess, Or How 32 Pieces on a Board Illuminated Our Understanding of War, Art, Science, and the Human Brain* (New York: Doubleday, 2006), David Shenk argues that "with the tweaking of a few pieces' powers of motion, it was an entirely new game. Suddenly, there were vastly more possibilities of play from the very start. Now the game was not only fast[er]. It was also nearly infinite." Shenk goes on to show that the estimated numbers of possible board configurations under modern chess rules is 10^{120}. As Shenk also observes: "By way of comparison, the total number of electrons in the universe is, as best physicists can determine, 10^{79}."

11. Murray, *A History of Chess*, 779.

12. Although it enjoyed a certain amount of popularity with printers during the early parts of the early modern era, Jacobus's text does not appear to have been published after the sixteenth century. In addition to Caxton's two versions, the text was printed in Latin in 1478, 1479, 1494, 1497, and 1505; in Italian in 1493 (with woodcuts) and 1534; in Dutch in 1479 and 1551; in German in 1477, 1483, 1536, and 1551; and in Spanish in 1549. See Carol S. Fuller, "A Critical Edition of *Le Jeu des Eschés, Moralisé*, Translated by Jehan de Vignay," (Ph.D. dissertation, Catholic University of America, 1974, app. B, 334, and Mark Weeks's "Chess Bibliography Before 1800": *http://mark_weeks.tripod.com/chwooi15/chwooi15.htm*. To my knowledge, the Caxton printing is still the only version available in English.

13. Murray, *A History of Chess*, 783.

14. These works include Luis Lucena's *Repetición de amores e arte de axedrez con CL iuegos de partido* (1497), Pedro Damiano's *Questo libro e da imparare giocare a scachi et de li partiti* (1512), Ruy López [de Segura]'s *Libro de la invención liberal y arte del juego del Axedrez* (1561), Horatio Gianutio of Mantia's *Libro del quale si tratta della Maniera di giocar' a Scacchi* (1597), and numerous notebooks by players who kept track of their moves. Murray describes these works in the latter parts of his *History of Chess*, specifically on pages 776–836. This is not to say that chess poems were never again popular. Arthur Saul's *The Famous Game of Chesse-Play* not only enjoyed popularity, it promoted the idea of play as a means to self-betterment. Yet poems like these tended to encourage people to learn the game and not to master the moral lessons that accompanied it. For an overview of Renaissance literature that mentions chess, see William Poole, "False Play: Shakespeare and Chess," *Shakespeare Quarterly* 55.1 (2004): 50–70.

15. Pedro Damiano, *Ludus scacchiae: Chesse-play*, trans. and ed. G.B. (London, 1597), A1. (Originally titled *(Questo libro e da imparare giocare a scachi de li partiti.)*

16. Ibid.

17. "To Sir Henry Wotton (Here's no more news)." John Donne, *The Satires, Epigrams, and Verse Letters*, ed. W. Milgate (Oxford: Clarendon Press, 1967), ll. 22–24.

18. *The Way of Perfection*, in *The Collected Works of St. Teresa of Avila*, vol. 2, trans. Kieran Kavanaugh and Otillio Rodriguez (Washington, D.C.: Institute of Carmelite Studies, 1980), 37–204, at 93–95. The paragraphs that include Teresa's references to the game appeared in chapter sixteen of *The Way of Perfection*. Teresa purportedly tore them out, although modern editors have continued to include them in their editions (editor's notes, 465).

19. François Rabelais, *Gargantua and Pantagruel*, trans. Burton Raffel (New York: Norton, 1990), and Francesco Colonna, *Hypnerotomachia Poliphili: The Strife of Love in a Dream*, trans. Joscelyn Godwin (London: Thames and Hudson, 1999). Florence Weinberg points out that in both instances music foregrounds the ways that chess corresponds to the harmony of spheres present in the larger universe. "Chess as a Literary Idea in Colonna's *Hypnerotomachia* and in Rabelais' *Cinquiesme Livre*," *Romanic Review* 70, 4 (1979): 321–35.

20. Gary Schmidgall has seen this moment as "not only a visual premonition of a happy union of husband and wife but also of a capable and prescient governmental style for the future Dukedom of Milan and Kingdom of Naples." "The Discovery at Chess in *The Tempest*," *English Language Notes* 23, 4 (1986): 11–16, at 13. Given Miranda's accusation that Ferdinand is cheating, I would question this reading of the scene as symbolic of future marital bliss. Nevertheless, I agree that the young lovers' game represents a specific model of power, one that is not merely an alternative to Prospero's negligence or to Antonio's tyranny. It should also be noted that, despite Marilyn Yalom's claim to the contrary, the lovers are *not* officially married by this point; Prospero has merely staged a pageant for their engagement and plans to attend their nuptials after they return to Naples; see *The Birth of the Chess Queen* (New York: HarperCollins, 2004), 223. Nevertheless, I agree that the young lovers' game represents a specific model of power, one that is not merely an alternative to Prospero's negligence or to Antonio's tyranny.

21. Nicholas Breton, "The Chesse Play," in *The Phoenix Nest*, 28–10, ed. R.S. of the Inner Temple (London, 1593), l. 8 and 10.

22. Ibid., ll. 49, 51–52.

23. William Cartwright, *The Game at Chesse: A Metaphoricall Discourse Shewing the Present Estate of this Kingdome* (London, 1643).

24. Breton, "The Chesse Play," ll. 71–72

25. This and the subsequent information about the appearance of certain words in Shakespeare come from John Bartlett, *A Complete Concordance to Shakespeare* (London: Macmillan, 1894; reprint New York: St. Martin's Press, 1984).

26. I do not wish to argue that the game necessarily led to the meanings these words acquired. According to the *Oxford English Dictionary*, the history of "pawn" as a security or pledge is "uncertain." It may have come from the French word *pan* or "pledge," which mean "cloth, piece, portion, or pane." It is thus possibly unrelated to the function of the pawn on the chessboard. Yet it is interesting to note that the term

was not commonly used in this sense until the late fifteenth and early sixteenth centuries, well after it had been used most often to describe a chess piece. Moreover, the fact that the same word marks both a financial/social agreement and a piece on a chessboard further indicates a cultural interest in the game's mimetic possibilities. By contrast, "check" comes directly from chess terminology. Yet like "pawn," the word was not, by the late sixteenth century, as commonly used in connection with the game as it was to indicate a restraint on action.

27. David Wallace, *Chaucerian Polity: Absolutist Lineages and Associational Form in England and Italy* (Stanford, Calif.: Stanford University Press, 1997), esp. 40–43. See also John E. Martin, *Feudalism to Capitalism: Peasant and Landlord in English Agrarian Development* (Atlantic Highlands, N.J.: Humanities Press, 1983).

28. As Lawrence Stone observes, late fifteenth- and early sixteenth-century England was a culture confronted with "an unprecedented social and geographical mobility which at the higher levels transformed the size and composition of the gentry. *The Family, Sex, and Marriage in England, 1500–1800* (London: Weidenfeld and Nicolson, 1977), 654. For more recent revisions of early modern absolutism, see Glenn Burgess's *Absolute Monarchy and the Stuart Constitution* (New Haven, Conn.: Yale University Press, 1996).

29. Even if this rise of individual sovereignty might have itself been sponsored by state paternalism, it ultimately led to the rise and protection of individual liberties. For a good overview of the double nature of Tudor-Stuart state and its "unresolved tension between negative libertarianism and paternalism," see Paul Cefalu's "Shakespeare's *Coriolanus* and the Consensual Nature of the Early Modern State," *Renaissance Forum* 4, 2 (2000), 1–14, at 1.

30. Benjamin Franklin, *The Morals of Chess*, in *Benjamin Franklin and Chess in Early America*, ed. Ralph K. Hagedorn (Philadelphia: University of Pennsylvania Press, 1958), 15–20.

31. The game was used by an artist for the cover of the *Chicago Tribune*'s "TV Week" section for January 8–14, 1995. The drawing shows a "Frasier" pawn confronting a "Rosanne" pawn. Around them are four other pawns that represent various television programs, while the caption above the board reads: "All the right moves: Shows jockey for position to win the ratings game." In 2002 chess was used to illustrate Edward W. Lempinen's "Is Osama Winning?" (*Salon.com*, September 6, 2002), an article about the attacks of September 11th of that year. In the cartoon-like image Osama bin Laden sits at a chessboard. In front of him are six miniaturized "pieces," three black (a suited George Bush, an American GI, and a figure dressed in "traditional" Arab attire) and three white (a coupled set of the World Trade Center towers, an exploding white SUV, and a capitol dome). The board is oriented toward the viewer, and it seems to invite him or her to play against bin Laden. Saussure uses chess as an analogy for the ways that language, like the rules of chess, preexists us. Ferdinand de Saussure, *Course in General Linguistics*, ed. Charles Bally and Albert Sechehaye, trans. Wade Baskin (New York: McGraw-Hill, 1959), 88–89.

Bibliography

Manuscripts, Manuscript Reproductions, Manuscript Copies, and Incunabula

Bancroft Library, University of California at Berkeley

fGV1320.A54. Facsimile manuscript reproduction of Alfonso X El Sabio, *Libros del ajedrez, dados y tablas*. 2 vols. Madrid: Vincent García Editores, S. A. Valencial—Ediciones Poniente, 1987.

Cleveland Public Library

789.0921 C4 Inc. (1458). Jacobus de Cessolis. *Das schachbuch des Jacobus de Cessolis: Codex palatinus latinus 961.*

789.0921 C475 Inc. (1475). Jacobus de Cessolis. *Solacium ludi schacorum.*

789.0921 C479L Inc. (1479). Jacobus de Cessolis. *Scaec spiel.*

789.0921 C483 Inc. (1483). Jacobus de Cessolis. *Schachzabelbuch.*

789.0921 D05 Inc. (1505) Jacobus de Cessolis. *Tractatus de scachis mistice interpretatus de moribus per singulos hominu status.*

789.0921 M. MS fourteenth c. Jean de Vignay. *La Moralité des nobles et du peuple sur le jeu des echetz.*

789.0921 M C3D. MS fourteenth c. Jacobus de Cessolis. *Incipit prologus in librum quem composuit frater Jacobus de Cessolis ordinis fratrum predicatorum de moribus hominum et officiis nobilium super ludo schacorum.*

789.0921 M C41L. MS fifteenth c. Jacobus de Cessolis. *Libellus de ludo scacchorum.*

789.0921 M C4L2. MS fourteenth c. Jacobus de Cessolis. *Multorum fratrum ordinis.*

789.0921 M C4L25. MS fifteenth c. Jacobus de Cessolis. *Hic incipit prologus super ludo scachorum.*

789.0921 M C4T. MS fifteenth c. Jacobus de Cessolis. *Incipit tractatus scacorum.*

789.0921 M DL Microfilm. MS fifteenth c. Jacobus de Cessolis. *In comincia el libro del gioco de scachi.*

789.0921 O493M Inc. (1493). Jacobus de Cessolis. *Libro di giuocho di scacchi.*

789.091 Ro. Copy of Bibliothèque Nationale MS 14,978. Guillaume de St. André. *Jeu des eschecs moralisés.*

789.0921 R1F. Photographic facsimile of Rouen MS 3066. Jean de Ferron. *Le Livre des eschecs moralisés.*

F 789.092 EC4. Photographic copies of parts of seven manuscripts of *Les echecs amoureux.*

GV 1442.C4 1480x. MS fifteenth c. Jacobus de Cessolis. *Libellus de ludo scacchorum.*

Q789.092 Al28E. Alfonso X. *Chess Manual.* John Griswold White's long-hand copy.

Q789.0921 Q9. Photographic copy of chess part of British Museum MS Bibl. Reg. 12 E. XXI (ff. 51a, 79a–104b). *Incipit tractus de scacario* and *moralitas de scaccario secundum dominum Innocentium Papam.*

Q789.0924 D819P. Photographic copy of Dresden Royal Library MS O.59. Jean de Vignay. *Le Livre des eschecs moralisés.*

Newberry Library, Chicago

MS. 55.5. MS fourteenth c. Jean de Ferron. *Le ieu des echez moralisiet.*

Folio Inc. 9323. William Caxton. *The Game and Playe of the Chesse* (1474).

Folio Inc. 9643. William Caxton. *The Game and Playe of the Chesse* (1483).

Regenstein Library, University of Chicago

MS. 392 MS fourteenth c. Jean de Ferron and Jean de Vignay. *Jeu des echecs moralisés.*

Primary Works

Aegidius Romanus (Giles of Rome). *On Ecclesiastical Power.* Ed. and trans. R. W. Dyson. Woodbridge: Boydell, 1986.

———. *The Governance of Kings and Princes: John Trevisa's Middle English Translation of the* De Regimine Principum *of Aegidius Romanus.* Ed. David C. Fowler, Charles F. Briggs, and Paul G. Remley. New York: Garland, 1997.

Alighieri, Dante. *De monarchia.* Trans. Richard Kay. Toronto: Pontifical Institute of Mediaeval Studies, 1998.

Anglo-Norman Lapidaries. Ed. Paul Studer and Joan Evans. Paris: Édouard Champion, 1924.

Aquinas, Thomas. *Aquinas: Selected Political Writings.* Ed. A. P. D'Entrèves. Trans. J. G. Dawson. Oxford: Basil Blackwell, 1948.

———. *On Kingship: To the King of Cyprus.* Trans. Gerald B. Phelan. Toronto: Pontifical Institute of Mediaeval Studies, 1949.

———. *The Political Ideas of Thomas Aquinas: Representative Selections.* Trans. and ed. Dino Bigongiari. New York: Hafner, 1953.

———. *St. Thomas Aquinas on Politics and Ethics.* Trans. Paul Sigmund. New York: Norton, 1988.

Aristotle. *The Politics*. Trans. Carnes Lord. Chicago: University of Chicago Press, 1984.

The Avowing of King Arthur. Ed. Roger Dahood. New York: Garland, 1984.

Le Bâtard de Bouillon: Chanson de geste. Ed. Robert Francis Cook. Geneva: Droz, 1972.

Boccaccio, Giovanni. *The Filocolo*. Trans. Donald Cheney. New York: Garland, 1985.

The Boke of Duke Huon of Burdeux. Ed. S. L. Lee. EETS e.s. 40, 41, 43, and 50. London, 1882–87. Reprint Millwood, N.Y.: Kraus Reprint, 1975.

Bonus Socius (Good Companion): XIIIth Century Manuscript Collection of Chess Problems. Ed. James F. Magee. Florence: Tipografia Giuntina, 1910.

Breton, Nicholas. "The Chesse Play." In *The Phoenix Nest*, 28–30. Ed. R.S. of the Inner Temple. London, 1593.

"The *Canterbury Interlude* and the Merchant's *Tale of Beryn*." In *The Canterbury Tales: Fifteenth-Century Continuations and Additions*. Ed. John M. Bowers. Kalamazoo, Mich.: Medieval Institute Publications, 1992.

Cartwright, William. *The Game at Chesse: A Metaphoricall Discourse Shewing the Present Estate of this Kingdome*. London, 1643.

Caxton, William. *Caxton's Own Prose*. Edited by N. F. Blake. London: Andre Deutsch, 1973.

La Chanson d'Aspremont: Chanson du geste du XIIe siècle. Ed. Louis Brandin. 2 vols. Paris: H. Champion, 1919–20.

Chaucer, Geoffrey. *The Complete Works of Geoffrey Chaucer*. Ed. W. W. Skeat. Oxford, 1894.

———. *The Riverside Chaucer*. 3rd ed. Gen. ed. Larry Benson. Boston: Houghton Mifflin, 1987.

Le Chevalier, Ogier de Danemarche, par Raimbert de Paris, poème du XIIe siècle: Publié pour la première fois d'après le MS de Marmoutier et le MS 2729 de la Bibliothèque du Roi. Paris, 1842.

Chrétien de Troyes. *Perceval; or, The Story of the Grail*. Trans. Ruth Hardwood Cline. Athens: University of Georgia Press, 1985.

———. *Le Roman de Perceval; ou, Le Conte du graal*. Ed. William Roach. Geneva: Droz, 1959.

———. *The Story of the Grail (Li Contes del Graal); or, Perceval*. Ed. Rupert T. Pickens. Trans. William W. Kibler. New York: Garland, 1990.

Christine de Pizan. *Book of the Body Politic*. Trans. and ed. Kate Langdon Forhan. Cambridge Texts in the History of Political Thought. Cambridge: Cambridge University Press, 1994.

———. *Le Livre du corps de policie*. Ed. Angus J. Kennedy. Paris: Honoré Champion, 1998.

———. *Le Livre de la mutacion de fortune*. Ed. Suzanne Solente. 4 vols. Paris: Editions A. and J. Picard, 1959.

———. *The Middle English Translation of Christine de Pisan's* Livre du Corps de Policie. Ed. Diane Bornstein. Heidelburg: Carl Winter, 1977.

Colonna, Francesco. *Hypnerotomachia Poliphili: The Strife of Love in a Dream*. Trans. Joscelyn Godwin. London: Thames and Hudson, 1999.

Le Conte de Floire et Blancheflor. Ed. Jean-Luc Leclanche. Paris: H. Champion, 1980.

The Court of Sapience. Ed. E. Ruth Harvey. Toronto: University of Toronto Press, 1984.

Damiano, Pedro. *Ludus scachiae: Chesse-play (Questo libro e da imparare giocare a scachi et de li partiti).* Trans. and ed. G. B. London, 1597.

The Dictes and Sayings of the Philosophers: A Facsimile Reproduction of the First Book Printed in England by William Caxton in 1477. London: E. Stock, 1877.

The Didot "Perceval" According to the Manuscripts of Modena and Paris. Ed. William Roach. Philadelphia: University of Pennsylvania Press, 1941.

Donne, John. *The Satires, Epigrams, and Verse Letters.* Ed. W. Milgate. Oxford: Clarendon Press, 1967.

Doon de la Roche: Chanson de Geste. Ed. Paul Meyer and Gédéon Huet. Paris: Edouard Champion, 1921.

The Early English Versions of the Gesta Romanorum. Ed. Sidney J. H. Herrtage. EETS e.s. 33. London: N. Trübner, 1879.

English Mediaeval Lapidaries. Ed. Joan Evans and Mary S. Serjeantson. EETS o.s. 190. London: Oxford University Press, 1933.

Evrart de Conty. "*The Chess of Love* (Old French Text with Commentary)." Trans. Joan Morton Jones. Ph.D. dissertation, University of Nebraska, 1968.

———. *Les Echecs amoureux: Eine altfranzösische Nachahmung des Rosenromans und ihre Englische Übertragung.* Ed. Ernst Sieper. Weimar: Emil Felber, 1898.

———. *Le Livre des eschez amoureux moralisés.* Ed. Françoise Guichard-Tesson and Bruno Roy. Montreal: Editions CERES, 1993.

Fitz Nigel, Richard. *Dialogus de Scaccario: The Course of the Exchequer.* Ed. and trans. Charles Johnson, with corrections by F. E. L. Carter and D. E. Greenway. Oxford: Clarendon Press, 1983.

Floire et Blancheflor. Ed. Margaret Pelan. Paris: Société d'édition: Les Belles lettres, 1937.

Floris and Blancheflour: A Middle-English Romance. Ed. A. B. Taylor. Oxford: Clarendon Press, 1927.

Fouke Fitz Warin. Ed. Louis Brandin. Paris: H. Champion, 1930.

Fouke le Fitz Waryn. Ed. E. J. Hathaway, P. T. Ricketts, C. A. Robson, and A. D. Wilshere. Oxford: Blackwell, 1975.

Franklin, Benjamin. "The Morals of Chess." In *Benjamin Franklin and Chess in Early America,* ed. Ralph K. Hagedorn, 15–20. Philadelphia: University of Pennsylvania Press, 1958.

Gesta romamorum. Ed. Hermann Oesterley. Berlin: Weidmann, 1872. Reprint Hildescheim: Georg Olms Verlagbuchhandlung, 1963.

Les Gius Partiz des Eschez: Two Anglo-Norman Chess Treatises. Ed. Tony Hunt. London: Anglo-Norman Text Society, 1985.

Gower, John. *Confessio Amantis.* Ed. Russell A. Peck. New York: Holt, Rinehart, and Winston, 1966. Reprint Medieval Academy Reprints for Teaching, Toronto: University of Toronto Press, 1980.

La Guerre de Metz en 1324: Poème du XIV siècle. Ed. E. de Bouteiller. Paris, 1875.

Guillaume de Lorris and Jean de Meun. *Le Roman de la rose.* Ed. Daniel Poirion. Paris: Garnier-Flammarion, 1974.

———. *The Romance of the Rose.* Trans. Charles Dahlberg. Princeton, N.J.: Princeton University Press, 1971.

Guy of Warwick *and Other Chapbook Romances*. Ed. John Simons. Exeter: University of Exeter Press, 1998.

Hoccleve, Thomas. *"My Compleinte" and Other Poems*. Ed. Roger Ellis. Exeter: University of Exeter Press, 2001.

———. *Regement of Princes*. Ed. Frederick J. Furnivall. EETS e.s. 72. London: Oxford University Press, 1897.

———. *The Regiment of Princes*. Ed. Charles R. Blyth, TEAMS series. Kalamazoo, Mich.: Medieval Institute Publications, 1999.

Jacobus de Cessolis. *The Buke of the Chess: Edited from the Asloan Manuscript*. Ed. Catherine van Buuren. Edinburgh: Scottish Text Society, 1997.

———. *Caxton's Game and Playe of the Chesse, 1474: A Verbatim Reprint of the First Edition*. Intro. William E. A. Axon. London: Elliot Stock, 1883.

———. "A Critical Edition of *Le Jeu des Eschés, Moralisé*, translated by Jehan de Vignay." Ed. Carol S. Fuller. Ph.D. dissertation, Catholic University of America, 1974.

———. *The Game of the Chesse*. Trans. William Caxton. Facsimile reprint by Vincent Figgins. London: Trübner, 1866.

———. "Jacobus de Cessolis: *Libellus de moribus hominum et officiis nobilium ac popularium super ludo scachorum*." Ed. Marie Anita Burt. Ph.D. dissertation. University of Texas, Austin, 1957.

———. *Le Jeu des éschaz moralisé: Traduction de Jean Ferron, 1347*. Ed. Alain Collet. Paris: Honoré Champion, 1999.

———. *Le Livre du jeu d'échecs, ou la society ideal au Moyen Age, XIIIeme siècle*. Trans. and ed. Jean-Michel Mehl. Paris: Editions Stock, 1995.

———. *Das Schachzabelbuch des Jacobus de Cessolis, O.P. in mittelhochdeutscher Prosa-Übersetzung*. Ed. Gerard F. Schmidt. Berlin: Erich Schmidt Verlag, 1961.

Jacobus de Voragine. *Legenda aurea*. Trans. William Caxton. London: J.M. Dent, 1900.

James VI and I, King. *Political Writings*. Ed. Johann P. Sommerville. Cambridge Texts in the History of Political Thought. Cambridge: Cambridge University Press, 1994.

James of Viterbo. *On Christian Government (De regimine Christiano)*. Ed. and trans. R. W. Dyson. Woodbridge: Boydell, 1995.

John of Salisbury. *Frivolities of Courtiers and the Footprints of Philosophers: First, Second, and Third Books and Selections from the Seventh and Eighth books of the* Policraticus. Trans. Joseph B. Pike. Minneapolis: University of Minnesota Press, 1938.

———. *Policraticus: Of the Frivolities of Courtiers and the Footprints of Philosophers*. Ed. and trans. Cary J. Nederman. Cambridge Texts in the History of Political Thought. Cambridge: Cambridge University Press, 1990.

———. *The Statesman's Book: Fourth, Fifth, and Sixth Books and Selections from the Seventh and Eighth Books of the* Policraticus. Trans. John Dickenson. New York: Russell and Russell, 1963.

Lancelot of the Laik *and* Sir Tristrem. Ed. Alan Lupack. TEAMS editions. Kalamazoo, Mich.: Medieval Institute Publications, 1994.

The Laws of the Salian Franks. Trans. and intro. Katherine Fischer Drew. Philadelphia: University of Pennsylvania Press, 1991.

Lefèvre, Raoul. *The Recuyell of the Historyes of Troyes.* Trans. William Caxton. Reproduced with a critical introduction by H. Oskar Sommer. London: D. Nutt, 1894.

The Legend of Guy of Warwick. Ed. Velma Bourgeois Richmond. New York: Garland, 1996.

Libelle of Englyshe Polycye: A Poem on the Use of Sea-Power, 1436. Ed. Sir George Warner. Oxford: Clarendon Press, 1926.

Lydgate, John. *The Pilgrimage of the Life of Man.* 1426. Based on Guillaume de Deguileville's *Pilgrimage of the Life of Man,* 1330 and 1355. Ed. F. J. Furnivall. London: Nichols and Sons, 1905.

———. *Reson and Sensuallyte.* Ed. Ernst Sieper. EETS e.s. 84, 89. London: Oxford University Press, 1901–3.

———. *Troy Book,* Ed. Henry Bergen, EETS e.s. 97. London: Kegan Paul, Trench, Trübner, 1906.

Mannyng, Robert. *Handlyng Synne.* Ed. Idelle Sullens. Binghamton, N.Y.: Medieval and Renaissance Texts and Studies, 1983.

Marsilius of Padua (Marsiglio de Padua). *Defensor pacis.* Ed. and trans. Alan Gewirth. New York: Columbia University Press, 1956. Reprint Medieval Academy Reprints for Teaching, Toronto: University of Toronto Press, 1980.

Meister Stephan. *Schachbuch.* Ed. W. Schlüter. Norden and Leipzig, 1889.

Middleton, Thomas. *A Game at Chess.* Ed. T. H. Howard-Hill. Manchester: Manchester University Press, 1993.

Mirk, John. *Mirk's Festial.* Ed. Theodore Erbe. EETS e.s. 96. London: Kegan Paul, Trench, Trübner, 1905.

The Mirror for Magistrates. Ed. Lily B. Campbell. Cambridge: Cambridge University Press, 1938. Reprint New York: Barnes and Noble, 1960.

Ogier le Dannoys: Roman en prose du XVe siècle. Facsimile reproduction by Knud Togeby. Munksgaard: Danske Sprog-og Litteraturselskab, 1967.

Penninc and Pieter Vostaert. *Roman van Walewein.* Ed. and trans. David F. Johnson. Garland Library of Medieval Literature 81 ser. A. New York: Garland, 1992.

Philippe de Mézières. *Le Songe du vieil pèlerin.* 2 vols. Ed. G. W. Coopland. Cambridge: Cambridge University Press, 1969.

Piers Plowman: The B Version. Ed. George Kane and E. Talbot Donaldson. London: Athlone Press, 1975.

Pseudo-Ovid. *The Pseudo-Ovidian De Vetula.* Ed. Dorothy M. Robathan. Amsterdam: A. M. Hakkert, 1968.

———. *La Vieille; ou, Les Derniers Amours d'Ovide (Poëme français du XIVe siècle traduit du Latin de Richard de Fournival).* Ed. Hippolyte Cocheris. Paris: August Aubry, 1861.

Les Quatre Fils d'Aymon ou Renaud de Montauban. Ed. Micheline de Combarieu du Grès and Jean Subrenat. Paris: Gallimard, 1983

Rabelais, François. *Gargantua and Pantagruel.* Trans. Burton Raffel. New York: Norton, 1990.

The Right Plesaunt and Goodly Historie of the Foure Sonnes of Aymon, Englisht from the French by William Caxton and Printed by him about 1489. Ed. Octavia Richardson. EETS e.s. 45. London: Trübner, 1885.

The Romance of Guy of Warwick: The Second or Fifteenth-Century Version. Ed. Julius Zupitza. EETS e.s. 25–26. London: Trübner, 1875–76.

The Romance of Perceval in Prose: A Translation of the E Manuscript of the Didot-Perceval. Ed. Dell Skeels. Seattle: University of Washington Press, 1966.

Le Rommant de Guy de Warwik et de Herolt d'Ardenne. Ed. D. J. Colon. Chapel Hill: University of North Carolina Press, 1971.

Ruodlieb. Trans. and ed. Gordon B. Ford, Jr. Leiden: E.J. Brill, 1965.

Saul, Arthur. *The famous game of chesse-play.* London, 1618.

Secretum Secretorum: Nine English Versions. Ed. M. A. Manzalaoui. EETS o.s. 276. Oxford: Oxford University Press, 1977.

Shakespeare, William. *The Tempest.* Ed. Stephen Orgel. Oxford: Clarendon Press, 1987.

Sir Gawain and the Green Knight. In *The Complete Works of the Pearl Poet,* trans. Casey Finch, ed. Malcolm Andrew, Ronald Waldron, and Clifford Peterson, 206–322. Berkeley: University of California Press, 1993.

The Song of Aspremont (La Chanson d'Aspremont). Trans. Michael A. Newth. New York: Garland, 1989.

The Tale of Beryn, with a Prologue of the Merry Adventure of the Pardoner with a Tapster at Canterbury. Ed. F. J. Furnivall and W. G. Stone. EETS e.s. 105. London: Kegan Paul, Trench, Trübner, 1909.

Teresa of Avila. *The Way of Perfection.* In *The Collected Works of St. Teresa of Avila,* vol. 2. Trans. Kieran Kavanaugh and Otillio Rodriguez, 37–204. Washington, D.C.: Institute of Carmelite Studies, 1980.

Twenty-Six Political and Other Poems. Part 1. Ed. J. Kail. EETS o.s. 124. London: KeganPaul, Trench, Trübner, 1904.

York (The Pinners): The Crucifixion. In *Medieval Drama: An Anthology.* Ed. Greg Walker. Oxford: Blackwell, 2000.

Secondary Works

Abraham, David H. "*Cosyn* and *Cosynage*: Pun and Structure in the *Shipman's Tale.*" *Chaucer Review* 11, 4 (1977): 319–27.

Adams, Jenny. "Exchequers and Balances: Anxieties of Exchange in *The Tale of Beryn.*" *Studies in the Age of Chaucer* 26 (2004): 267–97.

———. "'Longene to the Playe': Caxton, Chess, and the Boundaries of Political Order." *Essays in Medieval Studies* 21 (2004): 151–66.

———. "Pawn Takes Knight's Queen: Playing with Chess in the *Book of the Duchess.*" *ChaucerReview* 34, 2 (1999): 125–38.

———. "Pieces of Power: Medieval Chess and Male Homosocial Desire." *Journal of English and Germanic Philology* 103, 2 (April 2004): 197–214.

Adams, Robert. "The Concept of Debt in the *Shipman's Tale.*" *Studies in the Age of Chaucer* 6 (1984): 85–102.

Aers, David, ed. *Medieval Literature: Criticism, Ideology, and History.* New York: St. Martin's Press, 1986.

Alejandro, Roberto. *Hermeneutics, Citizenship, and the Public Sphere.* Albany: State University of New York Press, 1993.

Allen, Elizabeth. "The Pardoner in the 'Dogges Boure.'" *Chaucer Review* 36, 2 (2001): 91–127.

Althusser, Louis. "Ideology and Ideological State Apparatuses (Notes Towards an Investigation)." In *"Lenin and Philosophy" and Other Essays*, trans. Ben Brewster, 127–86. New York: Monthly Review Press, 1971.

Anderson, Perry. *Lineages of the Absolutist State.* London: N.L.B., 1974.

Armitage-Smith, Sydney, Sir. *John of Gaunt: King of Castile and Leon, Duke of Aquitaine and Lancaster, Earl of Derby, Lincoln and Leicester, Seneschal of England.* London: Westminster: A. Constable, 1904.

Astell, Ann W. *Political Allegory in Late Medieval England.* Ithaca, N.Y.: Cornell University Press, 1999.

Aurner, Nellie Slayton. *Caxton, Mirrour of Fifteenth-Century Letters: A Study of the Literature of the First English Press.* New York: Houghton Mifflin, 1926.

Baldwin, John W. *The Scholastic Culture of the Middle Ages, 1000–1300.* Lexington, Mass.: D.C. Heath, 1971.

Barkan, Leonard. *Nature's Work of Art: The Human Body as Image of the World.* New Haven, Conn.: Yale University Press, 1975.

Barron, Caroline, and Nigel Saul, eds. *England and the Low Countries in the Late Middle Ages.* New York: St. Martin's Press, 1995.

Bartlett, John. *A Complete Concordance to Shakespeare.* London: Macmillan, 1894. Reprint New York: St. Martin's Press, 1984.

Batt, Catherine. "Recreation, the Exemplary, and the Body in Caxton's *Game and Playe of the Chesse.*" *Ludica* 2 (1996): 27–43.

Beckwith, Sarah. "Ritual, Theater, and Social Space in the York Corpus Christi Cycle." In *Bodies and Disciplines: Intersections of Literature and History in Fifteenth-Century England*, ed. Barbara A. Hanawalt and David Wallace, 63–86. Minneapolis: University of Minnesota Press, 1996.

Bellamy, Elizabeth J. *Translations of Power: Narcissism and the Unconscious in Epic History.* Ithaca, N.Y.: Cornell University Press, 1992.

Benjamin, Walter. *Illuminations.* Ed. Hannah Arendt. Trans. Harry Zohn. New York: Schocken Books, 1969.

Bennett, Michael. *Richard II and the Revolution of 1399.* Stroud: Sutton, 1999.

Besamusca, Bart. "Gauvain as Lover in the Middle Dutch Verse Romance *Walewein.*" In *The Arthurian Yearbook II*, ed. Keith Busby, 3–12. New York: Garland, 1992.

Bird, Ruth. *The Turbulent London of Richard II.* New York: Longmans, Green, 1949.

Black, Antony. *Guilds and Civil Society in European Political Thought from the Twelfth Century to the Present.* Ithaca, N.Y.: Cornell University Press, 1984.

———. *Political Thought in Europe, 1250–1450.* Cambridge: Cambridge University Press, 1992.

Blades, William. *The Life and Typography of William Caxton, England's First Printer.* 2 vols. London: J. Lilly, 1861–63. Reprint New York: Burt Franklin, 1966.

Blake, N. F. *Caxton: England's First Publisher.* New York: Harper and Row, 1976.

———. *Caxton and His World.* London: Andre Deutsch, 1969.

————. "Continuity and Change in Caxton's Prologues and Epilogues: The Bruges Period." *Gutenberg-Jahrbuch* (1979): 72–77.

————. *William Caxton and English Literary Culture.* London: Hambledon Press, 1991.

Blakeslee, Merritt. "Lo Dous Joux sotils: La Partie d'échecs dans la poésie des troubadours." *Cahiers de Civilisation Médiévale, X^e-XIIe Siècles* 2–3 (1989): 213–22.

Bloch, R. Howard. *Medieval Misogyny and the Invention of Western Romantic Love.* Chicago: University of Chicago Press, 1991.

Bolens, Guillemette and Paul Beekman Taylor. "Chess, Clocks, and Counsellors in Chaucer's *Book of the Duchess.*" *Chaucer Review* 35, 3 (2001): 281–93.

————. "The Game of Chess in Chaucer's *Book of the Duchess.*" *Chaucer Review* 32, 4 (1998): 325–34.

Bolton, J. L. *The Medieval English Economy, 1150–1500.* London: J.M. Dent, 1980.

Bowers, John M. "Controversy and Criticism: Lydgate's *Thebes* and the Prologue to *Beryn.*" *Chaucer Yearbook* 5 (1998): 91–115.

————. "*The Tale of Beryn* and *The Siege of Thebes*: Alternative Ideas of *The Canterbury Tales.*" *Studies in the Age of Chaucer* 7 (1985): 23–50.

————. "Thomas Hoccleve and the Politics of Tradition." *Chaucer Review* 36.4 (2002): 352–69.

Britnell, R. H. *The Commercialisation of English Society, 1000–1500.* 2nd ed. Manchester: Manchester University Press, 1996.

Brooks, Christopher. "John of Salisbury and His World." In *The World of John of Salisbury*, ed. Michael Wilks, 1–20. Oxford: Basil Blackwell, 1984.

Brown, Peter. "Journey's End: The Prologue to *The Tale of Beryn.*" In *Chaucer and Fifteenth-Century Poetry*, ed. Julia Boffey and Janet Cowen, 143–74. London: King's College, 1991.

Brownlee, Kevin, and Marina Scordilis Brownlee, eds. *Romance: Generic Transformation from Chrétien de Troyes to Cervantes.* Hanover, N.H.: University Press of New England, 1985.

Bryan, Jennifer E. "Hoccleve, the Virgin, and the Politics of Complaint." *PMLA* 117, 5 (2002): 1172–87.

Burgess, Glenn. *Absolute Monarchy and the Stuart Constitution.* New Haven, Conn.: Yale University Press, 1996.

Burrow, J. A. "The Avowing of King Arthur." In *Medieval Literature and Antiquities: Studies in Honour of Basil Cottle*, ed. Myra Stokes and T. L. Burton, 99–109. Cambridge: D.S. Brewer, 1987.

Busby, Keith. *Gauvain in Old French Literature.* Amsterdam: Rodopi, 1980.

Butler, W. F. *The Lombard Communes.* London: T. Fisher Unwin, 1906.

Byrne, Robert. "Deep Blue Gently Shows It Has Developed a Nose for Nuances." *New York Times*, May 5, 1997, B, 3:1.

Callois, Roger. *Man, Play, and Games.* Trans. Meyer Barash. New York: Free Press of Glencoe, 1961.

Camille, Michael. "The King's New Bodies: An Illustrated Mirror for Princes in the Morgan Library." In *Kunstlerischer Austausch*, proceedings from the International Congress for Art History, Berlin, July 15–20, 1992, 373–405.

———. "Space and the Body: The *Jeu des Echecs Moralisées.*" Unpublished paper, 1991.

Carlson, David R. *English Humanist Books: Writers and Patrons, Manuscript and Print, 1475–1525.* Toronto: University of Toronto Press, 1993.

Carroll, Charles Michael. *The Great Chess Automaton.* New York: Dover, 1975.

Carruthers, Mary. *The Book of Memory: A Study of Memory in Medieval Culture.* Cambridge Studies in Medieval Culture. Cambridge: Cambridge University Press, 1990.

Cefalu, Paul. "Shakespeare's *Coriolanus* and the Consensual Nature of the Early Modern State." *Renaissance Forum* 4, 2 (2000): 1–14.

Chandler, David L. "Chess, Schmess! Computers Still Can't Handle the Tough Stuff." *Boston Globe,* May 13, 1997, A, 1:1.

Cherniss, Michael D. "Irony and Authority: The Ending of the *Roman de la Rose.*" *Modern Language Quarterly* 36 (1975): 227–38.

Coleman, Janet. *Medieval Readers and Writers, 1350–1400.* New York: Columbia University Press, 1981.

Coleman, Joyce. *Public Reading and the Reading Public in Late Medieval England and France.* Cambridge: Cambridge University Press, 1996.

Condren, Edward I. "On Deaths and Duchesses and Scholars Coughing Ink." *Chaucer Review* 10, 1 (1975): 87–95.

———. "The Historical Context of the *Book of the Duchess*: A New Hypothesis." *Chaucer Review* 5, 3 (1970): 195–212.

Connolly, Margaret. "Chaucer and Chess." *Chaucer Review* 29, 1 (1994): 40–44.

Constable, Olivia Remie. "Chess and Courtly Culture in Medieval Castile: An Analysis of the *Libro de Ajedrez* of Alfonso X, el Sabio." Unpublished paper, 2005.

Cooley, Franklin. "Two Notes on the Chess Terms in the *Book of the Duchess.*" *Modern Language Notes* 63, 1 (1948): 30–35.

Cooper, Helen, and Sally Mapstone, eds. *The Long Fifteenth Century: Essays for Douglas Gray.* Oxford: Clarendon Press, 1997.

Cosman, Madeleine Pelner. *The Education of the Hero in Arthurian Romance.* Chapel Hill: University of North Carolina Press, 1966.

Daly, Kathleen. "'Centre,' 'Power' and 'Periphery' in Late Medieval French Historiography: Some Reflections." In *War, Government and Power in Late Medieval France,* ed. Christopher Allmand, 124–44. Liverpool: Liverpool University Press, 2000.

David, Alfred. "Chaucerian Comedy and Criseyde." In *Essays on Troilus and Criseyde,* ed. Mary Salu, 90–104. Cambridge: D.S. Brewer, 1979.

Dawson, Anthony B. "*Women Beware Women* and the Economy of Rape." *Studies in English Literature* 27, 2 (1987): 303–20.

Day, John. *The Medieval Market Economy.* Oxford: Blackwell, 1987.

Delumeau, Jean. *Sin and Fear: The Emergence of a Western Guilt Culture, 13th to 18th Centuries* (*Le Péché et la peur,* 1983). Trans. Eric Nicholson. New York: St. Martin's Press, 1990.

de Roover, Raymond. *Business, Banking, and Economic Thought in Late Medieval and Early Modern Europe: Selected Studies of Raymond de Roover.* Ed. Julius Kirshner. Chicago: University of Chicago Press, 1974.

de Saussure, Ferdinand. *Course in General Linguistics.* Ed. Charles Bally and Albert Sechehaye. Trans. Wade Baskin. New York: McGraw-Hill, 1959.

Desmond, Marilynn. *Reading Dido: Gender, Textuality, and the Medieval Aeneid.* Minneapolis: University of Minnesota Press, 1994.

Di Lorenzo, Raymond D. "The Collection Form and the Art of Memory in the *Libellus super ludo schachorum* of Jacobus de Cessolis." *Mediaeval Studies* 35 (1973): 205–21.

Dinshaw, Carolyn. *Chaucer's Sexual Poetics.* Madison: University of Wisconsin Press, 1989.

Dollimore, Jonathan. "Introduction: Shakespeare, Cultural Materialism, and the New Historicism." In *Political Shakespeare: Essays in Cultural Materialism,* 2nd ed., ed. Jonathan Dollimore and Alan Sinfield, 2–17. Ithaca, N.Y.: Cornell University Press, 1994.

Driver, Martha W. *The Image in Print: Book Illustration in Late Medieval England and Its Sources.* London: British Library, 2004.

Duby, George. *The Knight, the Lady, and the Priest: The Making of Modern Marriage in Medieval France.* Trans. Barbara Bray. New York: Pantheon Books, 1983.

Dutton, Paul Edward. "*Illustre Civitatis et Populi Exemplum*: Plato's *Timaeus* and the Transmission from Calcidius to the End of the Twelfth Century of a Tripartite Scheme of Society." *Mediaeval Studies* 45 (1983): 79–119.

Dyer, Christopher. *Making a Living in the Middle Ages: The People of Britain, 850–1520.* New Haven, Conn.: Yale University Press, 2002.

———. *Standards of Living in the Later Middle Ages: Social Change in England, c. 1200–1520.* Cambridge: Cambridge University Press, 1989.

Eales, Richard. *Chess: The History of a Game.* New York: Facts on File Publications, 1985.

———. "The Game of Chess: An Aspect of Medieval Knightly Culture." In *The Ideals and Practice of Medieval Knighthood II: Papers from the Third Strawberry Hill Conference, 1986,* ed. Christopher Harper-Bill and Ruth Harvey, 2–34. Woodbridge: Boydell and Brewer, 1988.

Eberle, Patricia J., "Commercial Language and the Commercial Outlook in the *General Prologue.*" *Chaucer Review* 18, 2 (1983): 161–74.

———. "Mirror of Princes." In *Dictionary of the Middle Ages* vol. 8, ed. Joseph S. Strayer, 435. New York: Scribner's, 1987.

Ekelund, Robert B., Jr., Robert F. Hébert, Robert D. Tollison, Gary M. Anderson, and Audrey B. Davidson. *Sacred Trust: The Medieval Church as an Economic Firm.* Oxford: Oxford University Press, 1996.

Epstein, Steven A. *Genoa and the Genoese, 958–1528.* Chapel Hill: University of North Carolina Press, 1996.

Ferster, Judith. *Fictions of Advice: The Literature and Politics of Counsel in Late Medieval England.* Philadelphia: University of Pennsylvania Press, 1996.

Finnis, John. *Aquinas: Moral, Political, and Legal Theory.* Oxford: Oxford University Press, 1998.

Fisher, John H. "A Language Policy for Lancastrian England. *PMLA* 107, 5 (1992): 1168–80.

Fleming, John V. *Reason and the Lover.* Princeton, N.J.: Princeton University Press, 1984.

Forhan, Kate Langdon. "Polycracy, Obligation, and Revolt: Body Politic in John of Salisbury and Christine de Pizan." In *Politics, Gender, and Genre: The Political Thought of Christine de Pizan*, ed. Margaret Brabant, 33–52. Boulder, Colo.: Westview Press, 1992.

French, W. H. "Medieval Chess and the *Book of the Duchess.*" *Modern Language Notes* 64 (1949): 261–64.

Galpin, Stanley L. "*Les Eschez Amoureux:* A Complete Synopsis, with Unpublished Extracts." *Romanic Review* 11, 4 (1920): 283–307.

Geertz, Clifford. "Deep Play: A Few Notes on a Balinese Cockfight." In *The Interpretation of Cultures: Selected Essays by Clifford Geertz*, 412–53. New York: Basic Books, 1973. Originally pub. in *Daedalus* 101 (1972).

Genet, Jean-Philippe, ed. *Four English Political Tracts, of the Late Middle Ages.* London: Offices of the Royal Historical Society, 1977.

Gilbert, Jane. "Boyz Will Be . . . What? Gender, Sexuality, and Childhood in *Floire et Blanchflor* and *Floris et Lyriope.*" *Exemplaria* 9, 1 (1997): 39–61.

Gilchrist, J. *The Church and Economic Activity in the Middle Ages.* London: Macmillan, 1969.

Gill, Louise. "William Caxton and the Rebellion of 1483." *English Historical Review* 114, 445 (1997): 105–18.

Gonero, Valerie. *Parures d'or et de gemmes: L'Orfèvrerie dans les romans antiques du XIIe siècle.* Aix-en-Provence: Publications de l'Université de Provence, 2002.

Green, Richard Firth. *A Crisis of Truth: Literature and Law in Ricardian England.* Philadelphia: University of Pennsylvania Press, 1999.

———. "Legal Satire in *The Tale of Beryn.*" *Studies in the Age of Chaucer* 11 (1989): 43–62.

Greenblatt, Stephen. *Shakespearean Negotiations: The Circulation of Social Energy in Renaissance England.* Berkeley: University of California Press, 1988.

Guichard-Tesson, Françoise. "La Glose des *Echecs amoureux.* Un Savoir à tendance laïque: Comment l'interpréter?" *Fifteenth-Century Studies* 10 (1984): 229–60.

Harriss, Gerald L. "Political Society and the Growth of Government in Late Medieval England." *Past and Present* 138 (February 1993): 28–57.

Hatcher, John, and Mark Bailey. *Modelling the Middle Ages: The History and Theory of England's Economic Development.* Oxford: Oxford University Press, 2001.

Hattaway, Michael. "Drama and Society." In *The Cambridge Companion to English Renaissance Drama*, ed. A. R. Braunmuller and Michael Hattaway, 91–126. Cambridge: Cambridge University Press. 1990.

Heinemann, Margot. "Political Drama." In *The Cambridge Companion to English Renaissance Drama*, ed. A. R. Braunmuller and Michael Hattaway, 161–205. Cambridge: Cambridge University Press, 1990.

Held, David. *Political Theory and the Modern State: Essays on State, Power, and Democracy.* Stanford, Calif.: Stanford University Press, 1989.

Herzog, Michael B. "The *Book of the Duchess:* The Vision of the Artist as a Young Dreamer." *Chaucer Review* 22, 4 (1988): 269–74.

Hewson, John. "Saussure's Game of Chess." *Papers from the Fourth Annual Meeting of the Atlantic Provinces Linguistic Association*, ed. A. M. Kinloch, 108–16. Fredericton: University of New Brunswick, 1981.

Heydebrand und der Lasa, Tassilo von. *Zur Geschichte und Literatur des Schachspiels.* Leipzig: Veit, 1897.

Hindman, Sandra. *Sealed in Parchment: Rereadings of Knighthood in the Illuminated Manuscripts of Chrétien de Troyes.* Chicago: University of Chicago Press, 1994.

Holmes, Urban T. "The Adventures of Fouke Fitz Warin." In *Medium Aevum Romanicum: Festschrift für Hans Rheinfelder,* ed. Heinrich Bihler and Alfred Noyer-Weidner, 179–85. Munich: M. Hueber, 1963.

Hooper, David, and Kenneth Whyld. *The Oxford Companion to Chess.* Oxford: Oxford University Press, 1984.

Howard, Donald R. "Experience, Language, and Consciousness: *Troilus and Criseyde,* ll. 596–931." In *Medieval Literature and Folklore Studies: Essays in Honor of Francis Lee Utley,* ed. Jerome Mandel and Bruce A. Rosenberg, 173–92. New Brunswick, N.J.: Rutgers University Press, 1970.

Howard-Hill, T. H. "Political Interpretations of Middleton's *A Game at Chess* (1624)." *Yearbook of English Studies* 21 (1991): 274–85.

Huizinga, Johan. *Homo Ludens: A Study of the Play Element in Culture.* New York: Roy Publishers, 1950.

Hutson, Lorna. "Not the King's Two Bodies: Reading the 'Body Politic' in Shakespeare's *Henry IV,* Parts 1 and 2." In *Rhetoric and Law in Early Modern Europe,* ed. Victoria Kahn and Lorna Hutson, 166–98. New Haven, Conn.: Yale University Press, 2001.

Hyatte, Reginald. "The Manuscripts of the Prose Commentary (Fifteenth Century) on *Les Echecs Amoureux.*" *Manuscripta* 26, 1 (1982): 24–30.

———. "*Ovidius, Doctor Amoris*: The Changing Attitudes Towards Ovid's Eroticism in the Middle Ages as Seen in the Three Old French Adaptations of the *Remedia Amoris.*" *Florilegium: Carleton Papers on Late Antiquity* 4 (1982): 123–36.

Hyatte, Reginald, and Maryse Ponchard-Hyatte. *L'Harmonie des sphères: Encyclopédie d'astronomie et de musique extraite du commentaire sur* Les Echecs amoureux *(XVe s.) attribué à Evrart de Conty. Edition critique d'après les mss de la Bibliothèque Nationale de Paris.* New York: Peter Lang, 1985.

Ingham, Patricia Clare. "Masculine Military Unions: Brotherhood and Rivalry in *The Avowing of King Arthur.*" *Arthuriana* 6, 4 (1996): 25–44.

Jaeger, C. Stephen. *The Envy of Angels: Cathedral Schools and Social Ideals in Medieval Europe, 950–1200.* Philadelphia: University of Pennsylvania Press, 1994.

James, Mervyn. "Ritual, Drama, and Social Body in the Late Medieval English Town." *Past and Present* 98 (February 1983): 3–29.

Johnson, David F. "The Real and the Ideal: Attitudes to Love and Chivalry as Seen in *The Avowing of King Arthur.*" In *Companion to Middle English Romance,* ed. Henk Aertsen and Alasdair A. MacDonald, 189–208. Amsterdam: VU University Press, 1990.

Jonin, Pierre. "La Partie d'échecs dans l'épopée médiévale." In *Mélanges de langue et de littérature du Moyen Age et de la Renaissance offerts à Jean Frappier,* vol. 1, 483–97. Geneva: Droz, 1970.

Juel, Kristin E. "Loving the Creator and His Creations: Ethical Reflections on the Nature of Love in the Fourteenth-Century *Échecs Amoureux.*" Ph.D. dissertation, Indiana University, 2002.

Kaeppeli, Thomas. "Pour la biographie de Jacques de Cessole." *Archivum Fratrum Praedicatorum* 30 (1960): 149–62.

Kalning, Pamela. "Der Ritter auf dem Schachbrett: Ritterliche Tugenden im Schachbuch Konrads von Ammenhausen," (unpublished essay).

Kantorowicz, Ernst H. *The King's Two Bodies: A Study in Mediaeval Political Theology*. Princeton, N.J.: Princeton University Press, 1957.

Keats, Victor. *Chess, Jews, and History*. 3 vols. Oxford: Oxford Academia, 1994.

Kendrick, Laura. *Chaucerian Play: Comedy and Control in the* Canterbury Tales. Berkeley: University of California Press, 1988.

Kermode, Jenny. *Medieval Merchants: York, Beverley and Hull in the Later Middle Ages*. Cambridge: Cambridge University Press, 1998.

Kiser, Lisa J. *Truth and Textuality in Chaucer's Poetry*. Hanover, N.H.: University Press of New England, 1991.

Knapp, Ethan. *The Bureaucratic Muse: Thomas Hoccleve and the Literature of Late Medieval England*. University Park: Pennsylvania State University Press, 2001.

Knapp, Peggy. *Chaucer and the Social Contest*. New York: Routledge, 1990.

Knight, Charles. *William Caxton, the First English Printer: A Biography*. London: C. Knight, 1844.

Knowles, Christine. "Caxton and His Two French Sources: The *Game and Playe of the Chesse* and the Composite Manuscripts of the Two French Translations of the *Ludus Scaccorum*. *Modern Language Review* 49, 4 (1954): 417–23.

Kohler, Charles. "Traité du recouvrement de la Terre Sainte adressé, vers l'an 1295, à Philippe le Bel par Galvano de Levanto, Médecin Génois." *Revue de l'Orient Latin* 6 (1898): 343–69.

Kolata, Judith. "*Livre des Echecs Moralisés*." Master's thesis, University of Chicago, 1987.

Kraft, Christine. *Die Liebesgarten-Allegorie der* Echecs amoureux: *Kritische Ausgabe und Kommentar*. Frankfurt-am-Main: Peter Lang, 1977.

Kretzschmar, William. "Caxton's Sense of History." *Journal of English and Germanic Philology* 91, 4 (1992): 510–28.

Kuskin, William. "Caxton's Worthies Series: The Production of Literary Culture." *English Literary History* 66, 3 (1999): 511–51.

———. "The Erasure of Labor: Hoccleve, Caxton, and the Information Age." In *The Middle Ages at Work*, ed. Kellie Robertson and Michael Uebel, 229–60. New York: Palgrave Macmillan, 2004.

———. "Reading Caxton: Transformations in Capital, Authority, Print, and Persona in the Late Fifteenth Century." *New Medieval Literatures* 3 (2000): 149–83.

Krynen, Jacques. *Idéal du prince et pouvoir royal en France à la fin du Moyen Age (1380–1440): Etude de la littérature politique du temps*. Paris: Editions A. et J. Picard, 1981.

Lacy, Norris J. "The Design of the *Didot-Perceval*." In *Continuations: Essays on Medieval French Literature and Language in Honor of John L. Grigsby*, ed. Norris J. Lacy and Gloria Torrini-Roblin, 95–106. Birmingham, Ala.: Summa Publications, 1989.

———. "Gauvain and the Crisis of Chivalry." In *The Sower and His Seed: Essays on Chrétien de Troyes*, ed. Rupert Pickens, 155–64. Lexington, Ky.: French Forum Publishers, 1983.

Lawton, David. "Dullness and the Fifteenth Century." *English Literary History* 54, 4 (1987): 761–99.

Lecoy, Félix. "Guillaume de Saint-André et son *Jeu des échecs moralisés*." *Romania* 67 (1942): 491–503.

———. "Le *Jeu de echecs* d'Engreban d'Arras." In *Mélanges de philologie romane et de littérature médiévale offerts à Ernest Hœpffner*, 307–12. Paris: Les Belles Lettres, 1949.

Lempinen, Edward W. "Is Osama Winning?" *Salon.com.* September 6, 2002.

Lerer, Seth. "William Caxton." In *The Cambridge History of Medieval English Literature*, ed. David Wallace, 720–38. Cambridge: Cambridge University Press, 1999.

Levin, Richard A. "If Women Should Beware Women, Bianca Should Beware Mother." *Studies in English Literature* 37, 2 (1997): 371–89.

Lewis, C. S. *The Allegory of Love: A Study in Medieval Tradition.* London: Oxford University Press, 1936.

Lewis, P. S. *Later Medieval France: The Polity.* New York: St. Martin's Press, 1968.

Lindahl, Carl. *Earnest Games: Folkloric Patterns in the* Canterbury Tales. Bloomington: Indiana University Press, 1987.

Lopez, Robert S. *The Commercial Revolution of the Middle Ages, 950–1350.* Englewood Cliffs, N.J.: Prentice-Hall, 1971.

Madox, Thomas. *History and Antiquities of the Exchequer of the Kings of England, Second Edition.* 2 vols. London, 1769. Reprint New York: Augustus M. Kelley, 1969.

Mahoney, Dhira B. "Courtly Presentation and Authorial Self-Fashioning: Frontispiece Miniatures in Late Medieval French and English Manuscripts." *Mediaevalia* 21 (1996): 97–160.

Mann, Jill. *Chaucer and Medieval Estates Satire: The Literature of Social Classes and the* General Prologue *to the* Canterbury Tales. Cambridge: Cambridge University Press, 1973.

Martin, John. "Inventing Sincerity, Refashioning Prudence: The Discovery of the Individual in Renaissance Europe." *American Historical Review* 102, 5 (1997): 1309–42.

Martin, John E. *Feudalism to Capitalism: Peasant and Landlord in English Agrarian Development.* Atlantic Highlands, N.J.: Humanities Press, 1983.

Martines, Lauro. "Political Violence in the Thirteenth Century." In *Violence and Civil Disorder in Italian Cities, 1200–1500*, ed. Lauro Martines, 331–53. Berkeley: University of California Press, 1972.

Mathews, Johnye E. "The Black Knight as King of the Castle in *The Book of the Duchess*." *South Central Bulletin* 31, 4 (1971): 200–201.

Maus, Katharine Eisaman. *Inwardness and Theater in the English Renaissance.* Chicago: University of Chicago Press, 1995.

McNulty, Patricia. *St. Peter Damian: Selected Writings on the Spiritual Life.* London: Faber and Faber, 1959.

Medcalf, Stephen. "Motives for Pilgrimage." In *England in the Fourteenth Century: Proceedings of the 1991 Harlaxton Symposium*, ed. Nicholas Rogers, 77–108. Stamford, Conn.: Paul Watkins, 1993.

Mehl, Jean-Michel. "L'Exemplum chez Jacques de Cessoles." *Le Moyen Age: Revue d'Histoire et de Philology* 84 (1978): 227–46.

———. "Le Roi de l'Echiquier: Approche du mythe royal a la fin du Moyen Age." *Revue d'Histoire et de Philosophie Religieuses* 58 (1978): 145–61.

Mettlich, Joseph. *Die Schachpartie in der Prosabearbeitung der allegorisch-didaktischen Dichtung* Les Echecs amoureux. Münster: Aschendorffschen Buchdruckerei, 1907.

Morse, Ruth. "Understanding the Man in Black." *Chaucer Review* 15, 3 (1981): 204–6.

Muir, Dorothy. *A History of Milan Under the Visconti.* London: Methuen, 1924.

Murray, H. J. R. *A History of Chess.* Oxford: Oxford University Press, 1913.

Muscatine, Charles. *Chaucer and the French Tradition: A Study in Style and Meaning.* Berkeley: University of California Press, 1957.

———. "The Wife of Bath and Gautier's *La Veuve.*" In *Romance Studie. in Memory of Edward Billings Ham*, ed. Urban T. Holmes, 109–14. Hayward: California State College, 1967.

Nederman, Cary J. "A Duty to Kill: John of Salisbury's Theory of Tyrannicide." *Review of Politics* 50 (Summer 1988): 365–89.

———. "The Physiological Significance of the Organic Metaphor in John of Salisbury's *Policraticus.*" *History of Political Thought* 8, 2 (Summer 1987): 211–23.

Nguyen Van Cua, Pierre. "Le Roi et le tyran dans *Jeu des échecs moralisé* de Jacques de Cessoles." 2 vols. Dissertation, University of Rouen, France, 1993.

Nichols, Stephen G., Jr. *Romanesque Signs: Early Medieval Narrative and Iconography.* New Haven, Conn.: Yale University Press, 1983.

Nolan, Barbara. "The Art of Expropriation: Chaucer's Narrator in *The Book of the Duchess.*" In *New Perspectives in Chaucer Criticism*, ed. Donald M. Rose, 203–22. Oklahoma: Pilgrim Books, 1981.

Norbrook, David. "The Emperor's New Body? *Richard II*, Ernst Kantorowicz, and the Politics of Shakespeare Criticism." *Textual Practice* 10, 2 (1996): 329–57.

Olson, Glending. *Literature as Recreation in the Later Middle Ages.* Ithaca, N.Y.: Cornell University Press, 1982.

———. "The Misreadings of the *Beryn* Prologue." *Mediaevalia* 17 (1994): 201–19.

The Oxford Classical Dictionary. 3rd ed. Oxford: Oxford University Press, 1996.

Painter, George D. *William Caxton: A Biography.* New York: G.P. Putnam's Sons, 1977.

Patterson, Lee. *Chaucer and the Subject of History.* Madison: University of Wisconsin Press, 1991.

———. "Making Identities in Fifteenth-Century England: Henry V and John Lydgate." In *New Historical Literary Study: Essays on Reproducing Texts, Representing History*, ed. Jeffrey N. Cox and Larry J. Reynolds, 69–107. Princeton, N.J.: Princeton University Press, 1993.

———, ed. *Literary Practice and Social Change in Britain, 1380–1530.* Berkeley: University of California Press, 1990.

Pearsall, Derek. "Hoccleve's *Regiment of Princes*: The Poetics of Royal Self-Representation." *Speculum* 69 (1994): 386–410.

———. "Langland's London." In *Written Work: Langland, Labor, and Authorship*, ed. Steven Justice and Kathryn Kerby-Fulton, 185–207. Philadelphia: University of Pennsylvania Press, 1997.

Perkins, Nicholas. *Hoccleve's* Regiment of Princes: *Counsel and Constraint.* Cambridge: D.S. Brewer, 2001.

Pirenne, Henri. *Economic and Social History of Medieval Europe.* Trans. I. E. Clegg. New York: Harcourt, Brace, 1936.

Poole, William. "False Play: Shakespeare and Chess." *Shakespeare Quarterly* 55,1 (2004): 50–70.

Postan, M. M. *The Medieval Economy and Society: An Economic History of Britain, 1100–1500.* Los Angeles: University of California Press, 1972.

Reames, Sherry L. *The* Legenda Aurea: *A Reexamination of Its Paradoxical History.* Madison:University of Wisconsin Press, 1985.

Rebbert, Maria R. "The Celtic Origins of the Chess Symbolism in *Milun* and *Eliduc.*" In *In Quest of Marie de France, a Twelfth-Century Poet,* ed. Chantal A. Maréchal, 148–60. Lewiston, N.Y.: Edwin Mellen Press, 1992.

Rendall, Thomas. "Gawain and the Game of Chess." *Chaucer Review* 27, 2 (1992): 186–99.

Riddy, Felicity. "Giving and Receiving: Exchange in the *Roman van Walewein* and *Sir Gawain and the Green Knight.*" *Tijdschrift voor Nederlandse Taal-en Letterkunde* 112, 1 (1996): 18–29.

Robertson, D. W., Jr. "The *Book of the Duchess.*" In *A Companion to Chaucer Studies,* rev. ed., ed. Beryl Rowland, 403–13. New York: Oxford University Press, 1979.

———. *A Preface to Chaucer: Studies in Medieval Perspectives.* Princeton, N.J.: Princeton University Press, 1962.

Roseveare, Henry. *The Treasury: The Evolution of a British Institution.* London: Allen Lane, 1969.

Ross, Diane M. "The Play of Genres in the *Book of the Duchess.*" *Chaucer Review* 19, 1 (1984): 1–13.

Rossi, Marguerite. *Huon de Bordeaux et l'évolution du genre epique au XIIe siecle.* Paris: Honoré Champion, 1975.

Rowe, Donald W. "*Reson* in Jean's *Roman de la Rose:* Modes of Characterization and Dimensions of Meaning." *Mediaevalia* 10 (1984): 97–126.

Rowland, Beryl. "Chaucer as a Pawn in the *Book of the Duchess.*" *American Notes and Queries* 6, 1 (1967): 3–6.

———. "The Chess Problem in Chaucer's *Book of the Duchess.*" *Anglia* 80, 4 (1962): 384–89.

Rutter, Russell. "William Caxton and Literary Patronage." *Studies in Philology* 84, 4 (1987): 440–70.

Said, Edward. *The World, the Text, and the Critic.* Cambridge, Mass.: Harvard University Press, 1983.

Sanford, Eva Matthews. "The Lombard Cities, Empire, and Papacy in a Cleveland Manuscript." *Speculum* 12 (1937): 203–8.

Scanlon, Larry. "The King's Two Voices: Narrative and Power in Hoccleve's *Regement of Princes.*" In *Literary Practice and Social Change in Britain, 1380–1530,* ed. Lee Patterson, 216–47. Berkeley: University of California Press, 1990.

Schmidgall, Gary. "The Discovery at Chess in *The Tempest.*" *English Language Notes* 23 (1986): 11–16.

Schneider, Paul S. "'Taillynge Ynough': The Function of Money in the *Shipman's Tale.*" *Chaucer Review* 11, 3 (1977): 201–9.

Severs, J. B. "The Sources for the *Book of the Duchess.*" *Medieval Studies* 25 (1963): 355–62.

Shenk, David. *The Immortal Game: A History of Chess, Or How 32 Pieces on a Board Illuminated Our Understanding of War, Art, Science, and the Human Brain.* New York: Doubleday, 2006.

Shoaf, R. A. *Dante, Chaucer, and the Currency of the Word: Money, Images, and Reference in Late Medieval Poetry.* Norman, Okla.: Pilgrim Books, 1983.

Silva-Vigier, Anil de. *The Moste Highe Prince . . . John of Gaunt, 1340–1399.* Edinburgh: Pentland Press, 1992.

Simon, Eckehard. "The Provenance and Date of the Houghton Chessbook Manuscript and Its Miniatures." In *Essays in Honor of James Edward Walsh,* ed. William H. Bond. 29–42. Cambridge, Mass.: Goethe Institute of Boston and the Houghton Library, 1983.

Simons, Penny. "Pattern and Process of Education in *Le Conte du Graal,*" *Nottingham French Studies* 32, 2 (1993): 1–11.

Simpson, James. "Nobody's Man: Thomas Hoccleve's *Regement of Princes.*" In *London and Europe in the Later Middle Ages,* ed. Julia Boffey and Pamela King, 150–80. London: Westfield Publications in Medieval Studies, 1995.

———. "Spirituality and Economics in Passus 1–7 of the B-Text." *Yearbook of Langland Studies* 1 (1987): 83–103.

Smith, Adam. *Theory of Moral Sentiments.* Ed. Knud Haakonssen. Cambridge: Cambridge University Press, 2002.

Solente, Suzanne. "Le *Jeu des échecs moralisés,* source de la *Mutacion de fortune.*" In *Recueil de travaux offert à M. Clovis Brunel.* 2 vols. 556–65. Paris: Société de l'Ecole des Chartres, 1955.

Southern, R. W. *Scholastic Humanism and the Unification of Europe.* Vol. 1, *Foundations.* Oxford: Blackwell, 1995.

Stanbury, Sarah. "The Voyeur and the Private Life in *Troilus and Criseyde.*" *Studies in the Age of Chaucer* 13 (1991): 141–58.

Standage, Tom. *The Turk: The Life and Times of the Famous Eighteenth-Century Chess-Playing Machine.* New York: Walker, 2002.

Stevenson, Kay Gilliland. "Readers, Poets, and Poems Within the Poem." *Chaucer Review* 24, 1 (1989): 1–19.

Stone, Laurence. *The Family, Sex, and Marriage in England, 1500–1800.* London: Weidenfeldand Nicolson, 1977.

Strayer, Joseph. *The Reign of Philip the Fair.* Princeton, N.J.: Princeton University Press, 1980.

Strohm, Paul. *England's Empty Throne: Usurpation and the Language of Legitimation, 1399–1422.* New Haven, Conn.: Yale University Press, 1998.

———. *Hochon's Arrow: The Social Imagination of Fourteenth-Century Texts.* Princeton, N.J.: Princeton University Press, 1992.

———. *Politique: Languages of Statecraft Between Chaucer and Shakespeare.* Notre Dame, Ind.: University of Notre Dame Press, 2005.

Summit, Jennifer. "William Caxton, Margaret Beaufort and the Romance of Female Patronage." In *Women, the Book and the Worldly: Selected Proceedings of the St. Hilda's Conference, 1993,* vol. 2, ed. Lesley Smith and Jane H. M. Taylor, 151–65. Cambridge: D.S. Brewer, 1995.

Swanson, Jenny. *John of Wales: A Study of the Works and Ideas of a Thirteenth-Century Friar.* Cambridge: Cambridge University Press, 1989.

Sweezy, Paul, ed. *The Transition from Feudalism to Capitalism.* London: N.L.B., 1976.

Tatlock, John S. P., and Arthur G. Kennedy. *A Concordance to the Complete Works of Geoffrey Chaucer and to the* Romaunt of the Rose. Washington, D.C.: Carnegie Institute of Washington, 1927.

Taylor, Mark N. "Chaucer's Knowledge of Chess." *Chaucer Review* 38, 4 (2004): 299–313.

———. "How Did the Queen Go Mad?" Paper presented at the Thirty-Ninth International Congress on Medieval Studies, Kalamazoo, Michigan, May 2004.

Taylor, Steven M. "God's Queen: Chess Imagery in the Poetry of Gautier de Coinci." *Fifteenth Century Studies* 17 (1990): 403–19.

Thorndike, Lynn. "'All the World's a Chess-Board.'" *Speculum* 6 (1931): 461–65.

Tierney, Brian, and Sidney Painter. *Western Europe in the Middle Ages, 300–1475* (formerly entitled *A History of the Middle Ages, 284–1500*). 4th ed. New York: Knopf, 1983.

Tronzo, William L. "Moral Hieroglyphs: Chess and Dice at San Savino in Piacenza." *Gesta* 16, 2 (1977): 15–26.

Van der Linde, Antonius. *Geschichte und Litteratur des Schachspiels.* 2 vols. Berlin: J. Springer, 1874.

———. *Quellenstudien zur Geschichte des Schachspiels.* Berlin: J. Springer, 1881. Osnabrück: BiblioVerlag, 1968.

Vetter, Ferdinand. *Neue Mittheilungen aus Konrads von Ammenhausen Schachzabelbuch.* Aarau: H. R. Sauerländer, 1977.

von Neumann, John, and Oskar Morgenstern. *Theory of Games and Economic Behavior.* Princeton, N.J.: Princeton University Press, 1944.

Waley, Daniel. *The Italian City-Republics.* New York: McGraw-Hill, 1969.

Wallace, David. *Chaucerian Polity: Absolutist Lineages and Associational Forms in England and Italy.* Stanford, Calif.: Stanford University Press, 1997.

Ward, Charles Frederick. *The Epistles on the* Romance of the Rose *and Other Documents in the Debate.* Chicago: University of Chicago Press, 1911.

Weeks, Mark. "Chess Bibliography Before 1800." *http://mark_weeks.tripod.com/chwooi15/chwooi15.htm.* Accessed August 1, 2005.

Weinberg, Florence, "Chess as a Literary Idea in Colonna's *Hypnerotomachia* and in Rabelais' *Cinquiesme Livre.*" *Romanic Review* 70, 4 (1979): 321–35.

White, John Griswold. *A Manuscript Giving a Detailed Description of Chess Passages in Manuscripts Found in 145 European and Indian Libraries with the Names of Persons Underlined in Red Ink.* 2 vols. Cleveland: Cleveland Public Library, 1928.

Wilkinson, Charles. "A Thirteenth-Century Morality." *Bulletin: Metropolitan Museum of Art* n.s. 2, 1 (1943): 47–55.

Williams, Bernard. *Shame and Necessity.* Berkeley: University of California Press, 1993.

Williamson, Joan B. "Allegory in the Work of Philippe de Mézières." *Analecta Husserliana: Yearbook of Phenomenological Research* 41 (1994): 107–21.

———. "Jewels in the Work of Philippe de Mézières." In *Autour d'Eustache Deschamps: Actes du Colloque du Centre d'études médiEvales de l'Université de Picardie-Jules Verne, Amiens, 5–8 novembre 1998,* ed. Danielle Buschinger, 261–76. Amiens: Centre d'études médiévales, 1999.

Wilson, Robert H. "Caxton's Chess Book." *Modern Language Notes* 62 (1947): 93–102.

Wiseman, D. J. *Nebuchadnezzar and Babylon.* Schwich Lectures of the British Academy. Oxford: Oxford University Press, 1985.

Wood, Chauncey. *The Elements of Chaucer's* Troilus. Durham, N.C.: Duke University Press, 1984.

Yalom, Marilyn. *The Birth of the Chess Queen.* New York: HarperCollins, 2004.

Yeager, R. F. "Literary Theory at the Close of the Middle Ages: William Caxton and William Thynne." *Studies in the Age of Chaucer* 6 (1984): 135–64.

Zink, Michel. "Time and Representation of the Self in Thirteenth-Century Poetry." *Poetics Today* 5, 3 (1984): 611–27.

Index

Acknowledgments

This book, first drafted over the course of two Chicago winters, revised through several blazing Texas summers, and finished during a moderate Massachusetts autumn, was nurtured, challenged, and improved by various people in each of these locales. Most important in the Chicago contingent was Christina von Nolcken, my mentor and friend, whose enthusiasm for my work never seemed to flag, even when my own did. Anthony Perron, *meus magister optimus linguae Latinae*, merits special mention for his help with my translations of Jacobus de Cessolis. Others in Chicago (either there formerly or still residing currently) who read early drafts, sent me references, and pushed my argument in new directions include Garth Bond, Daniel Connolly, Karen Duys, Suzanne Edwards, Rachel Fulton, Anne Harris, Mike Goode, Nicole Lassahn, Mark Miller, Michael Murrin, Jolynn Parker, Anne Robertson, Larry Rothfield, Richard Strier, Andrea Walker, and Rebecca Zorach. I am deeply appreciative to all of you for your help.

When the book moved to Texas with me, it started to grow in new, and sometimes unruly, directions. The person most responsible for keeping it under control at this point was Robert Upchurch, my editor-in-chief, who always managed to tell me that my work was "fantastic" before showing me the many ways in which it wasn't. Also in Texas, Jacqueline Vanhoutte and Paul Menzer contributed their expertise in early modern culture, and in the case of the Paul, a deep knowledge of the entire category of metaphor. Karen Upchurch provided me with a good translation of parts of Alfonso's chess book; Edward J. López spent an unseemly amount of energy explaining game theory to me; and my research assistant Tanya Hooper proved to be a top notch reader. Finally, my friends and fellow band members, Corey Marks, Amy Taylor, Deborah Needleman Armintor, and Marshall Armintor, helped me to keep the whole project in perspective.

After arriving at the University of Massachusetts, I was invited to join an informal reading group that enthusiastically read and commented on my final chapter. I am grateful to the members of this group, Nancy Bradbury, Chick Chickering, Carolyn Collette, and Arlyn Diamond, to two members of the Five College Medieval Seminar, Craig Davis and Brigitte Buettner, and to my colleagues in my new department, in particular Stephen Harris and Joseph Black, for their feedback on various sections and their general support. Donald Maddox and Meriem Pages, also at UMass, have my deep gratitude for helping with several of my French translations; any errors that remain on this score will inevitably be in passages that they did not get a chance to see. And last but definitely not least, Ann Higgins, my research assistant during the final push, has gone above and beyond any reasonable call of duty. Thank you Ann, for making this book yours as well as mine.

Faculty members at other institutions who have helped me with my work on medieval chess, and on a few related topics, include Olivia Remie Constable, William Kuskin, Dhira Mahoney, Daniel O'Sullivan, Mark Taylor, William Tronzo, Daniel Magilow, and Pamela Kalning. David Shenk, an author whose book on chess will be released at around the same time as this one, has been kind enough to share his own research with me. I can only hope that he will share some of his readership with me as well. At the University of Pennsylvania Press, my manuscript was welcomed by Jerry Singerman, who shepherded it through the many stages of the publishing process. To him, Alison Anderson, Suzanne Dorf, the other editors at the press, Ann Astell, and one anonymous reader, I remain deeply grateful.

Financial support came from a variety of sources including grants from the American Council of Learned Societies, the University of Massachusetts Healey Endowment, and the University of North Texas Faculty Development Fund. Various parts of the book have already appeared in other forms: a portion of chapter four was published as "'Longene to the Playe': Caxton, Chess, and the Boundaries of Political Order," *Essays in Medieval Studies* 21 (2004), and two different sections of chapter three were published as "Pawn Takes Knight's Queen: Playing with Chess in Chaucer's *Book of the Duchess*," *Chaucer Review* 34, 2 (1999) and as "Exchequers and Balances: Anxieties of Exchange in *The Tale of Beryn*," *Studies in the Age of Chaucer* 26 (2004). I am also appreciative of the Newberry Library for allowing me to reproduce images from its collection.

Last but not least are the most personal debts. I give thanks to Lee Adams, Nancy Adams, Tim Chadsey, Guy Sternal, and Rebecca Sternal for their love and support. And most specially, I give my deepest appreciation and love to Jeff Sternal, who has read, commented on, and helped shape almost every page of this book.